CAUGHT IN THE ACT

THEATRICALITY
IN THE NINETEENTH-CENTURY
ENGLISH NOVEL

JOSEPH LITVAK

University of California Press
Berkeley · Los Angeles · Oxford

Portions of this book appeared in a slightly different form in the following publications:

ELH, vol. 53 (Summer 1986)
Texas Studies in Literature and Language, vol. 29, no. 2 (Summer 1987)
Nineteenth-Century Literature, vol. 42, no. 4 (March 1988).

They appear here by permission of the publishers.

University of California Press
Berkeley and Los Angeles, California

University of California Press, Ltd.
Oxford, England

Library of Congress Cataloging-in-Publication Data

Litvak, Joseph.
    Caught in the act : theatricality in the nineteenth-century English novel / Joseph Litvak.
    p.   cm.
    Includes index.
    ISBN 0-520-07452-1 (alk. paper). — ISBN 0-520-07454-8 (pbk. : alk. paper)
    1. English fiction—19th century—History and criticism. 2. Performing arts in literature. 3. Theater in literature. 4. Actors in literature. 5. Acting in literature. 6. e-uk.
    I. Title.
PR868.P44L5   1991
823'.809357—dc20
                                        91-10222
                                        CIP

Printed in the United States of America

9 8 7 6 5 4 3 2 1

The paper used in this publication meets the minimum requirements of American National Standard for Information Sciences—Permanence of Paper for Printed Library Materials, ANSI Z39.48-1984. ∞

Contents

To my mother and father,
Joann and Lawrence Litvak,
and to the memory of my grandmother,
Ann Iskow Grimes

Acknowledgments

Work on this book began in the summer of 1984, when, as the recipient of a summer stipend from the National Endowment for the Humanities, I went to London to do research that would result in a version of the chapter on *Mansfield Park*. I am happy to thank the NEH, as well as the Bowdoin College Faculty Research Committee and former Bowdoin President A. LeRoy Greason, for providing financial support.

Support of a different kind came from J. Hillis Miller, who planted the seeds of this book in the course of a conversation about an earlier project, and whose encouragement has meant a great deal to me. My dissertation adviser, the late Paul de Man, has left a body of work that continues to exemplify the kind of critical acuity to which I aspire.

Rosemarie Bodenheimer, Robert K. Martin, and Ruth Bernard Yeazell have commented helpfully on various chapters. In the final stages of this project, Mihoko Suzuki gave generously of her time and of her professional expertise. I am grateful as well to three anonymous readers for the University of California Press, whose suggestions have guided me in important ways as I revised the Introduction. Doris Kretschmer has been a marvelously astute editor; I greatly appreciate her interest in this project. I thank Betsey Scheiner for further editorial assistance, and Ellen Stein, whose copyediting was exemplary in its intelligence and precision.

At Bowdoin College, my colleagues Susan Bell, Joanne Feit Diehl, and Marilyn Reizbaum have given me invaluable encouragement and tactical advice. Helen Carson has done a superb job of helping to produce a presentable manuscript. It has been a pleasure to work with such capable research assistants as Robert Brewer, Jacob Kinnard, Gregory Merrill, and Paul Adelstein, the last of whom found the photograph that appears on the book's cover. I was pleasantly surprised to learn that this photograph is owned by the Bowdoin College Museum of Art, whose curator, Donald Rosenthal, promptly provided me with a reproduction of it.

That this book could not have been written without the intellectual inspiration of Eve Kosofsky Sedgwick should be evident to any reader of these pages; the influence of her friendship may be less palpable, but it has played no less significant a role in shaping the manuscript, and in determining its fate.

In the genre known as the acknowledgments, it is becoming almost conventional, at least among authors of a certain kind of book, to apologize for mentioning one's family. The antidomestic implications of this book notwithstanding, I am delighted to thank my parents, my grandparents, and my brothers, Daniel, Ronald, and Edward Litvak, for their sustained interest in and support of this project.

I cannot begin to express my gratitude to Lee Edelman. He has contributed to this book at every stage, from its groping initial conceptualization to its painful final polishing. He has been my ideal reader, my most demanding and most generous critic; every one of the pages that follow bears the trace of his careful and powerful intelligence. More mundanely but just as heroically, he has put up with more "scenes" than even this rather exhibitionistic author cares to remember. The book is a testimony to his insight and to his patience, both of whose proportions are, to say the least, spectacular.

An earlier version of Chapter 1 appeared in *ELH* 53 (Summer 1986). Part of Chapter 3 was published in somewhat different form in *Nineteenth-Century Literature* 42 (March 1988), and part of Chapter 7 was published in *Texas Studies in Literature and Language* 29 (Summer 1987). I thank the editors of these journals for granting permission to reprint this material.

Introduction

"Our society," Michel Foucault argued famously, "is one not of spectacle but of surveillance."[1] This book takes as its point of departure that rather stark representation of "our society," which, in Foucault's account, is also the society of the nineteenth century. That is, the readings offered here presuppose the *overtly* nontheatrical, even antitheatrical, character of the culture inhabited—indeed, to a certain extent, constructed—by the novels under analysis. Yet if these readings depart from that assumption in the sense of proceeding from it, they would also depart from it in the sense of leaving it behind—or would at least challenge it insistently and inventively enough so that a richer understanding of social interaction, both in the nineteenth century proper and in its lengthy, ongoing sequel, might begin to emerge in its place.

One of my primary concerns, accordingly, is to show how the novelistic tradition examined here unsettles the distinction between a society of spectacle and a society of surveillance. Of course, if *spectacle* is taken to imply extravagance and ostentation, then *spectacular* is probably not the first word one would apply to the works of Jane Austen, Charlotte Brontë, George Eliot, or even Henry James. On the contrary, just as this tradition marks the triumphant climax of the well-known rise of the novel, so it has been shown less to record than to help institutionalize what has been dubbed, almost as memorably, the fall of public man—a fall from the theatricality of eighteenth-century culture into the world of domesticity, subjectivity, and psychology, whose intimate, personalized scale, far from providing refuge from surveillance, installs it, with remarkable hospitality, in an apparently infinite number of snug little homes, where it can go about its business under cover of an endlessly idealizing

1. Michel Foucault, *Discipline and Punish: The Birth of the Prison*, trans. Alan Sheridan (New York: Vintage, 1979), p. 217.

misrecognition.[2] Thus, while recent studies of eighteenth-century English fiction deploy explicitly theatrical paradigms, it might seem anachronistic or merely wishful to look for theatricality in novels of the privatizing and privatized nineteenth century.[3] But I will demonstrate that, though such texts may be less showy than their eighteenth-century predecessors, their very implication in a widespread social network of vigilance and visibility—of looking and of being looked at—renders them inherently, if covertly, theatrical. After all, Foucault himself has to describe the cells of Bentham's Panopticon, the model of modern discipline, as "so many cages, so many small theatres, in which each actor is alone, perfectly individualised and constantly visible."[4] Foucault is obviously not promoting this displaced theatricality as compensation or consolation for the oppressiveness of the regime that contains it, nor is it my intention to celebrate the generalization of the carceral scene in nineteenth-century novels and their culture. The point, rather, is that, instead of simply precluding or negating spectacle, a society of surveillance entails certain rigorous spectacular practices of its own. Observing those practices at work in and around a series of nineteenth-century texts, the present study repeatedly emphasizes the *normalization* of theatricality, its subtle diffusion throughout the culture that would appear to have repudiated it.

2. See Ian Watt, *The Rise of the Novel: Studies in Defoe, Richardson, and Fielding* (Harmondsworth: Penguin, 1974) and Richard Sennett, *The Fall of Public Man* (New York: Knopf, 1977). Studies of the nineteenth-century novel that, variously inspired by Foucault, locate it in the history of privatization include Nancy Armstrong, *Desire and Domestic Fiction: A Political History of the Novel* (New York: Oxford University Press, 1987); John Kucich, *Repression in Victorian Fiction: Charlotte Brontë, George Eliot, and Charles Dickens* (Berkeley: University of California Press, 1987); D. A. Miller, *The Novel and the Police* (Berkeley: University of California Press, 1988); Mark Seltzer, *Henry James and the Art of Power* (Ithaca: Cornell University Press, 1984).

3. On theatricality in eighteenth-century fiction, see, for example, Terry Castle, *Masquerade and Civilization: The Carnivalesque in Eighteenth-Century English Culture and Fiction* (Stanford: Stanford University Press, 1986) and David Marshall, *The Figure of Theater: Shaftesbury, Defoe, Adam Smith, and George Eliot* (New York: Columbia University Press, 1986). Nina Auerbach has made a case for the theatricality of nineteenth-century literature and culture, most recently in *Private Theatricals: The Lives of the Victorians* (Cambridge: Harvard University Press, 1990). Auerbach's approach to nineteenth-century theatricality is quite different from mine, as I suggest at several points in this book.

4. Foucault, *Discipline and Punish*, p. 200. That spectacle and surveillance are by no means incompatible is demonstrated at length in Seltzer, *James and the Art of Power*, pp. 25–58, and suggested briefly in Jonathan Crary, "Spectacle, Attention, Counter-Memory," *October* 50 (Fall 1989): 105.

However cagey, then, however deficient in the Bakhtinian "carnivalesque" exuberance or (as rehearsed in the opening pages of *Discipline and Punish*) in the sheer Grand Guignol excess that one might associate with earlier manifestations of theatricality, the spectacles of surveillance pervade nineteenth-century fiction. Yet, another major concern of this book is to make clear that they thereby account not only for the peculiar efficacy of that fiction as an instrument of social regulation, as Foucauldian literary critics have argued, but also for its unpredictability, for its tendency *not* to accomplish—or not to accomplish quite as faithfully as might have been expected—the cultural task assigned to it.

If this book therefore maintains a certain distance from the Foucauldian interpretations to which it is nonetheless indebted, it also differs from, even as it intersects, another recently influential approach to nineteenth-century fiction. I am referring to a group of studies—focused somewhat more on American than on British novels, and somewhat more on the later than on the earlier or the middle nineteenth century—that link nineteenth-century fiction with precisely a "society of the spectacle," reading it as a commentary on, or as an accomplice of, the seductive new hegemony of advertising and of a necessarily *conspicuous* consumption.[5] Although some of the distinctive preoccupations of critics working in this mode—the marketplace, the commodification of the self—figure significantly here, I hope ultimately to project a more affirmative sense of "spectacle" than that which seems to inform their often scrupulously opaque, even deadpan, accounts. I intend no more to play up any "subversive" potential of consumerist theatricality than to glamorize the theatricality of surveillance. My aim, however, is to show how, if theatrical structures and techniques underlie or enable various coercive cultural mechanisms, the same structures and techniques can threaten those mechanisms' smooth functioning. In the process, I seek not to reclaim some primordial, anarchic essence of theatricality, but to reveal its pragmatic overdetermination, its perverse

---

5. Building upon such works as Jean Baudrillard, *La société de consommation* (Paris: Editions Denoël, 1970) and Guy Debord, *Society of the Spectacle* (Detroit: Black and Red, 1977), these studies include Rachel Bowlby, *Just Looking: Consumer Culture in Dreiser, Gissing, and Zola* (New York: Methuen, 1985); Amy Kaplan, *The Social Construction of American Realism* (Chicago: University of Chicago Press, 1988); Jennifer Wicke, *Advertising Fictions: Literature, Advertisement, and Social Reading* (New York: Columbia University Press, 1988).

capacity for doing more than just serving the interests of whatever political ideologies or cultural dispensations happen to have appropriated it.

Indeed, theatricality, as I develop it here, signifies not a single, unitary style or content, but a set of shifting, contradictory energies. Unlike "theater," which may denote a fixed place, institution, or art form, "theatricality" resists such circumscription, owing its value as a critical term to this very open-endedness. Nevertheless, the term is meant to have a specific force and to achieve specific effects in the readings that follow: it is directed not only against the coherent, stable subjectivity that the nineteenth-century novel supposedly secures for both its protagonists and its readers, but also against the domestic, domesticating closure—or, in the case of Henry James, against the aestheticization of that closure as the "house of fiction"—in which that subjectivity supposedly discovers its "natural" habitat. This double function may explain why this book is about "theatricality," rather than about, say, "textuality," in the nineteenth-century novel. For though the latter term would have (in fact, in the work of other critics, already has) lent itself admirably to the project of deconstructing subjectivity, the trope of "theatricality" enables us both to unpack subjectivity as performance and to denaturalize—to read as a *scene*—the whole encompassing space in which that subjectivity gets constituted: the intricate web of "romantic" bonds and family ties apparently consolidated by the novels in question.[6] In other words, if the self is treated here as not just a text but a contingent cluster of theatrical roles, then it becomes possible to make a spectacle of the imperious domestic, sexual, and aesthetic ideologies for which, and in which, it is bound. And that spectacle, I hope to show, often generates a number of spin-offs, unruly sideshows liable to cause further embarrassment for those forces in the novels (whether characters, author-effects, or other ideological emissaries) that would seem to uphold traditional family values.

One consequence of this interpretation of theatricality, then, is

---

6. A work whose aims are in many ways congruent with those of the present study is Joseph Allen Boone, *Tradition Counter Tradition: Love and the Form of Fiction* (Chicago: University of Chicago Press, 1987), which offers an astute discussion of the relations between marital ideology and narrative form, with special emphasis on the nineteenth-century novel.

that considerable attention is paid in the pages ahead not only to the ways in which theatrical energies are absorbed into what one might imagine, somewhat too organically, as a narrative's flow, but also to the ways in which such energies break or complicate that kind of natural-seeming teleology. Although I by no means see the-atricality as necessarily opposed to narrative—indeed, it often allows the latter to enfold it without any trouble whatsoever—at several crucial points here I invoke a distinction, most productively mobi-lized by feminist film theory, between the patriarchal, heterosexu-alizing pressure of narrative linearity, on the one hand, and the antilinear counterpressure of a feminist or gay spectacle or mas-querade, on the other.[7] The differences between nineteenth-century theatrical and twentieth-century cinematic categories should not, of course, be elided, but neither, as others have argued, should their continuities be denied, nor should we overlook the mediating role played by the nineteenth-century novel in the process of transmis-sion.[8]

This question of method bears not so incidentally on that of the book's scope. As a glance at the table of contents will confirm, I do not undertake a comprehensive study of theatricality in the nine-teenth-century English novel. A novelist like Thackeray, who might have seemed an obvious candidate for inclusion here, makes no appearance, and though I devote considerable space to the even more obvious Dickens, he has to share that space with those pre-sumably lesser figures, the "sensation" novelists. What mainly im-pels my reading of Dickens, in fact, is my conviction that the most

7. On the tension between phallocentric narrative and female spectacle, see Laura Mulvey, "Visual Pleasure and Narrative Cinema," in *Women and the Cinema: A Critical Anthology*, ed. Karyn Kay and Gerald Peary (New York: E. P. Dutton, 1977), pp. 412–28. For a discussion of the narrative disruptions effected by the cinematic represen-tation of the gay man, see Lee Edelman, "Imag(in)ing the Homosexual: *Laura* and the Other Face of Gender," in his *Homographesis: Essays in Gay Literary and Cultural Theory* (New York: Routledge, 1992). On subversive feminist and gay/lesbian the-atricality, see Judith Butler, *Gender Trouble: Feminism and the Subversion of Identity* (New York: Routledge, 1990), pp. 128–49.

8. On these intergeneric relations, see Peter Brooks, *The Melodramatic Imagination: Balzac, Henry James, Melodrama, and the Mode of Excess* (New Haven: Yale University Press, 1976); Thomas Elsaesser, "Tales of Sound and Fury: Observations on the Family Melodrama," in *Home Is Where the Heart Is: Studies in Melodrama and the Woman's Film*, ed. Christine Gledhill (London: British Film Institute, 1987), pp. 43–69; Gledhill, "The Melodramatic Field: An Investigation," ibid., pp. 5–39; William Rothman, *The "I" of the Camera: Essays in Film Criticism, History, and Aesthetics* (Cambridge: Cam-bridge University Press, 1988).

interesting theatricality in nineteenth-century English fiction is not necessarily the most "ebulliently" and most immediately recognizable. I focus more extensively on four other canonical novelists, who are at once more representative of their culture's overt, dominant antitheatricality and more plausibly motivated to rebel against it. For what these four more or less "psychological" novelists have in common, beyond their apparent willingness to produce (in their own distinctive ways, of course) the patriarchal, heterosexualizing narratives for which their culture has so insatiable a demand, is membership in groups (women and gay men, to be precise) that this culture, operating in no small part *through* such narratives, oppresses and marginalizes.

This book attempts to determine how the resulting conflicts of interest play themselves out—or fail to play themselves out—in these four authors' works. Thus, it suggests that when theatricality surfaces in the novels of Austen and Brontë, what gets performed is a complex disruption of the patriarchal narrative enterprise in which those authors are otherwise engaged, and that when James or one of his characters "makes a scene," what we observe is a gaily provocative acting up within and against the policing, pathologizing case histories that he simultaneously inscribes. Eliot would seem to stand out as the anomaly here, refusing the excesses of theatricality in favor of a "poetic" or theoretical metacommentary that would master them. Yet, as we will see, James turns out to have his own investment in dissevering the link between theory and theatricality, and in promoting the former as a defense against the latter.[9] Situating the gay male author at the end of a heterosexual female novelistic tradition, this book reads the Jamesian text as a stage on which that tradition's definitive resistances and compliances get recapitulated and reinterpreted in an especially condensed and telling way. It demonstrates that, though James's sexual and historical positioning may make him unusually anxious about inheriting a repertoire of female and feminist theatrical strategies, accounting for his apparent wish at times to transport himself into the magisterial, ostensibly

9. On the etymological and conceptual connection between theory and theatricality, see Jane Gallop, "Keys to Dora," in *In Dora's Case: Freud-Hysteria-Feminism*, ed. Charles Bernheimer and Claire Kahane (New York: Columbia University Press, 1985), p. 220, and Timothy Murray, *Theatrical Legitimation: Allegories of Genius in Seventeenth-Century England and France* (New York: Oxford University Press, 1987).

disembodied realm of aesthetic theory, the same positioning may explain his powerful identification with a certain figure of "the actress" and with the peculiar "commotion" she repeatedly causes.

Though it is easy, when writing about texts from an earlier century, to frame such ambivalences in terms of a tension between conscious complicity and unconscious subversiveness, as if the less official-looking aspects of an older text somehow had to exceed authorial awareness, I try not to draw too heavily on this particular implication of the return-of-the-repressed model. Not only does it aggrandize the critic at the expense of the author, but it prejudges and probably misrepresents a wide range of hermeneutic and historical issues, deluding us into thinking that we know what we mean when we talk about such things as authorship, agency, consciousness, and unconsciousness.[10] In short, I prefer not to create the impression that Austen, Brontë, Eliot, and James enact their *coups de théâtre* in spite of themselves; I try (not always successfully, I am sure) to give them credit for being as politically sophisticated and as rhetorically adroit as, for instance, late-twentieth-century academic critics.

Admittedly, the book's title might lead readers to expect that, if I do not set out to uncover what the authors *cannot* know, I have invested in the even more authoritarian fantasy of surprising them in their performance of what they would not want *us* to know. While I have no doubt occasionally given in, here again, to the all but irresistible interpretative temptations of voyeurism and sadism, it is important to note that I take my title from a passage in James's autobiography where, as we will see, he writes about catching *himself* in the act. If my critical gaze sometimes seems to recall the fascinated hyper-watchfulness of a certain style of pedagogue from the previous century, it should still be apparent that I aim not so much to expose or to embarrass the authors whom I "catch" as to show them in the process of catching and embarrassing *themselves*, of calling attention parodically or hyperbolically to their own agitated entanglement in the social scripts that determine them, and thus perhaps of agitating or rewriting those scripts from within.

If acting is a kind of interpretation, the reverse is equally true. Organized around the identification of figures in the novels and in

---

10. I am indebted to Eve Kosofsky Sedgwick for this insight.

their cultural milieu who function as precursors of contemporary reading practices, the book's main subtext is indeed about the theatricality of interpretation; and while the elaboration of this subtext means that, with varying degrees of sympathy, I (get to) catch other critics in the act, I make a point of catching myself as well. Depending upon the individual reader's tastes, these episodes of "self-consciousness" may embarrass her or him more or less than they embarrass me. In any case, the risk of appearing "self-important" or "pretentious" (terms the mere thought of which terrifies—which is to say, forms—the middle-class subject, not least the middle-class academic subject) seems worth running, for, despite the recent proliferation in literary and cultural studies of work on theatricality, vital questions about the performative effects of criticism itself—most basically, about *what* contemporary critics are performing, and about what or whom they are performing *for*—are only beginning to be posed.[11] If, as Foucault argued, "our society" is an extension of that of the nineteenth century, then we may learn some useful lessons from the acts of interpretation on view in some of that century's most surprisingly and acutely histrionic novels.

While one of the most sobering of those lessons would doubtless be how readily almost any would-be oppositional theatrics can be neutralized (if not sponsored from the outset) by the hegemonic

---

11. Notable writing on theatricality includes, in addition to the works mentioned above, Jean-Christophe Agnew, *Worlds Apart: The Market and the Theater in Anglo-American Thought, 1550–1750* (Cambridge: Cambridge University Press, 1986); Jonas Barish, *The Antitheatrical Prejudice* (Berkeley: University of California Press, 1981); Stanley Cavell, *Must We Mean What We Say?* (New York: Scribners, 1969); Michael Fried, *Absorption and Theatricality: Painting and Beholder in the Age of Diderot* (Berkeley: University of California Press, 1980); Stephen Greenblatt, *Renaissance Self-Fashioning: From More to Shakespeare* (Chicago: University of Chicago Press, 1980) and *Shakespearean Negotiations: The Circulation of Social Energy in Renaissance England* (Berkeley: University of California Press, 1988). An interesting subgenre is the growing body of work on cross-dressing; see, for example, Stephen Orgel, "Nobody's Perfect: Or, Why Did the English Stage Take Boys for Women?" *South Atlantic Quarterly* 88 (Winter 1989): 7–29, and Marjorie Garber, *Vested Interests: Cross-Dressing and Cultural Anxiety* (New York: Routledge, 1991). The beginnings of an analysis of criticism as performance may be observed in Armstrong, *Desire and Domestic Fiction* and "The Gender Bind: Women and the Disciplines," *Genders* 3 (Fall 1988): 1–23; Neil Hertz, *The End of the Line: Essays on Psychoanalysis and the Sublime* (New York: Columbia University Press, 1985); Alan Liu, "The Power of Formalism: The New Historicism," *ELH* 56 (Winter 1989): 721–71; Miller, *The Novel and the Police*; Eve Kosofsky Sedgwick, *Epistemology of the Closet* (Berkeley: University of California Press, 1990); Peter Stallybrass and Allon White, *The Politics and Poetics of Transgression* (Ithaca: Cornell University Press, 1986).

culture, the following chapters evince a reluctance to stop with that paradoxically comforting critical trope. To be sure, as anyone who has ever read an article on contemporary literary-critical discourse in, say, the *New York Times* can attest, it would be a mistake to underestimate the counterparodic genius of cultural orthodoxy. Perhaps the reading that persists in looking for—What should one call them?—transgressive openings in a text will always seem more naïve than the reading that eventuates in an ironic recognition of the capacity of Power to contain subversion; such a consideration may in fact explain the tentativeness with which some of my more optimistic formulations are proffered. At the same time, however, these readings proceed from the assumption that, by strategically reenacting certain scenes inscribed in the novels of Austen, Brontë, Eliot, and James, one may identify and release unsuspected energies of feminist and antihomophobic critique and revision, whose play our culture's theaters of oppression may not, for all their supervisory machinery, be able to keep within bounds.

1

The Infection of Acting
Theatricals and Theatricality in Mansfield Park

Though *Mansfield Park* seems the least inclusive or dialectical of Jane Austen's novels, it has failed to produce the critical unanimity that so unambiguous a work ought to permit.[1] Despite repeated attempts to lay the groundwork for scholarly consensus,[2] this ostensibly non-ironic novel continues to elicit incompatible commentaries. Paradoxically, its very dogmatism is what makes for disagreement: the question of why Austen, in championing the priggish Fanny Price, should appear to dishonor her own artistic verve, may be answered, it seems, in more than one way. Recent critics are divided between those for whom *Mansfield Park* is an emphatically anti-Jacobin, staunchly Christian work, and those who find in it a disguised yet all the more potent version of the feminist or anti-authoritarian message that other Austen novels develop less obliquely.[3] From this discord, one is tempted to conclude that the novel's dogma is somehow shakier than it ought to be. This chapter seeks not to determine once and for all whether the presiding genius of *Mansfield Park* is Edmund Burke or Mary Wollstonecraft, but to examine the central instability within the novel itself, the instability that renders such determination impossible. I will argue that the novel is neither un-

---

1. Lionel Trilling (*Sincerity and Authenticity* [Cambridge: Harvard University Press, 1971], pp. 75–80) opposes the "dialectical mode" of Austen's other novels to the "categorical" mode of *Mansfield Park*.

2. See, for example, Avrom Fleishman, *A Reading of Mansfield Park: An Essay in Critical Synthesis* (Baltimore: Johns Hopkins University Press, 1970) and Joel C. Weinsheimer, "*Mansfield Park*: Three Problems," *Nineteenth-Century Fiction* 29 (1974): 185–205.

3. For examples of the former view, see Marilyn Butler, *Jane Austen and the War of Ideas* (Oxford: Oxford University Press, 1975), pp. 219–49, and Gary Kelly, "Reading Aloud in *Mansfield Park*," *Nineteenth-Century Fiction* 37 (1982): 29–49. For examples of the latter view, see Margaret Kirkham, *Jane Austen, Feminism and Fiction* (New York: Barnes and Noble, 1983), pp. 93–120, and David Monaghan, *Jane Austen: Structure and Social Vision* (London: Macmillan, 1980), pp. 93–114.

equivocally conservative nor unequivocally progressive, but rather that it is governed by a conservatism so riddled with internal contradictions as to trouble the authoritarian temperament more radically than would the dialectical leniency of, say, *Pride and Prejudice* or *Emma*. To argue as much, however, will also mean showing the tenacity of that conservatism, qualifying any interpretation too eager to claim *Mansfield Park* as a document of humanistic amplitude.[4]

One recent call for a synthesis in Austen criticism asks us to imagine a "structure large enough to accommodate an affirmative text with a subversive subtext."[5] *Mansfield Park* reveals how precarious such a structure must, by definition, be. In a novel that abounds in talk of structures—of their erection, their improvement, and their dismantlement—the most problematic structure is the makeshift "theater" set up in the billiard-room of Mansfield Park. This structure literalizes a somewhat more abstract "structure"—the episode of the theatricals, the textual locus on which so much critical attention has centered. As Jonas Barish has pointed out, "the theatricals come charged with a mysterious iniquity that challenges explanation."[6] The "crux of the book,"[7] the theatrical episode disturbs us because we cannot see why *Austen* should have been so disturbed by an art form whose energies seem so similar to her own. Yet one might also say that it disturbs us even more insistently precisely because it *is* the crux of the book—because, that is, it has the power to become more than just a local structure, to spread perplexingly throughout the novel, just as the "theater" at Mansfield Park soon extends from the billiard-room, encompassing, of all places, Sir Thomas's study. The episode, which occupies the last third of the first volume, is abruptly terminated by his return from

4. In other words, this chapter attempts a kind of balancing act between two influential styles of novel-reading, the first associated with certain versions of feminism and deconstruction, the second emerging from the writings of Michel Foucault. If I have tried to maintain a sense of the subversive implications of theatricality without underestimating the capacity of authority to domesticate forces that might overturn it, I have also sought to suggest power's genius for self-preservation without promoting the monolithic view of power that often characterizes discussions of the nineteenth-century novel as a disciplinary practice.

5. David Monaghan, "Introduction: Jane Austen as a Social Novelist," in *Jane Austen in a Social Context*, ed. Monaghan (London: Macmillan, 1981), p. 7.

6. Jonas Barish, *The Antitheatrical Prejudice* (Berkeley and Los Angeles: University of California Press, 1981), p. 301.

7. Sybil Rosenfeld, "Jane Austen and Private Theatricals," *Essays and Studies* 15 (1962): 40.

Antigua: he wastes no time in eradicating all traces of the theatricals, not only ordering the sets to be torn down but going so far as to burn every copy of *Lover's Vows*, the play chosen for private performance. Despite this aggressive attempt at effacement, however, and despite the destruction of the theater as place, theatricality as topic turns out to pervade the novel. In this movement from a literal structure to a more metaphorical one, we witness a process of refinement, of increasingly subtle infiltration. After describing Sir Thomas's swift campaign of destruction, Austen informs us, slyly, that at least *one* remnant of the episode has escaped his ravages: Mrs. Norris has appropriated the curtain, surreptitiously removing it to her cottage, "where she happened to be particularly in want of green baize."[8] This appropriation and transformation might stand for that adaptability which allows the theater to survive and flourish in a less conspicuous form, reaching into the most unlikely recesses of the text.

Yet if this shift from theater to theatricality suggests the triumphant expansion of a "subversive subtext," we need to specify just what theatricality entails. As we will see, the political implications of theatricality in *Mansfield Park* are ineluctably ambiguous. Critics have tended to associate it with the most attractively self-dramatizing characters in the novel, Mary and Henry Crawford, thereby construing it in terms of metropolitan glamor and decadence. Theatricality has a less glittering side, however, and this variant turns out to be surprisingly consistent with the authoritarianism represented, in different ways, by Sir Thomas, Mrs. Norris, Fanny, and Edmund. Wavering between affirmative and subversive poles, the generalized, ubiquitous structure of theatricality begins to expose their relationship as one not of opposition but of almost systematic interdependence. An all-embracing theatricality would seem to threaten the very foundations of a novel whose heroine epitomizes what Tony Tanner calls "immobility,"[9] yet theatricality is in fact capable of such wide diffusion only because it has certain features that not merely conform to but even enable the novel's overriding

8. *Mansfield Park*, ed. Tony Tanner (Harmondsworth: Penguin, 1966), p. 210. Subsequent references to the novel will be to this edition, and will be included parenthetically in the text.

9. Introduction, *Mansfield Park*, ed. Tony Tanner (Harmondsworth: Penguin, 1966), p. 8.

conservatism. The question, in other words, is not so much "What motivated Austen's anti-theatricalism?" as "What motivated her to create the *impression* of anti-theatricalism?" Alien enough to give her pause yet not so alien as to resist the uses to which Austen puts it, theatricality in *Mansfield Park* affords the spectacle of a distinct overdetermination.

But what in the nature of theatricality allows supposedly rival ideologies to converge upon it? When Fanny Price and Henry Crawford offer their respective descriptions of the theatricals, we note the similarity of their language as much as the difference between their tones. Here is Fanny's view of the rehearsals:

> So far from being all satisfied and all enjoying, she found every body requiring something they had not, and giving occasion of discontent to the others.—Every body had a part either too long or too short;—nobody would attend as they ought, nobody would remember on which side they were to come in—nobody but the complainer would observe any directions.
>
> (p. 185)

Henry recalls the same experience with nostalgic relish:

> "It is as a dream, a pleasant dream!" he exclaimed, breaking forth again after a few minutes musing. "I shall always look back on our theatricals with exquisite pleasure. There was such an interest, such an animation, such a spirit diffused! Every body felt it. We were all alive. There was enjoyment, hope, solicitude, bustle, for every hour of the day. Always some little objection, some little doubt, some little anxiety to be got over. I never was happier."
>
> (p. 236)

Though one response suggests the bemused omniscience of detachment while the other evokes the giddiness of absolute involvement, both Fanny and Henry characterize the theatricals in terms of "discontent" or "anxiety." As Ruth Bernard Yeazell has written, theatricality provokes an "anxiety of boundary-confusion" that "is everywhere felt" in *Mansfield Park*.[10] Yet for Fanny and Henry the theater is not just an *object* of anxiety but the very *site* of anxiety, a site that crosses its own boundaries to figure the anxiety of the novel as a whole. For *Mansfield Park*, however much it may favor repose, is, as Yeazell notes, certainly one of the most anxious novels ever writ-

---

10. Ruth Bernard Yeazell, "The Boundaries of *Mansfield Park*," *Representations* 7 (Summer 1984): 137.

ten.[11] Anxiety may be the condition of all narratives, but here, in its generality as "a spirit diffused," it seems especially acute. Indeed, Fanny's composure is merely superficial, a defensive fiction: Austen tells us that, during the rehearsals, "her mind had never been farther from peace" (p. 180), that she is agitated by "many uncomfortable, anxious, apprehensive feelings" (p. 186), that she observes the preparations in a baffled state of "longing and dreading" (p. 187). Fanny is anxious about the theater precisely because she knows that it is less a structure toward which one can locate a safely external position than the fluctuating space in which all positions find their tenuous footing. A Henry Crawford may thrive within this milieu while a Fanny Price may inhabit it more unhappily, but neither the libertine nor the evangelical moralist can choose to function outside of it. In *Mansfield Park*, the theater, or the theatricality by virtue of which it disperses itself and colonizes the rest of the novel, becomes virtually synonymous with the inescapable context of all social existence and all political postures. Resembling Henry Crawford in abhorring "any thing like a permanence of abode" (p. 74), theatricality turns up where one least expects it—even in the innermost meditations of the self-effacing Fanny. Discussions of the theatricals have not stressed sufficiently their *privateness*: *Mansfield Park* is about the incursion of public values upon private experience, about the theatricality of everyday life, in which to say, with Fanny, "No, indeed, I cannot act" (p. 168), is already to perform, whether one wants to or not.

Like Fanny's anti-theatricalism, then, Austen's begins to emerge as a futile protest against the theatrical imperative—futile in large part because it is disingenuous, given the extent to which the political order of *Mansfield Park* depends upon a certain theatricality. Actual theaters may be circumscribed places that one can have demolished, but in its most generalized form theatricality, like Flaubert's divine artist, is present everywhere though visible nowhere. If this invisibility induces paranoia in the Tory mind, it also makes possible a more efficient policing of the social practices by which authority sustains itself. Austen, moreover, is not alone in recording

11. It is remarkable how frequently the word "anxious" and its various derivatives appear in the text. I suspect that a concordance of Austen's works would show that *Mansfield Park* draws more heavily than any of the other novels on the vocabulary of anxiety.

this ambiguity. *Mansfield Park*, which was published in 1814, figures in a broader cultural discourse about theatricality, a discourse shaped by authors whose differences appear even more irreconcilable than those between Fanny Price and Henry Crawford. Like Fanny and Henry, however, these real-life conservatives and progressives exhibit a striking kinship when they engage the problem of theatricality, which seems to inspire not only a number of tellingly recurrent images but also a certain rhetorical oscillation in writings otherwise divided along lines of political allegiance. By looking briefly at a few of these writings, we may arrive at a more precise sense of what theatricality meant in late-eighteenth- and early-nineteenth-century England, of how it tended to comprehend those who would comprehend it, and of how Austen's novel both reproduces and illuminates this predicament.

Our first two authors are evangelical ideologues whose wariness vis-à-vis the theater almost goes without saying. But here, as in *Mansfield Park*, the concern is less with the theater as an institution than with the possibility that the theater might have overstepped its institutional limits and invaded private life, establishing in private theatricals the symbol of an irreversible contamination. Indeed, in its recourse to metaphors of infection, Thomas Gisborne's *Enquiry into the Duties of the Female Sex* (1797) anticipates Austen's insight into the theater's refusal to stay within bounds. Gisborne identifies the ills of the modern stage, warning, "He knows little of human nature, who thinks that the youthful mind will be secured from the infecting influence of a vicious character, adorned with polished manners, wit, fortitude, and generosity, by a frigid moral, delivered at the conclusion, or to be deduced from the events of the drama."[12] Gisborne's slightly disorienting syntax already indicates an uncertainty characteristic of contemporary discussions of theatricality, for it is not at first clear whether the vicious character will infect the youthful mind *because* such a mind is adorned with polished manners and the like, or whether it will infect that mind *even though* it is so adorned. On closer inspection, it turns out that Gisborne intends

---

12. Thomas Gisborne, *Enquiry into the Duties of the Female Sex* (London: T. Cadell and W. Davies, 1797), pp. 171–72.

the former; in theatrical discourse as a whole, the polish that would serve as an antidote to poison often becomes indistinguishable from the poison itself. Metaphors of infection lead almost irresistibly to metaphors of seduction. As Tom Bertram, trying to justify the theatrical scheme to his father, says, the "infection" of acting "spread as those things always spread you know" (p. 200). But Gisborne's language, somewhat less vague than Tom's, suggests that "those things always spread" because the poison may beguile us into mistaking it for the cure.[13] Austen, after all, refers to acting not only as an "infection" but also as a "charm" (p. 154), and what "spreads" is nothing other than a play *about* seduction.

Gisborne uncovers the logic of this mixed metaphor when he explains why young women are particularly susceptible to the enchantments of playacting:

> A propensity to imitation is natural to the human mind, and is attended with various effects highly favourable to human happiness. . . . This propensity shows itself with especial strength in the female sex. Providence, designing from the beginning that the manner of life to be adopted by women should in many respects ultimately depend, not so much on their own deliberate choice, as on the interest and convenience of the parent, of the husband, or of some other connection, has implanted in them a remarkable tendency to conform to the wishes and examples of those for whom they feel a warmth of regard, and even of all those with whom they are in familiar habits of intercourse. . . . As the mind, in obeying the impulse of this principle, no less than in following any other of its native or acquired tendencies, is capable of being ensnared into errors and excesses; the season of youth, the season when the principle itself is in its greatest strength, and when it has yet derived few lessons from reflection and experience, is the time when error and excesses are most to be apprehended.[14]

Young women are even more liable to corruption than young men, since the very thing that keeps them healthy—their unusually strong "propensity to imitation"—can easily make them ill. Acting, whose essence is imitation, seduces by diminishing the distance between negative and positive terms—between poison and cure, sickness and health. Properly controlled, of course, the latent theatricality of the

---

13. For a discussion of the identity of poison and cure, see Jacques Derrida's remarks on the word *pharmakon* in "Plato's Pharmacy," in *Dissemination*, trans. Barbara Johnson (Chicago: University of Chicago Press, 1981), pp. 61–181.

14. Gisborne, *Enquiry*, pp. 115–17.

female sex, "implanted" in women by "Providence," can have a salutary effect, ensuring that they will "conform to the wishes and examples" of their (male) superiors. Yet at what point does the very act of "obeying" turn into its opposite, with the result that these no longer merely latent actresses are "ensnared into errors and excesses"? What is required, obviously, is a vigilant patrolling of the border between "good" acting and "bad" acting. Acting, however, in addition to blurring the lines between sickness and health, or between poison and cure, frustrates the attempt to define—let alone to patrol—the border between the safely domestic and the menacingly foreign, between the private and the public, between the inside and the outside. For no sooner has Gisborne asserted that Providence has implanted the "principle" of imitation in the female sex than he appears unsure whether this principle is "native or acquired." It may seem uncharitable to read vacillation into what is perhaps nothing more than a pseudophilosophical aside, yet this minor rhetorical fluttering hints at the boundary-confusion that becomes a leitmotif of the literature on theatricality.

We encounter this theme again in another tract directed at saving young women from themselves. In *Strictures on the Modern System of Female Education* (1799), Hannah More animadverts more harshly than Gisborne on the theatricalization of private life. Where Gisborne sees theatricality as a merely potential danger—as the aggravation of otherwise healthy "tendencies"—More describes it as a disease in its advanced stages, at least "among women of rank and fortune": "If the life of a young lady, formerly, too much resembled the life of a confectioner, it now too much resembles that of an actress; the morning is all rehearsal, and the evening is all performance."[15] More blames this vitiating penetration of the public into the private on a more specific form of crosscultural trespass: the "modern apostles of infidelity and immorality," among whom she must number Elizabeth Inchbald, the translator and adapter of August von Kotzebue's *Lovers' Vows,* have strengthened their attacks on female virtue by enlisting the subversive services of German literature. Yet what might strike others as grounds for clemency invites More's sharpest censure: "In many of these translations, certain

15. Hannah More, *Strictures on the Modern System of Female Education*, 2 vols. (London: T. Cadell and W. Davies, 1799), 1:115.

stronger passages, which, though well received in Germany, would have excited disgust in England, are wholly omitted, in order that the mind may be more certainly, though more slowly, prepared for the full effect of the same poison to be administered in a stronger degree at another period."[16]

In the preface to her translation of *Lovers' Vows*, Inchbald defends her omissions and modifications by appealing to her own theatrical savvy, to her sense of what will play in Germany but not in England.[17] According to More, however, such changes are designed precisely to undermine rather than recognize the differences between the two nationalities. As in so much right-wing literature of the period, the poison of theatricality is inseparable from the poison of foreignness—specifically, of the revolutionary doctrines threatening to spread to England from the continent.[18] Theatricality destroys the body politic by destroying that body's immune system, which, like all such systems, consists in the ability to distinguish between the native and the foreign, between self and other. The most insidious translation is that which seems so reassuringly familiar as to prevent us from identifying and repelling the alien substance. Here, the poison owes its seductive power not to its polished exterior but to its deceptive folksiness: the *Unheimliche*, or unsettling, masquerades as the *Heimliche*, or cozy. Interestingly, one of the ways in which Jane Austen signals the gravity of the theatrical infection is by having Edmund say of the Grants, through whom Mary and Henry Crawford were introduced into the Bertram family circle, "They seem to belong to us—they seem to be part of ourselves" (p. 211). If even the normally watchful Edmund has trouble distinguishing between insiders and outsiders, then the immune system of Mansfield Park has clearly broken down.

Against such calamities, More counsels a renewed alertness. But

16. More, ibid., 1:42.
17. See Elizabeth Inchbald, Preface and Remarks, *Lovers' Vows: Altered from the German of Kotzebue* (London: Longman, Hurst, Rees, and Orme, 1808), pp. 3–9.
18. The xenophobia of the age appears not only in the political journalism of periodicals like *The Anti-Jacobin* and the *Porcupine and Anti-Gallican Monitor*, both of which published negative reviews of *Lovers' Vows*, but also in the literary theory of Wordsworth's Preface to the second edition of *Lyrical Ballads* (1800), with its denunciation of "sickly and stupid German tragedies," which satisfy a "degrading thirst after outrageous stimulation." *Poetical Works*, ed. Thomas Hutchinson, rev. Ernest de Selincourt (London: Oxford University Press, 1975), p. 735.

if her tone seems particularly melodramatic—apparent improve-
ments in the translation serve in fact to poison the mind "more
certainly, though more slowly"—then some of this straining to
equate less with more and better with worse may indicate that she
herself has become a victim of what she would contain. For her
rhetoric of suspicion rests upon a logic of paradox, whereby quan-
titative differences disappear and everything ends up as its opposite.
Is not this inability to differentiate one of the primary symptoms of
the theatrical disease? Indeed, even as More rails against the tendency of upper-class young women to resemble actresses, her own
prose draws heavily on theatrical metaphors, referring repeatedly,
for example, to the duties that a young Christian woman must "perform." It is worth noting that, earlier in her career, More had been
a playwright, a friend and ardent admirer of Garrick, and a member
in good standing of the London theatrical community; regardless of
her present sympathies, her writing bears the marks of this past.[19]
Yet where Gisborne might distinguish between moral and immoral
performance, More's new militancy excludes this possibility, as if to
cover the traces of its own infection. Once again, the attempt to
situate oneself outside the anxious world of playacting merely produces more anxiety, more evidence of one's inextricable implication
in that world.

Gisborne seems more inclined to acknowledge what More prefers
to repress—namely, that all social experience presupposes some degree of theatricality. But, as we have seen, to acknowledge the con-
tagion is not to escape its effects: in its own, admittedly milder,
discrepancies, Gisborne's language joins More's in illustrating the
plight of an authoritarianism compelled to come into contact with
forces it would rather regulate or pronounce upon from a distance.
The awkward position of these two evangelical conduct-book writers
recalls that of Edmund Bertram, who, in order to halt the spread of
the theatricals, has to plunge into their midst, playing the highly
compromising role of Mary Crawford's lover in the Mansfield production of Kotzebue's play. Yet if Gisborne and More exemplify the
difficulties of a certain conservatism in coping with theatricality, we
would expect a liberal and more sophisticated writer to approach

19. For a discussion of More's career in the theater, see Mary Gwladys Jones,
Hannah More (Cambridge: Cambridge University Press, 1952), pp. 25–40.

the subject with something like urbane equanimity. This attitude does in fact characterize William Hazlitt's essay, "On Actors and Acting" (1817), a shrewd and lively rejoinder to the enemies of the stage. Oddly enough, though, Hazlitt's defense shows some of the same instabilities that we have noticed in the language of the detractors.

Where Gisborne and More accuse the theater—or at least the theater in its present form—of encouraging immorality, Hazlitt recommends it as the "best teacher of morals" because the "truest and most intelligible picture of life." Matters become more complicated, however, when he proceeds to explain how theatrical mimesis effects this moral education: "It points out the selfish and depraved to our detestation; the amiable and generous to our admiration; and if it clothes the more seductive vices with the borrowed graces of wit and fancy, even these graces operate as a diversion to the coarser poison of experience and bad example, and often prevent or carry off the infection by inoculating the mind with a certain taste and elegance."[20] As in the previous texts, seduction and infection seem to invoke each other almost automatically, but here their relationship is more intricate. If, for Hazlitt, polish is not the poison but indeed the antidote, these "borrowed graces of wit and fancy" participate in what looks like a homeopathic program. For, as Gisborne and More would remind us, wit and fancy, or the "taste and elegance" with which they "inoculate" the mind, may *become* seductive vices in their own right. Hazlitt appears to share this view, insofar as he contrasts the theatrical graces with the *"coarser* poison" of vices not wearing this borrowed "clothing."

Yet the mixed metaphor itself may signal a deeper trouble. Though Hazlitt began by affirming the morally instructive properties of mimesis, the process he is now describing has to do neither with mimesis nor with instruction, but with a kind of seduction of the mind itself. Adorning rather than imitating reality, wit and fancy "prevent or carry off the infection" of the mind by seductive vices by seducing it toward other, less coarse ones. Not only is the mind seduced: it is also reduced, demoted to the role of a passive object that can only submit to being "diverted" toward the lesser of two

20. "On Actors and Acting," in Hazlitt, *Essays*, ed. Rosalind Vallance and John Hampden (London: Folio Society, 1964), p. 23.

evils. By way of arguing for the salutary influence of the theater, Hazlitt resorts to the somewhat disconcerting image of the playgoer as patient, and in so doing comes surprisingly close to Gisborne's ideology of social control, with its notion of latent theatricality as the basis of female "conformity." Of course Hazlitt's politics permit him to speak in less sinister terms: when he says of actors, "The height of their ambition is to be *beside themselves*,"[21] he celebrates the freedom of the "improvised self,"[22] the Protean exuberance of a Henry Crawford. Alongside this overall humanism, however, Hazlitt's apparent endorsement of theatricality as a means of manipulation becomes all the more significant, for it testifies to the readiness with which theatrical forms lend themselves to disciplinary purposes.[23]

Perhaps the congestion of Hazlitt's language symptomatizes uneasiness in the face of inconsistency, or perhaps the clutter was designed as a "diversion," at once an alternative to and a distraction from this inconsistency. In either case, though, Hazlitt's unstable rhetoric reveals yet another peculiarity of the theatrical discourse to which *Mansfield Park* contributes. Where Gisborne and More worried that the theater might encroach upon everyday life, Hazlitt's tergiversations point to the difficulty of keeping everyday life from encroaching upon the theater. It is not that Hazlitt rejects representation: as we have seen, he bases—or tries to base—his defense of the theater on a plea for its mimetic value. Yet in order to sustain one's view of the theater as an "epitome, a bettered likeness of the world,"[24] one has to bar from this idealized enclosure the more cynical calculations that too often prevail in everyday life; such cynicism may accord with pragmatic schemes of social regulation, but it hardly becomes a large-spirited humanism. The theater can be a bettered likeness of the world only by remaining free from ideo-

---

21. Hazlitt, ibid., p. 22.

22. Leo Bersani, *A Future for Astyanax: Character and Desire in Literature* (Boston: Little, Brown, 1976), p. 76.

23. It is perhaps more than anecdotally interesting that in 1815—the year after *Mansfield Park* appeared—Hazlitt himself published a less than enthusiastic review of *Lovers' Vows*. "The whole of this play," he wrote, "which is of German origin, carries the romantic in sentiment and story to the extreme verge of decency as well as probability" (*A View of the English Stage; or, A Series of Dramatic Criticisms*, ed. W. Spencer Jackson [London: George Bell and Sons, 1906], p. 113).

24. Hazlitt, "On Actors," p. 22.

logical complicities *with* that world, complicities that would jeopardize its ability to imitate and to instruct. In explaining how the theater operates as a guardian against *moral* infection, however, Hazlitt opens it to just this kind of *ideological* infection. Moreover, if the theater starts to look a little more like the world, the world starts to look a little more like the theater; as the different poisons play upon the mind, it becomes hard to tell where reality ends and art begins.

Together, Gisborne, More, and Hazlitt delineate the landscape of dis-ease in which *Mansfield Park* takes place. To situate the novel in this context, though, is not necessarily to arrive at a clearer understanding of what Jane Austen really thought about the theater. Much of the criticism of *Mansfield Park* tries to solve the mystery of the author's intention, but the point of the preceding survey is that theatricality wreaks havoc on intentions. Whether they stand on the left or on the right, authors who set out to elucidate the problem soon find themselves baffled by unexpected complexities. Hazlitt undertakes to offer a liberal paean to actors and acting, and yet cannot help being pulled in the direction of authoritarianism. Contrary to our assumptions about the lawlessness of theatricality, the subject seems to impose an almost inexorable rightward drift.[25] Yet, contrary to what we might assume about drifts to the right, the texts of our evangelical authors betray a remarkable restlessness. Calling for an attentive monitoring of the theatrical impulse, Gisborne succeeds in showing why such monitoring may be impracticable. More, for her part, continues the sermon against theatricality as the enemy

25. In a single issue of the moderately liberal periodical *The Theatrical Inquisitor* 2 (May 1813), we find yet another illustration of this point. An anonymous article entitled "On the Origin and Progress of Theatrical Amusements in England" describes how the theater "became the source of an amusement classical and elegant at the same time that it was in the highest degree improving and attractive" (206). Only a few pages later, another anonymous piece fulminates about the dangers of masquerades: "a masquerade is the school of elegant instruction in all the mysteries of wantonness" (214). Admittedly, the masquerade is a minor and specialized form of theater, not a synonym for the theater in general. But the recurrence of the word "elegant" in a sardonic rather than an honorific register points to the problematic nature of the vaccine Hazlitt prescribes, and to a widespread early-nineteenth-century ambivalence about theatricality, even (or especially) among those in the protheatrical camp.

within, unwittingly providing evidence of the lengths to which a discourse will go in concealing the signs of its own occupation. As a novel about theatricality, *Mansfield Park* dramatizes both the conservative appropriation of theatrical forms and the way these forms endanger the very interests that appropriate them, threatening to turn the captors into captives.

Just how does conservatism appropriate theatricality? Following Hazlitt, we might see a certain homeopathic logic at work in the novel. The patriarchal authority who "keeps every body in their places" (p. 182), Sir Thomas embodies a cunningly manipulative authority, one that will not hesitate, for example, to exile Fanny to Portsmouth in the name of a "medicinal project upon [her] understanding, which he must consider as at present diseased" (p. 363). Though the theatrical scheme suggests a flouting of his authority, since it is conceived and begun during his absence and in spite of the likelihood of his disapproval, the theatricals may function quite differently, as a kind of medicinal project upon Mansfield Park itself, which a conscientious authority must also consider as diseased. For even before the Crawfords arrive, Mansfield Park suffers from an overdose of theatricality. Indeed, the regime in question seems more like a parody of authority than like authority in the strict sense. Sir Thomas has delegated too much power to the officious Mrs. Norris, who, with her "love of directing" (p. 45), views the household as a showcase for her own talents of management and domestic economy. Small wonder that she becomes such an energetic sponsor and supervisor of the theatricals. She has already assisted in the education, or miseducation, of Sir Thomas's daughters, Maria and Julia, who typify the sort of "accomplished" young women about whom Hannah More complains:

> The Miss Bertrams were now fully established among the belles of the neighbourhood; and as they joined to beauty and brilliant acquirements, a manner naturally easy, and carefully formed to general civility and obligingness, they possessed its favour as well as its admiration. Their vanity was in such good order, that they seemed to be quite free from it, and gave themselves no airs; while the praises attending such behaviour, secured, and brought round by their aunt, served to strengthen them in believing they had no faults.
>
> (p. 68)

Actresses in everything but the title, Maria and Julia manifest their illness by concealing it. Just as, for Mrs. More, the poison of subversive ideas works most effectively when introduced under a familiar disguise, so the height of vanity is to "seem quite free from it," and the perfection of theatrical artifice is an apparent artlessness.

Given this state of affairs, why not attempt to cure like with like, "treating" theatricality itself with doses of more theatricality?[26] Obviously, Sir Thomas has nothing to do with the theatrical scheme. I am not intimating that he masterminds and controls it in some implausibly subterranean way. Yet, as the major authority *within* the book, he may well represent the authority *behind* the book—namely, Jane Austen herself. As he states at the outset, it is his duty to "authorize" (p. 47) various practices and relationships at Mansfield Park, and this responsibility echoes a more fundamental author-izing.[27] Perhaps Austen not only authors but also authorizes the theatrical episode, working out in terms of narrative structure a medicinal project or experiment upon the diseased body politic of Mansfield Park and, by extension, of the English gentry as a whole.[28] The injection of the Crawfords—and, to a lesser extent, of Mr. Yates—would serve to shock the system of Mansfield Park into protecting itself against such intruders. The infection that they bring would have the theatricals as its most alarming symptom, but this attack would culminate in a return to health. Indeed, the episode does seem to have some of the desired effect, for it ends with the banishment of Yates, the retreat of the Crawfords, and the departure of Maria and Julia, and initiates both the rise of Fanny and the fall of Mrs. Norris.

The only trouble with this scheme is that it scants the considerable distance between the end of the theatrical episode and the end of the novel itself: two whole volumes stand between the ostensible purgation and the complete recovery of Mansfield Park from the evils that have plagued it. However daring the homeopathic experiment, the disease lingers. For the Crawfords are only temporarily

---

26. It is perhaps significant that the first major discoveries in homeopathic medicine took place in the late eighteenth century.

27. For a discussion of the relationship between authorship and authority as viewed by women writers, see Sandra M. Gilbert and Susan Gubar, *The Madwoman in the Attic: The Woman Writer and the Nineteenth-Century Literary Imagination* (New Haven: Yale University Press, 1979), pp. 3–99.

28. For a reading of the theatrical episode along these lines, see Fleishman, *A Reading*, pp. 24–29.

repelled by Sir Thomas's displeasure; their exclusion, in fact, lasts for a mere two chapters. Moreover, it is immediately after this drastic attempt at cleansing that Edmund makes his remark about how the Grants, half-sister and half-brother-in-law of the Crawfords, "seem to be part of ourselves."[29] And instead of taking steps to resolve this familial identity crisis, Sir Thomas actually exacerbates it, trying to maneuver Fanny into marrying Henry Crawford. Sir Thomas does not seem to recognize the Crawfords as the real "daemon[s] of the piece" (p. 435), as the chief perpetrators of the "bustle and confusion of acting" (p. 205). Like Maria and Julia, whose vanity is so advanced that it conceals itself, Mary and Henry are such adroit actors that they know how to dissemble their theatrical busy-ness. As a result, they are soon readmitted, while the less skillful Mr. Yates, who "bustles" more discernibly, is cast out. Of course, Yates is not merely a scapegoat, since it was he, after all, who carried the infection of acting from Ecclesford to Mansfield in the first place. But this very sanctioning of a covert theatricality at the expense of an overt one inheres in the deeper logic of the narrative: the theatricals serve not as a homeopathic cure—although Austen might want us to view them as one—but as a "diversion," as Hazlitt would say, from the subtler and more comprehensive theatricality that persists long after Sir Thomas has reclaimed his study.

Jane Austen diverts our attention from this theatricality so that we may not notice how indispensable a role it plays in the rehabilitation of Mansfield Park. The reason that the Crawfords, who, through metonymic slippage, "seem to belong to us," and the bustling Mrs. Norris, who "seemed a part of" Sir Thomas (p. 450), are not expelled until the end of the novel is not that it takes so long to eliminate theatricality, but that theatricality requires this much time to, as it were, take effect. By the end of the novel, these characters have done their work so well—have "implanted" theatricality so firmly—that they themselves no longer need to remain at Mansfield: they have not so much overstayed their welcome as outlived their usefulness. A sort of sideshow, the homeopathic experiment fails because it was never intended to succeed.

29. In "Three Problems," Weinsheimer comments: "The Crawfords are not some extrinsic evil that ascends from London to violate the pure children of Mansfield; rather, the Crawfords' appeal is based on tendencies latent in Edmund and in the whole Bertram family" (p. 203).

Theatricality inhabits Mansfield Park before, during, and after the theatrical episode. Are there differences, though, between the theatricality of the Miss Bertrams and the theatricality of the Crawfords, or between the theatricality of the Crawfords and the theatricality of Fanny? We may begin to answer this question by suggesting that, where Fanny's cousins embody a dangerously centrifugal sociability, Fanny installs a steadfast and almost inaccessible inwardness at the other end of the narrative continuum. Mary and Henry Crawford do not so much stand between these two extremes as upset the very dichotomy on which this model is predicated. Mary, for example, is the subject of numerous tortured conversations between Fanny and Edmund, in which they struggle to decide whether her apparent irreverence indicates some profound flaw in her nature or merely the unfortunate effect of the company she keeps. We can understand Fanny and Edmund's perplexity: on the one hand, Mary displays what looks like genuine warmth and affection for others; on the other hand, Austen often emphasizes the enormous amount of technique that underlies this display, as when, at Fanny's coming-out party, Mary takes great pains to tell everyone what (she thinks) he or she wants to hear. In her artful artlessness, she puts even Maria and Julia to shame, seducing not only Edmund but many a suspicious, if not cantankerous, critic as well.[30]

Yet her brother is an even better actor, in whom play and seriousness are inseparably intertwined. Thus Fanny, whose mind tolerates only either/or distinctions, is at a loss to interpret his amorous behavior toward her:

> How could *she* have excited serious attachment in a man, who had seen so many, and been admired by so many, and flirted with so many, infinitely her superiors—who seemed so little open to serious impressions, even where pains had been taken to please him—who thought so slightly, so carelessly, so unfeelingly on all such points—who was every thing to every body, and seemed to find no one essential to him? . . . Every thing might be possible rather than serious attachment or serious approbation of it toward her. She had quite convinced herself of this before Sir Thomas and Mr. Crawford joined them. The difficulty was in maintaining the conviction quite so ab-

---

30. Marvin Mudrick, for example, defends Mary Crawford as the wronged would-be heroine of the novel, even though she is in many ways similar to Emma Woodhouse, for whom he has a distinct dislike. See *Jane Austen: Irony as Defense and Discovery* (Princeton: Princeton University Press, 1952), pp. 155–80.

solutely after Mr. Crawford was in the room; for once or twice a look seemed forced on her which she did not know how to class among the common meaning; in any other man at least, she would have said that it meant something very earnest, very pointed. But she still tried to believe it no more than what he might often have expressed towards her cousins or fifty other women.

(p. 309)

An inveterate player of roles—a man who is "every thing to every body"—Henry seems incapable of meaning what he says. How could such semiotic promiscuity coexist with the "seriousness" that Fanny keeps invoking? And yet Crawford presents the anomaly of one who not only combines role-playing with sincerity but reveals sincerity as an *effect* of role-playing. Fanny is bewildered by Crawford because she assumes that, if one is not serious, then one must be acting, manipulating conventions rather than speaking from the heart.[31] Austen's *style indirect libre*, however, discloses more than Fanny's consciousness can contain: words and deeds that one can "class among the common meaning" or insert into a conventional slot are not those that *lack* sincerity but those that convey it. Though he seems to personify an illicit deviation from the norm of seriousness into the no-man's-land of artifice and conventionality, Henry in fact exposes seriousness as a product of artifice and conventionality. He is the exception that infects the rule.

What is infectious in Henry, moreover, is not the unmanageable indeterminacy that Fanny sees in him, but something surprisingly close to the ideals of hierarchy and propriety that we associate with a character like Sir Thomas. For although Henry enters the novel trailing clouds of undecidability—as befits one whom Leo Bersani

31. Some of the novel's best readers follow Fanny in endorsing the dichotomy of theatricality and sincerity, according to which Henry Crawford can only fall into the first category. For Tony Tanner (Introduction, *Mansfield Park*, p. 21), "he is really amusing himself by *playing* at being the honest devoted suitor. He is acting, albeit unconsciously." And while Kenneth L. Moler (*Jane Austen's Art of Allusion* [Lincoln: University of Nebraska Press, 1968], p. 143) thinks that Henry is "consciously playing the role of the reformed rake, as he has played other roles in the past," he and Tanner are in essential agreement when it comes to indicting Henry for representing "the external, the superficial, [and] the social" rather than "more solid and substantial values" (p. 127). One of the central claims of this chapter is that these "values" are inherently implicated in "the external, the superficial [and] the social." For some suggestive remarks about antitheatricalism as a reaction to the inescapability of "the social," see Barish, *Prejudice*, p. 349.

calls an "ontological floater"[32]—the aim of the authoritarian appropriation of theatricality is to demystify it, to shift its focus from
glamorous excess to a more pedestrian trading in certain codified
procedures. Where before there was the prospect of reckless, infinite
self-invention, now we find an almost mechanical shuffling and
reshuffling of a limited repertory of tricks of the trade. Once the
more or less spectacular attack of the theatricals has subsided, the
novel can address itself to the task of domesticating the theatrical
Crawfords—not, as More would have it, in order more certainly,
though more slowly, to subvert Mansfield Park, but in order to rob
them of their subversive power. By the end of the novel, potentially
subversive impulses—which Austen groups under the heading of
the "itch for acting" (p. 147)—will have been converted into props
of authority.

The conquest of the Crawfords is a crucial intermediate phase in
the ideological conflict enacted in the novel. For if Mary and Henry
emblematize at first the anarchy of the unbounded self, they magnify
the objectionable theatricality of Maria and Julia, who, as Sir Thomas
finally admits, "had never been properly taught to govern their
inclinations and tempers" (p. 448). The triumph of Fanny at the end
of the novel symbolizes the triumph of governance over a selfhood
run wild, but the demystification of Mary and Henry marks the
turning point in that war. And though Fanny is appalled by the way
the Crawfords reduce sincerity to a convention, she herself represents the consummation of that process. Of course, we have identified artful artlessness as the most distinctive trait of the Bertram
sisters, yet their theatricality is too dispersive, too outer-directed, to
comply with the novel's centripetal ethos. The burden of the middle
section of the novel is to stage the theatricalization of the self in
such a way that theatricality virtually disappears into that inner
space, submerged in the form of rigorously inculcated habits of mind
and modes of response. *Mansfield Park*, that is, attempts to move
backward from Gisborne's theatrical young women, "ensnared into
errors and excesses," to the latent actresses whose "propensity to
imitation," carefully shaped and supervised, becomes the very guarantee of their virtuous "conformity." Lending themselves to a dem-

32. Bersani, *A Future*, p. 76.

onstration of how the theatrical self may be redefined, the Crawfords enable this corrective movement from the theatrically extroverted Maria and Julia to the theatrically introverted Fanny.

When Henry reads aloud from Shakespeare, for example, Fanny's involuntary absorption in the performance signifies more than just the transitory power of actor over spectator. An important lesson is being impressed upon her mind:

> In Mr. Crawford's reading there was a variety of excellence beyond what she had ever met with. The King, the Queen; Buckingham, Wolsey, Cromwell, all were given in turn; for with the happiest knack, the happiest power of jumping and guessing, he could always light, at will, on the best scene, or the best speeches of each; and whether it were dignity or pride, or tenderness or remorse, or whatever were to be expressed, he could do it with equal beauty.—It was truly dramatic.—His acting had first taught Fanny what pleasure a play might give, and his reading brought all his acting before her again; nay, perhaps with greater enjoyment, for it came unexpectedly, and with no such drawback as she had been used to suffer in seeing him on stage with Miss Bertram.
>
> (PP. 334-35)

Up until now, reading, for Fanny, has represented an escape from the public exposure implicit in acting. Whenever the eroticism of the rehearsals impinges too painfully upon her claustral sensibility, Fanny withdraws into the chill of her fireless room, where her books offer the solace of silent and purely spiritual intercourse.[33] It is not surprising that at her greatest crisis during the theatrical episode— the point at which she nearly capitulates to the company's request that she read the part of the Cottager's wife—Fanny can think only of returning to her room. She has, of course, been helping the others learn their lines by reading opposite them, but what is disturbing about this request is that it makes reading look all too much like a form of acting. It is one thing to rehearse with individual actors, quite another to read aloud as a member, however temporary, of the entire cast. Reading aloud points to an infection of reading proper by the very values it ought to exclude. Fanny's desire to maintain a polarity between reading and acting manifests itself throughout the novel, since any kind of heightened attention in the rooms be-

---

33. One of the most common criticisms of private theatricals was that they permitted an "unrestrained familiarity with persons of the opposite sex" (Gisborne, *Enquiry*, p. 184).

low—any compulsion to look at and to be looked at—merely reinstates the theatrical threat on a less obvious level. Yet Henry's reading aloud once again undermines her cherished opposition: as Lady Bertram says, "It was really like being at a play" (p. 336). "His reading [brings] all his acting before [Fanny] again," revealing the didactic purposiveness of both pursuits. For where, before, her retreats to the converted schoolroom that is her own apartment were a way of "shrinking again into herself" (p. 335), as if in flight from the free play of wandering libido, now she realizes that Henry's "acting taught . . . what pleasure a play might give."

His acting teaches her a more essential lesson as well—that the act of shrinking into oneself, of cultivating inwardness, has certain inevitable histrionic implications. All along, in eschewing acting, Fanny has in fact been playing a role, albeit "sincerely." As Sandra M. Gilbert and Susan Gubar point out, "Fanny silently plays the role of the angel by refusing to play."[34] From Henry's performance, she learns not the necessity of acting but the impossibility of *not* acting. Many critics have cited Henry's remarks about the inability of most preachers to deliver an impressive sermon as a sure sign of his moral turpitude: he is actually a "bad reader" (and thus a bad person), the argument runs, because he is "not concerned with belief, only with applause or admiration."[35] This sort of reasoning, however, may tell us more about the conduciveness of Austen's novels to moral position-taking than about the ideological ironies that generate their moralism.[36] For Henry's preoccupation with the "rules and trick" (p. 338) of preaching merely foregrounds the obsessive and omnipresent conventionality upon which the moral system of the entire novel depends. Whatever taint we may detect in Henry's tendency to see theatricality in everything—even in the religious vocation that is the novel's purported theme—turns out to color the authoritarian vision of *Mansfield Park* as a whole, especially as that vision is entrusted to Sir Thomas.

Indeed, if Henry's cynicism—or, what is even worse, his conflation

34. Gilbert and Gubar, *Madwoman*, p. 166.
35. Kelly, "Reading Aloud," p. 39.
36. For discussions of the ways in which *Mansfield Park* resists the demand for moral certainty, see D. A. Miller, *Narrative and Its Discontents: Problems of Closure in the Traditional Novel* (Princeton: Princeton University Press, 1981), pp. 21–22 and 55–57, and Martin Price, *Forms of Life: Character and Moral Imagination in the Novel* (New Haven: Yale University Press, 1983), pp. 65–89.

of cynicism and conviction—offends our moral good taste, Sir Thomas's medicinal projects should strike us as equally exploitive. If they do not, it is only because the novel has succeeded in concealing its indebtedness to what it pretends to disown. One almost senses a collusion between Henry and Sir Thomas, for while the former would seduce Fanny into marriage, the latter expends considerable energy in encouraging this seduction. Any difference between the two male characters lies in Austen's presentation of their strategies. In the case of Henry, she chooses to italicize, literally, his conscious use of rhetorical convention. When, for example, he tells Fanny that he has had William promoted to second lieutenant, he "used such strong expressions, was so abounding in the *deepest interest*, in *twofold motives*, in *views and wishes more than could be told*, that Fanny could not have remained insensible of his drift" (p. 304; Austen's emphasis). In the case of Sir Thomas, Austen adopts a coy tone in order to cast a somewhat more benign light on the same manipulativeness. At the end of Fanny's party, when Sir Thomas orders her, in the presence of Crawford, to go to bed—" 'Advise' was his word, but it was the advice of absolute power" (p. 285)—Austen comments tellingly on the devices whereby patriarchal authority perpetuates itself: "In thus sending her away, Sir Thomas perhaps might not be thinking merely of her health. It might occur to him, that Mr. Crawford had been sitting by her long enough, or he might mean to recommend her as a wife by shewing her persuadableness" (p. 286).

Readers of Austen's last complete novel know what an ominous ring the word "persuasion" can acquire. In "shewing her persuadableness," Sir Thomas puts Fanny on stage, exhibiting her just as Henry exhibits himself, deploying theatrical technique as craftily as his younger collaborator. In fact, he may be even shrewder, since he is manipulating both actress (Fanny) and audience (Henry). Displaying Fanny in the role of the obedient young woman, Sir Thomas in effect concocts, for Henry's benefit, a preview of and invitation to the marriage he seeks to bring about. With his keen sense of timing—he judges that "Mr. Crawford had been sitting by [Fanny] long enough"—and his eye for the symbolically resonant detail, Sir Thomas is the novel's preeminent juggler of theatrical conventions. Fanny's dramatic exit is merely the finale to an entire evening of skillfully directed moves, one that began with her "practising her steps about the drawing-room" (p. 278), looking perhaps more like one of Hannah More's amateur actresses than like one of Gisborne's demure mimics. The ball in her honor, conceived and staged by her uncle, constitutes her official entrance into society, the moment at which the ugly duckling steps into the spotlight to discover herself a swan. It is thus a thoroughly theatrical event, but instead of receiving the stigma that one might think it merits, it functions both as a pivotal point in the heroine's development and as a validation of the "absolute power" by which that development has been supervised: Sir Thomas "was pleased with himself for having supplied every thing else [but Fanny's beauty];—education and manners she owed to him" (p. 282).

Fanny, however, does not seem fully to appreciate the extent of her debt to Sir Thomas, for she of course rebels against his plan for her to marry Crawford, leading many commentators to propose that she is perhaps not so docile after all. Admittedly, her secret yet unwavering devotion to her cousin Edmund, in spite of her suitor's relentless blandishments and her uncle's merciless charge of "*ingratitude*" (p. 319; Austen's emphasis), seems to adumbrate a rejection of theatrical management and a brave defense of the inviolate self. But we would do well to consider the long-range effects, as well as the immediate consequences, of this recalcitrance. Fanny's insubordination precipitates the medicinal project according to which Sir Thomas dispatches her to the petit bourgeois chaos of Portsmouth, where she learns to esteem rather than disdain the theatricality of the Mansfield Park regime. After only a week amid the filth and anarchy of the parental abode, where "Nobody was in their right place, nothing was done as it ought to be" (p. 381), she longs for the scrupulous decorum of her uncle's home, where his insistently watchful authority "keeps every body in their place." If Fanny showed a regrettable tendency to disobey theatrically organized power, her exile serves as a valuable reminder of the virtues of such theatricality. Sir Thomas's project upon her diseased understanding is a success, not because Fanny relinquishes her claim to an unassailable self, but because she realizes that that very integrity is possible only on the intensely supervised stage of Mansfield Park. Ultimately, that is, she acknowledges her debt to Sir Thomas, and to the elegant conventionality for which, and by which, he stands:

> Her eagerness, her impatience, her longings to be with them, were such as to bring a line or two of Cowper's Tirocinium for ever before her. "With what intense desire she wants her home," was continually

on her tongue, as the truest description of a yearning which she could not suppose any school-boy's bosom to feel more keenly.

(p. 420)

The citational mode of Fanny's yearning is itself a token of the experiment's success. It demonstrates that Austen's most inward heroine is also, as many readers have observed, her most bookishly formulaic.[37] Whenever she feels the urge to dive deep into her innermost self, Fanny comes up with a handy touchstone, usually borrowed from Cowper. She is most herself when she is quoting someone else.[38]

It might be objected that theatricality is not the same thing as conventionality, that, although Fanny may think in clichés, she does not therefore acquiesce to the theatrical imperative. Yet the contention of this chapter is that, in the case of *Mansfield Park*, theatricality is in fact identified with conventionality to such a degree that the two terms eventually become synonymous. That theatricality-as-conventionality replaces theatricality-as-subversion reveals itself most vividly in the shift from metaphors of infection and of seduction to metaphors of debt and repayment. By the end of the novel, an omniscient authority has placed this world sufficiently under its control so that it may be said to own its subjects just as a conventional utterance or gesture owns a fixed and stable meaning. In marrying Edmund instead of Henry Crawford, Fanny indeed helps Sir Thomas to consolidate his empire and to protect his property from dispersion at the hands of outsiders. In keeping the family circle closed, she affirms repetition over difference, and legitimates Sir Thomas's patriarchal program: "Sir Thomas saw repeated, and for ever repeated reason to rejoice in what he had done for them all" (p. 456). At last, after the disappointments arising from the "grievous mismanagement" (p. 448) of his own daughters, he sees in Fanny a handsome return on his investment: "Fanny was indeed the

37. See Kenneth L. Moler, "The Two Voices of Fanny Price," in *Jane Austen: Bicentenary Essays*, ed. John Halperin (Cambridge: Cambridge University Press, 1975), pp. 172–79.

38. In *Jane Austen and the War of Ideas*, pp. 245–49, Marilyn Butler locates the "failure" (p. 249) of *Mansfield Park* in the undue weight given to Fanny's consciousness, especially in the second half of the novel: "In the anti-Jacobin novel consciousness must be treated critically, lest it inadvertently lets in the enemy, subjectivism. Jane Austen has put much ingenuity into having her cake and eating it, but she has not succeeded" (p. 248). Yet by ignoring the conventional frame Austen has placed around Fanny's consciousness, Butler misses the subtlety and scope of the novel's strategy of appropriation.

daughter that he wanted. His charitable kindness had been rearing a prime comfort for himself. His liberality had a rich repayment" (p. 456). "Prizing" in Fanny "more and more the sterling good of principle" (p. 455), Sir Thomas prizes as well the sterling good of principal.

Indeed, in the final chapter of the novel one has the impression that its protagonist is less Fanny than Sir Thomas himself, or the "governing body" that he represents.[39] Fanny and Edmund live happily ever after, but they do so in order to repay the authority that created them. As we have said, Sir Thomas may be viewed as an agent of Jane Austen, insofar as both appear to endorse the fortification of a conservative social order. Just here, however, where this order seems to have prevailed over the forces of subversion, authority starts to look oddly vulnerable. We would not be the first to notice a rather mechanical quality to this last chapter, which Austen begins with a perfunctory remark about her "impatien[ce] to restore every body . . . to tolerable comfort" (p. 446), and which she punctuates with other disquieting glimpses of the novelist ostentatiously in a hurry to tie up loose ends. When did Edmund transfer his love from Mary Crawford to Fanny?: "exactly at the time when it was quite natural that it should be so, and not a week earlier" (p. 454). What became of the prodigal older son, Tom?: "He became what he ought to be" (p. 447). Austen takes greater trouble to describe the fates of Maria and Julia, the Crawfords, and Mrs. Norris, but her own somewhat noisy interventions are all too reminiscent of this last character's theatrical bustle. No sooner has Sir Thomas expelled his demonic counterpart—whose "anxiety for every body's comfort" (p. 196) mocks his own need to keep everybody in "their place"—than Mrs. Norris returns in the form of the anxious, "impatient," comfort-oriented author herself. Not only does Mrs. Norris parody the authority of Sir Thomas; as Gilbert and Gubar have written, she is a "parodic surrogate for the author, a suitable double whose manipulations match those of Aunt Jane."[40] In the embarrassing moment when the ordinarily discreet Jane Austen advances to the proscenium to ring down the curtain on the final scene of her drama, we witness something like a return of the repressed.

The lesson of *Mansfield Park*, it seems, is that subversive theat-

---

39. The term comes from Joseph M. Duffy, "Moral Integrity and Moral Anarchy in *Mansfield Park*," *ELH* 23 (1956): 75.
40. Gilbert and Gubar, *Madwoman*, p. 171.

ricality can *only* be repressed, temporarily neutralized by a concerted effort of demystification. This process can occur, however, precisely because theatricality is not a single, unitary phenomenon but an already self-divided set of practices capable of serving both reactionary and subversive causes. If it can serve both, it can betray both, offering at best a precarious purchase on whatever interpretation of reality it has been recruited to promote. *Mansfield Park* has been praised as a psychological study that uncovers the impurity of even the most admirable motives, yet it also performs a political analysis, yielding insight into the necessary inconsistency of any ideological position that appropriates theatricality for its own purposes. A final reference should illustrate this point. When Edmund decides that duty compels him to give up his censorious stance and join in the theatricals, he tries to persuade Fanny, and himself, that this about-face produces only the *"appearance* of . . . inconsistency" (p. 175; Austen's emphasis). He explains that, if he does not play the romantic lead opposite Mary Crawford, someone from outside the immediate circle will. Thus he must act so that he "can be the means of restraining the publicity of the business, of limiting the exhibition, of concentrating our folly" (p. 176). And, of course, his folly *is* concentrated, not only in the sense of being circumscribed but also in the sense of being intensified. For in becoming an accomplice to the theatrical scheme, Edmund loses some of his status as moral paragon, incurring the disapproval of both Fanny and his father. He may genuinely wish to "limit the exhibition," but he may also wish to exhibit his desire for and to Mary Crawford. Acting (the word itself is suggestive)[41] in what he imagines is his father's interest, he manages at the same time to accommodate certain designs of his own, designs that may be at odds with the preservation of law and order. In Edmund's inconsistent behavior, authority nearly subverts itself. Faced with this emergency, Jane Austen summons Sir Thomas back to Mansfield Park—so that authority may attempt, yet again, to include what could disrupt it.

41. For a discussion of the theatricality implicit in the very notion of an act, see Barbara Johnson, *The Critical Difference: Essays in the Contemporary Rhetoric of Reading* (Baltimore: Johns Hopkins University Press, 1980), pp. 65–66.

2

The Governess as Actress
The Inscription of Theatricality in Jane Eyre

Why do you like Miss Austen so very much? I am puzzled on
that point. What induced you to say that you would have rather
written *Pride and Prejudice* or *Tom Jones*, than any of the Waverley
Novels?

I had not seen *Pride and Prejudice* till I read that sentence of
yours, and then I got the book. And what did I find? An accurate
daguerreotyped portrait of a commonplace face; a carefully fenced,
highly cultivated garden, with neat borders and delicate flowers;
but no glance of a bright, vivid physiognomy, no open country,
no fresh air, no blue hill, no bonny beck. I should hardly like to
live with her ladies and gentlemen, in their elegant but confined
houses. These observations will probably irritate you, but I shall
run the risk.

Charlotte Brontë, to G. H. Lewes

"Elegant but confined":[1] Brontë's formula epitomizes a certain way
of dismissing Jane Austen's work. Had Brontë read *Mansfield Park*
rather than *Pride and Prejudice*, moreover, her assessment might
have been even less charitable, for while "elegance" serves in *Pride
and Prejudice* as a kind of atmospheric *compensation* for confinement,
the demystifying narrative of *Mansfield Park* makes "elegance" the
very *mode* of confinement. As we saw in the last chapter, the demystification enacted in that novel requires a distinctly inhospitable
domestication, whereby the glamor or subversive éclat of a free-
wheeling, insouciant theatricality is replaced by an "elegance" or
decorum that, far from softening the disciplinary standard upheld
by the forbidding Fanny Price, efficiently enforces it, "keep[ing]
every body in their place." So dampening is the effect of this de-

---

1. Quoted in Clement Shorter, ed., *The Brontës: Life and Letters*, 2 vols. (1908; rpt.
New York: Haskell House Publishers, 1969), 1:387.

mystification that we are grateful when, at the end of the novel, the narrator uncannily impersonates the bustling Mrs. Norris, permitting an almost grotesque officiousness to unsettle the smooth surface of her prose. Once we could enjoy the rakish seductions of Mary and Henry Crawford; now that a rigorous "elegance" is the order of the day, we find ourselves oddly cheered by mere intimations of comic meddlesomeness. Yet this vulgar travesty of the powers that be is more than just a consolation prize: it reminds us forcibly of the energies that had to be repressed or contained in order for the reign of decorum to be secured, and it thereby compels us to recognize the shakiness of this dispensation. As the curtain descends on the happy household of Edmund and Fanny Bertram, we are allowed to glimpse the outlines of a sequel that begs to be written, in which, say, The Return of Mary Crawford overtakes the scrupulous disenchantments effected by Part One.

Although Charlotte Brontë is clearly impatient with Austenian confinement, it would seem rather inappropriate to characterize any of her novels as a "carnivalesque" rewriting of Austen such as that described above. In differing from Austen, Brontë hardly seems interested in taking her cue from the ways in which Austen differs from herself. A powerful polemicist, Brontë instead establishes the terms not only for a certain confinement of Austen herself but also, as a result, for her own liberating entry into the history of the novel. Asserting the superiority of "open country" and "fresh air" (fresh *Eyre?*) to her predecessor's "carefully fenced, highly cultivated gardens," Brontë prescribes the distinction that would take hold in more or less canonical accounts of the development of the English novel.[2] Raymond Williams, for example, though by no means a canonical critic, seems to endorse Brontë's version of literary history when he writes:

> A certain worldliness, readily understandable in earlier periods (though never, I think, as persuasive as is made out), made for the qualification of love; found its value as social exchange and respect, as most coolly in Jane Austen. . . . What was directly expressed in Blake and in Keats and in different ways in Shelley and Byron seems to have gone underground, before the 1840s, in fiction and even in

2. On the Austen-Brontë dichotomy in Victorian criticism, see Elaine Showalter, *A Literature of Their Own: British Women Novelists from Brontë to Lessing* (Princeton: Princeton University Press, 1977), pp. 102–05.

drama; indeed is literally underground in the dark images of the Gothic and in the produced straining extravagances of melodrama. The achievement of the Brontë sisters, before we say anything else, is that in different ways they remade the novel so that this kind of passion could be directly communicated.[3]

Williams articulates a widespread, commonsensical understanding of what happens to the English novel around the time of, indeed through the intervention of, Charlotte Brontë and her sisters: their novels breathe "passion" and "love" into what has seemed a rather "coolly" restrictive tradition of "worldliness." Yet it is not hard to see how Williams complicates his account by tracing the latent or "underground" Romantic impulses liberated by the Brontës not only to the "dark images of the Gothic" but also to the "produced straining extravagances of melodrama." In other words, although it is tempting to honor Brontë by describing her difference from Austen as an escape from the constricting elegance associated with the tyranny of "manners"—from the various forms of "social exchange" and compulsory indirection that come under the heading of "theatricality"—her "remaking" of the novel involves the rehabilitation of elements that have themselves had, as it were, a theatrical career, and that may continue, even after their recovery, to bear the marks of that history. Indeed, one of the charges Brontë had to answer in her defense of *Jane Eyre* (1847) was that of being too "melodramatic."[4] Admittedly, the "produced straining extravagances of melodrama" represent a different theatricality from either Mary and Henry Crawford's libertine glamor, the ultimate elegance of the Bertrams' cool (not to say chilly) regime, or even Mrs. Norris's noisy managerial style. Moreover, we should not simply assimilate the theatrical implications of Brontë's first-person narratives to those of Austen's third-person narrative. I want to argue, however, that the expressive openness and "directness" of Brontë's novels is significantly bound up, after all, not only with melodramatic extravagance but also with the other embarrassing kinds of theatricality she and many of her critics discern in Austen. Brontë's "achievement" owes at least as much to these forces of "qualification" as to its sources in Blake, Shelley, Keats, and Byron.

3. Raymond Williams, *The English Novel: From Dickens to Lawrence* (New York: Oxford University Press, 1970), p. 61.

4. Shorter, ed., *The Brontës: Life and Letters*, 1:386.

Theatricality and its subsidiary metaphors have enjoyed considerable prominence in a number of recent, skeptically driven critical
projects. Derrida's delineation of "the scene of writing" and Foucault's work on the (ostensibly nonspectacular) stagecraft of modern
power are perhaps the most obvious examples of and models for
the deployment of "theatricality" as a trope of demystification,
whereby the apparently immediate and unproblematic can be resisted or preemptively framed on the grounds of its factitiousness
or its unsuspected ideological complicity. In proposing to read
Brontë's fiction in the light of theatricality, I am not, however, merely
seeking to add yet another supposedly invulnerable repository of
truth and presence to the ever-growing list of compromised master-
pieces. Not *merely*, since, if one hopes to do more than just repeat
a by now familiar and even respectable critical gesture, one cannot
simply dispense with it, as though supplementation equaled transcendence. If *Jane Eyre* and *Villette* are in some sense founding texts
in the tradition of the novel, this is not for the reasons Williams and
others adduce, but because they embody so graphically two apparently antithetical yet interdependent functions of the novel in modern culture: on the one hand, they represent a potent identification
of novel-writing and novel-reading with the creation, consolidation,
and safeguarding of an autonomous subjectivity; on the other hand,
they situate that subjectivity in an inescapable, ever-menacing context of surveillance, suspicion, circumvention, and unmasking.[5] That
is, they dramatize the inevitability—for the author, for the protagonist, and, perhaps less saliently but no less crucially, for the critic—
of a certain will to demystify: demystification is not what happens
to the novel (although the critic may feel as if he or she were exercising that prerogative) but what happens *in* and *through* the novel.
In her preface to the second edition of *Jane Eyre*, for example, Brontë
admits that one of her aims has been "to pluck the mask from the
face of the Pharisee," "to scrutinize and expose, to raise the gilding
and show base metal under it."[6] And if it still seems somewhat

    5. This characterization of the cultural role of the novel is derived from a series
of essays by D. A. Miller, collected in *The Novel and the Police* (Berkeley: University
of California Press, 1988).
    6. Charlotte Brontë, *Jane Eyre*, ed. Q. D. Leavis (Harmondsworth: Penguin, 1966),
pp. 35, 36. All quotations from the novel are taken from this edition. Subsequent page
numbers will be included parenthetically in the text.

surprising that she should have seen Thackeray, of all contemporary novelists, as a kindred spirit (signaling her admiration by dedicating this edition to him), this improbable affinity points up the central imperative of truth-telling, satirical or otherwise, in Brontë's fiction. More powerfully than Thackeray's works, however, or than the somewhat later instances of the sensation novel and the detective novel, Brontë's texts epitomize the contagious dialectic of *evasion* and *exposure* that will henceforth loom large in the novel, even (or especially) when it is less overtly "psychological" or "Romantic."

For where the narrative of sensation or detection typically enacts a linear movement toward transparency and closure, the plots of Brontë's novels notoriously refuse the comforts of linearity, intensifying the demand for demystification precisely by frustrating it.[7] For all their vaunted commitment to direct communication, and despite their author's reputation as one who "pours forth her feelings . . . without premeditation,"[8] these novels virtually institutionalize the *obstacles* to unmediated and unpremeditated expression and understanding. If they stand out as emblematic demonstrations of the will to unveil, they do so because they install opacity as a permanent fixture of the novelistic world. In the veritable theater of self-fashioning that they constitute, theatricality-as-display and theatricality-as-deception articulate the conflictual masquerade of the modern novel, which seems, in its cult of interiority, to have left its theatrical prehistory far behind. Brontë's novels stand as memorials to the process whereby the novel as cultural production absorbs and covers over the traces of its historically and politically *supplementary* relation to the theater, of its genealogy as repetition-in-difference. "The inscription of theatricality" denotes the ambiguity of this process: to inscribe theatricality is at once to replicate it and to displace it, incorporating this generic other and at the same time disguising it. In the nineteenth century, the novel becomes a crypt in which theatricality lies concealed, but only half-concealed, since this very encrypting bespeaks an intrinsically theatrical subterfuge.

7. For a provocative discussion of the nonlinearity of Brontë's plots in terms of the dynamics of Brontëan desire, see John Kucich, *Repression in Victorian Fiction* (Berkeley: University of California Press, 1987), pp. 60–68.

8. From the *Westminster Review*'s 1860 review of *Mill on the Floss;* cited in Showalter, *A Literature of Their Own*, p. 104. On passionate expression in Brontë as a mode of opacity, see Kucich, *Repression in Victorian Fiction*, pp. 40–51.

But though one cannot, therefore, choose *not* to reenact the ritual of demystification, there is another, more interesting reason why I hope "not merely" to deconstruct Brontëan subjectivity. *Mansfield Park* shows that demystification, far from being a neutral cognitive process, in fact serves a highly coercive ideological purpose, however unpredictably or unreliably. For their part, Brontë's novels extend this insight, by unfolding a multiplicity of dramas in which demystification turns out to have a specific, though often overdetermined, political and erotic agenda of its own. It is important to point out that this discovery does not necessarily discredit the diverse acts of unveiling at work in—or in response to—the text. What it does is to open up a range of performative possibilites behind a series of cognitive scenes, to present them *as scenes*, rather than as so many disinterested projects of reception taking place passively and invisibly out, as it were, in the audience.[9]

Though the question of theatricality figures importantly in all of Brontë's novels, I will be concerned here with only two—the most famous and the one most deadeningly pasteurized and homogenized for absorption into the collective unconscious, *Jane Eyre*, and the last and the one most bristlingly "textual" and "complex," *Villette* (1853). Of these two, the latter would appear to be the logical place to begin showing how theatricality, as in *Mansfield Park*, spreads from the assigned locus of the literal stage to encompass not only spectators but participants in transactions—for example, reading, writing, teaching, lovemaking—supposedly untainted by theatrical obliquity. *Villette*, after all, thematizes theatrical issues overtly and recurrently, and, with its cosmopolitan, or at least Continental, setting, seems more likely than *Jane Eyre* to illustrate a suitably corrosive confrontation between the domestic, the private, and the in-

---

9. An interesting context for Brontë is suggested by Edward Said, *The World, The Text, and the Critic* (Cambridge: Harvard University Press, 1983). In "many modern novels," writes Said, "The very problematic of textuality is neither eluded nor elided, but made into an explicit intentional and constitutive aspect of the narrative. Sterne comes to mind immediately, but so do Cervantes, Proust, Conrad, and many others. The point is that these motifs, which are the very ones in a sense constructed by Derrida's criticism, already exist in narrative not as a hidden (hence inadvertent) element but as a principal one. Such texts cannot therefore be deconstructed, since their deconstruction has already been begun self-consciously by the novelist and by the novel. Thus this aspect of narrative poses the challenge, as yet not taken up, of what there is to be done *after* deconstruction is well under way, after the *idea* of deconstruction no longer represents elaborate intellectual audacity" (p. 193).

ward—the world, in short, of "the governess"—and the foreign, the public, and the centrifugal—the world, in short, of "the actress." But I want to discuss *Jane Eyre* first, not only in deference to chronology but also because this less obviously theatrical text has concomitantly more power to illustrate the ways in which theatricality gets camouflaged, in which the novelistic space denies its theatrical structure by internalizing it. In *Villette*, as we will see, the governess—a role that Brontë herself had of course played in real life—in fact turns into an actress; and if that progression, from one Victorian female paradigm to its apparent opposite, is not quite as definitive or as thematically coherent as it is in, say, *Vanity Fair*, its greater conspicuousness in relation to the economy of roles in *Jane Eyre* suggests that we may have more to learn, at least initially, from the governess whose acting is never even momentarily literal, but always furtively and disingenuously figurative—that is, highly characteristic of theatricality in the nineteenth-century novel.

Brontë may have disliked Austen—and she may not even have begun to read her until after *Jane Eyre* was published—but in one sense her novels seem oddly reminiscent of *Mansfield Park*: Fanny Price might well be seen as the precursor of Brontë's "undelightful" heroines.[10] Where Fanny insists, "No, indeed, I cannot act," Jane Eyre rebuffs Rochester's attempt to objectify her by warning him, "I will not be your English Céline Varens" (p. 298). Céline Varens, of course, is the French opera dancer with whom Rochester had the liaison that, to the dismay of many Victorian readers, he has recounted to Jane, and that, his rather half-hearted denials notwithstanding, has apparently resulted in the birth of little Adèle, Jane's pupil at Thornfield Hall. And as in *Mansfield Park*, the use of theatrical themes and imagery in *Jane Eyre* seems mainly homeopathic. For, though Rochester's theatrical escapade plays a paradoxically crucial role in the narrative insofar as it motivates Jane's presence at Thornfield, and though one could argue that, as the "miniature"· (p. 170) of her mother, Adèle introduces the "French" disease of theatricality into the domestic interior of the novel, Rochester provides more reassuring terms for the metaphorical recuperation of theatricality: "I . . . took the poor thing out of the slime and mud

---

10. Matthew Arnold, *The Letters of Matthew Arnold to Arthur Hugh Clough*, ed. Howard Foster Lowry (London and New York: Oxford University Press, 1932), p. 132.

of Paris, and transplanted it here, to grow up clean in the wholesome soil of an English country garden" (p. 176). As everyone knows, the climate of the house itself can hardly be called "wholesome"; but the force of passages such as this one is to suggest that whatever dangers are lurking nearby have nothing to do with the French connection: it is rather the much more fiery Spanish or Creole presence of Bertha Mason that should give us pause. This transplant or graft provides an exemplary graph of how a certain potentially hazardous foreign substance may be subsumed safely within a domestic order. Most references to theatricality in the novel have a similarly diminishing effect, as in the "miniaturization" of Adèle whereby we are invited to dismiss her, as Blanche Ingram does when she greets her with the exclamation, "Oh, what a little puppet!" (p. 202).

Unlike *Mansfield Park*, however, where the reduction of theatricality to convention becomes the normative, if covert, gesture of the novel itself, here the novel defines itself over and against that reduction. At the beginning of the novel, for example, when Mrs. Reed refuses to release Jane from the red-room, the heroine explains, "I was a precocious actress in her eyes" (p. 49); the implication is that Jane's oppressor is too brutishly enslaved by commonplace assumptions about artifice and sincerity to understand her. Or when, in a more metacritical register, the narrator writes that "a new chapter in a novel is something like a new scene in a play" (p. 125), the perfunctory, merely approximate character of that "something like" effectively empties the analogy of any disruptive potential. Indeed, the subsequent stage directions that tell us what to imagine in this "scene" underscore not the distractions of decor but the prevailing intimacy that obtains in the relationship between narrator and reader.[11] The rhetorical parallel becomes a hygienic bar separating the novelistic from the theatrical. Thus, if a certain theatrical infection *does* take hold in *Mansfield Park*, *Jane Eyre* would appear to inoculate itself more consequentially: a conventionalizing rhetoric would render the text immune from that very conventionality, mak-

---

11. In *The English Novel*, Williams observes: "What matters throughout is this private confidence, this mode of confession: the account given to a journal, a private journal, and then the act of writing includes—as it were involuntarily, yet it is very deliberate and conscious art—the awareness of the friend, the close one, the unknown but in this way intimate reader: the reader *as* the writer, while the urgent voice lasts" (p. 70). Williams is aware that what also matters here is the dissimulation of the act of writing *as act*, of the performance of the reader *as performance*.

ing this novelistic world safe for authenticity, freedom, and direct communication.

That a legitimate domain has been secured for the founding of a unitary, autonomous self is the enabling assumption of the most influential feminist reading of *Jane Eyre*. In the chapter that serves as the iconic centerpiece of *The Madwoman in the Attic*, Sandra M. Gilbert and Susan Gubar rechristen the narrative as "Plain Jane's Progress," as a "pilgrimage toward selfhood," culminating in Jane's exorcism of her "truest and darkest double," the demonic Bertha Mason.[12] But while the animalistic Bertha figures so centrally in this psychoanalytic allegory, any minatory allure that might attach to such culpably *social* female characters as Céline, Adèle, and Blanche gets minimized here: functioning merely as so many "important negative 'role-models' for Jane," these characters "suggest problems she must overcome before she can reach the independent maturity which is the goal of her pilgrimage" (p. 350). The teleology of this interpretation privileges Jane's "unseduceable independence in a world of self-marketing Célines and Blanches" (p. 353). Whatever their importance as "negative 'role-models,'" these sexually com- modified women never exceed the thematic determination of prob- lems-to-be-overcome, and therefore never loom much larger than the puppet-like Adèle. Characterizing the latter, along with her mother and Blanche, as "denizen[s] of Vanity Fair" (p. 350), Gilbert and Gubar ask, "May not Adèle, the daughter of a 'fallen woman,' be the model female in a world of prostitutes?" (p. 350), but they see little likelihood of Jane's taking this model seriously. If, on the one hand, these characters—to whose numbers we may add Jane's frivolous, "stylish" cousin Georgiana, who is at one point compared to "waxwork" (p. 257); the hypocritically fashionable Brocklehurst women; and even the "coquettish" (p. 394) Rosamond Oliver—typify a certain proverbial construction of female sexuality in terms of both acting and prostitution,[13] on the other, heavier hand, the very brit-

---

12. Sandra M. Gilbert and Susan Gubar, *The Madwoman in the Attic: The Woman Writer and the Nineteenth-Century Literary Imagination* (New Haven: Yale University Press, 1979), pp. 367, 360. Subsequent references to this work will appear parenthet- ically in the text.

13. As we will see when we turn to *Daniel Deronda*, this construction has figured prominently in recent feminist criticism of George Eliot. For discussions that contex- tualize the stereotype(s) more generally, see Nina Auerbach, *Woman and the Demon: The Life of a Victorian Myth* (Cambridge: Harvard University Press, 1982); Jonas Barish,

tleness or blankness (Blanche-ness?) of the stereotype guarantees, as in the novel itself, that the woman who "sings and dances for her supper" will never turn into anything more subversive than "a clockwork temptress invented by E. T. A. Hoffmann" (p. 350). Insofar as Jane's developmental drama is seen to center on her confrontation with the Madwoman in the Attic, not with the Dancer in the Boudoir or the Coquette in the Parlor, there is little reason to doubt her when she says, "I will not be your English Céline Varens." Not only will Jane Eyre never turn into Becky Sharp, something of a "clockwork temptress" herself; more important, she is saved from the contemptible world of "social exchange" in which Jane Austen's "elegant but confined" female characters are doomed to circulate.

But Brontë's novel betrays a remarkable fascination with the very world and worldliness that she would soon patronize in Austen. Admittedly, Brontë seems to set up the "lady" merely to have Jane unmask her as already disreputably masked—to have Jane debunk her, that is, as her ostensible opposite, the "prostitute." Yet if, in "plucking the mask," Jane reveals not naked truth but *another mask*, however "base," then the project of debunking—of "scrutinizing" and "exposing"—cannot be described as simply antitheatrical: it may in fact be impelled surreptitiously by something like a desire for theatricality. Precisely by encouraging us, for instance, to concur with Jane in her decision that Blanche Ingram is "beneath jealousy" (p. 215) because, though "very showy," she is "not genuine" (p. 215), the narrative also compels us to join Jane in emulating the "ceaseless surveillance" (p. 215) to which Rochester subjects Blanche; and, as we discover, the act of surveillance seems almost inevitably to precipitate the would-be demystifier into a volatile state of both "ceaseless excitation and ruthless restraint" (p. 216). Just as Fanny Price's refusal to participate in the theatricals at Mansfield Park fails to exempt her from the theatrical dis-ease of mingled "longing and dreading," so too does Jane discover the instability of the binary opposition between spectator and spectacle. Jane's longish dramatization of her surveillance is all the more worth quoting because of its appropriately turbid logic.

The Antitheatrical Prejudice (Berkeley: University of California Press, 1981); Joan Rivière, "Womanliness as a Masquerade," *International Journal of Psychoanalysis* 10 (1929): 303–13.

"Why can she not influence [Rochester] more, when she is privileged to draw so near him?" I asked myself. "Surely she cannot truly like him, or not like him with true affection! If she did, she need not coin her smiles so lavishly, flash her glances so unremittingly, manufacture airs so elaborate, graces so multitudinous. It seems to me that she might, by merely sitting quietly at his side saying little and looking less, get nigher his heart. I have seen in his face a far different expression from that which hardens it now while she is so vivaciously accosting him; but then it came of itself: it was not elicited by meretricious arts and calculated manoeuvres; and one had but to accept it—to answer what he asked without pretension, to address him when needful without grimace—and it increased and grew kinder and more genial, and warmed one like a fostering sunbeam. How will she manage to please him when they are married? I do not think they will manage it; and yet it might be managed; and his wife might, I verily believe, be the very happiest woman the sun shines on."

(p. 216)

If it is not "jealousy" that troubles Jane, neither is it exactly altruistic sorrow on behalf of Rochester, destined though he appears to be for a loveless marriage. Instead, one gathers that Jane's anxiety stems from the fact that only she seems to have recognized the disparity between her own superior "genuineness" on the one hand and Blanche's "meretricious arts and calculated manoeuvres" on the other. But though she knows that Blanche would do better by "merely sitting quietly at his side," Jane is soon agitating herself by imagining how she might "manage" as Rochester's wife. Indeed, the previous paragraph shows Jane vacillating between visions of out-Blancheing Blanche and of adopting an even subtler, more "pacifistic" strategy:

When she failed, I saw how she might have succeeded. Arrows that continually glanced off from Mr. Rochester's breast and fell harmless at his feet, might, I knew, if shot by a surer hand, have quivered keen in his proud heart—have called love into his stern eye, and softness into his sardonic face; or, better still, without weapons a silent conquest might have been won.

(p. 216)

These passages suggest that it is not enough merely to write Blanche off as a bad or insufficiently inspired actress, although—more accurately, *because*—the spectacle of her failure is gratifying indeed. As she keeps missing her target here, she exemplifies better than she knows the novel's insistent formulation of theatricality as an endless, dizzying dialectic of power and subservience, whereby to act is to be simultaneously empowered and vulnerable. Commanding Rochester to sing for her, she adds, "If you don't please me, I will shame you by showing you how such things *should* be done" (p. 208). Or again: "Both her words and her air seemed intended to excite not only the admiration, but the amazement of her auditors: she was evidently bent on *striking* them as something very dashing and daring indeed" (p. 208; emphasis added).

Blanche's performance, of course, "excites" something other than "admiration" and "amazement": its (unintended) effect is precisely the drama of "ceaseless excitation" traversing Jane Eyre, which excitation, merged with "ruthless restraint," constitutes both an internalization and an intensification of the agonistic theatricality already demonstrated by Blanche. As we can see from the long passages in which Jane criticizes Blanche's histrionic technique, Blanche's punitive, self-aggrandizing, but also oddly self-abasing agenda in fact gets appropriated and enacted in the consciousness of her silent observer, the governess hiding "behind the window-curtain" (p. 205). Blanche boasts of how, as a child, she "took care to turn the tables" on such "nuisance[s]" (p. 206), but here it is rather Jane Eyre who turns the tables on her, for the ruthlessness of Jane's self-restraint enables the ruthlessness of her rhetorical triumph over the hapless Blanche.

Indeed, the "ceaseless excitation and ruthless restraint" that Blanche's egregiously miscalculated assault on Rochester triggers in Jane represents a complicated, "striking" play not only of self-pity and envy (if not "jealousy") but also of self-congratulation, disdain, and a vindictiveness whose voyeuristic pleasure is only barely moralized. Satirical demystification—the adversarial uncovering of Blanche's inept theatrical "calculations" as such—emerges here as an ardent vicariousness that does not so much undermine as upstage it.[14] The novel offers many such scenes of overdetermined specta-

---

14. Jane's performance here might lend itself to discussion in terms of what René Girard, in *Deceit, Desire, and the Novel: Self and Other in Literary Structure*, trans. Yvonne Freccero (Baltimore: Johns Hopkins University Press, 1972), calls "mimetic desire." For a feminist and antihomophobic reframing of Girard's model, see Eve Kosofsky Sedgwick, *Between Men: English Literature and Male Homosocial Desire* (New York: Columbia University Press, 1985), esp. pp. 21–27. The important, complicated question of lesbian (and/or female homosocial) desire and identification in Brontë's novels requires careful analysis; unfortunately, such analysis is somewhat beyond the scope of the present study.

torship on Jane's part, scenes that, far from constituting mere detours in her "pilgrimage toward selfhood," both articulate that trajectory and provide the measure for the weight, volume, and density that define the "selfhood" in question. If the product of this narrative—the elaborated subjectivity named "Jane Eyre"—is in fact ultimately theatrical, that theatricality entails far more than the protagonist's arriving at a proper stance toward the various "role models" placed in her way. To be sure, Jane Eyre's selfhood *is* formed against the relatively flat backdrop composed by more conventionally theatrical characters like Blanche, Céline, and Adèle. This does not mean, however, that Jane is the "opposite" of those characters; rather, they serve as pretexts or contexts, enticingly pregnant blanks, in relation to which her "surveillance" manifests itself as a self-charging ("exciting"), at once sadistically and masochistically "ruthless," performance in its own right. Nor does this performance occur only when Blanche, Céline, Adèle, or any other "merely" stylish woman is on stage. That, before her marriage to Rochester, Bertha Mason was "a fine woman, in the style of Blanche Ingram" (p. 332), should point to an important link between Jane's "truest and darkest double" and those blanched or whitened female characters whose worldly falseness and vacuity come laden with a paradoxical power to induce in the heroine extravagant spectacles of self-construction.[15] The latter may be puppets, but, like their counterparts in *Vanity Fair*, they are all "magnified puppets" (p. 217), as Jane describes two other characters, and therefore "provoking puppet[s]" (p. 302) as well, as Rochester provokingly calls Jane herself. In appreciating Brontë's impressive revision of the novel as a genre, we should not underestimate the role played in that revision by a vigorously magnified and repeatedly projected meretriciousness, saliently but not exclusively embodied in non-English women,[16] and invested with a provocative (i.e., at once energizing and irritating) glamor and even pathos by virtue of its very contemptibility. The worse the acting—and, in *Jane Eyre*, almost all acting promises to be delectably "bad"—

15. Although it does not touch directly on *Jane Eyre*, Nina Auerbach's "Alluring Vacancies in the Victorian Character," *Kenyon Review* 8 (1986), 36–48, might be consulted in this regard.

16. Other examples in Brontë's fiction include Zoraïde Reuter in *The Professor*, and Ginevra Fanshawe, Pauline Home, and Zélie St. Pierre in *Villette*; Alfred de Hamal in *Villette* is a significant male version of this usually female type.

the better the show. Nothing succeeds (for Jane) like failure (on the part of her showy, worldly Others).

Much as we should acknowledge the extent to which Jane is constructed in and by these complicated power-plays, we must also take into account the considerable rhetorical effort involved in occluding this entire process. In other words, if I have been emphasizing thus far the "excitation" and even the empowerment that attends Jane's surveillance, I want now to focus on the "restraint" that turns that ex-citation back *in* upon itself, that makes expansiveness look like inwardness, so that Brontëan exteriority (the outdoorsiness of "open country," "fresh air," etc.) becomes indistinguishable from Brontëan interiority. It is as though Brontë were fending off Austen even before having read her: where mere *intro*version might recall Austen at her most oppressively "confined," unchecked *extro*version might suggest Austen at her most culpably social. Brontë avoids both of these pitfalls by means of a certain invagination. In a brilliant recent study of repression in Victorian fiction, John Kucich has written:

> The most striking thing about expressions of passion in Brontë's fiction is that they are most often histrionic—the performance of a mask that conceals, rather than reveals, an interior condition of desire. For Charlotte Brontë, passion implies the existence of an aroused, hypersensitive self that it simultaneously withholds. In her Byronically passionate male characters—and also in her female protagonists, though in more ephemeral ways—passion is a means of distancing others in order to preserve a desirable state of inward tension. By marking an inward instability, an eccentricity of the self to itself, passionate expression actually defeats any knowledge of its nature by others, and marks itself in opposition to them, rather than as a fusional impulse. . . . [P]assionate expression is a mark of estrangement and distance, of self-elaboration in isolation, which brings it very close to the Brontëan repression we usually think of as its adversary.[17]

Kucich's account of the virtual interchangeability of "passion" and "repression" in Brontë's fiction as a whole confirms my own sense of the inextricable entanglement of "excitation" and "restraint" in Jane Eyre's many acts of surveillance: as Kucich would suggest, the "inward tension" that defines Jane's spectatorship arises not from

17. Kucich, *Repression in Victorian Fiction*, pp. 40–41.

a war of polar opposites but rather from the repeated collapsing of an opposition. Yet my argument differs from Kucich's in two respects. First, I want to claim that, although the complicity of "excitation" or "passion" and "restraint" or "repression" seems to establish the solipsistic isolation that Kucich identifies as Brontë's most distinctive effect, the "inward instability" of Jane Eyre at any rate is more social and more political than Kucich will allow, not so much an escape from Foucauldian relations of power as a heightened reinscription of them. Second, while I obviously agree that Brontëan passion is mainly histrionic, I want to look at the ways in which the histrionic, which Kucich rightly associates with the "mask that conceals," is itself masked by Brontë. These two points may seem to contradict each other, the one claiming greater sociality in Brontë, the other arguing for greater reticence. But in fact I will also argue that Brontë is most responsive to social pressures precisely when she herself restrains and dissembles the dramas that her heroine at the same time rehearses so excitedly.

The persistence of a certain critical tradition begun by Brontë herself would indeed persuade us that the ruthless restraint that is an integral component of Brontëan theatricality functions instead as a guarantee *against* theatricality, that the dropping of a curtain in front of these dramas succeeds nonetheless in not looking like a theatrical effect at all: it seems instead to consecrate "the depth" (p. 46) or the "visionary hollow" (p. 46) that the cagey heroine first sights during her imprisonment in the red-room, and whose mapping and furnishing will be the program of the ensuing narrative. Protestations of antitheatricality thus proliferate unsurprisingly throughout the book, although they reach a kind of crescendo during the period immediately before the aborted wedding, when Jane is at pains to keep rejecting the "stage-trappings" (p. 288) of courtship. (And when, soon after that non-ceremony, Jane famously leaves Thornfield, she does so to avoid the implicitly theatricalizing fate of becoming the latest in Rochester's series of mistresses.) Perhaps the oddest of all Jane's deflections is her impatient observation that Rochester, who wants to deck her out in prenuptial finery, "would yet see me glittering like a parterre" (p. 296). While the immediate reference seems to be to the sense of "parterre" as an ornamental (or "Austenian") arrangement of flower beds, one cannot help noticing, in this context of disavowal, the more specifically theatrical reference as well. Though prepared, even eager, to cast herself as the spectator par excellence—Mrs. Reed, for example, could never tolerate her niece's "continual, unnatural watchings of one's movements" (p. 260)—the heroine would evade any interpretation of her spectatorship as a spectacle in itself, meticulously effacing (or covering up) any hints of "glitter" in her ceaselessly vigilant prose.[18]

Accordingly, the narrative must obey a stringent logic of decor— and of decorum—in converting the shining plane of the red-room mirror, or the showy plain of an ostentatious audience, into a semi-matte surface that will reflect only the visionary recessiveness (and "depth") of an unimpeachably plain Jane. The lineaments, as well as the risks, of this logic may be glimpsed in a letter Brontë wrote describing how, during a rare trip to London, she and her sister Anne visited the opera in the company of their publishers:

> We attired ourselves in the plain, high-made country garments we possessed, and went with [George Smith and his sisters] to their carriage, where we found Mr. Williams. They must have thought us queer, quizzical-looking beings, especially me with my spectacles. I smiled inwardly at the contrast, which must have been apparent, between me and Mr. Smith as I walked with him up the crimson-carpeted staircase of the Opera House and stood amongst a brilliant throng at the box door, which was not yet open. Fine ladies and gentlemen glanced at us with a slight, graceful superciliousness quite warranted by the circumstances. Still, I felt pleasantly excited in spite of headache and sickness and conscious clownishness, and I saw Anne was calm and gentle, which she always is.[19]

Here, in an uncanny blurring of the distinction between fiction and reality, the author reenacts the role performed by her newly celebrated fictional surrogate, inheriting Jane's excitement and reliving her restraint as headache, sickness, and embarrassment. Like Jane's response to Blanche, Brontë's internal drama masters and exceeds, in complexity, interest, and above all, emotional seriousness, the external scene that occasions it. In this edgy encounter with the

---

18. Williams writes, "People still have to fight past the governess to get to the Brontë sisters. I mean fight past the image, the depressing image, that is still taken for granted. . . . Seen from the middle-class way round, and especially from the male middle-class way, the governess as a figure is repressive, unfeminine, dowdy. . . . I don't know how much I now need to insist on breaking the image: that deforming image which obscures—and is meant to obscure—a particular and general repression" (*The English Novel*, pp. 62–63).

19. Shorter, ed., *The Brontës: Life and Letters* 1:437.

London beau monde, the brilliance of the throng becomes a foil for
the transcendent display of the provincial author's (self-)conscious-
ness. What is remarkable in this account is its delicate balance between a scrupulously half-shamefaced exhibitionism and the trem-
ulous yet invincible *inwardness* it nonetheless affirms. Where the
gaze of her publishers and the "elegant young ladies"[20] who ac-
company them threatens to turn Brontë into a spectacle, she trans-
forms her own conveniently deglamorizing "spectacles" not only
into a powerful instrument of vision but also into a protective barrier
behind which a private drama of contemplation may take place
unobserved. Thus shielded, she is free to "fe[el] pleasantly excited"
but, more important, to "smile . . . inwardly," quietly appropriating
much of the "superciliousness" she ascribes to her sophisticated,
but only superficially perceptive, beholders. By means of an ingenious reversal, not unlike that practiced by Jane Eyre in her surveillance of Blanche Ingram, the mere snobbery associated with
"fine ladies and gentlemen" gets introjected and refined as the "genuine" (paradoxical, spiritual, virtually inexpressible) loftiness of the
"high-made" "country spinster," as Brontë calls herself elsewhere.[21]
Even the possibility of humiliation risked by the acknowledgment
of "clownishness" gets preempted, thanks to Brontë's absorptive
emphasis on her "consciousness" of it.[22]

This biographical vignette recalls still another scene from the
novel that Brontë had just published. In this scene, a similar recuperation is performed, but with a telling difference. Soon after her
arrival at Lowood, Jane, having dropped and broken her "slate," is
first "exposed to general view on a pedestal of infamy" (p. 99) but
then, like her model of self-abasement, Helen Burns, "completely
cleared from every imputation" (p. 106) of guilt. In a typically Brontëan pattern, humiliation only serves to establish the victim's un-
fathomable depth of receptivity, which "no language can describe"

20. Ibid.
21. Ibid., 443.
22. I allude here to Michael Fried's *Absorption and Theatricality: Painting and Beholder in the Age of Diderot* (Berkeley: University of California Press, 1980). In Fried's
work, "absorption" comprises a range of aesthetic techniques aimed at counteracting
or dissembling theatricality, which, as I understand it—particularly with the help of
the polemical essay, "Art and Objecthood," in Gregory Battcock, ed., *Minimal Art:
A Critical Anthology* (New York: E. P. Dutton, 1968)—characterizes an inferior kind of
art.

(p. 99): the degradations of the outside ironically reaffirm the inviolability of the inside.[23] Yet, despite the well-known autobiographical nature of her fiction, as well as the crafty literariness of her autobiographical writings, Charlotte Brontë will take chances in her private correspondence that she spares the central character in her more public work as a novelist. For Brontë's drama of appropriation and reversal unfolds in a literal theater, too palpably social a place, whereas Jane Eyre enacts this scenario under the aegis of *displacement:* all of her "theatergoing" and all of her "acting" occur either within the overtly disciplinary space of the schoolroom or within the covertly disciplinary space of (someone else's) home. Where Charlotte Brontë hides behind her spectacles in an actual *site* of spectacles, her fictional creation hides behind surfaces in settings less apt to invest them homonymically with a compromising glitter.[24]

The "treacherous slate" (p. 97) that Jane accidentally breaks is only one of many such surfaces, although its fracture and symbolic reconstitution prove exemplary: hoping to "escape notice" (p. 97) by using it to "conceal [her] face" (p. 97), the heroine finds herself betrayed by the very object that should have protected her; but instead of branding her as a "liar" (p. 98), as Brocklehurst would have it, her "obtrusive" (p. 97) exposure and consequent shaming

23. The paradigmatic scene in this regard would be that in which Helen Burns, having been found guilty of untidiness, is transformed into an exemplary text: "Next morning Miss Scatcherd wrote in conspicuous characters on a piece of pasteboard the word 'Slattern,' and bound it like a phylactery round Helen's large, mild, intelligent, and benign-looking forehead. She wore it till evening, patient, unresentful, regarding it as a deserved punishment" (p. 105).

24. In "Film and the Masquerade: Theorising the Female Spectator," *Screen* 23 (September–October 1982): 83, Mary Ann Doane has shown how, in the mainstream cinema, women's "spectacles" are a dangerous signifier: "Glasses worn by a woman in the cinema do not generally signify a deficiency in seeing but an active looking, or even simply the fact of seeing as opposed to being seen. The intellectual woman looks and analyses, and in usurping the gaze she poses a threat to the entire system of representation. It is as if the woman had forcefully moved to the other side of the specular." Hence the necessity, Doane argues, of the moment in films when the bespectacled woman removes her glasses, and is thereby almost magically "transformed into spectacle, the very object of desire" (p. 83). Yet the danger flirted with in Brontë's letter is more ambiguous, since Brontë's glasses threaten not only the dominant system of representation but also, given the potentially contaminating context, Brontë herself: she does not need to take off her spectacles to risk *becoming* a spectacle. Doane calls the cinematic cliché of "girls who wear glasses" a "heavily loaded moment of signification, a social knot of meaning" (p. 83). By keeping Jane Eyre out of the social spaces that she herself dares to enter, Brontë tends to disguise the ways in which the heroine is caught up in such social knots.

produce the opposite effect of wiping the slate clean, restoring to Jane the medium on which she may hence inscribe the indescribable signs of her integrity. And since the slate—a surface whose associations with pedagogical compulsion, happily enough, clear *it* from any suspicion of borrowed glamor—is both what one writes *on* and what one hides *behind*, self-inscription is identified with self-effacement, thereby allowing the autobiographer to elude any "imputation" of theatricality. Writing, we are asked to believe, even writing about oneself, is not like acting: it is what one does *instead* of acting. The form of "restraint" typically adopted in *Jane Eyre*, then, appears less voluntary, and less ambiguous, than that imposed in the passage about the "spectacles," just as writing forgoes its associations with the social luster of professional authorship—especially *successful* professional authorship—to assume instead the protective covering of (home)work. If less ambiguous, however, this strategy is nothing if not paradoxical, for while the relative abjection of Jane Eyre seems to bar her from "society" in the seductive, specialized sense of a pleasure-seeking elite, it would also have the enabling effect of exempting her from society as a whole.

In order to examine more closely the process thanks to which Jane can say, equivocally, "I appeared a disciplined and subdued character" (p. 116), let us return to Jane's surveillance of Blanche, paying particular attention to the way Brontë frames and thus, oddly enough, detheatricalizes it. It is important to recognize that, by placing Jane "behind the window-curtain"—by having her "shr[i]nk . . . into the shade" (p. 205), like Fanny Price—Brontë discreetly draws a veil in front of the heroine's performance, occulting its rivalrous histrionics and offering it instead as further evidence of an otherwise inarticulable inwardness. Indeed, if the entire episode of the Ingrams' visit threatens to become an Austenian comedy of manners, Brontë neutralizes that danger through an equally Austenian countermeasure, according to which the heroine, furtively but avidly consuming the all-too-glittering spectacle of aristocratic role-playing, thereby demonstrates the vast, even inestimable capacity of her own consciousness.[25] (It is this kind of *gourmandise*, one suspects, that

25. Robert B. Heilman has written: "The introduction of comedy as a palliative of straight Gothic occurs on a large scale when almost seventy-five pages are given to the visit of the Ingram-Eshton party to mysterious Thornfield; here Charlotte, as often in her novels, falls into the manner of the Jane Austen whom she despised."

has earned Brontë her reputation for what Matthew Arnold, albeit disgustedly, called "hunger, rebellion, and rage."[26]) Throughout this episode, whenever Jane might seem to be standing in front of a curtain (whether "literally" or "figuratively"), the narrative recontextualizes her so that she ends up standing *behind* one. As the Ingrams and their party approach the house, Jane watches them from the window, "taking care to stand on one side, so that, screened by the curtain, I could see without being seen" (p. 195). When she comes downstairs to introduce Adèle to the guests, Jane is relieved to be screened once again:

> Fortunately, there was another entrance to the drawing-room than that through the saloon where they were all seated at dinner. . . . The crimson curtain hung before the arch: slight as was the separation this drapery formed from the party in the adjoining saloon, they spoke in so low a key that nothing of their conversation could be distinguished beyond a soothing murmur.
>
> (pp. 199–200)

Yet Jane's inability to overhear their conversation actually has the same effect as her unimpeded visual consumption: in both cases, what is ultimately secured for her is a saving opacity. And that *her* opacity is both the antithesis and the double of *their* meretricious brilliance becomes clear a few paragraphs later:

> A soft sound of rising now became audible; the curtain was swept back from the arch; through it appeared the dining-room, with its lit lustre pouring down light on the silver and glass of a magnificent dessert-service covering a long table; a band of ladies stood in the opening; they entered, and the curtain fell behind them.
>
> (p. 200)

As soon as this "band of ladies," having made a lavishly lit entrance, stands in front of the curtain, that curtain looks very much like a curtain on a stage, and the ladies appear bathed in all the culpable "lustre" of the will to dazzle: for a brief but resonant moment, the decorative match between the "crimson-carpeted staircase" of the opera house and the crimson curtain of the private home hints at

---

"Charlotte Brontë's 'New Gothic,' " in *The Brontës: A Collection of Critical Essays*, ed. Ian Gregor (Englewood Cliffs, N.J.: Prentice-Hall, 1970), p. 98.

26. Matthew Arnold, *Letters of Matthew Arnold*, ed. George W. E. Russell (New York: Macmillan, 1896) 1:34.

the larger and more problematic resemblance between public theater and an unstably "domesticated" theatricality. As long as it is Jane, however, who stands in the same spot, both she and the backdrop look quite different: far from setting her *off*, as a foil does a jewel, the curtain sets her *apart*, marking her distance from and inaccessibility to the resplendent company on the other side. Like Charlotte Brontë's spectacles and the young Jane Eyre's slate—like a whole series of Brontëan surfaces, for that matter—the curtain validates the self not by revealing it but by obscuring it. Always a consumer (rather than an object to be consumed), Jane will not perform the "ladylike" function of being served up like some temptingly unwholesome "dessert." Even though she and the "band of ladies" occupy the same position in front of the curtain, Brontë manipulates this "screen" so that, in the space of a single page, it serves—or appears to serve—two radically incompatible purposes. By virtue of the author's scenic legerdemain, an anamorphic illusion splits the screen-as-enhancing-backdrop from the screen-as-protective-cover, thereby disrupting any visible continuity between the "ladies" who stand *flamboyantly* before the former and the governess who stands *meekly* before—which is to say, behind—the latter.[27]

This is by no means the only place in the novel where Brontë stages as a distinction, even as an opposition, what might easily look like a similarity. In the novel's crucial opening scene, Jane is pun-

---

27. Brontë's investment in this distinction is suggested in this passage from a letter she wrote to her publisher, William Smith Williams, after her visit to London:

> An existence of absolute seclusion and unvarying monotony, such as we have long—I may say, indeed, ever—been habituated to, tends, I fear, to unfit the mind for lively and exciting scenes, to destroy the capacity for social enjoyment.
>
> The only glimpses of society I have ever had were obtained in my vocation of governess, and some of the most miserable moments I can recall were passed in drawing-rooms full of strange faces. At such times, my animal spirits would ebb gradually till they sank quite away, and when I could endure the sense of exhaustion and solitude no longer, I used to steal off, too glad to find any corner where I could really be alone. Still, I know very well, that though the experiment of seeing the world might give acute pain for the time, it would do good afterwards; and as I have never, that I remember, gained any important good without incurring proportionate suffering, I mean to try to take your advice some day, in part at least—to put off, if possible, that troublesome egotism which is always judging and blaming itself, and to try, country spinster as I am, to get a view of some sphere where civilised humanity is to be contemplated.
>
> (Shorter, ed., *The Brontës: Life and Letters* 1:443)

ished for her want of a properly "sociable and childlike disposition, a more attractive and sprightly manner" (p. 39), by her exclusion from the Reeds' family circle:

> A small breakfast-room adjoined the drawing-room, I slipped in there. It contained a bookcase; I soon possessed myself of a volume, taking care that it should be one stored with pictures. I mounted into the window-seat: gathering up my feet, I sat cross-legged, like a Turk; and, having drawn the red moreen curtain nearly close, I was shrined in double retirement.
>
> (p. 39)

If not crimson, this curtain is at least red, and its power to induce a corresponding blush of embarrassment in the would-be "unsociable" text has not gone unexploited. In a recent reading of *Jane Eyre*, Gayatri Chakravorty Spivak performs an adroit deconstruction of this scene, uncovering it as precisely a theatricalization of selfhood: grounded in this "scene of the marginalization and privatization of the protagonist," the subsequent narrative may proceed to naturalize "[t]he battle for female individualism" as it "plays itself out within the larger theater of the establishment of meritocratic individualism, indexed in the aesthetic field by the ideology of 'the creative imagination.' "[28] Rather like Jane Austen when she surfaces as the disruptively parodic Mrs. Norris, Spivak unpacks that ideology by deploying the theatrical metaphor in a frankly deidealizing way.

Nor are she and Kucich, who also emphasizes Brontë's histrionics, the only critics to have insisted on pulling back the curtain that Brontë draws in front of her protagonist. Terry Eagleton, in his demythifying book on the Brontës, also seeks, in the aggressively noisy manner of the finale of *Mansfield Park*, to show theatricality writ large in a work that endeavors tirelessly to write it small. Eagleton anticipates my questioning of the heavily advertised contrast between Jane Eyre and a character like Blanche Ingram:

> Jane, who shares Blanche's liking for "devilish" men, knows better than she does how they are to be handled—when to exert her piquant will and when to be cajolingly submissive. . . . Jane moves deftly between male and female roles in her courtship of Rochester; unlike

---

28. Gayatri Chakravorty Spivak, "Three Women's Texts and a Critique of Imperialism," *Critical Inquiry* 12 (Autumn 1985): 244.

Blanche, who is tall, dark, and dominating like Rochester himself, she settles astutely for a vicarious expression of her own competitive maleness through him. She preserves the proprieties while turning them constantly to her advantage, manipulating convention for both self-protection and self-advancement.[29]

While they have very different critical styles and even different political agendas—one traditionally "Marxist," the other more ambitiously "Marxist-feminist"—both Eagleton and Spivak direct the corrosive trope of "theatricality" against what they see as a certain (petit-)bourgeois success story. Instead of joining Gilbert and Gubar in celebration of "plain Jane's progress," these two critics read that narrative as an allegory of the brilliant career of bourgeois or bourgeois-feminist ideology in general, a career whose success has depended in large part on its ability to mask or dull its very brilliance. Both, therefore, take us behind the scenes of this exemplary tale, exposing Brontë's painstakingly achieved antitheatrical illusion so as to reveal what goes on behind the scenes—on the far side of the curtain—as an elaborate, highly tendentious scene in itself.

It should be clear by now that my own approach to the novel is closer to the demystifying school of Brontë criticism than to the celebratory one. But my aim in acknowledging and describing these prior interpretations has not been merely to take my place in line, a place that all too easily becomes a hiding place, a place *behind*. If it is important not to "cover up for" Charlotte Brontë by covering up theatricality along with her, it is equally important not to cover oneself in the prestigious mantle woven and worn by previous unmaskers. As we have seen, a certain unmasking is already dramatized in the novel itself: but what is most instructive about Jane's desire to "pluck the mask" from Blanche, just as Brontë would "raise the gilding" (p. 36) from her own miniaturized Vanity Fair, is that the ensuing act of demystification, precisely because of the "excitation" it induces in the demystifier, has to subject itself to "ruthless restraint." As we have also seen, the ruthlessness of this restraint affects both the object and the subject of demystification, although we have devoted more attention to the latter, since potentially vi-

29. Terry Eagleton, *Myths of Power: A Marxist Study of the Brontës* (New York: Barnes and Noble, 1975), pp. 30–31.

olent self-discipline continues to seem somewhat anomalous in a novelist who invokes images of "open country" and "fresh air" to advertise her art.

As for the literary critic, it ought not to surprise us that his or her "ruthlessness" should find an external object, whether in the canonical text, in its author, in its protagonist, or in some composite scapegoat: as popular usage implies, "criticism" has a certain reputation for being mean. In its relentlessly prosecutorial style, Eagleton's reading, for one, epitomizes this destructive tendency—a tendency perhaps less obvious to academic critics than to those outside the profession. For though many of us are intermittently or vaguely aware of the aggressivity that informs our work in general, we may ignore not only the *ceaselessness* of its ruthless excitations but also the professional deformation whereby we restrain or repress them, to say nothing of the ruthlessness with which we do so. Indeed, our very ignorance of that deformation betokens the thing it both "actively" disregards and "passively" fails to know.[30] If these quotation marks would blur the hierarchical distinction between a deliberate *act* of ignoring and an involuntary *state* of unknowing, this is because I want to bring contemporary demystifying critics—who, in their apparent self-possession, might recall the reserved but savvy, ironic, and newly empowered Charlotte Brontë we glimpsed at the opera— a little closer to that even less glamorous and even more carefully guarded avatar of "the writer," the governess named Jane Eyre. For if Jane represents the writer *disciplined*, it is hard to tell whether that discipline is self-discipline or rather the effect of certain imperious external constraints, whether it is administered willingly or

30. In this chapter's concerns with interpretive vicariousness, compulsory self-masking, and *Schadenfreude*, the reader may discern the influence of Eve Kosofsky Sedgwick's recent work on "the epistemology of the closet." Especially pertinent here are her discussion of the performative effects of ignorance in "Privilege of Unknowing," *Genders* 1 (Spring 1988): 102–24, and her analysis of the connections in Proust between the closet as spectacle and the closet as viewpoint in "Epistemology of the Closet (I)," *Raritan* 7 (Spring 1988): 39–69, and "Epistemology of the Closet (II)," *Raritan* 8 (Summer 1988): 102–30. Consideration of this influence could open out into consideration of the question of the relationship between gay and antihomophobic strategies of interpretation, on the one hand, and novels that are (apparently) about female heterosexual desire, on the other hand. Since the question is a large and complicated one, I can only broach it here. I hope in some future project to discuss the links between "the closet," a figure for the construction of gay and lesbian knowledge and identity, and "the attic," which Gilbert and Gubar have established as a figure for feminist knowledge and identity.

unwillingly, consciously or unconsciously. Indeed, as we have seen, Brontë's disciplining of the self that writes has the peculiar consequence of transforming what ought to look like a subjection to social control into what looks instead like a savingly asocial or at least antisocial condition. Likewise, those of us who practice a deidealizing literary criticism most eloquently attest our embeddedness in the social precisely when, "accepting" the restraints of our discipline, we discreetly withdraw from the scene of our own readings.

Critics' techniques of withdrawal can be as sophisticated as those practiced by, or upon, Brontë's heroine. Eagleton's reading may itself be a study in the "competitive maleness" he identifies in Jane, yet its deftly self-distancing effect of analytic *mise en abîme* at the same time renders it an impressive exercise in the art of "vicarious expression" he attributes to her as well. Spivak, for her part, thematizes the veiling of her own authorial performance as a pragmatic refusal to theatricalize the "author" of the novel along with its protagonist: she chooses "rather strategically to take shelter in an essentialism which, not wishing to lose the important advantages won by U.S. mainstream feminism, will continue to honor the suspect binary oppositions—book and author, individual and history."[31] And it is no doubt clear that my dilation upon other critics' defenses has served a dilatory and defensive purpose in its own right. One might argue, moreover, that this chapter's relative generality or even diffidence thus far with respect to the specific social—for example, sexual and class—determinants of Jane's behavior has served as a not-so-reliable screen for certain rather undelightful social aggressivities of my own. Yet I hope that it will not seem merely defensive if I suggest, first, that this diffidence is in large part a temporary response to the necessity for a preliminary analysis of Brontë's own evasion of social specification, and, second, that the interpretive ruthlessness it would occlude is itself a response to my fear that, as a teacher who writes, as a disciplined subject, far from being safely superior to Brontë's literary governess, I am in fact insufficiently differentiated from her.

In the next section of this chapter, I will attempt to specify the social role that, precisely by virtue of its Brontëan "unsociability," the demystifying school of literary criticism has in common with

31. Spivak, "Three Women's Texts," p. 244.

the "disciplined ... character" known as Jane Eyre.[32] It might be objected that, even if this analogy demonstrates a structural affinity, it may seem to overlook the obvious difference between the overwhelming "subjectivity-effect" of Brontëan discourse and the constitutive facelessness of most academic criticism. Yet I hope that what follows will be justified by its delineation of a performative dimension that academic "objectivity" might share, surprisingly enough, with Brontëan "subjectivity." For if we can see what it is that *effects* that "subjectivity," we may be able to see not only how effectively it responds to social pressures, but also how closely the decorum of criticism maintains an active repression not unlike Jane Eyre's. If, in our more or less ruthless unmasking of that unmasker in the text, a certain transferential logic apparently compels us to repeat the double gesture whereby Jane catches others in the act of theatricality while at the same time concealing the traces of her own theatrical implication, we can at least attempt to analyze that logic, to interrogate the motives that sustain us in this productive inconsistency. We can ask, that is, not only how a curtain gets drawn in front of a certain drama of reading, but also why and on whose account it may be useful, as Spivak suggests, thus partially "to ignore the lessons of deconstruction."[33] Obviously, not all dramas of reading are the same, and the annals of recent criticism would no doubt show that there are many ways of "ignoring" deconstruction while seeming to honor it. The point is not to totalize diverse readings of Brontë's novel, much less to collapse those readings into the equally spurious totality of the different readings performed *in* the novel. Rather, I hope to consider some of the strategies that governesses who write may share with other teachers who, in different ways, take up the pen to inscribe theatricality in the novel.

32. Undoubtedly, the analogy I am proposing invites what D. A. Miller, in *The Novel and the Police*, p. 193, has called the "mortifying charges (sentimentality, self-indulgence, narcissism) which our culture is prepared to bring against anyone who dwells in subjectivity longer or more intensely than is necessary to his proper functioning as the agent of socially useful work." Instead of trying to answer those charges, I refer the reader to the source of this quotation, Miller's essay on *David Copperfield*, 192–220, where they are shrewdly problematized as functions of the culture of the "open secret." In its argument—although not, perhaps, in its performance—that essay is less sanguine than the present chapter about the destabilizing effects of deconstructive practice.

33. Spivak, "Three Women's Texts," p. 244.

In the middle of the Ingrams' stay at Thornfield, the theatricality that suffuses the episode finds its most "direct expression" in the charades that the company performs. "They spoke of 'playing charades,' " Jane tells us, "but in my ignorance I did not understand the term" (p. 211). As is the case with Jane's other professions of "ignorance," and with the professional "ignorance" or self-effacing "restraint" commonly assumed by professors of literature in their role as writers of criticism, we are confronted not with the inertness of a mere lack or negation but with a powerfully signifying opacity. Positing a gap at the level of cognition, this assertion of "ignorance" comes heavily charged with performative potential. Though Jane's "ignorance" excuses her from participating in the charades, as Rochester invites her to do, it provides her with the leading role in a far more important, if more covert, play.

A few pages before Jane recounts the stages of her "ceaseless surveillance," we join her in a less obviously anxious phase of her spectatorship, watching the charades along with her. What is most striking about this lengthy and thematically pregnant passage is not Jane's response to it but rather her apparent *neutrality*: the narrative here consists primarily of description, forgoing the evaluative and meditative exfoliations that characterize so many other passages in the novel. This relative neutrality indicates, of course, that Jane's countertheatrical screen is already in place. But the obscurity thus procured for her—an obscurity that Jane would rather have us read as *obtuseness*—has an uncanny analogue in the obscurity generically inherent in the charades themselves: spectator and spectacle are linked in a complicity that Brontë manages artfully to dissemble, mainly by diverting our gaze from the narrator and fixing it instead on the *tableaux vivants* executed in front of her. So subtle is this distraction that, unless the reader pays particular attention to architectural details that the critical eye is trained merely to scan as so much stage direction, he or she will not notice that the stage for this performance is nothing other than the drawing-room in which Jane has been stationed so as to seem quintessentially *nontheatrical*. "The drawing-room, as I have before observed, was raised two steps above the dining room" (p. 212); we have probably *not* observed, however, that it was Jane, before it was the dazzling band of ladies, who loomed on such a platform, and that it was she, not they, who thus stood poised for unveiling within the confines of the room's implicitly dramatic arch. At any rate, when the curtain rises, now enlisted in an avowedly (if amateurishly) theatrical enterprise, it discloses three consecutive, elaborately mounted tableaux: the first representing "the pantomime of a marriage" (p. 212) between Rochester and Blanche; the second, a small triumph of orientalist *mise en scène*, depicting the same two characters as "Eliezer and Rebecca" (p. 213) beside a well; the third displaying a "begrimed" (p. 213) Rochester in a prison cell. At the end of this sequence, the members of the audience solve the charade, whose three scenes denote "Bridewell Prison." As if to proffer further evidence of her "ignorance," however, Jane does not pause to underscore the semantic implications of this signifier; instead, when the other spectators ascend the stage to perform their own charade, she continues to watch Rochester and Blanche, who, though now spectators themselves, remain spectacularized as a result of Jane's increasingly excited and ruthless—but at the same time supposedly naïve and out-of-it—vigilance.

Indeed, a generalized interchangeability of spectator and spectacle seems by now to be one of the defining features of both Brontëan and Austenian theatricality. Yet, we have also seen how much of Brontë's (and, to a somewhat lesser extent, of Austen's) energy goes into the masking of the heroine's participation in these reversals. In the passage in question, it is precisely Jane's muteness with respect to the charade's meaning that deflects attention from any similarity between that nonresponse and the "dumb show" (p. 212) enacted before our eyes, or between her inscrutability as an observer and the "darkness" (cosmetically as well as hermeneutically guaranteed) of the charade itself. The rules of the game require that the "diviners" (p. 214) become actors in their turn, but Jane appears exempt from this otherwise obligatory transformation of cognition into performance. Just as Brontë severs the connection between opacity and the blinding glitter that might resemble it too closely for comfort, so she forestalls any recognition of the symmetrical relationship between Jane's illegibility and that of the enigmatic tableaux: whereas the latter are made to suggest a potentially uncontrollable *excess* (of meaning), the former is manipulated so as to look like an antithetical and merely static *lack* (of interpretation). The danger readily illustrated for Jane is that she might end up like the interpreters in the audience, forced into excessive performance herself: "interpretation," after all, is also another name for "acting."

In playing dumb, however, Jane in fact does something quite specific, albeit without appearing to do anything at all. What Jane's "ignorance" does is nothing less than to articulate the rhetorical and social topography of the novel. For this "ignorance" is itself artic-ulated or internally divided. On the one hand, it functions as an index of class inferiority, marking Jane's distance from the "showy" aristocrats in whose sophisticated games she must not participate. On the other hand, insofar as she *chooses* not to participate, it may be inferred that Jane's "ignorance" affords her a certain privilege as well. If "ignorance" stands out as one of the novel's favorite sig-nifiers for *social* repression or restraint, it also belongs to an appar-ently antithetical set of valuations, in which negativity turns into a virtue, in which privation gets cathected as a positive force. That is, the very minimalness of Jane's social literacy, and the attendant exiguity of her social surface, become the ground for her *rhetorical* authority, an authority signaled early in the novel when, with a kind of grudging admiration, another character says of the young heroine, "I never saw a girl of her age with so much cover" (p. 44). Figured as "so much cover," Jane's density, which we have identified as a certain obtuseness, can be transvalued as a kind of protopoetic com-paction analogous to the Freudian dream-work, with its "complex" effects of condensation, displacement, and overdetermination.

"You can't judge a book by its cover": Jane's "ignorance" renders her both unknowing and, more honorifically, unknowable; it can associate her both with unconsciousness—construed rather flatly as a lack of information or experience—and with the unconscious— construed much more generously as an active, if occulted, source of meaning and energy. Jane's bookish cover adumbrates the subver-sive potential that lies hidden within the socially and psychologically repressed, a potential all the greater for being "linguistic" rather than "real." Emblematically, when Rochester calls Jane "inexplica-ble" and "uncanny" (p. 289), the prestigious resonance of these epithets cancels out the negativity of their prefixes. Invested with an aura of textuality that befits a titular heroine, Jane Eyre challenges us to penetrate her cover, to join Rochester in thinking, "An unu-sual—to me—a perfectly new character, I suspected was yours: I desired to search it deeper and know it better" (p. 340). And when, under such (implicitly violent) hermeneutic pressure, Jane proudly proclaims, "But I have a veil—it is down" (p. 272), she is trading on the conventional wisdom that detects in victimhood and repression a blessing in disguise.

Because of its cunning mobilization of "ignorance," *Jane Eyre* is indeed one of the major sites of the convention—central to modern ideology, political and literary—that dissociates rhetorical (and ontological) power from social power, producing a chiasmus in which the inferiority of oppressed or marginalized groups virtually guarantees their latent, but all the more disruptive, eloquence, while the politically and economically powerful, trading eloquence for elegance, surrender their linguistic hegemony and assume a corrupt idiom that is itself "merely" conventional. Under this chiastic dispensation, the episode of the charades, for example, can never become an effective locus of what a "subversive" literary criticism might wish to see as Derridean free play. However seductively "textual" it may seem, this potentially disseminative interlude is reduced to the status of a trivial pursuit: textuality has been dissociated from theatricality, the former imbued, oddly enough, with an almost logocentric inexpressibility and depth—as in, "I desired to search it deeper"—and the latter deflated, rendered superficial and frivolous. Like the private theatricals in *Mansfield Park*, the charades end up signifying nothing more subversive than the fabled vacuity and/or promiscuity of the upper classes, who represent "social exchange" at its most mindless. In contrast, Jane's wise "ignorance" at once saves her from this linguistic fate and affiliates her with the mystifyingly exalted community of those who, could they speak, would utter the *parole pleine* of truth and authenticity. For if Jane is flanked on one side by Vanity Fair—by "a world of self-marketing Célines and Blanches"—she adjoins on the other side the more figurative but therefore more formidable community of the dispossessed and the incarcerated—the world most aptly symbolized by Jane's "truest and darkest double," The Madwoman in the Attic. As Gilbert and Gubar's canonizing title implies, Bertha is indeed the internalized—the interned—character par excellence; and when, in the famous, ominous scene of her nocturnal visit to Jane's room, she throws Jane's bridal veil over her face, the first Mrs. Rochester reminds her successor of the considerable mystique that attaches to those who know how to remain under cover, even when, as in this instance, they are on the loose.

I am suggesting that Jane's inwardness, far from constituting an end in itself, performs a specific kind of cultural work. To say that Jane functions as an ideological placeholder would exaggerate, but not misstate, her representational role. By cultivating an inaccessible interiority, Jane ultimately and crucially protects not herself but the larger chiastic rewriting of power relations that her "ignorance" makes possible. That the demand for this intermediacy issues not only from within the novel but, perhaps more importunately, from extratextual sources may become clear if we consider a contemporary review of *Jane Eyre*, a review that is also a telling discussion of the lot of the Victorian governess. The reviewer, Elizabeth Rigby, writes:

> The line which severs the governess from her employers is not one which will take care of itself, as in the case of a servant. If she sits at table she does not shock you—if she opens her mouth she does not distress you—her appearance and manners are likely to be as good as your own—her education rather better; there is nothing upon the face of the thing to stamp her as having been called to a different state of life from that in which it has pleased God to place you; and therefore the distinction has to be kept up by a fictitious barrier which presses with cruel weight upon the mental strength or constitutional vanity of a woman.[34]

As we will see when we turn to Rigby's specific remarks on *Brontë's* governess, her compassion does not preclude the most stringently prescriptive attitude toward its objects. For though she laments the "cruel weight" resulting from the very groundlessness or arbitrariness of "the line which severs the governess from her employers," what concerns Rigby about this "fictitious" distinction is less the suffering its peremptoriness imposes upon the former than the danger to which its tenuity exposes the latter. "The distinction *has to be* kept up": otherwise, the "employer" addressed both as the *destinataire* ("you") and as the real subject of this discourse might find himself—and more important, the "ladies" of his social class—uncomfortably close to the marketplace from which the governess has emerged. As M. Jeanne Peterson, Mary Poovey, and Nancy Armstrong have shown, the Victorian governess virtually embodied the

34. Elizabeth Rigby, "*Vanity Fair*—and *Jane Eyre*," *Quarterly Review* 84 (December 1848): 177.

deconstructibility of her culture's opposition between "lady" and "prostitute." An irremediably vexing symptom of tensions within middle-class life, "[s]he was educated to be a 'nosegay' to adorn her 'papa's drawing room,' and as a governess she had sold herself as an ornament to display her employer's prestige."[35] What makes the governess so unwelcome a presence within the middle-class home is her accentuation not of the pathetic disparity between her intended fate and her real one, but rather of the more painful *affinity* between "nosegay" and "ornament" as tropes of quasi-theatrical ostentation.

Constantly threatening to uncover the precariousness of the polarization of idealized female domesticity on the one hand and dreaded female commerce on the other, the governess always already plays an intermediate role—a *disturbingly* intermediate role as deconstructive thorn-in-the-side—that necessitates her ideological refashioning in a more *reassuringly* intermediate role as emblem of interiority. Almost intrinsically a site of "social exchange"—a figure for the transgressive circulation of social meanings—the governess must be reconceived in a way that re-covers her and that thereby covers up her exacerbating potential. If she cannot help occupying a liminal position in the class and gender system of Victorian culture, then perhaps that position can be buttressed or hypostatized so as to separate the identities it might otherwise conjoin. Thus, Rigby's apparently empathetic discourse, regretting the "fictitious barrier which presses with cruel weight upon the mental strength or constitutional vanity of a woman," simultaneously constitutes both that barrier and the woman whose task is henceforth to "keep it up." And if, in bearing, internalizing, and so eventually *becoming* this ruthless restraint, the disciplined governess must repress the "vanity" of her theatrical (i.e., female) nature, the compensation for this

35. M. Jeanne Peterson, "The Victorian Governess: Status Incongruence in Family and Society," in Martha Vicinus, ed., *Suffer and Be Still: Women in the Victorian Age* (Bloomington: Indiana University Press, 1972), p. 11. Mary Poovey's *Uneven Developments: The Ideological Work of Gender in Mid-Victorian England* (Chicago: University of Chicago Press, 1988) contains a chapter on the governess and *Jane Eyre* that builds upon Peterson's research in ways similar to my own, although Poovey does not explicitly address the questions of the governess's theatricality and of her significance for contemporary writer-teachers. I regret that Poovey's fine book was published after I had written most of this chapter, and that I was therefore unable to incorporate into it a sustained dialogue with her reading of the novel. Also see Nancy Armstrong, *Desire and Domestic Fiction: A Political History of the Novel* (New York: Oxford University Press, 1987), pp. 78–79, on the transgressive potential of the governess.

pressing upkeep is a ceaseless excitation of her "mental strength," which impresses upon her the profundity of the subjectifying (i.e., female) work she performs, and brings comfort to the "employers" whose homes she thereby defends.

Admittedly, it might appear rather odd to view Jane Eyre's pivotal "ignorance" as consistent with the kind of disciplinary fiction dictated by Rigby. After all, the product of the former—a triptych with Bertha on one side, Céline, Adèle, and Blanche on the other side, and Jane in the middle—does not seem ideally congruent with the aim of the latter—a hierarchy with the "lady" on top, the "prostitute" on the bottom, and the long-suffering governess in the middle. The two models appear to have nothing more in common than the same medial figure. Rigby in fact disliked *Jane Eyre*, denouncing its heroine as "the personification of an unregenerate and *undisciplined* spirit" (emphasis added).[36] Nor is it particularly difficult to understand this hostility: in unmasking Blanche as a "bad" actress—as a more respectable, home-grown version of Céline—Brontë's heroine inscribes the very confusion that Rigby would prohibit. But before we decide that Brontë's deconstructive unmaskings are automatically "subversive," let us consider—as Rigby does not—the way in which they might actually promote Rigby's project.

I would argue that, while one might want to read it as a gesture of defiance, Brontë's fictional work goes a long way toward constructing the fictitious barrier Rigby prescribes; the novel's debunking of certain binary oppositions may thus serve as a kind of alibi. Indeed, Brontë's defensive strategy is even shrewder than Rigby's. For where Rigby, though reinforcing the boundary that barely differentiates the governess from her employer, would thereby merely hold the line between the still more unsettlingly similar categories of (domestically theatrical) "nosegay" and (commercially theatrical) "ornament," Brontë redraws the social map by superimposing on the vulnerable opposition between home and marketplace what looks like a more radical opposition between an interior now defined as "psychological" and an exterior now defined as "social." That is, since Blanche Ingram (the "lady") already bears too great a resemblance to Céline Varens (the "prostitute"), Brontë deconstructs both of them into the same inferior category, and provides, on the far side

36. Rigby, "*Vanity Fair*," p. 173.

of the governess, the heavy ballast of the id-like Bertha. That Bertha is "demonic" rather than "ladylike," moreover, hardly detracts from her stabilizing power: her very extremity testifies to the vastness of the psychic space capable of containing her. And contain her is just what Jane Eyre does, constituting, by virtue of her own "depth," a barrier behind which the Madwoman lurks as the internalized or repressed "truth" of the redomesticated female subject. Rigby would defend upper-middle-class and would-be upper-middle-class women on the basis of social privilege alone, a privilege she knows to be threatened by its beneficiaries' lack of any corresponding physical, intellectual, or psychological distinction: she admits that, in "appearance," "manners," and "education," the governess is likely to be equal if not superior to her employers. Brontë, however, places *her* governess at the frontier of a brave new world of female subjectivity, a world that can include not only the demonic Bertha, at its furthest limit, but also, in its great normative middle distance, the same women Rigby protects, though less effectually, without benefit of Brontë's empowering cover of redefined and expanded "privacy."[37]

Brontë's governess, then, figures not an alternative to confinement but a better *form* of confinement, one that offers both shelter and a semblance of liberation. A novel that seems to organize itself into a series of rooms and houses, *Jane Eyre* may be said to comprise three main symbolic spaces, which we can call "Gothic," "Brontëan," and "Austenian," to give a more authoritative sound to the madwoman/governess/prostitute triad. And if the Brontëan enclosure, characterized by the dense psychic layering that makes it a barrier as well, nonetheless seems compatible with effects of "open country" and "fresh air," this is because Brontë positions her heroine strategically between the unspeakably "dark" recesses inhabited and personified by Bertha Mason, and the discreditably "glittering" exteriority inhabited and personified by Blanche, Céline, Adèle and company.[38] Polarizing two distinct sets of literary conventions—on the one hand, "the dark images of the Gothic," in Raymond Wil-

---

37. My account of Brontë's construction of "subjectivity," and of the madwoman's ideological usefulness within that construction, owes much to Armstrong, *Desire and Domestic Fiction*, esp. pp. 186–213.

38. One thinks here of Austen's (rather apprehensive) description of her own mode—or at least that of *Pride and Prejudice*—as "light and bright and sparkling."

liams's phrase; on the other, the "worldliness" epitomized by Jane Austen—the Brontëan heroine is thus also confined and implicitly conventionalized by them, if only through metonymic contact. And yet, the structure so produced persists in looking like an *escape* from structures and conventions and constraints—in short, from the sorts of alterity that usually count, in modern critical parlance anyway, as "the social." To be sure, the intermediate space that Brontë maps out seems to exhibit a distinct antigravitational tendency toward the Gothic attic. But Brontë's psychologizing appropriation of that place and of the literary tradition it emblematizes, an appropriation that critics have recognized for some time now, is "novel" only in the sense that a novel, as *Mansfield Park* has shown us, is itself a conventional structure in which a theater lies concealed. The Brontëan middle, and the disjunction it signifies, are as socially determined, and as socially performative, as both the Gothic upstairs and the more overtly stagy Austenian downstairs.

Nowhere is Brontë more effective in her public relations, of course, than when she persuades even her most socially sensitive critics that her fiction furnishes an essentially private site in which, as if for the first time, "passion" can be either "directly expressed" (Williams again), or, as Kucich would have it, *indirectly* expressed but with an even more antisocial result. As I have been suggesting, *Jane Eyre* can perform its ideological duty only if it disguises that performance. Early in Jane's relationship with Rochester—who incarnates social power in this novel and who also, it turns out, is himself a master of disguise—that imperious employer gives her a lesson both in the task she will be expected to carry out and in the proper means of domesticating or effacing it. In this virtually primal scene of instruction, Rochester tells Jane the story of how Adèle came to be "transplanted" from France to England. It is this narration, as we have noted, that particularly scandalized Victorian readers. Rigby, for example, complains of how Rochester "pours into [Jane's] ears disgraceful tales of his past life, connected with the birth of Adèle."[39] But just as the transplant in question intends a homeopathic effect, supposedly defending the world of the novel against the theatricality that Adèle represents, so this narrative-within-a-narrative goes out of its way to declare its innocuousness.

39. Rigby, *"Vanity Fair,"* p. 164.

Rochester, in fact, pauses in the middle of his story to reassure Jane of her immunity from it: "I know what sort of mind I have placed in communication with my own: I know it is one not liable to take infection" (p. 174). Always a quick learner, Jane echoes her teacher's "knowledge" when, musing on his story, she remarks that "there was probably nothing at all extraordinary in the substance of the narrative itself" (p. 177). If Rochester has greater faith in Jane's "mental strength" than Rigby has, his disciplinary procedure requires that premise as fundamentally as Rigby's ideological fiction needs the support that it too presses into service; and while the placidity of Rochester's pupil and the tremulousness of Rigby's governed governess may seem incommensurate, Jane, as we have seen, is indeed capable of the agitation—what Rochester in fact forecasts for her here as "whirl and tumult, foam and noise" (p. 173)—that, in complementing her outward calm, proves her interiority to be so usefully receptive.

The "substance" of Rochester's narrative is his affair with Céline Varens. Rochester tells Jane of how Céline betrayed him and abandoned Adèle, whom he subsequently rescued from "the slime and mud of Paris." In narrating his discovery of Céline's faithlessness, Rochester stages his spectatorship in a way that seems to anticipate Jane's equally vengeful acts of consumption. Waiting for his "opera inamorata" (p. 173) one night on the "balcony" (p. 172) outside her boudoir, he sees her returning to her hotel with another man. "Prepar[ing] an ambush," he "dr[aws] the curtain" (p. 175) in front of the balcony window, through an aperture of which he may thus, like Jane, "see without being seen." But that Rochester is in fact demonstrating the necessary *difference* between himself and Jane is signaled by the conspicuous absence from his surveillance of any of the voyeuristic titillation that animates hers. For whatever "excitation" he may have been feeling subsides at the very point where he would seem most susceptible to it—as soon, that is, as he begins to witness the spectacle of his betrayal and ridicule: "They [Céline and her lover] began to talk; their conversation eased me completely: frivolous, mercenary, heartless, and senseless, it was rather calculated to weary than enrage a listener" (p. 175). And if the frivolity of the scene is matched by the boredom of the spectator—if Rochester refuses to get excited—he exempts himself equally from the rigors of restraint. For he responds to this potentially enraging experience not only by coming out into the open, but then by concluding this particular charade with a brisk finesse all the more pointed for the bad acting that serves as its foil:

> Opening the window, I walked in upon them; liberated Céline from my protection; gave her notice to vacate her hotel; offered her a purse for immediate exigencies; disregarded screams, hysterics, prayers, protestations, convulsions; made an appointment with the vicomte for a meeting at the Bois de Boulogne. Next morning I had the pleasure of encountering him; left a bullet in one of his poor etiolated arms, feeble as the wing of a chicken in the pip, and then thought I had done with the whole crew.
>
> (pp. 175–76)

It turns out, of course, that Rochester cannot quite dismiss "the whole crew": instead, he is forced to transplant the noxiously Parisian Adèle into what he (rather misleadingly) calls "the wholesome soil of an English country garden" (p. 176). Yet insofar as Rochester persists in denying that he is Adèle's father, this transplant neatly figures appropriation as disavowal, and inscription as erasure. And if the graft in question thus has a dismissive effect after all, that effect derives not so much from the aristocratic insouciance of Rochester's irony as from the domesticating receptivity of Jane's "mind," whose capacity for assimilation his didactic narrative has been seeking to establish. For in this lesson, Rochester has implicitly but forcefully been impressing upon the governess the need for her governance, not just of her "protégée" (p. 176), Adèle, but also of the mind he has posited in her, and therefore of the potential promiscuity of social exchange—of the social in the most dangerously inclusive sense—that his own Byronic circulation appears to signify. Jane dutifully notes of this and other "conferences" (p. 177):

> I, indeed, talked comparatively little, but I heard him talk with relish. It was his nature to be communicative; he liked to open to a mind unacquainted with the world, glimpses of its scenes and ways (I do not mean its corrupt scenes and wicked ways, but such as derived their interest from the great scale on which they were acted, the strange novelty by which they were characterized); and I had a keen delight in receiving the new ideas he offered, in imagining the new pictures he portrayed, and following him in thought through the new regions he disclosed, never startled or troubled by one noxious allusion.
>
> (p. 177)

As an upper-class man, Rochester obviously has greater mobility— and less anxiety about it—than does, say, an upper-class woman.

Not so differently from a writer like Rigby, however, Rochester still insists on the necessity of a fictitious barrier to hold "the world" in place, to regulate the flow of social meanings. What better barrier than his newly employed governess, who, equipped with a disciplined, densely structured mind, positively "delight[s] in receiving," and absorbing, all the "tumult" that the narratives of his Byronic theatricality can "open to" her. Indeed, Jane sees herself not as a captive audience but as an expansive consciousness privileged to capture the "novelty" that informs Rochester's "scenes." Subsuming these scenes "in thought," containing these tableaux by "imagining" them, Jane affirms the psychological novel's ability to suppress the "corrupt" and "noxious" associations of the material it incorporates.

For though Jane denies even the corrupt *content* of Rochester's stories (to say nothing of their corrupting *influence*), we may prefer to view that denial as part of a cover-up, in whose distinctive methods Rochester himself has been giving her careful on-the-job training. In narrating for Jane the "frivolous" but admittedly "slimy" scene of Céline's unmasking, for instance, he has also allegorized for her edification, and thus for the strengthening of the social order itself, the appropriately antiseptic, antitheatrical—one might even say "novelizing"—response to it. As if to drive home the lesson he has been teaching, moreover, Rochester, in the middle of recounting this meretricious French melodrama (or is it a farce?), "portrays" what thus becomes a kind of scene within a scene; and the embedded scene not only has the same infectious potential as the foreign affair, but indeed strikes dangerously close to home:

> He ground his teeth and was silent: he arrested his step and struck his boot against the hard ground. Some hated thought seemed to have him in its grip, and to hold him so tightly that he could not advance—
>
> We were ascending the avenue when he thus paused; the hall was before us. Lifting his eyes to its battlements, he cast over them a glare, such as I never saw before or since. Pain, shame, ire—impatience, disgust, detestation—seemed momentarily to hold a quivering conflict in the large pupil dilating under his ebon eyebrow. Wild was the wrestle which should be paramount; but another feeling rose and triumphed: something hard and cynical; self-willed and resolute: it settled his passion and petrified his countenance: he went on—
>
> "During the moment I was silent, Miss Eyre, I was arranging a point with my destiny. She stood there by that beech trunk—a hag like one of those who appeared to Macbeth on the heath at Forres. 'You like Thornfield?' she said, lifting her finger; and then she wrote in the air a memento, which ran in lurid hieroglyphics all along the

house front, between the upper and lower row of windows, 'Like it if you can! Like it if you dare!' "

(pp. 173–74)

An inscription of the novel's Gothic subtext, this passage also records the theatrical implications of that subtext, which the novel frames more often as its buried, repressed, incarcerated "truth," as a signified so private and internal as to *transcend* theatricality, intimating instead a realm of peculiarly logocentric écriture, of unspeakable textuality. Indeed, if—to borrow Gilbert and Gubar's admirable pun—Bertha Mason has to be shut up, this is because the novel cannot risk the contradiction of too obvious or too frequent a staging of its deepest and "darkest" secret; and if the witch of Thornfield nonetheless manages the occasional escape, what these sorties display more crucially, as we have seen, is Jane's ability—far greater than Grace Poole's—to front for and thereby recontain her. As Rochester's pupil and narratee, Jane is in fact being trained in this recuperative function. What completes the lesson, however, is not so much Rochester's Macbeth-like exchange with his "destiny" as Adèle's interruption of it, or rather the exemplary use to which Rochester puts that interruption:

> Adèle here ran before him with her shuttlecock.
> "Away!" he cried harshly; "keep at a distance, child; or go in to Sophie!" Continuing then to pursue his walk in silence, I ventured to recall him to the point whence he had abruptly diverged—
> "Did you leave the balcony, sir," I asked, "when Mdlle Varens entered?"
> I almost expected a rebuff for this hardly well-timed question: but, on the contrary, waking out of his scowling abstraction, he turned his eyes towards me, and the shade seemed to clear off his brow.

(p. 174)

A certain "abruptness" indeed renders the passage itself oddly resistant to naturalistic interpretation. Paternal (or, as Rochester insists, nonpaternal) resentment is not enough to account for the "harshness" with which he "rebuffs" Adèle. Adèle's sudden appearance, moreover, seems as unmotivated as the verbal violence that greets it. I would argue that her interruption acts, in its own almost comically contingent way, as a kind of shuttlecock in its own right, providing an accidental though no less unwelcome link between the inscription of Céline on the one hand and the inscription of (and by) the "hag" on the other. Intruding on Rochester's quasi-

Shakespearean scene, and issuing from the tonally and thematically disparate story of the actress-prostitute who is her mother, Adèle figures the threat of a relay between the very rhetorical registers the novel strives to segregate. As a result of such a relay, it might become difficult, if not impossible, to distinguish between the Gothic and the Austenian, between the psychological and the social, between the internal and the external, between the unconscious and the "calculating," between the uncanny and the frivolous, between the demonic and the merely "mercenary."

For despite their respective excesses, it is not so much any intrinsic content that makes both the story of Céline and the dialogue with the hag so potentially harmful; rather, the real danger lies in the possibility that they will infect *each other*. Hence Rochester's command: "Keep at a distance, child; or go in to Sophie!" In ordering Adèle to *go in*, he prepares her for the domesticating discipline he is busy teaching her teacher. That the object of his anger is female should not come as a surprise, since the object of his instruction is female as well. Rochester makes an example of Adèle, repelling her for having enacted the very boundary-crossing that her governess, as formed by his pedagogy, must prevent, precisely by upholding the fictitious barrier of her own inwardness. And the arbitrariness of that weighty charge is merely hinted at by the apparent arbitrariness with which Rochester treats Adèle.

Again, though, Jane learns her lesson well. "Recalling" Rochester from his Gothic-Shakespearean seizure to the story of Céline, she need not fear the same treatment Adèle has just received, since the very recalling re-marks—rather than compromises—the boundary in question. Jane has understood the responsibilities of her "post" (p. 176)—or, more specifically, her responsibilities *as* post, as both support and marker. Indeed, the pupil's progress is registered immediately and gratifyingly on the teacher's face, as "the shade seemed to clear off his brow." Through this clearing, Jane's readiness for her appointed work finds its index on her master's closely watched, heavily meaning-laden countenance. I would suggest, moreover, that the precondition for—or the necessary counterweight to—the novel's insistent and intensive representational heightening of the worldly, if world-weary, Rochester is precisely the heaviness and density of Jane's internalizing discourse. The point is not just the obvious one that Rochester is on display only because Jane's first-person narrative has produced him; rather, I am arguing almost the opposite case, that the social power for which Rochester stands has in a sense produced or called forth the narrative *in* or *on* which he stands. *Jane Eyre* is thus a kind of command performance that, rigorously veiling its performative exigencies and efficacies, militates not only against a possible slippage of class boundaries within the division of female symbolic labor, but also against an inordinate confusion or extravagance of meanings within a certain world of male social exchange as well.

In other words, the theatrical glamorization of a wealthy and powerful man like Rochester depends upon the antitheatrical subordination of a poor and powerless woman like Jane Eyre. For example, if Rochester's fantasm of "lurid hieroglyphics" already threatens a parodic or hyperbolic collapse of Gothic inscription into the "hysterics" of the bad boulevard drama that frames it, and if that framing itself sets the stage for contamination, Rochester can indulge with impunity in these deconstructive flirtations, because, after all, he has trained the governess to keep up the very distinctions that, as his class and gender entitle him to do, he plays at breaking down.[40] It is he who owns the shuttlecock, and who determines both its frolicsome appearance and its abrupt disappearance. He knows, that is, that after the scene of Jane's instruction, she will know how to separate—how to mark the incongruity between—the less clearly disciplinary scenes that he has been combining in an almost "carnivalesque" way. We have already noted the docility of the words with which she begins this cleanup operation:

> As he had said, there was probably nothing at all extraordinary in the substance of the narrative itself: a wealthy Englishman's passion for a French dancer, and her treachery to him, were everyday matters enough, no doubt, in society; but there was something decidedly strange in the paroxysm of emotion which had suddenly seized him when he was in the act of expressing the present contentment of his mood, and his newly revived pleasure in the old hall and its environs. I meditated wonderingly on this incident.
>
> (p. 177)

40. A rather different, though oddly pertinent, discourse on the relations among hieroglyphics, theater, and cruelty is to be found in the writings of Antonin Artaud, and in their interpretation by Jacques Derrida. See Artaud, *The Theater and Its Double*, trans. Mary Caroline Richards (New York: Grove Press, 1958), and Derrida, "The Theater of Cruelty and the Closure of Representation," in *Writing and Difference*, trans. Alan Bass (Chicago: University of Chicago Press, 1978), pp. 232–50.

"Meditat[ing] wonderingly," Jane thereby in effect reinstates the basis for Rochester's "newly revived" domestic "contentment," a sense of security located narratively, and regrounded discursively, in the space *between scenes.*

It is tempting, of course, to relieve Jane of this socially useful but unglamorous work of interposition, so that the novel's apparently "carnivalesque" theatrics may be imagined as extending not only to her but—as if *through* her—to "the reader" as well. Helena Michie, for instance, writes:

> Reading *Jane Eyre* is a veritable masquerade in which neither the reader nor the character can consistently tell the difference between mask and reality. Throughout the novel both Jane and Rochester try on a series of disguises and personae that grow more and more complex at the point of apparent unveiling. Jane's "discovery" that Rochester is the gypsy, for instance, only complicates matters and generates new questions about their respective roles. For Jane, even more than Rochester, the novel is a series of costume fittings that focus on the central contradictions between heroine and dependent.[41]

Though, as I began by suggesting, Brontë's novels are indeed far more theatrical than either she or some of her most influential critics would have us believe, I have been arguing for most of this chapter that *Jane Eyre*, at any rate, has to restrain or to conceal its heroine's theatricality. And if Jane's consequent subjectification provides a cover for the women of the employers' class—women whose domesticity might otherwise seem perilously close to the conditions of social exchange from which it would signify an escape—this subjectification also works to neutralize the more expansive and promiscuous social exchange mythically enacted by upper-class men, whose circulation constitutes not one side of the social map but rather an incessant movement back and forth across it.

What this means in terms of Michie's argument is that Rochester may be seen to "try on a series of disguises and personae" to the precise extent that Jane may not. Rochester may play the gypsy, but Jane must play the spectator. In that showy set-piece of a scene, he is free to transform his body into a site of contradictions, where the

---

41. Helena Michie, *The Flesh Made Word: Female Figures and Women's Bodies* (New York: Oxford University Press, 1987), p. 49.

maleness of his scrutinizing gaze collides with the femaleness of his "masquerade," or where the temporary "darkness" of his gypsy persona underscores the permanent "darkness" of both his person and his character, and thus seems to deconstruct the opposition between the psychic "darkness" of Gothic repression (Bertha) and the much less scary hermeneutic "darkness" of the charades (Blanche). But the reason these intimations of heteroglossia seem neither threatening nor particularly liberating is that Jane can be counted upon to resist them: "I believe you have been trying to draw me out—or in; you have been talking nonsense to make me talk nonsense" (p. 231). Such obdurate perspicacity keeps the focus of the narrative *away* from Jane's "costume fittings" and from the "central contradictions between heroine and dependent," ostentatiously investing Rochester alone with the authority to embody social contradictions yet thereby debunking such contradictions as so much "nonsense." For if the festive destabilizing of sexual, racial, and generic categories comes oddly to seem the exclusive right of the powerful, the tendentious casting of the "aristocracy" in that role makes "subversion" look even more archaic and innocuous, especially in light of what Gilbert and Gubar call Jane's "unseduceable independence."[42]

To maintain the illusion of this independence from an ultimately inconsequential world of profligate social exchange, Brontë usually *avoids* the analogy between reading and masquerade. The numerous scenes in the novel that center on the more or less aggressive or painful analysis of others employ textual rather than theatrical metaphors.[43] Significantly, the art form with which the heroine is associated is not acting but painting, which is associated in turn with both writing and "discipline" (p. 191).[44] And when Jane—under theatricalizing pressure—leaves Thornfield, she assumes not a mask but

---

42. Although Terry Castle's *Masquerade and Civilization: The Carnivalesque in Eighteenth-Century English Culture and Fiction* (Stanford: Stanford University Press, 1986) advances an excessively celebratory interpretation of its subject, overemphasizing the "subversive" powers of masquerade, see pp. 90–92 for a lucid discussion of the generally conservative effects of " 'downward' travesty" or "the imitation of the powerless by the powerful."

43. For examples, see pp. 283, 380, and 407.

44. For a fascinating analysis of the painting-drawing-writing-theatricality-pain nexus, but in relation to a textual and tonal milieu as distinct from Brontë's as that of Artaud, see Michael Fried, "Realism, Writing, and Disfiguration in Thomas Eakins's *Gross Clinic*," *Representations* 9 (Winter 1985): 33–104.

an "*alias*" (p. 363). Indeed, one could interpret each of her successive displacements in the course of the novel—from Gateshead Hall to Lowood School to Thornfield Hall to Moor House to Ferndean—as a way of extricating her from a situation in which her antitheatrical cover is in danger of being blown. When, for example, she escapes from St. John Rivers to return to Rochester, she is escaping not just lovelessness and authoritarianism, but an increasingly specular power-play, in which the histrionics of the play threaten to surpass the intensities of the power. Breaking away with the declaration, "*My* powers were in play and in force" (p. 445), she marshals the near-redundancy of "power . . . in force" to put "play" in its place, and to prefigure her final absorption into the asocial utopia of Ferndean.

By means of such strategies of absorption and displacement—strategies similar to those we have discussed in *Mansfield Park*—Brontë inscribes an even more sophisticated and elaborate technology of the self than Austen does. Yet the fantasy that Michie articulates, whereby, as in Austen's parodic curtain call as Mrs. Norris, that technology may be undone and the novel may be reconceived—and, even better, experienced—as a masquerade, finds an unlikely source of encouragement in Rigby's exuberantly punitive review of the novel. I have said that Rigby thought the character of Jane Eyre "undisciplined," inadequate for the task of keeping up the fictitious barrier in front of a problematic domesticity. Not surprisingly, this inadequacy manifests itself as a certain theatricality: Brontë's governess might sometimes *look like* "a noble, high-souled woman," but Rigby—perhaps getting back at Brontë for having theatricalized the "lady"—exposes Jane as a "flippant, fifth-rate, plebeian actress."[45]

Against my claim that Brontë's discipline of the governess constitutes an even sturdier barrier than the one Rigby demands, Rigby would insist on the failure of that fiction. And, much as one would censure the appalling class animus that informs Rigby's attack, one must admit that she may have a point. For there is often a sense in which Jane's inwardness borders on—indeed, collapses into—the very staginess or bad acting from which it would distinguish itself. (Presumably, if Jane's acting were better than "fifth-rate," one would

45. Rigby, "*Vanity Fair*," p. 171.

not notice it as acting, but would see only the noble, high-souled woman she now strains to impersonate.) "One" somehow knows what Rigby means when she writes, "One feels provoked as Jane Eyre stands before us."[46] Impelled by an unmistakable ardor of discreditation, Rigby of course adduces her own examples; more decorously and discreetly, we might point to some of the "soliloquies" Jane delivers in the course of the book.[47] Yet, if the "failure" implicit in Blanche Ingram's bad acting proves inseparable from Jane's "success" as a heroine, perhaps we should pause to consider the possible virtues of Jane's own bad acting, before lining up behind Rigby to take potshots at the would-be impostor.

We have already noted the Brontëan invagination whereby openness becomes inwardness, but we placed that process under the heading of "restraint." When Rigby remarks that "governesses are said to be sly . . . but Jane out-governesses them all," she identifies a reversal of that process—a turning outward of the inside—and she indicts it as precisely a refusal of restraint: "little Becky"—Becky Sharp of course, 1847's other famous governess-turned-actress— "would have blushed for her."[48] It is not always easy, however, to tell whether Jane is outside-in, or inside-out.[49] When Jane resists Rochester's pseudocarnivalesque efforts "to draw [her] out—or in," the obstinacy of her "self"-disciplinary in-folding overmasters the prepositional equivocation. But in other scenes, such as the humiliation or the unmasking of Blanche, where Jane's excitation tends not to seem *fully* complicit with her restraint, a certain effect of "out-governessing" suggests that Brontë may be playing a game of *fort/da* with the disciplinary techniques that her work generally enforces.

Without going so far as to call that effect "subversive" or "carnivalesque," we can at least differentiate it from the sort of deconstruction or demystification that ruthlessly restrains or ignores its own performance. There is of course no guarantee that demystifi-

46. Ibid., p. 167.
47. The one most vulnerable to ridicule is the one on pp. 117–19, on how to find a job as a governess. What makes it so embarrassing to the academic critic, at any rate, is its all-too-specific staging of "careerism."
48. Rigby, "*Vanity Fair*," p. 169.
49. I am tempted here to amend a (notorious) remark of Freud's in his case history of Dora, and to suggest that the question of whether a governess is outside-in or inside-out can naturally not be a matter of indifference. See Sigmund Freud, *Dora: An Analysis of a Case of Hysteria*, ed. Philip Rieff (New York: Collier, 1963), p. 84.

cation-as-masquerade will not be reenfolded within the disciplinary apparatus. Yet it may be useful to recall another one of our clusters of metaphors, and to remember that, precisely as a central figure in the chiastic redrawing of the social map, Jane Eyre's compulsory "ignorance" already carries within itself an unpredictable potential for the very social exchange that it works ostensibly to segregate as "prostitution" or to trivialize as "aristocratic" errancy. Chiasmus, after all, is the rhetorical schematization of exchange. The intermediary can be both a protective barrier and a dangerously effective conductor of "antithetical" meanings. Like Jane Eyre, contemporary deconstructive teacher-critics, especially those who profess "strategically" "to ignore the lessons of deconstruction," are positioned, just as "strategically," between what is idealized as a transcendent (though not exactly "Gothic") realm of truth and authority, to which we are thought to have privileged access—one has only to recall recent right-wing defenses of "the canon" and of "the Western tradition"—and what is projected—by left and right alike—as a degrading (though not exactly "Austenian") marketplace. Because *our* intermediate space is both as necessary to the culture and as potentially deconstructive of it as is the intermediate space demarcated and maintained by Jane Eyre, we might learn from her a certain "sly," if not "flippant," way of occupying it.

I am implying not that deconstructive literary critics should simply become more theatrical—whatever that would mean—but that, by recognizing certain parallels between our own cultural instrumentality and that of a Victorian teacher-writer-unmasker like Jane Eyre, we might also recognize certain opportunities—under the very cover of our discipline—to be more socially and politically "provoking" than we sometimes think we are. In its very latency as a critical option, deconstruction-as-performance may have greater power to disturb than does deconstruction-as-cognition. In her dazzling essay on Freud's case history of Dora, Jane Gallop suggests that "for psychoanalysis to be a site of radical contestation, Freud must assume his identification with the governess."[50] For the governess, unlike the phallic mother (or, for that matter, the mad-

50. Jane Gallop, "Keys to Dora," in *In Dora's Case: Freud-Hysteria-Feminism*, ed. Charles Bernheimer and Clare Kahane (New York: Columbia University Press, 1985), p. 215.

woman), is not only a troublesome source of sexual demystification, but in herself a demystifying emblem of social, and sexual, exchange. Criticism—especially deidealizing criticism—is often depicted as a stripping away of masks, but the critic—at least the academic critic— also *wears* a mask: the mask of the governess. Not by penetrating or—only somewhat less abusively—by lifting Jane Eyre's cover, but by turning it inside-out so that it becomes visible as a mask, "the reader"—more often than not an alias for the professor of literature— expresses, covertly, his or her desire to "out-governess them all": not merely to act out his or her role in the social script, but to act it *badly*, so as to transform a barrier and a surveillance post into a site, if not of radical contestation, then of an excitation that is not inevitably its own restraint.

3

Scenes of Writing,
Scenes of Instruction
Authority and Subversion in Villette

As to the anonymous publication, I have this to say: If the withholding of the author's name should tend materially to injure the
publisher's interest, to interfere with the booksellers' orders, etc.,
I would not press the point; but if no such detriment is contingent
I should be much thankful for the sheltering shadow of an incognito. I seem to dread the advertisements—the large-lettered "Currer
Bell's New Novel," or "New Work by the Author of *Jane Eyre*."

> Charlotte Brontë, in a letter to her publisher, George Smith

I submit, also, to the advertisements in large letters, but under
protest, and with a kind of ostrich longing for concealment.

> Brontë, writing again to Smith, three days later

In 1966, Jacques Derrida published the essay that would be translated
into English as "Freud and the Scene of Writing";[1] nine years later,
in a pointedly polemical swerve from Derrida, Harold Bloom posited
a "primal scene of instruction."[2] In substituting "instruction" for
"writing," Bloom signaled his rejection of the deconstructive problematic of textuality in favor of what he took to be, precisely, more
primal questions of poetic influence and originality. It is not my aim
here to determine which "scene"—Derrida's or Bloom's—in fact
takes precedence over the other. Rather, I want to reexamine the

1. Brontë's letters are quoted in Clement Shorter, ed., *The Brontës: Life and Letters*,
2 vols. (1908; rpt. New York: Haskell House, 1969) 2:282, 283. Derrida's essay is included
in *Writing and Difference*, trans. Alan Bass (Chicago: University of Chicago Press,
1978).
2. The most relevant texts by Bloom are *A Map of Misreading* (New York: Oxford
University Press, 1975), esp. 41–62, and *Poetry and Repression: Revisionism from Blake
to Stevens* (New Haven: Yale University Press, 1976), esp. pp. 52–82.

relationship between "writing" and "instruction" *as scenes*, scenes that Bloom's revisionism works to disarticulate, and to do so by introducing into this agon between critical fathers the figure of a woman writer for whom those scenes have a crucial interdependence.

As I suggested in the previous chapter, Charlotte Brontë is in some sense a major precursor (to use Bloom's term) of a certain kind of modern writer-teacher; in this chapter, I hope to look more carefully at how, in *Villette* (1853), theatricality—the common denominator of Derrida's and Bloom's theorizing—brings the activities of writing and teaching/learning into productively unsettling contact with each other. Often serving to prevent such contact, "theory" can end up idealizing or hypostatizing the terms it would isolate. When, for example, Bloom speaks of "instruction," he clearly has something grander in mind than the often tedious business of pedagogy depicted in Brontë's text; likewise, when Derrida writes of "writing," his strategic avoidance of literalistic reductions of the term sometimes leads to a certain formalizing abstraction. The suspended relationship between criticism and pedagogy will therefore be rearticulated here in the context not only of a difference in genders, but also of a difference in genres: where Derrida stages "writing" through the interpretation of psychoanalytic texts, and where Bloom stages "instruction" through the interpretation of poetic texts, Brontë stages both in her own *novelistic* text, whose local specificities may suggest ways in which to frame the professing of literary theory as itself a literary genre, with powerful (if not exactly magisterial) performative motives and effects.

Before turning to the analysis of *Villette*, however, I want to comment briefly on the relationship between this chapter's title and its subtitle. If the title recalls the critical dyad of Derrida and Bloom, the coupling of "authority and subversion"—familiar from the chapter on *Mansfield Park*—should evoke the more recent "new historicist" discourse about the politics of literature, where "authority" tends to be associated with the name of Foucault and "subversion" with that of Mikhail Bakhtin.[3] In the course of the reading that

3. The subtitle in fact alludes to a particular (and particularly influential) new historicist essay, Stephen Greenblatt's "Invisible Bullets: Renaissance Authority and Its Subversion, *Henry IV* and *Henry V*," in *Political Shakespeare: New Essays in Cultural Materialism*, ed. Jonathan Dollimore and Alan Sinfield (Ithaca: Cornell University

follows, it should become evident that I do not see these two oppositions as parallel or homologous; instead, I would hope that each
pairing would cut across the other as if *diagonally*. For while the
more recognizably political terms of the subtitle are intended to
check the potential for theoretical essentialism in the terms of the
title, the latter are intended to complicate the too-easy polarity of
the former—a polarity that asserts itself even when, as often happens
in new historicist practice, the terms are presented as asymmetrical.
It is possible, of course, to reduce the Derrida-Bloom antithesis to
a choice between revolutionary and conservative literary theories.
Where Derrida's mobilizations of écriture have impelled (and perhaps been impelled by) various Marxist and feminist insurgencies,
Bloom's counteremphasis on the oedipal pathos of "instruction" has
seemed increasingly to bespeak a politically motivated contempt for
such contestatory politicizing of literary studies. Yet what should
emerge, through the subsequent discussion of Brontë's novel, is a
sense of how the interplay or overlap between scenes of writing and
scenes of instruction may prevent us from deciding too quickly
whether a text is "authoritarian" or "subversive," "complicit" or
"contestatory." Though deconstruction, among other teachers,
would remind us that these binary oppositions are as inevitable as
more classically philosophical ones, Brontë's text—even as it opposes
a certain severe Protestant consciousness to a more "playful" French,
or Franco-Belgian, sensibility—compels us at least to refine our vocabulary, to come up with more versatile and more acute ways of
describing the relations between literary performance on the one
hand and social-political performance on the other.

Brontë, of course, advertises her work in such a way as to make
it seem particularly resistant to such heuristic use. Gillian Beer has
observed that "Charlotte Brontë was the most introspective of all
Victorian novelists."[4] Although the previous chapter should have

---

Press, 1985), pp. 18–47. The present chapter's reading of *Villette* should make clear
why I have omitted Greenblatt's "its" from my allusion. I first encountered the notion
that "Bakhtin and Foucault might serve as antithetical models for the discursivity of
culture" in a discussion of Greenblatt's work (among that of others) by Jonathan
Goldberg, "The Politics of Renaissance Literature: A Review Essay," *ELH* 49 (Summer
1982): 533.

4. Gillian Beer, " 'Coming Wonders': Uses of Theatre in the Victorian Novel," in
English Drama: Forms and Development, ed. Marie Axton and Raymond Williams (Cambridge: Cambridge University Press, 1977), p. 185. For another excellent discussion of

problematized Brontë's "introspectiveness," the epigraphs to the present chapter make clear that, well after the spectacular success of *Jane Eyre*, Brontë was indeed still playing the role of the governess. In these quotations from her letters concerning the marketing of *Villette* (which followed the publication of *Shirley* in 1849), Brontë, her deglamorizing "spectacles" still firmly in place, continues to figure authorship in terms of self-"concealment" rather than of self-revelation. By 1852, when those letters were written, Brontë's attachment to these dull "spectacles" has in fact been generalized as the wish for the even murkier "shadow of an incognito," and the "fictitious barrier" imposed upon the governess has become the barrier of fiction itself, behind which the governess-novelist would withdraw.

It should be easy enough, at this point, to expose that barrier as a piece of theatrical scenery. But instead of repeating that gesture from the previous chapter, let us consider a surprisingly similar antitheatrical pose on the part of a contemporary of Brontë's who had achieved great success precisely as an actress. After describing how, in order to save her father and his Covent Garden Theatre from financial ruin, she performed on his stage in the role of Juliet, Fanny Kemble concludes her account of her triumphant debut:

> And so my life was determined, and I devoted myself to an avocation which I never liked or honored, and about the very nature of which I have never been able to come to any decided opinion. . . .
>
> At four different periods of my life I have been constrained by circumstances to maintain myself by the exercise of my dramatic faculty; latterly, it is true, in a less painful and distasteful manner, by reading, instead of acting. But though I have never, I trust, been ungrateful for the power of thus helping myself and others, or forgetful of the obligation I was under to do my appointed work conscientiously in every respect, or unmindful of the precious good regard of so many kind hearts that it has won for me; though I have never lost one iota of my intense delight in the act of rendering Shakespeare's creations; yet neither have I ever presented myself before an audience without a shrinking feeling of reluctance, or withdrawn from their presence without thinking the excitement I had undergone unhealthy, and the personal exhibition odious.
>
> Nevertheless, I sat me down to supper that night with my poor,

---

the theater as the ambivalently charged "other" of the Victorian novel, see Nina Auerbach, "Alluring Vacancies in the Victorian Character," *Kenyon Review* 8 (1986): 36–48.

rejoicing parents well content, God knows! with the issue of my trial; and still better pleased with a lovely little Geneva watch, the first I had ever possessed, all encrusted with gold work and jewels, which my father laid by my plate and I immediately christened Romeo, and went, a blissful girl, to sleep with under my pillow.[5]

Kemble's inability "to come to any decided opinion" about the theater reveals itself throughout this passage, not only in the elaborately qualified disavowal of the second paragraph, but also in the overdetermined symbolism of the third, where the dutiful daughter pockets the reward for her "painful and distasteful" self-sacrifice. Accepting the token of paternal gratitude and approval, the young Kemble also manages a sly (and possibly unwitting) mischievousness in christening the prize "Romeo" and taking it off to bed. Perhaps this gesture bespeaks an otherwise inexpressible pride in the "personal exhibition" that her moralism compels her to find "odious." But even if, to the contrary, it implies her resentment of having been "constrained" into such odious exhibition, this would-be antitheatrical protest remains couched in theatrical terms. For in going to sleep with "Romeo"—under the legitimating auspices of the canonical Shakespeare—she extends into the family circle the very drama in which she has just performed, and thus mocks parental authority even as she defers to it.

Of course, this feat is made easier by the fact that she has performed not only for the sake of, but also with, her parents—while her father played Mercutio, her mother played Lady Capulet—so that, for her, the theatrical profession (or "avocation," as she would minimize it) represents a peculiar combination of submissive and transgressive possibilities. To "do [her] appointed work conscientiously in every respect" is to violate the canons of respectability enforced by society at large; to rebel, however covertly or belatedly, against "the obligation [she] was under" is to win back that respectability. As confining as this quadruple bind may seem, it may also permit an oddly compensatory rhetorical slippage, so that, in recounting her experience on the stage, Kemble can move rapidly, almost indiscernibly, between censorious and covertly celebratory registers. How, for example, are we to take her statement that she

5. Frances Ann Kemble, *Records of a Girlhood*, 2nd ed. (New York: Henry Holt, 1879), pp. 220–21.

went to sleep "a blissful girl"—as an instance of bemused dismissal or of fond remembrance? That these apparently incompatible attitudes may cohere in a single narrative utterance points to the way in which the subject of the theater produces instabilities, one might even say a certain "excitation," in a text by an author who, if she cannot resolve her indecision, would at least subordinate it to a commanding rhetoric of moral integrity.

Kemble's *Records of a Girlhood* (1878), the memoir in which the passage above appears, is a remarkable and neglected work of Victorian autobiography, and its author a significant figure not only for nineteenth-century theatrical and social history, but for literary history as well. Kemble can serve to bring into focus some complexities in *Villette*.[6] For if Brontë's anxieties about the theatricality of authorship match Kemble's distaste for public exposure, the author who would not become an "actress" and the actress who in fact became an author also resemble each other in their guilty fascination with the object of their fear and loathing. In *Villette*, as in Kemble's *Records*, the theater and its metaphorical extension, theatricality, prove capable of arousing profoundly and intricately mixed feelings because of their own ideologically heterogeneous character, their availability to both authoritarian and subversive discourses. Of course, we have already studied this overdetermination not only in *Jane Eyre*, but also in *Mansfield Park* and the nonnovelistic texts clustered around it. What the passage from Kemble illustrates (and what *Villette* amplifies) is an effect of this overdetermination to which we have not yet devoted much attention: when conservative cultural forces require the containment or inscription of theatricality (within structures such as the self, the family, the autobiographical narrative, the novel), the possibility arises that this normalizing move will generate its own inversion, and that the process of inscription will itself come to seem theatrical.

Like her namesake, Fanny Price, Kemble seems to hypothesize a

---

6. In *Literary Women* (Garden City, N.Y.: Doubleday, 1976), p. 188, Ellen Moers suggests the juxtaposition of Kemble's *Records* with *Villette*, both of which she sees as belated responses to that sensational early-nineteenth-century figuration of the writer/actress, Madame de Staël's *Corinne*. For a richly informative account of the shifting cultural perception (and social status) of the actress in the course of the Victorian period, see Christopher Kent, "Image and Reality: The Actress and Society," in *A Widening Sphere: Changing Roles of Victorian Women*, ed. Martha Vicinus (Bloomington: Indiana University Press, 1977), pp. 94–116.

series of gradations that would guard her against the de-gradations of acting: if, while acting is "unhealthy," "reading" is "less painful and distasteful," then *writing about acting* must place one at an even more safely privatized remove. Yet the rhetorical slippage in Kemble's account exemplifies the way in which the supposedly sanitizing process of recording or writing down one's theatrical experiences may fail to *keep* them down; in the oscillations of her prose, the act of "righting" theatricality becomes shiftily and dizzyingly theatrical in its own right. Appearing to distance her theatrical career from her narrative of it, Kemble at the same time *continues* that career at and on another stage, by displacing her earlier performance into what thus becomes a scene of writing.

Although Brontë and Kemble both write theatrically about (or, more exactly, against) the theater, it is important not to erase the differences between them, the most obvious of which is that Kemble had prolonged first-hand experience of her subject. But it is just as important not to hypostatize that experience as literal and primary, in contradistinction to Brontë's, which thus becomes figurative and derived. What might seem most exceptional in Kemble's case—the understanding, by virtue of belonging to one of England's greatest theatrical families, of the theater as at once deviant and normative—in fact manifests itself throughout *Villette* as the irreversible entanglement of a disciplinary theatricality with a transgressive or potentially feminist theatricality. While the resulting undecidability has prompted certain critics to regard *Villette* as uncannily modern or radical, the comparison of Brontë with Kemble suggests a particularly Victorian inflection of this modernity, a mutually unsettling relationship between the terms "Victorian" and "modern."[7]

If Kemble's inability to reach a decision about the theater offers a determinate context for *Villette*'s indeterminacy, the ironies uncovered in our brief reading of Kemble hint that there might be considerable room for contestatory maneuvering within this apparently limiting framework—maneuvering all the more effective, perhaps, for taking place in the "sheltering shadow" of the dominant,

7. Readings that stress the modern or even postmodern aspects of *Villette* include Nina Auerbach, "Charlotte Brontë: The Two Countries," chapter 12 in Auerbach, *Romantic Imprisonment: Women and Other Glorified Outcasts* (New York: Columbia University Press, 1985), pp. 195–211, and Christina Crosby, "Charlotte Brontë's Haunted Text," *Studies in English Literature* 24 (1984): 701–15.

patriarchal ideology, and thus for passing as "unconscious." Remaining undecided *about* the theater may in fact be a socially acceptable way of participating in the undecidability *of* the theater, of moving inventively within the contradictions of a certain Victorian construction of theatricality itself. If, in its wobbliness and self-division, that construction oddly resembles the more recent notion of écriture, writing about the theater—whether as a former actress or as an "ostrich"-like novelist—may necessarily mean occupying not a stably extratheatrical vantage point but rather what Freud, speaking precisely of "the unconscious," called "another scene."[8]

Despite its author's "ostrich longing for concealment," *Villette*, unlike *Jane Eyre*, makes no secret of its obsession with the theater and theatricality. This obsession becomes most obvious in the numerous episodes of acting and theatergoing that punctuate the narrative and that constitute so many flamboyant, though not exactly extraneous, "set-pieces."[9] Yet Brontë's insistent concern with theatrical issues is also evident in the way that theatrical imagery and vocabulary virtually permeate the text, providing it with its self-consciously meta-Gothic machinery, encoding the action as a series of "scenes" and "spectacles," defining the characters in terms of their "roles," even populating the narrator-heroine's claustral and jealously guarded consciousness with a stock company composed of such allegorical players as Impulse, Temptation, Reason, Imagination, Hope, and Desire. And since the novel interprets theatricality not just as a form of extravagance but also as a system of artifice and deception, the narrative itself may properly be called theatrical insofar as Lucy Snowe deploys a whole repertoire of evasive and duplicitous tactics in telling—and not telling—her story. A thorough study of the theater and its diffusion throughout *Villette* would require far more space than this chapter will allow. For now, we must content ourselves

8. For a rigorous discussion of "the relation of psychoanalysis to theatricality," see Philippe Lacoue-Labarthe, "Theatrum Analyticum," *Glyph* 2 (1977): 122–43.

9. The theatricality of the episodes themselves is suggested by Robert Bernard Martin, who refers to them as "a series of big scenes, almost set-pieces" (*The Accents of Persuasion: Charlotte Brontë's Novels* [New York: Norton, 1966], p. 155).

with examining some of the more telling excitations that the theatrical problem induces in the text.[10]

This problem manifests itself most tellingly in the way in which the novel's thematics of acting and spectatorship overlap and merge continually with its thematics of teaching and governance. Like Jane Eyre, and like Brontë herself in her earlier life, Lucy Snowe devotes her quotidian energies to the business of pedagogy: in the course of the novel, she moves from governess to schoolteacher to proprietor and director of her own school. Yet, while the narrative keeps positing an opposition between the disciplinary activity of the governess/teacher on the one hand and the flamboyant career of the actress on the other hand, it also keeps undermining this opposition, so that Lucy is at once the self-effacing antithesis and the unlikely double of a character such as the "demoniac" (p. 339) Vashti or the narcissistic Ginevra Fanshawe, whose chief skills are "music, singing, and dancing" (p. 151).

That Vashti and Ginevra inhabit the same culpably public sphere points to another one of the major differences between *Villette* and *Jane Eyre*. For if much of the official ideological labor of the latter consists in the segregation of the "demoniac" from the (merely) frivolous, the former displays a curious nonchalance not only about the mixing of those two registers but also about Lucy's frequent excursions into the composite space thus constituted. As we will see when we touch on the "Gothic" subplot revolving around the figure of "the nun," the generic and social barriers that were imposed in *Jane Eyre* seem considerably more permeable and provisional in the later novel. The fact that the teacher here appears less closely tied to her intermediate post may have something to do with the novel's foreign setting: *Villette* would seem to present us with an instance of ideology on holiday, as it were, no longer so concerned with the policing of domestic relations, where "domestic" applies to both the household and the nation. This relative relaxation of disciplinary constraints may also have something to do with the different career moves of the two pedagogical heroines: while Jane Eyre does spend

10. In his introduction to the Penguin edition of *Villette*, ed. Mark Lilly (Harmondsworth: Penguin, 1979), p. 13, Tony Tanner claims that "oscillation" is "a keyword in considering the novel." I will be referring to this edition throughout the chapter. Subsequent references will appear parenthetically in the text.

time as a schoolteacher, what defines her more centrally is her activity as a governess; conversely, while Lucy starts out as a governess, she quickly assumes the more public, and more frankly histrionic, role of the schoolteacher.

In other words, if the novel's primary spatial foci are the schoolroom and the theater, it conflates these two venues as much as it
separates them, so that each in its own way becomes a scene of
instruction. On the one hand, Madame Beck's *pensionnat* seems to
require, for its proper administration, a certain calculated deployment of theatrical effects; the most sustained example of this theatricalization of power is the episode of the school play in chapter 14;
the most recurrent, the tendency of the narrative to frame the teacher's *estrade* as a stage. On the other hand, Lucy's visits to the theater
tend to have a didactic, rather heavily allegorical character; in the
epistemologically anxious world of the novel, the theater becomes
a meaning-fraught arena where one goes to Learn Lessons. And if
we expect a dialectical resolution to emerge from the novel's third
overcharged space, the hated yet surreptitiously admired Catholic
Church, we can only be disappointed, for this indulgently tyrannical
institution merely replicates the tension at work in each of the other
spheres, disseminating its supposedly corrupt teaching as the "subtle
essence of Romanism" that "pervades" (p. 195) Madame Beck's
school, and exhibiting the incursion of theatricality in the "painted
and meretricious face" (p. 516) of its decadent pageantry.

Yet it would be a mistake to see these more or less open displacements as signs of deconstructive "subversion": when ideology
goes on holiday, it unwinds only to expand its reach. When, as so
often happens in *Villette*, ostensible opposites end up imitating each
other, and potential alternative spaces turn out to have been mirages,
the most noticeable effect is not usually one of heady destabilization
but of stasis or even imprisonment. Many critics have commented
upon the oppressive atmosphere of *Villette*: despite, or perhaps because of, the heroine's upward mobility, the same paternalistic structure seems to contain and neutralize every incipient attempt at resistance or bid for autonomy, and repetition seems to preempt any
move toward genuine difference.[11] For this reason, the novel's motif

---

11. In her perceptive reading of *Villette* in *Women, Power, and Subversion: Social
Strategies in British Fiction, 1778–1860* (Athens: University of Georgia Press, 1981), pp.

of female androgyny or transvestism—as when Lucy dresses partly as a man for the school play, or when we are told that Madame Beck "did not wear a woman's aspect, but rather a man's" (p. 141)— appears not so much daringly iconoclastic as grimly expressive of the ambitious woman's confinement to male impersonation.[12] At these moments, theatricality itself wears an aspect that alternates painfully between the liberation of role-playing and the conventionality that circumscribes and ironizes any such improvisatory freedom.

A number of critics have also observed that, although Lucy rightly views the mannish Madame Beck as her adversary, she in some sense resembles and even surpasses this simulacrum of both "first minister" and "superintendent of police" (p. 137), mastering the art— amply if inadvertently demonstrated by her unobliging mentor—of transforming theatrical spectatorship into a technology of surveillance.[13] " 'Surveillance,' 'espionage,' these were her watch-words" (p. 135), Lucy says of the way Madame Beck manages her *pensionnat*; but these are the watch-words (the pun is all too appropriate) of Lucy's narrative as well. By the end of the novel, when Lucy sets up her own school—thanks, of course, to Monsieur Paul—she has already proven herself a formidable rival of Madame Beck, in whose establishment she has studied and internalized a complex "system for managing and regulating" (p. 135) others, a system that Lucy even uses to manage and regulate her relationship with the reader.

For Lucy's famous "perversity," however protomodernist a nar-

---

86–124, Judith Lowder Newton tends to locate the novel's subversiveness in its theme of "the working life and of self-enhancing power," as opposed to the constricting values of female "love and self-sacrifice" (p. 103). Though the working life can suggest an escape from the Victorian ideology of love and marriage, the power such work affords is by no means obviously self-enhancing. For this reason, I prefer to look for subversiveness less in the novel's thematic opposition of work to love and marriage than in the cunning and indirection of its narrative strategies. For a particularly acerbic reading of Lucy Snowe's social and economic ascent, see Terry Eagleton, *Myths of Power: A Marxist Study of the Brontës* (New York: Barnes and Noble, 1975), pp. 61–73.

12. For a discussion of the paradoxical advantages of female cross-dressing in *Villette*, see Sandra M. Gilbert and Susan Gubar, *The Madwoman in the Attic: The Woman Writer and the Nineteenth-Century Literary Imagination* (New Haven: Yale University Press, 1979), p. 413.

13. On the similarity between Lucy and Madame Beck, see, for example, Margot Peters, *Charlotte Brontë: Style in the Novel* (Madison: University of Wisconsin Press, 1973), p. 91, and Mary Jacobus, "The Buried Letter: Feminism and Romanticism in *Villette*," in *Women Writing and Writing about Women*, ed. Jacobus (New York: Barnes and Noble, 1979), p. 45.

rative it may appear to generate, derives its logic from the material exigencies of a more or less abject power struggle distinctively enacted between women, who can overcome their disenfranchisement and claim some of the prerogatives of male authority only by battling each other in a game of silence and indirection. Lucy's narrative stance is modeled on the "pantomime" (p. 131), performed on her first night at the school, in which she colludes and competes with her employer: while Madame Beck inspects Lucy and her belongings, Lucy, "feign[ing] sleep" (p. 131), spies on her. As Tony Tanner points out, "the spier spied on is not an uncommon situation in this world" (p. 19).

Yet it is not just the characters who feel the unpleasant effects of the manipulative and antagonistic voyeurism that dominates *Villette:* to the extent that reading here is not so much a "masquerade" (to use Helena Michie's term) as itself a kind of spying—an equation that the novel does not fail to underline—we repeatedly find ourselves inserted in the discomforting, even humiliating, position of Madame Beck, by the kind of rhetorical one-upmanship in which Lucy excels.[14] And though this experience is bound to be different for male and female readers, the difference may be more elusive than we would think, since to be cast as the outwitted Madame Beck is to be characterized as at once "too masculine" and "not masculine enough," as a monstrous conjunction of the illegitimately "male" and the inescapably "female."[15]

The most notorious instance of the way the reader is made to perform as the narrator's dupe occurs at the beginning of volume 2, where Lucy reveals that the alluring "Dr. John" is the same person as Graham Bretton. By the time she finishes explaining why she has left us in the dark, along with Graham, Lucy has instilled in *us* the very suspicion and anxiety from which we may have thought we could enjoy a safe readerly detachment. Lucy recognized Graham long before this revelation, but

14. The association of reading with spying is established, for example, by such intrusive acts as Madame Beck's examination of Lucy's letters from Dr. John, and M. Paul's regular inspections of the contents of Lucy's desk.

15. The gender of the reader posited by Lucy's asides is usually left unspecified, but in the course of one of these not particularly friendly addresses (p. 422), she lifts the veil to identify her reader as male. Full treatment of the interesting and complicated question of how the narrator constructs and negotiates her relationship with her audience lies beyond the scope of this chapter.

to *say* anything on the subject, to *hint* at my discovery, had not suited my habits of thought, or assimilated with my system of feeling. On the contrary, I had preferred to keep the matter to myself. I liked entering his presence covered with a cloud he had not seen through, while he stood before me under a ray of special illumination, which shone all partial over his head, trembled about his feet, and cast light no farther.

(p. 248)

Like Madame Beck's system of management and regulation on which it is based—and which it seeks rivalrously to "assimilate"—Lucy's "system of feeling" sustains a veiled yet watchful subjectivity, one that functions primarily by gathering information about (and withholding it from) other selves, "cast[ing] light no farther" than a "tremblingly" furtive scopophilia will allow. Lucy repeatedly invokes the sheltering shadow of an incognito, not for herself, but to hide from the reader the identities of other characters.[16] These acts of renaming, however, keep her "covered with a cloud" of mystery as well—"Who *are* you, Miss Snowe?" (p. 392), we wonder with Ginevra Fanshawe—and this opacity is as aggressively (and pruriently) strategic as it is defensively sheltering.

In this light, as we have already rather suspected, Charlotte Brontë's own wish for a sheltering shadow betokens not an antitheatrical posture, but indeed an intensely theatrical penchant for disguise and dissimulation.[17] If she refuses to make a spectacle of herself, Brontë merely ends up exchanging theatrical self-display for theatrical self-concealment. Dreaming of what in effect would be a *second* incognito—for the putatively androgynous pseudonym, "Currer Bell," had of course served initially as a mask in its own right—

16. The name "Lucy Snowe," which Brontë at one point changed to "Lucy Frost," is itself highly overdetermined, and thus a kind of shadow in its own right, as suggested by the author's defense of it with reference to "the '*lucus a non lucendo*' principle"; see Shorter, ed., *The Brontës: Life and Letters* 2:286. The name functions in a complex signifying chain, which includes ideas of coldness, blankness, light, dark, abstraction, contradiction, repetition, and so forth.

17. Brontë is of course no more identical with Lucy Snowe than she is with Jane Eyre. Throughout this chapter, however, I assume a certain *allegorical* link between Brontë and Lucy (just as I posited certain telling continuities between Brontë and Jane). Critics have often pointed out the author's differences from, and even dislike of, Lucy, and much more needs to be said about the by-no-means-unproblematic relations between author and protagonist. Yet the tendency to enumerate dissimilarities may bespeak a will to dissociation that itself needs to be analyzed. For now, at any rate, I would contend that the novel remains more instructive as a (highly oblique) portrait of the artist than as a case history.

Brontë imagines an "anonymity" that, while keeping her out of the public eye, would enable her to eye the public with redoubled efficacy. Without going so far as to portray Brontë as the agent of some kind of Victorian Big Brother, we should emphasize here her predilection for the trappings of patriarchal power—the power to objectify and scrutinize others while exempting oneself from similar treatment.

Becoming trapped inside a borrowed costume is indeed one of the risks that Sandra M. Gilbert and Susan Gubar suggest when they argue that, in Brontë's novels, "escape becomes increasingly difficult as women internalize the destructive strictures of patriarchy."[18] Impersonating Madame Beck's impersonation of a first minister-cum-superintendent of police, Lucy also mimes her author's response to Robert Southey's advice that, since "literature cannot be the business of a woman's life," she content herself with "writ[ing] poetry for its own sake; not in a spirit of emulation, and not with a view to celebrity."[19] Her obedient promises to Southey and herself notwithstanding, Brontë, as we know, does not ultimately follow this advice. Yet, though she does not restrict her literary activity to the writing of poems, and though she does publish, Brontë's intractability is as problematic as Kemble's acquiescence. For she figures her "business" as an author in terms that imply a certain compromise, whereby she engages in the forbidden act of "emulation" but emulates what looks like the permissible "business of a woman's life."

As we have seen, that is, Brontë models her novel-writing persona not on the attention-craving actress, but on the correctly self-denying pedagogue, a role she knows well. For Brontë and for Southey, as for certain contemporary schools of literary criticism, writing suggests a kind of naughty "celebrity" that verges on notoriety, and that can be avoided only if writing emulates not the (bad) emulation typical of acting but the (good) emulation proper to learning and teaching. What is inscribed or contained here is thus a particular characterization of writing itself. Barred from the pursuit of literary

---

18. Gilbert and Gubar, *Madwoman in the Attic*, p. 400.

19. Shorter, ed., *The Brontës: Life and Letters*, 1:128. For a perceptive discussion of Brontë's art in light of the conflicts expressed in her correspondence with Southey, see Carol T. Christ, "Imaginative Constraint, Feminine Duty, and the Form of Charlotte Brontë's Fiction," *Women's Studies* 6 (1979): 287–96.

fame, the novelist-as-teacher settles for the humbler privilege of disciplinary license, renouncing theatricality as a mode of self-exposure to recover it, in far less glamorous form, as an obliquely and tenuously empowering paradigm for supervision. Assuming the gray uniform of the schoolmistress is as close as she will get to putting on the patriarchal trousers. If the female novelist achieves moral respectability by investing herself in an educating heroine rather than a performing one, she also takes political shelter—but ambiguous shelter, since what protects her at the same time contains her— under an ideological system that inscribes and appropriates theatricality as a metaphor for governance.[20]

But the distance between a governess and a governor, or between a mistress and a master, is as great as that between Madame Beck, or Lucy, and a real minister or police superintendent.[21] Lucy makes this distance explicit when she writes: "That school offered for [Madame Beck's] powers too limited a sphere; she ought to have swayed a nation: she should have been the leader of a turbulent legislative assembly" (p. 137). Yet if an energizing turbulence is denied these two ambitious women in the larger political sphere, it shows up not only in the theatricalized schoolroom, but in the textual politics of this bildungsroman itself. When Lucy describes how Madame Beck forced her to take over as the school's English teacher, she admits, "I shall never forget that first lesson, nor all the under-current of life and feeling it opened up to me" (p. 142). But when Lucy mounts the *estrade*, she gains access not so much to "life and feeling" in their unmediated form as to energies of *enactment* that the inscription of theatricality has had to keep under or keep down. The "undercurrents" "opened up to" her remind us that the scene of instruction is still a *scene*, and that the act of writing about teaching is still an *act*.

Admittedly, the intrinsic fluidity of the pedagogical theater is not always cause for celebration: *Villette* frames the scene of instruction as a hazardously volatile space, in which the autocratically "histrionic lessons" (p. 197) of a teacher like Paul Emanuel risk degen-

---

20. My terms here derive from Ellen Moers, who offers chapters on "Performing Heroinism" and "Educating Heroinism" (*Literary Women*, pp. 173–210 and 211–42).

21. I owe this formulation to a long and dazzling footnote in an essay by Gayatri Chakravorty Spivak, "Finding Feminist Readings: Dante–Yeats," *Social Text* 3 (Fall 1980): 74, n. 2.

erating into "the ravings of a third-rate London actor" (p. 455). Moreover, the teacher's vulnerability is matched by his or her own power
to inflict violence. Though the staginess of teaching may at times
diminish its disciplinary impact, it serves more often to secure it.
Indeed, what makes Lucy's "first lesson" so memorable is the almost
terroristic efficacy of the *coups de théâtre* with which she silences
the "mutinous mass" (p. 143) of her pupils. And while this inaugural
scene of instruction is also, as it happens, a scene of writing, the
writing in question takes place under the oppressive heading of
"dictation" (p. 144): what surfaces here is not—or at least, not yet—
the decentering force of écriture; rather, we seem to be back in the
Lowood schoolroom of *Jane Eyre*, where writing is a form of manual
labor, not an act of disruption.

If the scene nonetheless has the capacity to intimate a reversal
of the inscription of theatricality into the theatricality of inscription,
this is because the repetition implicit in the process of dictation
figures the more ambiguous repetition that the narrative itself performs. For though, as I have argued, the repetitiveness produced by
the novel's collapsing of oppositions is more claustrophobic than
liberating, the novel also uses repetition in a less constraining way,
as an integral component of its distinctive narrative structure. I have
referred to its "obsessive" concern with theatricality, but I want now
to qualify this quasi-psychoanalytic term. As Karen Lawrence has
shown, while *Villette* apparently lends itself to discussion in terms
of the Freudian narrative theory elaborated by Peter Brooks and
D. A. Miller, that model, especially as represented by Brooks, may
be limited by its androcentrism.[22] I would merely point out one
aspect of Brooks's theory that Lawrence does not discuss, but that

22. Karen Lawrence, "The Cypher: Disclosure and Reticence in *Villette*," *Nineteenth-Century Literature* 42 (March 1988): 448–66. Lawrence's fine essay also shares
the concern of the present chapter with the interplay between theatrical and scriptive
metaphors in Brontë's novel. The works to which she refers are Peter Brooks, *Reading
for the Plot: Design and Intention in Narrative* (New York: Random House, 1985), and
D. A. Miller, *Narrative and Its Discontents: Problems of Closure in the Traditional Novel*
(Princeton: Princeton University Press, 1981). For another feminist alternative to
Brooks, Lawrence recommends Nancy K. Miller, "Emphasis Added: Plots and Plau-
sibilities in Women's Fiction," in *The New Feminist Criticism: Essays on Women, Literature and Theory*, ed. Elaine Showalter (New York: Pantheon, 1985), pp. 339–60. For
a discussion of Brooks and other male-centered narrative theorists, see also Joseph
Allen Boone, *Tradition Counter Tradition: Love and the Form of Fiction* (Chicago: University of Chicago Press, 1987), pp. 71–73.

supports her thesis. It is significant that Brooks draws on the Freudian topos of the child's game of *fort/da*, which I invoked in the previous chapter to describe Brontë's rather impertinent way of "playing with" the very disciplinary machinery of which her work seems to be an instance. Yet Brooks, following Freud, tends to see the reversals and repetitions in the game of *fort/da* as essentially conservative functions under the aegis of the death-drive: the mastery that the child achieves in "staging" over and over the disappearance (*fort*) and return (*da*) of a toy—interestingly, Freud himself uses the theatrical term (*inszenieren*)—seems akin to the quiescence achieved through death.[23]

To be sure, it would not be terribly difficult to subordinate *Villette*'s narrative structure, which obsessively stages and restages the disappearance and return of the theater, to this reading of "Freud's Masterplot," as Brooks calls it. In an article on the image of Rachel Félix in *Villette* and other Victorian novels, John Stokes has identified repetition as a salient feature of dramatic criticism in the period, even or especially in the writing of so distinguished a critic as George Henry Lewes, Brontë's would-be mentor (and, as we will see, an important interpreter of theatricality to George Eliot).[24] While Stokes thus argues for "the superiority of novels [to criticism] when it comes to rendering the evanescence of theatrical experience," in its general outlines, at any rate, *Villette* may recall all too well the "homogenizing tendency"[25] that Stokes finds in the discourse of dramatic criticism. But though Brontë participates in that discourse more compromisingly than Stokes would allow, her stance within it at the same time suggests a saving difference. For if Jane Eyre's occasional appearance of "out-governessing the governess" can create a little too much excitement in both the text and many of its readers, Lucy Snowe's emulative project of out-teaching the teacher involves, as I will show in the next section, a more importunate pattern of doings and undoings, a more persistently unsettling play of *fort* and *da* than Jane's less perverse narrative will accommodate. Much as they

23. For the development of this argument, see in particular "Freud's Masterplot: A Model for Narrative," in Brooks, *Reading for the Plot*, pp. 90–112. The relevant text by Freud is *Beyond the Pleasure Principle*.

24. John Stokes, "Rachel's 'Terrible Beauty': An Actress Among the Novelists," *ELH* 51 (Winter 1984): 771–93.

25. Ibid.: 790.

would effect a binding (a term Brooks favors) of potentially provocative "under-currents," the obsessive comings and goings of the
theatrical motif in *Villette,* both in and out of school, may also imply
a peculiarly *feminist* strategy of repetition that "opens up" the master's discourse, and the master's plot, from within. Interestingly, in
French, the language that Brontë disseminates so lavishly throughout this francophobic text, *répétition* means, among other things,
"rehearsal." As "drama critics" in their own right, both Brontë and
Kemble (who herself cunningly repeats theatricality in another
place) anticipate the French feminism of Luce Irigaray, the theorist
of "mimicry," against a certain Freudianism, as repetition with a
difference:

> To play with mimesis is . . . , for a woman, to try to recover the
> place of her exploitation by discourse, without allowing herself to be
> simply reduced to it. It means to resubmit herself—inasmuch as she
> is on the side of the "perceptible," of "matter"—to "ideas," in par-
> ticular to ideas about herself, that are elaborated in/by a masculine
> logic, but so as to make "visible," by an effect of playful repetition,
> what was supposed to remain invisible: the cover-up of a possible
> operation of the feminine in language. It also means to "unveil" the
> fact that, if women are such good mimics, it is because they are not
> simply resorbed in this function. *They also remain elsewhere:* another
> case of the persistence of "matter," but also of "sexual pleasure."[26]

The episode of the school play is the novel's first major staging of
its theatrical concerns. The centerpiece of Madame Beck's *fête,* the
vaudeville, like the ball that follows and elaborates upon it, could
be read as a virtual object lesson in Foucauldian paradox. In its
apparent raciness, the play dramatizes the libidinal intrigues taking
place in the *pensionnat,* all the better to control them. Likewise, the
ball, which entails the seemingly scandalous introduction of young
men into the girls' school, actually enhances the authority of the
school's Machiavellian "directress" (p. 213). As Lucy observes, "the
admission of these rattlesnakes, so fascinating and so dangerous,
served to draw out madame precisely in her strongest character—
that of a first-rate *surveillante*" (p. 213). Just here, however, we begin

26. Luce Irigaray, *This Sex Which Is Not One,* trans. Catherine Porter with Carolyn
Burke (Ithaca: Cornell University Press, 1985), p. 76.

to notice a certain danger within the paradox itself. For if Madame Beck's strength as a *surveillante* needs to be "drawn out," then she cannot help crossing the all-important line between spectator and "character," thereby opening herself up to a surveillance of which she should be the sole practitioner. Though perhaps intermittently necessary, these displays of power can imperil the very authority they seek to reinforce, whether that authority is represented by a schoolmistress (or -master), a teacher in that school, or—as we will see—a king.

At this point, in any case, it is worth noting that the *vaudeville* itself effaces the division between audience and spectacle, compromising the neat hierarchy whereby those who *see* exercise epistemological and political mastery over those who *are seen*. And it is none other than Lucy, by her own definition the spectator par excellence, who sets this process in motion when she bows to pressure from M. Paul and agrees to replace one of his actresses in the role of a fop. Having mentioned the more sobering implications of Lucy's partial cross-dressing, of her confinement to male impersonation, we must now acknowledge that her half-male, half-female attire does in fact engender a disturbing little drama—a drama that disturbs both hierarchies of gender *and* hierarchies of power. It does so, however, not by functioning as a static representation, but by instigating a dynamic circulation of erotic subtexts between "actors" and "audience." For when Lucy steps onto the stage as the fictional surrogate of the Count de Hamal, wooing Ginevra away from the fictional surrogate of Dr. John, she in effect *rewrites* the script so as to release from its formulaic lineaments a veritable orgy of overdetermined triangularity. Suddenly discovering that Ginevra is "acting *at*" (p. 210) the real Dr. John, Lucy aims her own performance, at once seductively and vindictively, at the same target, turning the beholder into a spectacle in his own right:

> The spectacle seemed somehow suggestive. There was language in Dr John's look, though I cannot tell what he said; it animated me: I drew out of it a history; I put my idea into the part I performed; I threw it into my wooing of Ginevra. In the 'Ours,' or sincere lover, I saw Dr John. Did I pity him, as erst? No, I hardened my heart, rivalled and out-rivalled him. I knew myself but a fop, but where *he* was outcast *I* could please. Now I know I acted as if wishful and resolute to win and conquer. Ginevra seconded me; between us we half-changed the nature of the *rôle*, gilding it from top to toe. Between

the acts M. Paul told us he knew not what possessed us, and half expostulated, 'C'est, peutêtre plus beau que votre modèle,' said he, 'mais ce n'est pas juste.' I know not what possessed me either; but somehow, my longing was to eclipse the 'Ours:' *i.e.*, Dr John. Ginevra was tender; how could I be otherwise than chivalric? Retaining the letter, I recklessly altered the spirit of the *rôle*. Without heart, without interest, I could not play it at all. It must be played—in went the yearned-for seasoning—thus flavoured, I played it with relish.

(p. 210)

Lucy's own improvisatory "drawing out" of a history refuses merely to copy the *modèle* prescribed by M. Paul; though still a repetition—after all, Lucy "retain[s] the letter" if not the "spirit"— her performance is a repetition that displaces the original. Surprised by her own histrionic and revisionary prowess, Lucy mimes the unfolding of the novelist-as-pedagogue into the novelist-as-actress-as-(re)writer. "Cold, reluctant, apprehensive, I had accepted a part to please another: ere long," she recognizes, "warming, becoming interested, taking courage, I acted to please myself" (p. 211). Simultaneously autoerotic, homoerotic, and heteroerotic, Lucy's bold reinterpretation pluralizes the "sexual pleasure" Irigaray associates with female mimicry. Critics have labored indeed to untangle the relational possibilities of Brontë's polymorphous scenario, in which a woman dressed from the waist up as a man plays the effeminate suitor of a coquette who plays herself; in which this female quasi-male-impersonator acts for one man (M. Paul), and both for and against another (Dr. John); in which the inextricably interwoven strands of rivalry and desire running through the "real-life" drama are further knotted by its "recklessly" innovative reworking on stage.[27]

Lucy's supposedly uncharacteristic role-playing does more than just bestow upon her a "character" whose stereotypically masculine "strength" temporarily installs her in Madame Beck's *souliers de silence:* what is at stake here is not merely the reversal or reapportionment of traditional gender roles. Similarly, the doubling of actors as viewers of their audience, and thus of this audience as a spectacle in itself, does not just shore up the specular symmetry implicit in any theatrical confrontation. In each case, the terms of a classic

27. For a lucid enumeration of the various erotic relations implied by this scenario, see Eagleton, *Myths of Power*, p. 70.

antithesis (male versus female, actor versus spectator) are turned back upon themselves to yield a peculiar structural confusion. Breaking down sexual and aesthetic polarities, Lucy "breaks character" so as to divide and multiply characters—both her own and others'— and to produce an unmanageable proliferation of plots, whose point is its very excessiveness, its refusal to be straightened out into a single coherent narrative line. Staging a miniature yet appropriately unruly carnival at the center of Madame Beck's authoritarian, self-promoting *fête*, Lucy—like Brontë—"draws out" the precariousness inherent in a regime that uses a disciplinary theatricality to neutralize a transgressive theatricality. For this antithesis, it turns out, is no more absolute than the others: in each version of theatricality, its opposite remains uneasily latent.

Given the contestatory energies implied by this scene, it comes as no great surprise that Lucy should resolve immediately to renounce them:

> A keen relish for dramatic expression had revealed itself as part of my nature; to cherish and exercise this new-found faculty might gift me with a world of delight, but it would not do for a mere looker-on at life: the strength and longing must be put by; and I put them by, and fastened them with the lock of a resolution which neither Time nor Temptation has since picked.
>
> (p. 211)

Where Fanny Kemble can admit to her "intense delight" in acting only by sublimating it as "reading" and by subsuming it beneath the authorizing aura of "Shakespeare," Lucy is compelled to "put by" her dramatic propensities altogether: the disruptive forces would seem to have been recontained without any trouble, and the ghost of Robert Southey to have triumphed after all. But Lucy's claim to have stifled her theatrical instincts is not entirely accurate. Although she evades M. Paul's invitation to dance at the ball, barely saving herself from this "second performance" (p. 221), later the same evening Lucy finds herself once again "venturing out of what [she] look[s] on as [her] natural habits" (p. 222), when she presumes to discuss Ginevra with Dr. John.[28] And like so many *final* "farewell

---

28. The word "habits" connects Lucy's "natural" reticence with the image of the nun, which is central to the novel. That the nun's habit turns out to be a kind of theatrical costume points to the radically theatrical "nature" of Lucy's anti- or untheatricality.

performances," this infraction inaugurates a whole series of such lapses—not so much into histrionics "pure and simple" as into the more insidious hybridization of *scenes* of writing/instruction—lapses which create precisely the undecidability that prevents us from knowing whether Lucy "really" wants to give up the bad and "unnatural" habit of acting but keeps getting overcome by "Temptation," or whether "Temptation" is merely another one of Lucy's roles, which she performs with "keen relish," even while impersonating a "mere looker-on at life," an innocent bystander.

On the one hand, the major theatrical episodes in the novel—the *vaudeville*, the visit to the art gallery to see "The Cleopatra," the concert, the performance by Vashti, the climactic *fête* in the park— all share what might be viewed as a certain self-canceling tendency: assembling major characters, precipitating recognitions and resolutions, they seem designed to pull the various loose thematic ends of the narrative together so as to have done with theatrical excess once and for all. On the other hand, to the extent that these totalizing gestures themselves partake of a certain theatricality—by no means a monolithically conservative one—they seem either disingenuous or misguided. Purifying theatricality of its anarchic traces, for example, means rehabilitating the opposition between a powerful (and invisible) spectator and a strangely passive actor or object of surveillance, an opposition that the *vaudeville* has dramatically discredited. To be sure, when Lucy accompanies Dr. John and his mother to the concert attended by the king and queen of Labassecour, she conscientiously expresses the obligatory fear of self-exhibition—recoiling from her unfamiliarly colorful mirror image, staying "in the shade and out of sight" (p. 292)—and indeed makes a point of ridiculing most of the performers and congratulating herself on being the only observant member of an audience composed of dim-witted Labassecouriens. But if Lucy reduces the entire scene— including the other spectators as well as the performers—to the status of an anthropologically interesting tableau, her most ambitious act of observation—her reading of the family drama, the "mournful and significant . . . spectacle" (p. 291), taking place between the king and the queen—is also her most ambiguous.

For though this reading typifies the analytic program of a supervisory authority bent on demystifying everything but itself, it also entails a sympathetic identification of reader with "text."[29] In the "strong hieroglyphics" of melancholia she sees "graven as with iron stylet" (p. 290) on the king's face, Lucy perceives not only the markings of a power that subjugates him, but also a reflection of her own susceptibility to "that strangest spectre, Hypochondria" (p. 290). Yet the destabilizing force of this reading goes beyond the sentimentality of shared suffering. For Lucy proceeds to suggest:

> Perhaps he saw her [Hypochondria] now on that stage, over against him, amidst all that brilliant throng. Hypochondria has that wont, to rise in the midst of thousands—dark as Doom, pale as Malady, and well nigh strong as Death. Her comrade and victim thinks to be happy one moment—"Not so," says she; "I come." And she freezes the blood in his heart, and beclouds the light in his eye.
>
> (p. 290)

As in the revisionary *vaudeville* presented six chapters earlier, Lucy turns the either/or logic of dichotomy—in this case, the dichotomy between master and slave, ruler and subject—into the trickier acrobatics of both/and, where the individual performers are internally contradictory as well as expansively volatile. It is not just that, in projecting herself onto the king, and implicitly assuming his text-like receptivity, Lucy at once diminishes his power and augments her own; by animating the Hypochondria that haunts them both, she compounds the complexity, and upsets the symmetry, of the power-play. For if Lucy's demystification of the king is both sympathetic and aggressive, it aligns her on the one hand with the real queen, his "kind, loving, elegant" (p. 290) wife, and on the other hand with the ghostly queen or cruel goddess who renders him "her comrade"—note the equivocation—"and victim." Moreover, since Hypochondria is anthropomorphized first as a figure who writes her power on the king's face and then as a figure who performs on a stage, she can reenact the embodiment of the novelist-as-actress, a representation supposedly prohibited after the school play, when Lucy vowed never to act again. Here, of course, she does not take the stage literally. But she does so fantasmatically, through her treble identification with the vulnerably conspicuous king, that "good an-

29. For an interesting reading of the episode of the concert as an anti-patriarchal debunking on Lucy's part, see Gilbert and Gubar, *Madwoman in the Attic,* p. 421.

gel" (p. 291) his wife, and above all the avenging artist (herself trebled by association with Doom, Malady, and Death) born of her own afflicted imagination; and these multiple projections, in their versatility, may be even more unsettling than Lucy's more overt role-playing. The theater here is more than just a scene of instruction or—what comes to the same thing—a scene of disciplinary inscription, in which Lucy presents herself as a page to be written upon by the social realities of Labassecour. Both text *and* author, both spectator *and* specter, both king and queen at once, Lucy inscribes a mind-boggling one-woman show.

However, as part of a pattern that quickly becomes familiar to readers of *Villette*, the managerial imperative wastes no time in announcing itself, reinvesting the theatrical metaphor with the values of vision and comprehension, so that, by the end of the concert, after Ginevra has sneered at him and his mother, Dr. John can "speak the plain truth" (p. 302) and proclaim the demise of his infatuation. But in the lottery that follows the concert, Dr. John wins a woman's head-dress, and Lucy a cigar-case; she refuses to exchange prizes with him, treasuring her metonym of masculinity "to this day" (p. 300). And while she says that "it serves . . . to remind [her] of old times" (p. 300), it seems more significant as a souvenir of that earlier episode in the narrative itself, when Lucy's explicitly theatrical cross-dressing initiated a chiastic narrative confusion not unlike this more recent one, which Dr. John's manly claims of insight and self-possession seek to overrule.

The subsequent trajectory of Dr. John's love story, wherein he replaces the coquettish (i.e., irresponsibly theatrical) Ginevra with the doll-like (i.e., compliantly theatrical) Paulina Home as the object of his affections, may be taken to epitomize the ideological campaign of the narrative as a whole.[30] But in its parts—especially those parts that seem to bear a totalizing function—*Villette* continues to resist this pressure toward domestication. The remaining theatrical episodes become increasingly hypertense and elaborate in their staging of Lucy—and her author—as at once writer and text, and if these figurations of simultaneous power and servitude are too ambiguous to inspire easy optimism, their very ambiguity begins to seem sig-

---

30. For an example of Paulina's non-threatening theatricality, see the *pas de fée* she performs in the presence of her father and her future husband (p. 364).

nificantly troublesome, a growing and irremediable irritant. Admittedly, the relation of these problematic moments to the overarching narrative is itself undecidable: in one reading (perhaps inspired by Brooks), such continual returns to the scene of the crime—the crime of theatrical excess—may signal a repetition-compulsion on the part of the text, a need to master a disquieting stimulus; in another reading (perhaps inspired by D. A. Miller's more recent, Foucauldian work),[31] the same recurrence could be seen as a device whereby the text confidently rehearses its technique of producing, and just as deftly withdrawing, whatever might appear to unnerve it; in yet a third reading (perhaps inspired by Irigaray), this pattern could point to the text's delight in reviving and reliving tensions it pretends to disown. But again, it is precisely because it is so difficult to determine the text's competence in, or attitude toward, this play of *fort/da* that these scenes of return, taken together, seem so provoking; Lucy Snowe turns Jane Eyre's bad acting into a bad habit—a virtual system, a Method, as it were—that her narrative cannot (or will not) kick.

Three chapters after the concert, in any case, Lucy is back in the theater, this time drawn by the magnetism of the renowned actress Vashti who, repeating her real-life model, Rachel Félix, is herself repeated, as we will see, in the texts of Eliot and James. Lucy's response to the performance by Vashti is advertised as one of almost self-parodic ambivalence:

> It was a marvellous sight: a mighty revelation. It was a spectacle low, horrible, immoral.
>
> (p. 339)

It is as though Brontë wished to control her own indecision about the theater, and about Rachel-Vashti, by presenting it in such crudely schematic form.[32] The surrounding paragraphs, however, suggest why the actress might invite, and defy, such defensive simplification:

31. This work has been collected in Miller, *The Novel and the Police* (Berkeley: University of California Press, 1988). For an example of the kind of reading I have mentioned, see the essay in that volume entitled "From *roman policier* to *roman police:* Wilkie Collins's *The Moonstone*," pp. 33–57.

32. The letters in which Brontë describes her impressions of Rachel, whose acting she observed in London in 1851, constitute a kind of rehearsal for the Vashti chapter in *Villette*. "Rachel's acting," she writes to one correspondent, "transfixed me with wonder, enchained me with interest, and thrilled me with horror" (Shorter, ed., *The*

What I saw was the shadow of a royal Vashti: a queen, fair as the day once, turned pale now like twilight, and wasted like wax in flame. . . . I found upon her something neither of woman nor of man: in each of her eyes sat a devil. These evil forces bore her through the tragedy, kept up her feeble strength—for she was but a frail creature; and as the action rose and the stir deepened, how wildly they shook her with their passions of the pit! They wrote HELL on her straight, haughty brow. They tuned her voice to the note of torment. They writhed her regal face to a demoniac mask. Hate and Murder and Madness incarnate, she stood. . . .

Suffering had struck that stage empress; and she stood before her audience neither yielding to, nor enduring, nor in finite measure, resenting it: she stood locked in struggle, rigid in resistance.

(p. 339)

Recapitulating and combining in her very person the king, the queen, and Hypochondria, the "sinister and sovereign Vashti" (p. 341) also, as many critics have noted, serves as a potent, heavily freighted image for both Lucy and Brontë as female artists. Eve Kosofsky Sedgwick, for example, reads "this drama of substance and abstraction" as an allegory of almost sadomasochistic self-inscription: "Vashti is herself at work creating a character, so that the rigor and wastage of individuation, redoubled in her, spread out as well to capture Lucy, the suddenly fixed viewer."[33] Doubling, redoubling, fascination, repulsion, sovereignty, suffering, strength, and frailty mingle and collide in this overwrought portrait of the artist, which makes a mockery of the neatly balanced antithesis that would crop and frame it. Unavailable to the relatively sophisticated grammar of both/and alone, Vashti evokes not only that structure but also the rhetorical convolution of neither/nor/nor. Hardly a reassuring apotheosis of the novelist-as-actress, this "maenad" with "angel's hair" (p. 340) nonetheless figures the spectacularly profitable (and spectacularly expensive) possibilities of multiple negation and self-contradiction.

Vashti indeed seems to exemplify Irigaray's theory of female mimicry, whereby "to play with mimesis is . . . , for a woman, to try to

---

Brontës: Life and Letters 2:252). For an astute reading of the Vashti episode as Brontë's revision of George Henry Lewes, who not only had written extensively about Rachel but also had attempted to supervise Brontë's own career, see Stokes, "Rachel's 'Terrible Beauty' ": 779–83.

33. Eve Kosofsky Sedgwick, "The Character in the Veil: Imagery of the Surface in the Gothic Novel," *PMLA* 96 (1981): 267.

recover the place of her exploitation by discourse, without allowing herself to be simply reduced to it." Vashti's performance suggests that, if one is inscribed in a constraining social text, one can at least act out the various processes of one's textualization, thereby achieving a certain leverage with which to displace that preexistent order. To the extent that this visit to the theater constitutes yet another scene of instruction, it is one in which Lucy learns from Vashti (as Irigaray might have learned from Vashti) how to stage "a possible operation of the feminine in language." Just as Vashti turns herself into a receptive surface on which "the passions of the pit . . . [write] HELL," so Lucy suffers her acquaintances to superimpose their received ideas—sexist, class-bound, sentimentalizing—upon her; but, like Vashti, she manages at the same time to rewrite the parts others would make her play, "neither yielding to" them nor "enduring" them, but "rigid"—indeed, perverse—"in resistance." When Vashti's performance is cut short by a fire she herself seems to have caused, Lucy may be said not only to take over for *her* but also to take up the stylus where Hypochondria left off, for now she in fact represents the scene of her own writing: " 'Fire!' rang through the gallery. 'Fire!' was repeated, re-echoed, yelled forth: and then, and faster than pen can set it down, came panic, rushing, crushing,—a blind, selfish, cruel, chaos" (p. 342). The act of describing the fire seems suddenly to be taking place not retrospectively, but at the same time as the event itself. And as the time of the narration collapses into the time of the narrative, the roles of novelist (Brontë) and teacher (Lucy) and actress (Vashti) "repeat" and "re-echo" one another in a potentially productive textual "chaos."

To be sure, what is produced, after the inevitable demystifying dismissal of the fire as the result of a minor accident involving "some loose drapery" (p. 347), is nothing more immediately redeemable than more chaos. But if the remainder of the narrative has little trouble displaying Lucy as "a rising character" (p. 394), her professional progress has performative implications that an exemplarily self-disciplined novel of education would deny. If the "show-trial" (p. 492) in chapter 35 offers us yet another view of the writer-teacher on stage, this time subjected to a "forced examination" (p. 496), it also shows Lucy triumphing over her boorish examiners, not so much by demonstrating her knowledge as by inscribing a defiant satire on "Human Justice." Lucy has every reason to be as "content

... with the issue of [this] trial" as Kemble says her parents were (and as she herself may have been, though for different reasons) with the outcome of her own. Once again, Lucy converts what could have been a merely disciplinary scene of instruction, in which the female teacher is framed as a student, into a scene in which writing is both work *and* play. And, once again, the English teacher seems to combine self-inscription with self-dramatization. For Lucy's text about Justice is not *just* a satire; indeed, as M. Paul might complain, "ce n'est pas juste." "Human Justice" starts out as a "blank, cold abstraction" (p. 495), much like the often blank, cold Lucy Snowe herself. Suddenly inspired, however, by her recognition of her examiners as the two men who had frightened her on the night of her arrival in Villette, Lucy revises Justice as a "red, random beldame with arms akimbo" (p. 496); in the process, she may also be sketching a colorful and unsettling (if not exactly flattering) portrait of herself as a destructive female artist. Turning the "trial" into a "show" of her own, Lucy teaches her arrogant would-be teachers a lesson.

The novel's showiest frustration of its own apparently straitlaced pedagogy, however, occurs at the end, in the scene of Lucy's drugged excursion to the illuminated park. To move from writing and instruction to the other critical dyad informing the present chapter: this long, climactic episode might almost be read as a symbolic encounter between the Bakhtinian carnival and the Foucauldian prison, an encounter in which the two spaces, like the theater and the schoolroom, clash and merge and displace each other, in what thus becomes a vertiginous dialectic of "Imagination" and "Truth."

Stimulated into reverie by a drug that was intended to stupefy her, Lucy escapes from the "prison" (p. 548) of Madame Beck's school and wanders to the park, which in its festive aspect appears to her "a land of enchantment" (p. 550). Seeing her friends pass before her in a weirdly alienating light, Lucy resorts again to the theatrical metaphor: "Throughout this woody and turfy theatre reigned a shadow of mystery; actors and incidents unlooked-for, waited behind the scenes" (p. 556). But this is as much the language of paranoia as of liberatory excess, and neither Lucy nor the reader is terribly surprised to discover, at the "confines" (p. 556) of this theater, the "secret junta" (p. 558) made up of Madame Walravens, Madame Beck, and Père Silas. For indeed, this *fête* "was not considered a show of Vanity Fair, but a commemoration of patriotic sacrifice. The Church patronized it, even with ostentation" (p. 558).

Nor should it surprise us that the play of ambiguity does not stop here, but extends into Lucy's reading of the "love scene" (p. 566) between M. Paul and his ward, Justine Marie: as in earlier readings, Lucy's "unveiling" of the truth, to use Iragaray's term, is itself a product of fantasy; once more, Lucy is not just "excluded spectator," but, as Mary Jacobus notes, *"metteur en scène* in a drama of her own making."[34] And while the *literal* unveiling of "the NUN" as de Hamal seems to have been dictated by a selective, stage-managing rationalism that would turn nunnery into mummery, the residues of transgressive theatricality persist all the way into the novel's notoriously inconclusive ending, where Brontë, having cast M. Paul as Lucy's "king" (p. 587)—But what, at this point, is a king?—and sent him to "Guadaloupe," at once kills him off and brings him back alive, playing the game of *fort/da* not only with this newly crowned monarch, but also, outrageously, with her own authoritarian father, who pressed her for a "happy" ending. As Elizabeth Gaskell, Brontë's friend and biographer, tells us: "All she could do in compliance with her father's wish was so to veil the fate in oracular words, as to leave it to the character and discernment of her readers to interpret her meaning."[35] Closer here to an actor's mask than to part of a nun's habit, the "veil" becomes a sheltering shadow of undecidability, beneath which, if she so chooses, Brontë can do a kind of conjuring trick: she can make M. Paul—as well as his resident sponsor, the Reverend Patrick Brontë—go away and come back and go away again. We end, as we began, with an instructive scene of ambivalent daughterly inscription. Like Fanny Kemble rehearsing the events of her opening night, Charlotte Brontë, on closing her novel, provides a valuable lesson in the ironic theatricality of "indecision," and in the complex, often surprisingly double-edged symbolism of that patriarchal theater known as the nineteenth-century family. "In compliance with her father's wish," the author veils not

34. Jacobus, "The Buried Letter," p. 52.
35. Elizabeth Gaskell, *The Life of Charlotte Brontë*, ed. Alan Shelston (Harmondsworth: Penguin, 1975), p. 484.

only M. Paul's fate but her own subversive performance as well. Covertly enacting both regicide and patricide, Brontë gets away with murder.

At the beginning of this chapter, I acknowledged (and predicted) the difficulty of getting around or beyond the authority-subversion polarity. In so doing, however, I also indicated the need for better and more various ways of talking about the political affiliations and social consequences of the peculiar kind of "performance" that takes place in and as a literary (or literary-theoretical) text. The reading conducted here has attempted partially and very preliminarily to answer that need by demonstrating some of the complicated, shifting relations among theatricality, pedagogy, and writing in Brontë's novel, relations whose effects cannot simply be reduced to a binary opposition between transgression and containment. In concluding this chapter, and in anticipating the discussion of Dickens and sensationalism in the next, I would like to draw out, as Brontë would say, one other potentially particularizing strategy suggested, though not yet identified, here.

When Lucy resorts to cross-dressing in the *vaudeville* for Madame Beck's *fête*, she calls attention to a process that, as other examples in this chapter should have confirmed, traverses the text—what Christina Crosby, in her shrewd reading of *Villette*, calls "a wide range of substitution and slippage" concerning gender identity.[36] Crosby's paradigm for this process—although "paradigm" may not be the best word to use when a promiscuous *contiguity* is the order of the day—is the surprising connection between the neurotically introspective Lucy on the one hand and the vacuously superficial Count de Hamal on the other, a connection implied not only by Lucy's performance as the fop in the school play, but also by the fact that these apparently antithetical characters are both associated with the figure of "the nun": while this figure functions resonantly as a "metaphor" for Lucy's own repression, that evocativeness gets "flattened out" retroactively when Lucy learns, near the end of the novel, that "the nun" was merely the theatrical disguise de Hamal

36. Crosby, "Charlotte Brontë's Haunted Text": 708.

assumed in order to gain access to Ginevra inside the *pensionnat*.[37] With remarkable dexterity, Crosby exploits this connection to achieve a kind of deconstructive flattening out of her own, a sophisticated (con)textualization of earlier feminist readings of the novel, which tend to inflate the psychological meaningfulness they ascribe to Lucy. Treating the conventional Gothic figure of "the nun" as a textually constitutive "none"—less as an emblem of plenitude and interiority than as a floating signifier, a ghostly harbinger of *différance*—Crosby claims for *Villette* a more "radical"[38] feminism than has hitherto been recognized in it. "Invagination" would indeed describe the general strategy of a reading that in effect turns Lucy Snowe inside-out.

Like the critics discussed in the previous chapter, Crosby uses theatrical tropes—tropes of costumes and of role-playing—so as to debunk the Gothicizing metaphysics of Brontëan presence. Unlike some of those critics, however, she links theatricality not only with a certain textual flatness, but with a certain "play" as well.[39] Yet though she in turn links this play with the Irigarayan notion of a *speculum de l'autre femme*,[40] she has little to say about the "sexual pleasure" that Irigaray sees as being "unveiled" by a feminist "play[ing] with mimesis." It is worth noting, therefore, that, while conventionally mediated, all the veilings and unveilings performed in *Villette*, like all the dressings and cross-dressings, intimate various *unconventional* forms of sexual desire or sexual experience, forms that the term "androgyny" would merely reconventionalize. Instead of rehearsing the travesty of "the nun," or of returning to another already-cited example of gender slippage, such as the non-exchange of prizes in the scene of the concert, I would like to look briefly at one more passage, in which the slippery configuration of writing, acting, and instruction hints at "under-currents" of sexual and textual pleasure (or even of pain) that the sensation novel, for its part,

37. I take the term "flattened out" from Crosby, ibid.: 705, who uses it to show how this debunking is reinforced by the explanatory letter that Ginevra leaves for Lucy.

38. Ibid.: 703.

39. For example: "The mobility of meaning in Brontë's text is never a lure away from complexity, but is an Imaginary with a difference: its series of refracted images is always in play, always producing new configurations, without origin or end" (ibid.: 715).

40. Ibid.: 713.

will specialize in "exciting," and that a responsive teacher-critic might be able to mobilize as well.

This passage occurs in chapter 28, shortly after Lucy has caused M. Paul's cherished *lunettes* to shatter, in the middle of one of his lessons, no less. As though advancing this rather castratory flirtation, the narrative has Lucy push her luck by keeping her distance from M. Paul when he arrives at the *pensionnat* to deliver one of his occasional dramatic readings; and he exposes himself to further danger by his very choice of material:

> For his misfortune he had chosen a French translation of what he called "un drame de Williams Shackspire; le faux dieu," he further announced, "de ces sots païens, les Anglais." How far otherwise he would have characterized him had his temper not been upset, I scarcely need intimate.
>
> Of course, the translation being French, was very inefficient; nor did I make any particular effort to conceal the contempt which some of its forlorn lapses were calculated to excite. Not that it behoved or beseemed me to *say* anything; but one can occasionally *look* the opinion it is forbidden to embody in words. Monsieur's [new] lunettes being on the alert, he gleamed up every stray look; I don't think he lost one: the consequence was, his eyes soon discarded a screen, that their gaze might sparkle free, and he waxed hotter at the north pole to which he had voluntarily exiled himself, than, considering the general temperature of the room, it would have been reasonable to become under the vertical ray of Cancer itself.
>
> (pp. 416–17)

Against Fanny Kemble's faith in the prophylactic properties of "reading" (as opposed to acting) and of "Shakespeare" (as opposed to less prestigious cultural icons), this passage frames the reading of Shakespeare as a notably risky undertaking, much like acting itself at its most "painful and distasteful." Admittedly, the riskiness may have something to do with the fact that much gets lost in (French) translation. Yet M. Paul's French serves, oddly enough, to align him with none other than Vashti. Indeed, if this is presumably a scene of instruction—in which it is not quite clear who is the teacher and who is the student—it is also a scene of writing—in which, likewise, it is hard to know just who writes and who (or what) gets written. On the one hand, after his less-than-successful reading M. Paul "seem[s] to be occupied in making marginal notes to his 'Williams Shackspire' " (p. 417). On the other hand, the more consequential act of inscription here would appear to be that whereby

Lucy rewrites the incendiary Vashti ("wasted like wax in flame") as the blazing Paul ("wax[ing] hotter at the north pole"), or vice versa. Displacing Vashti's "demoniac" performance into Paul's "contemptible" one, Lucy, like Jane Eyre, experiences much of the pungent "excitement" of bad acting. And the observation that *Paul's* pain affords *Lucy* pleasure only begins to address the thinly veiled erotics of the scene. For if the "pain" is not all on his side, neither is the "pleasure" all on hers. Part of what gets Paul hot, as it were, is the excitement of attacking not only "Williams Shackspire," but also Lucy, ostensibly through her compatriots. Conversely, she must sense a certain arousing sting in hearing herself classed among "ces sots païens, les Anglais."

We could speculate further about Lucy's affect in response to *this* slippage, in which she is typed in the terms that she herself ordinarily applies to Paul and his culture; about the surreptitious gratification she might derive from the inadvertently carnivalesque (if "forlorn") Frenching of the immortal Shakespeare; about the implications of the blurring of gender that results from the recasting of Paul as Vashti or of Vashti as Paul; about the *frisson* that might attend the sheer fact of conducting such a highly charged sexual power play behind the "screen" of institutional ceremony. But it will have to be enough for now merely to signal these complexities, which perhaps seem insufficiently public or momentous to found a significant textual politics, much less a "subversive" textual politics. I would argue, and indeed hope to show in the next chapter, that such undercurrents are worth identifying, since, precisely to the extent that they precede or exceed the stark and sweeping opposition between "authority" and "subversion," they constitute the micropolitics of theatricality in the nineteenth-century novel. It may be difficult, even impossible, to resist the temptation to decide whether a given novel is "authoritarian" or "subversive"; yet that project may also be as unrewarding, finally, as trying to separate the "French" scene of writing from the "English" scene of instruction. If what we have been given to read, after all, is an (unspecified) "drame de Williams Shackspire," we might as well attempt to become better (more specific) readers of that grotesquely *composite* text and play.

4

Dickens and Sensationalism

Of all the canonical English authors, Dickens would seem to be the one obvious and inevitable candidate for inclusion in a book on theatricality in the nineteenth-century novel. If, according to Gillian Beer, Charlotte Brontë is "the most introspective [i.e., the least apparently theatrical] of all Victorian novelists," Dickens might stand as Brontë's antithesis, as Beer in fact suggests when she writes: "More than any other Victorian novelist, Dickens draws upon the theatre's power of *manifestation* in his subject matter, characterisation, and in the activities of his style. His style is spectacle."[1] Beer expresses a critical consensus or commonplace, which is routinely supplemented or supported with references to Dickens's life-long fascination with the theater, his passionate involvement in amateur theatricals, and his equally zealous commitment, late in his career, to the public readings that may have hastened his death: whether or not they would celebrate it, most students of nineteenth-century English fiction would probably agree to recognize the existence, indeed the overwhelming visibility, of what Robert Garis (hardly a fan himself) has called "the Dickens theater."[2]

Yet, precisely because of Dickens's evident preeminence as a theatrical novelist, he figures less centrally in the present study than do authors whose attitudes toward the theater are more ambivalent. For the emphasis here falls not so much on theatricality *tout court* as on the *resistance* to theatricality—on the ways in which certain nineteenth-century novels, aligning themselves with such values as inwardness, privacy, propriety, and sincerity, attempt to suppress

1. Gillian Beer, " 'Coming Wonders': Uses of Theatre in the Victorian Novel," in *English Drama: Forms and Development*, ed. Marie Axton and Raymond Williams (Cambridge: Cambridge University Press, 1977), p. 179. The remark about Brontë, quoted in the previous chapter, comes from p. 185.

2. Robert Garis, *The Dickens Theatre: A Reassessment of the Novels* (London: Oxford University Press, 1965).

or to conceal theatrical energies, images, and techniques, even as they appropriate them. If, for example, the dissimulation of theatricality in *Jane Eyre* has turned out to be a theatrical strategy in its own right, it is the contradiction or tension between theatrical and antitheatrical pressures—not the presence of theatricality "itself"— that we have found most interesting. Compared to the "Austen theater" and the "Brontë theater," which are intriguingly displaced or disguised, broken up or covered over, the "Dickens theater" must seem rather unpromisingly—that is, unproblematically—up-front; no one should have any trouble finding it. The difficulty, for us at any rate, lies in finding something to *say* about it. What can one do with a novelist who could proclaim, "Every writer of fiction, though he may not adopt the dramatic form, writes in effect for the stage"?[3]

The mock pathos of the question, of course, should indicate its partial disingenuousness. Just as other critics have hardly been at a loss for words when it comes to discussing theatricality in Dickens, I too wish to comment, albeit somewhat elliptically, on the place of the theater in his work. Though I devote less space to Dickens than to Austen, Brontë, Eliot, or James, it is not quite true that he is therefore less "central" to this study. After all, to situate a discussion of Dickens in the middle of this book is not exactly to marginalize him. If Dickens, along with his contemporaries in sensation fiction, serves to fill the interval between the book's two halves, this intermediacy goes beyond the function of mere *divertissement*. While a critic like Garis would see Dickens, to say nothing of the sensation novelists (of whom Garis says precisely nothing), as in fact representing a rather distasteful diversion from the course of "what is highest in art,"[4] a standard exemplified signally by, among others, Austen, Eliot, and James, I would argue that, from Garis's point of view, Dickens may be all too close to these presumably more "serious" artists: if Dickens's novels constitute a betrayal of some putative high-cultural respect for "the inner life,"[5] the betrayal takes the form less of perfidy than of revelation, whereby Dickensian staginess calls attention to the ways in which the idealized interiority

3. Charles Dickens, speech to the Royal General Theatrical Fund, March 29, 1858; cited in Paul Schlicke, *Dickens and Popular Entertainment* (London: Allen and Unwin, 1985), p. 33.
4. Garis, *The Dickens Theatre*, p. 37.
5. Ibid., pp. 41–62.

is already staged, and thus betrayed in the first sense of the word, even in the exalted works of Austen and company.

For this reason, Dickens's intermediate position here might almost be regarded as pivotal, and this privileged placement might indeed be seen to *honor* Dickens's claim that "every writer of fiction . . . writes in effect for the stage." But if one aim of this chapter (as of the book as a whole) is to abbreviate the distance between a novelist who is "for the stage" and others who seem to be "against" it, then I will also want to suggest that, even in as protheatrical a novelist as Dickens, the "effects" of writing for the stage are not always as coherent or as unambivalent as we might expect them to be. In his richly informative book, *Dickens and Popular Entertainment*, Paul Schlicke, writing from an ideological stance that is the exact opposite of Garis's elitism, praises Dickens's theatricality as aggressively as Garis derides it: "Central to his role as an artist, integral with his social convictions, rooted in his deepest values, and a source of lifelong delight, popular entertainment reaches to the core of Dickens's life and work."[6] Convincingly as Schlicke demonstrates the importance of this intrinsically popular (and populist) theatricality in Dickens, however, he keeps encountering certain disturbing inconsistencies in the works he chooses to study. For example, in discussing as early and as supposedly upbeat a novel as *Nicholas Nickleby* (1839), a novel that was inscribed to Dickens's friend, the great actor W. C. Macready, Schlicke can neither evade nor explain away the problem of Nicholas's uneasiness about his association with Crummles's troupe of actors; he must also acknowledge that the players are "inappropriately rejected"[7] when, near the end, the narrative exiles them to America. One should infer from such inconsistencies not that Dickens is antitheatrical after all, but that "writing in effect for the stage" comprises *different* effects to the extent that "the stage" comprises *different*—and at times incompatible—constructions of theatricality. Dickens resembles the other novelists in this book not in any fear of the theater and its diffusions but in the heterogeneity of his theatrical ideology and practice.

In this chapter, I will be concerned to map, through a brief look at a rather arbitrary selection of texts, both the internal fissures and

6. Schlicke, *Dickens and Popular Entertainment*, p. 4.
7. Ibid., p. 85.

overdeterminations of "the Dickens theater" and the adjacent, in many ways similar force-field constituted, in the 1860s, by the notably (or notoriously) theatrical genre of the sensation novel. While the traditional view is that Dickens's novels display an increasing pessimism, I would propose that "dark" or "pessimistic" works like *Great Expectations* (1861) and *Our Mutual Friend* (1865) in fact represent a refinement of the more self-divided theatrical technology of their ostensibly sunnier predecessors. And while criticism has recognized affinities between Dickens's later works and the productions of writers like Wilkie Collins, Mary Elizabeth Braddon, and Mrs. Henry Wood,[8] I hope to show, in the third section of this chapter, how sensationalism both avails itself of Dickens's technology and reintroduces, into what might thus appear to be an intolerably and inexorably efficient textual-political apparatus, a potentially saving excess or unreliability.

Dickens's third novel, the much-dramatized *Nicholas Nickleby*, suggests itself as a chief exhibit in any case for the buoyant and prodigious—one might even say carnivalesque—theatricality of Dickens's early work. "Dickens's fascination with the world of the theatre," Michael Slater observes, "is manifest everywhere in his writings, but nowhere given such joyous scope as in *Nicholas Nickleby*."[9] And yet, for the reasons that even Schlicke has to register, both the joyousness and the scope of the novel's protheatricality may be somewhat restricted. For the hero's evident misgivings about his involvement with the Crummles troupe, and the ultimate removal of that troupe from the novel, betoken a larger pattern of segregation within the novel. "In the final analysis," Schlicke admits, "the rejection of Crummles is consonant with his isolation from the rest of the book."[10] It is as though, well before the narrative dis-

8. See, for example, Patrick Brantlinger, "What Is 'Sensational' about the 'Sensation Novel'?" *Nineteenth-Century Fiction* 37 (June 1982): 1–28; Winifred Hughes, *The Maniac in the Cellar: Sensation Novels of the 1860s* (Princeton: Princeton University Press, 1980); Alexander Welsh, *George Eliot and Blackmail* (Cambridge: Harvard University Press, 1985).

9. Michael Slater, Introduction, *Nicholas Nickleby* (Harmondsworth: Penguin, 1986), p. 15. Subsequent references to the novel will be to this edition, and will be included parenthetically in the text.

10. Schlicke, *Dickens and Popular Entertainment*, p. 86.

patches Crummles and company to America, it had already set up a sort of internal colony within which to contain them. That the account of Nicholas's experiences as a member of the troupe merely constitutes a more or less discrete textual interlude is of course attributable to the novel's loose, episodic structure. But generic or formal considerations alone cannot explain the persistent effect of a rigorous separation between the theatricality of Crummles and his players, on the one hand, and the main interest of the novel—the violent, persecutory relations between Nicholas and Ralph Nickleby—on the other. What makes this separation so peculiar, moreover, is that it is hard to tell whether the "utopia" of the theatrical world is thereby being protected from the more extensive, conspicuously *dys*topian realm presided over by Ralph, or vice versa.

Nor does it help to call the latter space "antitheatrical." For though Ralph is indeed something of a killjoy, he is not only a highly theatrical character in his own right—we can identify him easily enough with the stereotypical villain of Victorian melodrama—but one who is himself fascinated, if not by the world of the theater, then by the theater of the world. Confronted with a great financial loss, and with the frustration of one of his nefarious schemes, the usurer regrets most painfully—and most theatrically—the consequent loss of opportunities for sadistic capitalization on the theatricality of others:

> Ten thousand pounds! How many proud painted dames would have fawned and smiled, and how many spendthrift blockheads done me lip-service to my face and cursed me in their hearts, while I turned that ten thousand pounds into twenty! While I ground, and pinched, and used these needy borrowers for my pleasure and profit, what smooth-tongued speeches, and courteous looks, and civil letters they would have given me! The cant of the lying world is, that men like me compass our riches by dissimulation and treachery, by fawning, cringing, and stooping. Why, how many lies, what mean and abject evasions, what humbled behaviour from upstarts who, but for my money, would spurn me aside as they do their betters every day, would that ten thousand pounds have brought me in!
>
> (pp. 837–38)

At once relishing and assailing "the cant of the lying world"—relishing it *because* it is so eminently assailable—Ralph shifts the charge of "dissimulation and treachery" onto his victims, imaging the world they inhabit as a veritable theater of duplicity. If this ruthlessly excited critique of worldliness makes Ralph sound like Charlotte Brontë on a particularly bad day, it also voices the specifically male, and male-volent, theatrical ethos that occupies much of the novel. For the dog-eat-dog world view that Ralph implies here gets enacted most recurrently and spectacularly in his relationship with his nephew. Borrowing from recent Foucault-inspired readings of Dickens, we could call the theatricality inherent in that relationship "panoptic" or "paranoid."[11] "Across my path, at every turn, go where I will, do what I may, he comes!" (p. 813). Ralph is speaking here, but it could just as easily be Nicholas, since one of the features of this specular scenario is precisely the interchangeability of hunter and hunted.

To be sure, Ralph and Nicholas are not completely interchangeable: one could hardly overlook the Manichean distribution of roles in this family drama. Yet it is telling that, within the all-too-comprehensive framework of the panoptic or paranoid plot, one opposition that does *not* come into play, as it were, is that between the grinding theatricality of surveillance and one-upmanship associated with Ralph and the supposedly life-enhancing theatricality of "joy" and extravagance associated with Crummles. Certainly, the vitality and generosity of the players stand in sharp contrast to the meannesses relentlessly perpetrated by Ralph. But the point is that those virtues *merely* stand—that they have no more than a static relation to the novel's more compelling and more consuming theatrical agenda.

Insofar as the collision fails to take place, any argument for the "carnivalesque" effect of Crummles and his players must remain merely wishful. Unlike, say, *Villette*, *Nicholas Nickleby* keeps its "Bakhtinian" theatricality at more than arm's length from its "Foucauldian" theatricality, so that to call the former "Bakhtinian" or "carnivalesque" at all is itself misleading. Since the "utopianism" of that theatricality consists mainly in its relegation to a rather inconsequential place apart—apart from the much larger theater in which the novel's central conflict unfolds—it would be more accu-

---

11. I have in mind Eve Kosofsky Sedgwick, *Between Men: English Literature and Male Homosocial Desire* (New York: Columbia University Press, 1985), especially the chapters on *Our Mutual Friend* and *The Mystery of Edwin Drood;* and D. A. Miller, *The Novel and the Police* (Berkeley: University of California Press, 1988), especially the chapter on *Bleak House*.

rate, if less politically stimulating, to call the distant and oddly abstract site thus constituted "ludic."[12] For while the players are indeed incessantly playful, there is relatively little at stake in their play. Working to limit their theatricality to what may be imagined as precisely a more manageable (because spatially and temporally fixed) "stage," the *circumscription* of their textual existence—the narrowness and the literally provincial remoteness of the scope allotted for their performances—guarantees that their subversions will subvert nothing.

In the previous chapter, of course, I attempted to gesture beyond, or perhaps beneath, the dichotomy of subversion versus authority, indicating the need for more plural and discriminate ways of analyzing theatrical (and literary) politics. What I am arguing here is not that the theatricality represented by the Crummles troupe fails to be "genuinely" subversive, but rather that, like the authority-subversion dualism itself, at least as it is often deployed, it fails to be very useful, not to say very interesting. In a general sense, for example, it is possible to read as "subversive" the much-quoted passage in which Crummles bids Nicholas farewell:

> Mr. Crummles, who could never lose any opportunity for professional display, had turned out for the express purpose of taking a public farewell of Nicholas; and to render it the more imposing, he was now, to that young gentleman's most profound annoyance, inflicting upon him a rapid succession of stage embraces, which, as everybody knows, are performed by the embracer's laying his or her chin on the shoulder of the object of affection, and looking over it. This Mr. Crummles did in the highest style of melodrama, pouring forth at the same time all the most dismal forms of farewell he could think of, out of the stock pieces.
>
> (p. 478)

Crummles's flagrant *offstage* hamminess in some sense deconstructs the opposition between the "psychological" inside and the "social" outside ("how many spendthrift blockheads [would have] done me lip-service to my face and cursed me in their hearts") presupposed by Ralph Nickleby's theatricality of "dissimulation and treachery." Yet, although this passage might scandalize a reader like Robert

---

12. The allusion here is to the important work of Johan Huizinga, *Homo Ludens: A Study of the Play Element in Culture* (New York: Harper and Row, 1970). Although the concept of "play" has a rich and capacious significance for Huizinga, it is more reassuring, less potentially disruptive, than a concept like Bakhtin's "carnival."

Garis, it seems far less corrosive, given its Dickensian context, than such otherwise similar acts as Henry Crawford's reading aloud and Jane Eyre's soliloquizing. In Dickens's text, in other words, the contradiction between Crummles's "deconstructive" theatricality and Ralph's more "conservative" theatricality, however disturbing that contradiction may appear from a certain ideological perspective, simply does not amount to much, thematically or otherwise.

There is one other way, however, in which the passage quoted above might seem to signify. For when Crummles's flamboyant farewell occasions in Nicholas "profound annoyance," we sense the possibility of productive contact between the Nicholas-Ralph plot and the Nicholas-Crummles plot—between, that is, a tortuously oedipalized relationship and what would seem to be its sweetly uncomplicated antithesis. And yet, despite the encouragement offered to this view by Nicholas's rather ill-timed tirade against the "literary gentleman" at the farewell supper for the Crummles family in chapter 48—a not-so-veiled attack by Dickens on playwrights who had plagiarized his works, including the present one—the would-be deidealizing critic is hard put to generate much friction from the contiguity between Nicholas's earlier annoyance and his later indignation, since, as a moderately close reading of the novel will show, it is not about to stage a relativizing dialogue between its paranoid theatricality and its joyously (and asexually) ludic theatricality. At best, one can use the evidence at hand to cast further doubt on too unqualified a view of Dickens as an enthusiastic partisan of popular entertainment. Writing for (or about) at least *two* distinct and incommensurable stages—the one so isolated as to risk the inertia of literality, the other so insidiously generalized as to resemble a pervasive and almost invisible malignancy rather than a determinate textual locus—Dickens "in effect" prevents them from overlapping with, and consequently from having much of an effect upon, each other.

Thus, while it may still be true that, as Gillian Beer says, Dickens's "style is spectacle," the disjunctive representation of theatricality in *Nicholas Nickleby*, at any rate, presents a challenge to the homogenizing tendency of many accounts of the Dickens theater. In place of a total theatrical system which offers itself up for either celebration or condemnation, we discover in that text a set of discontinuous theatricalities: the nonrelation between theatrical themes or topoi raises questions about the supposedly organic linkage between those topoi on the one hand and theatricality as a "style" or discursive mode on the other hand. Such questions loom large in a novel from Dickens's middle period like *Hard Times* (1854). As Catherine Gallagher has shown, "the book has an excessively metaphoric style, as well as a metaphoric structure, and its style becomes one of its themes."[13] Far from signaling the happy synthesis of stylistic and thematic levels, however, that thematization ends up intensifying the sense of fracture within the Dickens theater. For if, in Gallagher's words, *Hard Times* "simultaneously flaunts and discredits its metaphoricality,"[14] which we might specify as a ludic theatricality at the level of style, that self-criticism points to the possibility of a *non*thematized theatrical style—a style held in reserve, exempt from the discreditation visited upon the overtly interrogated ludic theatricality; a style that corresponds, not surprisingly, to the panoptic theatrical theme so crucial both here and in *Nicholas Nickleby*. In *Hard Times*, that is, a disjunctiveness of stylistic theatricalities may replicate the earlier novel's disjunctiveness of thematic theatricalities.

It will of course seem perverse to suggest that this novel, so explicitly and programmatically directed *against* the culture of panopticism, is in fact secretly complicit with it. One might object that, though the novel may undermine the ludic values it means to uphold, it certainly has no intention of upholding panoptic ones. As is well known, *Hard Times* constitutes an attack on utilitarianism, the very doctrine that, in the writings of Bentham, provides the precise model for Foucault's elaboration of "an indefinitely generalizable mechanism of 'panopticism' " within post-Enlightenment Western culture.[15] The novel would thus lend itself not only to a Foucauldian reading but also, more interestingly, to a reading of Foucault. My aim here is not to conduct either of those readings, but merely to point out some of the ways in which Dickens's text (perhaps like Foucault's) surreptitiously allows for and depends

13. Catherine Gallagher, *The Industrial Reformation of English Fiction: Social Discourse and Narrative Form, 1832–1876* (Chicago: University of Chicago Press, 1985), p. 160.

14. Ibid., p. 166.

15. Michel Foucault, *Discipline and Punish: The Birth of the Prison*, trans. Alan Sheridan (New York: Vintage, 1979), p. 216. See pp. 195–228 for an extended discussion of Bentham, the Panopticon, and panopticism.

upon a certain panoptic *remainder* after the critique of panopticism has been performed.[16] For where *Nicholas Nickleby* erects a barrier between its panoptic and ludic theatricalities, *Hard Times*, more intricately, at once stages a sort of "dialectical" interplay between them and withholds from that interplay the cognitive power and organizational privilege that may hence redound upon the narration itself. From a perspective like Gallagher's, this leftover panopticism might look like another incriminating trace of a failed (because self-contradictory) ideological project; but in the diachronic context of the technological development to which the novel contributes, this "failure" may constitute a step on the road to "success."

What makes the relationship between Gradgrind's panopticism and the ludic sphere of the circus appear "dialectical" is that, instead of merely substituting the latter for the former, the novel appropriates ludic values so as to humanize the mechanisms of control and surveillance. This strategy is exemplified synecdochally in the sequence of the plot, whereby Sissy Jupe, the clown's daughter, is first taken into the Gradgrind family and then permitted to exercise her mitigating influence upon Gradgrind and his daughter Louisa. In the last paragraph of the novel, the narrator recapitulates the strategy: we are left with an image of Sissy "thinking no innocent and pretty fancy ever to be despised; trying hard to know her humbler fellow-creatures, and to beautify their lives of machinery and reality with those imaginative graces and delights, without which the heart of infancy will wither up, the sturdiest physical manhood will be morally stark death, and the plainest national prosperity figures can show, will be Writing on the Wall."[17] As this passage makes clear, the novel does not call for the triumph of "fancy" over "machinery and reality"; rather, it calls upon "fancy" to "beautify" "machinery and reality." Despite the intensity of its antiutilitarian rhetoric, *Hard Times* recommends not so much an end to panoptic culture as the consolidation of a kinder, gentler panopticism. It is

16. That such "skepticism" may reinforce the administrative machinery it seems to dismantle is one of the main implications of D. A. Miller's reading of *Bleak House* in *The Novel and the Police*, although Miller does not apply this insight to Foucault himself. He hints in passing at its relevance to *Hard Times*, in a footnote to that essay, p. 100.

17. Charles Dickens, *Hard Times*, ed. David Craig (Harmondsworth: Penguin, 1982), p. 313. Subsequent references to the novel will be to this edition, and will be included parenthetically in the text.

as though Ralph Nickleby had adopted one of the Crummles children, so that the joy thus enlisted, gradually turning the villain into a nice guy after all, might ultimately improve the image of the power he deploys.

Even in a fairly obvious thematic way, then, *Hard Times* is not quite as hard on its times as one might think. Yet, as is often the case with such liberal concessions, the "dialectic" that makes the book so accommodating tends to break down—to borrow Bakhtin's distinction—into something less harmoniously "dialogic."[18] In other words, instead of, or in addition to, the compromise formation that the novel seems to intend, it produces collisions like those that failed to occur in *Nicholas Nickleby*; the standoff between panoptic and ludic theatricalities that we noted in the earlier novel is here replaced by certain kinds of pile-up that are all the more interesting for appearing not to be what the author has in mind.

Other critics have observed some of these collisions, analyzing, for instance, the grotesque displacement of circus imagery into the description of industrial Coketown (p. 65), the odd similarity between the obnoxious and spuriously "self-made" Bounderby and the lovable and fancifully "made-up" circus folk, and the way the innocence and fun of Sleary's horse-riding get repeated, in the climactic scene of the Gradgrind family reunion, in the mode of "grim farce."[19] If such effects suggest that the theatricality of Sleary's troupe, unlike the otherwise comparable theatricality of Crummles's, may legitimately be called "carnivalesque," the disruptive contact that they attest works both ways: the panoptic can relativize the

18. See Mikhail Bakhtin, *Problems of Dostoevsky's Poetics*, ed. and trans. Caryl Emerson (Minneapolis: University of Minnesota Press, 1984): "The unified, dialectically evolving spirit, understood in Hegelian terms, can give rise to nothing but a philosophical monologue. And the soil of monistic idealism is the least likely place for a plurality of unmerged consciousnesses to blossom. In this sense the unified evolving spirit, even as an image, is organically alien to Dostoevsky. Dostoevsky's world is profoundly *pluralistic*" (p. 26). Bakhtin states the contrast more pithily in a note cited by Emerson in the preface: "Dialogue and dialectics. Take a dialogue and remove the voices . . . remove the intonations . . . carve out abstract concepts and judgments from living words and responses, cram everything into one abstract consciousness—and that's how you get dialectics" (p. xxxii).

19. The latter phrase is from Gallagher, *The Industrial Reformation*, p. 158; she discusses the ironies of this scene on pp. 157–58. On the description of Coketown, see ibid., p. 160, and Schlicke, *Dickens and Popular Entertainment*, pp. 179–80; on the similarity between Bounderby and the circus performers, see Gallagher, p. 162, and Schlicke, pp. 175–78.

ludic as much as the ludic can relativize the panoptic. That is, while contact with Sleary can make the sober discourse of "fact" sound a little slurred and silly, contact with the Gradgrinds and Bounderby can make Sleary seem a little sleazy. These collisions are also collusions, where the connotations of "playing together" are no longer merely "innocent and pretty." As participants in actual carnivals might confirm, there is something sinister as well as liberating about the carnivalesque.

If the novel does not quite succeed in bringing off its "dialectic" without a hitch, however, it is not content to settle for the symmetrical unsettling whereby, for instance, the world of the schoolroom (and of the factory) and the world of show penetrate and parody each other. In *Villette* (which was published the year before *Hard Times*), Brontë does not settle for such a consoling structure either: as we saw at the end of the previous chapter, the play of "authority" and "subversion" in Brontë's text inscribes not a neutralizing specularity but a risky micropolitics of sexual overdetermination. In *Hard Times*, Dickens confounds symmetry by inscribing a rather different sexual politics, in which the ludic parody of panopticism gets gendered as female, so that, unlike its converse, it can more easily be made a spectacle of and then ejected from the novel. I am referring to the narrator's treatment of Mrs. Sparsit, Bounderby's déclassée housekeeper. A somewhat marginal character, Mrs. Sparsit is subjected to curiously intense and elaborate narrative framing. The narrative sets her up, that is, in ways and for reasons that demand consideration, for the excessively gleeful framing and abjection of this character go a long way toward securing the unproblematized panopticism that Dickens reserves for his own use.

As with all the evildoers in his novels, Dickens provides us with abundant reasons for wanting to see Mrs. Sparsit humiliated and banished: we have no trouble convicting her of being malicious, self-serving, snobbish, reactionary, sexually manipulative, and so on. But what indicts her most decisively, if not most palpably, is the way in which she combines all of these vices in her self-appointed project of spying on Louisa Gradgrind and Louisa's would-be seducer, James Harthouse. For in thus playing detective—and the word "play" is crucial here—Mrs. Sparsit unbecomingly, indeed illicitly, arrogates to herself—and thereby mocks—the privilege of surveillance that should ultimately accrue not so much to the operators of the "beautified" or rehabilitated social "machinery" as to the author who prescribes its reform. Insofar as she would assume a position of empowered spectatorship, Mrs. Sparsit must herself be exposed as "an interesting spectacle" (p. 258) instead:

> Now, Mrs. Sparsit was not a poetical woman; but she took an idea, in the nature of an allegorical fancy, into her head. Much watching of Louisa, and much consequent observation of her impenetrable demeanour, which keenly whetted and sharpened Mrs. Sparsit's edge, must have given her as it were a lift, in the way of inspiration. She erected in her mind a mighty Staircase, with a dark pit of shame and ruin at the bottom; and down those stairs, from day to day and hour to hour, she saw Louisa coming.
>
> It became the business of Mrs. Sparsit's life, to look up at her staircase, and to watch Louisa coming down. Sometimes slowly, sometimes quickly, sometimes several steps at one bout, sometimes stopping, never turning back. If she had once turned back, it might have been the death of Mrs. Sparsit in spleen and grief.
>
> (pp. 226–27)

Taking this "allegorical fancy . . . into her head," Mrs. Sparsit embodies—one might say with a vengeance—what Mark Seltzer has called "the fantasy of surveillance."[20] Yet vengeance therefore finally belongs to Dickens, who, in staging her detective work as a Gothic "erection" "inspired" self-damningly by projective wish-fulfillment, effectively pulls the rug out from underneath it. Though ungrounded in the "innocent and pretty" impulses informing the kind of "fancy" that the novel affirms, Mrs. Sparsit's "fancy" is not quite as epistemologically shaky as Dickens would have us believe: her staircase does have some foundation in "fact." As we might expect, however, Louisa does "turn back," and just in the nick of time, with the welcome result that the nosy Mrs. Sparsit's fondly and presumptuously contrived structure comes tumbling down all around her. In previous chapters, we have seen how the positions of spectator and spectacle may be reversed, but the present reversal has a particular punitive force. When Louisa flees from Harthouse's advances and seeks her father's protection, a disappointed Mrs. Sparsit gets shown up by the only "detective" this text will authorize, and shown off by that author as proof of his superior power of surveillance:

20. Mark Seltzer, "*The Princess Casamassima*: Realism and the Fantasy of Surveillance," in his *Henry James and the Art of Power* (Ithaca: Cornell University Press, 1984), pp. 25–58.

> But, Mrs. Sparsit was wrong in her calculation. Louisa got into no coach, and was already gone. The black eyes kept upon the railroad-carriage in which she had travelled, settled upon it a moment too late. The door not being opened after several minutes, Mrs. Sparsit passed it and repassed it, saw nothing, looked in, and found it empty. Wet through and through: with her feet squelching and squashing in her shoes whenever she moved; with a rash of rain upon her classical visage; with a bonnet like an over-ripe fig; with all her clothes spoiled; with damp impressions of every button, string, and hook-and-eye she wore, printed off upon her highly-connected back; with a stagnant verdure on her general exterior, such as accumulates on an old park fence in a mouldy lane; Mrs. Sparsit had no resource but to burst into tears of bitterness and say, "I have lost her!"
>
> (p. 238)

That final lament not only caps this account of Mrs. Sparsit's defeat but also hints at another, perhaps especially arousing, reason why she must be defeated in the first place. As Gallagher observes, "to fancy" has a sexual as well as an epistemological meaning.[21] Mrs. Sparsit's hatred of Louisa, whom she at one point apostrophizes, with uncertain sarcasm, as "my dearest love" (p. 235), may not be entirely separable from the love that dare not speak its name. The authorial law that requires her abjection—to complete her punishment, Bounderby ultimately fires her—does so, in any case, to fend off precisely the kind of overdetermined sexual politics that we signaled in *Villette* and that, as we will see, looms so large in the sensation novel. Like Lucy Snowe and her rival, Madame Beck, Mrs. Sparsit threatens to inscribe—or, worse, to disclose—elements of fantasy, motives of desire, in any surveillance whatsoever, including its more discreet, respectable, and male-sponsored versions. Denying such overdetermination by making a mockery of her mockery, Dickens at the same time asserts the prerogatives of inscription as exclusively and unproblematically his own. "With damp impressions . . . printed off upon her highly-connected back," Mrs. Sparsit, who would have become an "author" in her own right, becomes instead a mere text, testifying to the sovereignty of her creator. Like the prisoner in Kafka's penal colony, she must bear upon her body the lesson she has failed to learn otherwise. By ignoring the "Writing on the Wall," she in effect sentences herself to being written on and written off.

---

21. Gallagher, *The Industrial Reformation*, p. 164.

As we know from Freud, of course, denial (*Verneinung*) "is a way of taking account of what is repressed."[22] One might thus argue in Dickens's defense (as though he needed defending) that his punishment of Mrs. Sparsit is itself an instance of the transgression it would both censure and forestall. It would follow from such an argument that, while (or because) *Hard Times* underwrites a covert authorial panopticism, it equally maintains a covert ludic, even an authentically subversive, theatricality. Although this might be an appealing proposition, I would resist its implicit symmetry by pointing to the redundancy of the process whereby Dickens spectacularizes Mrs. Sparsit: as we have seen, the ludic parody of panopticism that she enacts is already inscribed in the collisions that take place elsewhere in the text, and that get framed much less hysterically. If Freud suggests that denial has its ambivalent ironies, he also concludes, less reassuringly, that it "belongs to the instinct of destruction."[23] To claim, moreover, that Mrs. Sparsit's offense consists not in mobilizing the carnivalesque, but in mobilizing it in the wrong way, would be to miss the point of the carnivalesque itself, which, unlike, say, the hermeneutic circle, presumably refuses to be adjudicated in terms of "right" and "wrong" modalities. Where *Nicholas Nickleby* gives us pause to the extent that, permitting Ralph and associates to upstage Crummles and company, it simply seems more interested in the former than in the latter, *Hard Times*, though more politically interesting, suggests that the political interests invested in the Dickens theater may not be quite the same as those it purports to serve.

Of course, what makes a text like *Hard Times* more "interesting," at least for late-twentieth-century critics, is precisely the suspicion that it engenders in us. Rather like Mrs. Sparsit, we may enjoy a somewhat wishful relation to the objects of our surveillance, getting "as it were a lift" from the very ideological complicities that would seem to mark a fall. This explains why a late novel such as *Great Expectations*, with its even more advanced system of representational discipline, can be seen as at once disturbingly "pessimistic" and gratifyingly "successful" as a work of art. I am by no means pro-

---

22. Sigmund Freud, "Negation," in *General Psychological Theory: Papers on Metapsychology,* ed. Philip Rieff (New York: Collier, 1976), p. 214.
23. Ibid., p. 216.

posing that *Great Expectations* implicitly constitutes a sort of belated tribute or apology to the spirit of Mrs. Sparsit. Indeed, although much of the novel's "comedy" might appear to be aimed at the fanciful character of social machinery—one thinks, for example, of the description in chapter 20 of the cult-like adoration that makes the lawyer Jaggers look like a contemporary rock star—the novel both demonstrates and exemplifies the way in which that machinery harnesses the irony and playfulness that supposedly elude it.

For in the thoroughly mechanized world that the novel portrays, the ludic can neither stand outside (or on the margins of) social constraint nor disrupt it from within. Where Crummles's troupe, however ineffectual, at least has its own well-defined textual purview, and where Sleary's horse-riding, however compromised, at least *seems* to occupy a symbolic "neutral ground" (p. 55), *Great Expectations* offers no equivalent focus or site of putatively nonpanoptic theatricality. Though Mr. Wopsle's career as an actor—especially as it achieves a climax of sorts in the famous scene of his performance as Hamlet—might seem to suggest itself for this purpose, Wopsle's theatrics are absorbed by the paranoid or crime plot that they thereby fail to oppose. For example, one of the more impressive ways in which the young Pip's fear of authority is reinforced is through Wopsle's reading of *George Barnwell*; a few chapters later, Wopsle may be seen regaling his fellow villagers, a little too self-delightingly, with his dramatic reading of a report of a murder; and as if to clinch the point that his antic disposition subserves rather than subverts the book's paranoid plot, it is in the course of one of his later, even more ludicrous performances that Wopsle spots the archvillain, Compeyson, sitting in the audience behind Pip.[24] That scene of recognition, ominously playing up the by-now-familiar ambiguity whereby spectators become spectacles and vice versa, makes clear what has been implicit in the novel all along: namely, that the various comic turns executed by Wopsle, as well as by numerous other characters, never really demarcate a significant oppositional stage, but stay firmly within the confines of the theater of surveillance and suspicion. As in *Hamlet*, a pre-text upon which, as Edward

24. For a discussion of the novel's male-paranoid plot and its emblematic imagery of "coming from behind," see Eve Kosofsky Sedgwick, *Between Men*, pp. 131–32. In the same book, Sedgwick offers lengthier analyses of that plot as it is rehearsed in *Our Mutual Friend* and *The Mystery of Edwin Drood*.

Said has shown, Dickens tropes elaborately in this novel,[25] the embedded entertainment functions mainly as a pretext for entrapment, thus showing itself to be trapped within a larger, oppressively male-centered scenario of competition, persecution, and revenge.

The plotter at the center of the novel's mysterious plots, Compeyson is of course punished himself when he drowns in attempting (successfully, as it turns out) to persecute Magwitch. Yet, unlike Mrs. Sparsit, who would also usurp certain authorial prerogatives, Compeyson, whom Peter Brooks calls "the novel's hidden arch-plotter,"[26] enjoys the privilege of inconspicuousness, instead of being held up drippingly as a cautionary figure of fun: even when, as in the recognition scene, Compeyson actually makes an appearance, he looks distinctly "like a ghost."[27] Though Compeyson pays for his transgressions with his life, so that Mrs. Sparsit's humiliation and dismissal appear mild in comparison, Dickens seems oddly deferential toward this potential rival. This apparent inconsistency can easily be explained in terms of "male bonding," in all the figurative and literal senses in which the book allows us to imagine that term; what is somewhat less self-evident (though, even so, not much of a secret in this frankly "pessimistic" work) is that the textual network in which Dickens pulls so many strings coincides to a remarkable degree with the criminal system over which Compeyson reigns. When Brooks argues that "the criminally deviant, transgressive plot . . . [has] priority over all the others"[28] in the novel, he points to the connection between the supposedly legitimate machinery of social control—instantiated here by the machinery of narration—and the supposedly illegitimate practices of coercion and constraint that in fact relate to the former not as parody but as paradigm. It is as

25. See Edward Said, "Criticism between Culture and System," in his *The World, the Text, and the Critic* (Cambridge: Harvard University Press, 1983), pp. 196–218. Said's staging of the scene in which Wopsle plays Hamlet makes it illustrate and comment upon certain differences between Derrida and Foucault; he seems to suggest that, while the scene activates Derridean motifs of dissemination, subversion, and so on, it also shows how novelistic framing can play at undermining textual and political authority even as it more consequentially acts out a Foucauldian will to power.

26. Peter Brooks, *Reading for the Plot: Design and Intention in Narrative* (New York: Random House, 1985), p. 133.

27. Charles Dickens, *Great Expectations*, ed. Angus Calder (Harmondsworth: Penguin, 1982), pp. 398, 399. Subsequent references to the novel will be to this edition, and will be included parenthetically in the text.

28. Brooks, *Reading for the Plot*, p. 130.

though the "world" of reformed panopticism that we encountered in *Hard Times* turned out to have modeled itself not upon the humanized Gradgrind family, but upon the "world" of Ralph Nickleby—a figure whose insidiously diffusive power and influence Dickens indeed seemed to admire a bit too much.[29]

Thus, the paranoia that Compeyson activates in Pip (it "was as if I had shut an avenue of a hundred doors to keep him out, and then had found him at my elbow," [p. 399]) gets generalized throughout the narrative, virtually structuring Pip's (and almost everyone else's) entire social experience. So widespread is this paranoia, so nearly does it attain to the status of universality, that it has the ironic effect of erasing the boundary line between the social and the psychological. Indeed, as the veritable lingua franca of this paranoid world, irony supplies paranoia with a certain cognitive credibility even as it drains paranoia of its affective coloring. When Estella speaks to Pip in her usual deflationary tone, he reacts with a pathos that would disguise the obviousness, not to say the banality, of the news she brings: "Her reverting to this tone as if our association were forced upon us and we were mere puppets, gave me pain; but everything in our intercourse did give me pain" (p. 288). What is "painful" here is how routine, how automatic, this "pain" has become. And just as that sensation or affect seems to have been emptied of its individuating potential, so the ludic reference, which might at least appear to intimate a compensatory public or collective dimension, instead conveys the very irony that flattens it out as "mere" puppetry.

Here and throughout the novel, irony, far from introducing a saving levity, has all the heaviness of the convict's leg-iron with

---

29. In a provocative discussion of *Great Expectations*, as well as of *The Woman in White* and *East Lynne*, Laurie Langbauer argues that these novels tend to identify the totalizing social system with the figure of the mother; see "Women in White, Men in Feminism," *Yale Journal of Criticism* 2 (Spring 1989): 219–43. Though I agree that characters like Molly in *Great Expectations* and Mrs. Catherick in *The Woman in White* are more important than they might at first seem, their importance strikes me as being more in the nature of missing links—hence of elements of the system—than in the nature of manipulators and emblems of the system itself. However decisive they may be in the piecing together of their books' plots, their subordinate roles in these linear patterns are not allowed to achieve synecdochic force. The function of standing for the mechanism of which one—*anyone*, no matter how powerful—is after all merely a part (even an ultimately repudiated part) is reserved almost exclusively for unsavory male characters like Compeyson and, in *The Woman in White*, Fosco.

which Orlick attacks Mrs. Joe. Describing his childhood, Pip rationalizes his paranoid projections, even as he appears to make light of them:

> I think my sister must have had some general idea that I was a young offender whom an Accoucheur Policeman had taken up (on my birthday) and delivered over to her, to be dealt with according to the outraged majesty of the law. I was always treated as if I had insisted on being born, in opposition to the dictates of reason, religion, and morality, and against the dissuading arguments of my best friends. Even when I was taken to have a new suit of clothes, the tailor had orders to make them like a kind of Reformatory, and on no account to let me have the free use of my limbs.
>
> (p. 54)

To the extent that it becomes a structural or "stylistic" feature of the narrative itself, the rhetorical technique that would seem comically to put such discipline at a distance underlies a whole *technology* of discipline, where law and order are now maintained at the level of textual self-regulation. The self-conscious obliquity that in this passage signifies facetiousness pervades the narrative, displaying a quasi-mechanical insistence, and culminating in the double bind of the novel's second, "happier" ending. That "happiness" is questionable, of course, because the irony that has been systematizing the text from the beginning now leaves its distinctive mark in the notorious undecidability of Pip's fate: not only is it impossible to know what it means that he "saw no shadow of a future parting from" Estella (p. 492), but even if we could know, it would be impossible to determine whether the result—either union or separation—were desirable or not. Instead of opening up alternatives to or within the strictures of social organization, irony—sometimes imagined, in its defensive character, as salutary, even life-giving—has become one of those strictures, the rhetorical equivalent of the Accoucheur Policeman.

Yet, if the Dickens theater thus finally appears to achieve the coherence of a totalizing system, the potentially depressing implications of that triumph may nonetheless be mitigated by a recognition of the precariousness implicit in its genealogy. As a textual machine, *Great Expectations* indeed seems more efficient than *Hard Times*, but that efficiency may well have something to do with the later novel's adoption of a first-person narrative mode, in which the author's own self-betraying power-plays—such as that which we inferred from his treatment of Mrs. Sparsit—are not so much transcended as merely camouflaged by his identification with the protagonist. More ambiguously, the efficiency of *Great Expectations* also depends, as we have seen, upon its persistent collapsing of the ludic into the panoptic. Although the result of this procedure here is the assimilation of playful or even contestatory energies, such collapsing, as Dickens's counterparts in sensation fiction show, can have unpredictable consequences.[30] While it can flatten out and thereby vitiate certain forces of possible resistance, it can also reinscribe them in a context that hence becomes all the more vulnerable to them. As we saw at the end of the previous chapter, the flatness of conventionalized theatricality may facilitate a promiscuous slippage or play of signifiers, which may in turn trace within the text a provocatively unconventional micropolitics of sexuality. Though, even in sensation fiction, collapse by no means guarantees such effects, it can certainly help to produce them, shaking up the kind of novelistic "stage" that a writer like Dickens manages ever more stringently.

It is well known that Dickens and Wilkie Collins were friends and collaborators—that, for example, Dickens acted in Collins's play, *The Frozen Deep* (1857), that Collins published in *Household Words* and *All the Year Round*, and that the stimulating example of Collins's *The Woman in White* (1860) accounts significantly for Dickens's shift, in

30. In "Women in White," Langbauer reads *Great Expectations* and the sensation novel in the light of her project of "questioning the strategy of collapse itself": 221. She concludes that, "As feminists, many of us have up to now focused on the ways that the collapse of gender can be subversive, but we need to focus too on the conservative power of such strategies": 237. Her emphasis thus falls on that conservative power—a power that, indeed, must not be disregarded and that I will take into account in the discussion below. Yet I want also to argue against a premature foreclosure of consideration of the "subversive"—I prefer to say, more modestly, "complicating"—effects of collapse. Indeed, one way to prevent such foreclosure is by resisting the temptation to think of rhetorical strategies as simply "conservative" or "subversive"; this rather stark binarism may not be able to account for some of the more noteworthy, if not the most readily identifiable, turns of a text's political performance. Another way to prevent such foreclosure is by avoiding the somewhat restrictive binarism of gender that Langbauer assumes, and that enables her to do some serious collapsing of her own, in this case collapsing of issues of sexuality into issues of masculine/feminine definition.

Great Expectations, toward tighter narrative construction. The friendship and collaboration between Dickens and Collins may be taken, moreover, as an emblem of the close connection between the Dickensian oeuvre and sensation fiction as a whole. If Dickens is the most obviously theatrical Victorian novelist, the sensation novel is the most obviously theatrical Victorian subgenre. Critics have long recognized its affinities with stage melodrama; as Patrick Brantlinger points out, "Most of the writers of sensation novels also wrote melodramas, and best sellers like *East Lynne* and *Lady Audley's Secret* were quickly dramatized." Underscoring the avowed theatricality of the form, Brantlinger cites Collins's claim that "the Novel and the Play are twin-sisters in the family of Fiction."[31]

Yet, at least in the case of Collins, the theatricality of the sensation novel is no more homogeneous or univocally joyous than the theatricality of Dickens. To tease out the family romance implicit in Collins's metaphor, and to hint at the anxiety that it so smoothly dissembles, one might recall the relationship in *The Woman in White*—the parent, as it were, of sensation novels—between Laura Fairlie and the eponymous Anne Catherick, who, though not exactly twins, are half-sisters whose uncanny resemblance to each other grounds the complex machinations of the novel's plot. Without going so far as to allegorize these half-sisters as representatives of the specific literary genres whose family ties Collins affirms, we can see that their kinship, essential as it may be to the proper functioning of the narrative, also symptomatizes a larger *im*propriety that the narrative seeks to overcome.

For, as living proof of Philip Fairlie's premarital sexual indiscretions, as an unfortunate and unwitting token of how "the sins of the fathers shall be visited upon the children,"[32] Anne Catherick is only one embodiment—and not even the most spectacular one—of a radical disorder within "the family of Fiction" that this text undertakes to treat. Like the Bertrams in *Mansfield Park*, the Fairlie family suffers from a general confusion between the "proper" and the "improper," a confusion as to what belongs inside it and what is foreign to it. And, as in Austen's novel, that confusion takes the

---

31. Brantlinger, "What Is 'Sensational'?": 4–5.
32. Wilkie Collins, *The Woman in White*, ed. Julian Symons (Harmondsworth: Penguin, 1985), p. 575. Subsequent references to the novel will be to this edition, and will be included parenthetically in the text.

literary form of too palpably intimate—too sisterly, one might say—
a relationship between "the Novel" and "the Play." The focus here
is less on Anne Catherick than on such other members of the extended family as the repellently "womanish" (p. 66) Frederick Fairlie
and the disconcertingly mannish Marian Halcombe, both of whom
attest to a blurring not only of gender roles but also—by virtue of
their hyper-self-conscious performances—of the distinction between
the novelistic (or realistic) "naturalness" ascribed to those roles and
the theatrical necessity of *playing* them in the first place. The problems exhibited by the family of *this* fiction thus point to conflicts
within Collins's supposedly happy "family of Fiction" as a whole.

Indeed, the narrative conducts a family practice in which gender-
confusion—the text's most conspicuous sign of trouble—can be cured
only through a resolution of genre-confusion. The literal promiscuity
of the father—"the spoilt darling of society" (p. 574)—has produced
more than just Anne Catherick: on a more displaced or figurative
level, it has generated a series of metaphorical promiscuities, of
confusions or collapses, which, manifesting themselves theatrically
as the transindividual spoilage associated with a certain "decadence," necessitate a particularly drastic *anti*theatrical therapy. Unlike
Mansfield Park, moreover, *The Woman in White* does not seem interested in substituting a more acceptably discreet theatricality for the
theatricality that it rejects. For the sake of its own well-being, "the
family of Fiction," *chez* Collins, may end up disowning one of its
"twins."

Yet, if *The Woman in White* is not as inclusive as Collins's theoretical pronouncement would lead us to believe, neither is it as
severely exclusive as the previous paragraphs might seem to imply.[33]
In his acute reading of the novel, D. A. Miller has shown how, even

---

33. In her chapter on the sensation novel in *A Literature of Their Own: British
Women Novelists from Brontë to Lessing* (Princeton: Princeton University Press, 1977),
pp. 153–81, Elaine Showalter differentiates between the "conventional" sensationalism
of Collins and the "subversive" sensationalism of female writers such as Braddon
and Wood. At the end of the chapter, however, she qualifies her appraisal of the
subversiveness of the female sensationalists. On the refusal of both individual sensation novels and of the subgenre in general to yield up either a univocally "subversive" or a univocally "conservative" meaning, see Elizabeth K. Helsinger, Robin
Lauterbach Sheets, and William Veeder, *The Woman Question: Society and Literature
in Britain and America, 1837–1883,* 3 vols. (New York: Garland, 1983) 3: 125–26; Jonathan
Loesberg, "The Ideology of Narrative Form in Sensation Fiction," *Representations* 13
(Winter 1986): 115–38.

as it develops an "aversion therapy" directed against aberrations of gender and sexuality, it "risks" exposing as equally aberrant the normative (i.e., patriarchal, heterosexual) Victorian family itself.[34] This ambiguity is amply embodied by Count Fosco, who, as Miller suggests, constitutes a sort of transitional object for the narrative that (barely) contains him. On the one hand, this dandiacal foreigner, with his "effeminate tastes and amusements" (p. 245) and his resemblance to "a fat St. Cecilia masquerading in male attire" (p. 250), has clear affinities with the freakishly "androgynous" members of the Fairlie household. On the other hand, Fosco's intimidatingly adroit "management" (p. 244) of his once-refractory wife—"The rod of iron with which he rules her never appears in company—it is a private rod, and is always kept upstairs" (p. 244)—typifies the "ironically" phallocratic power he will exercise over almost everyone else in the novel as well. As archvillain and arch-plotter, Fosco indeed has a supervisory, totalizing agency that, like Compeyson's in *Great Expectations,* makes him look like a figure, however sinister, for the norm-enforcing novelist himself. But where Compeyson scarcely appears at all, the "immensely fat" (p. 240) Fosco figures so prominently as virtually to (dis)figure not only the novelist but this full-figured novel itself. One might therefore argue that his greatest crime, the one for which he must die, is the flamboyance with which he theatricalizes, and thereby compromises, panoptic power—the "mountebank bravado" (p. 611) with which, all but chewing the scenery, he acts out what should have remained invisible. "The Count is a miserable spy—!" (p. 318), cries Laura, with justified, if insufficiently circumspect, indignation. More diffidently, but no less accurately, Fosco's illiterate cook, evincing the folk wisdom that gives her eyes to see what some of her betters are slower to notice, sizes up her employer as being "more like a play-actor than a gentleman" (p. 422). Taken separately, however, these charges seem self-evident to the point of innocuousness: it is only their *combination* that indicates the enormity of the Count's crime. Rather like a more skillful and more self-possessed Mrs. Sparsit, Fosco offends by mixing the quasi-authorial functions of espionage and inscription with a style marked by "loud theatrical emphasis and profuse theatrical

---

34. Miller, *The Novel and the Police,* p. 166. The point that I paraphrase is articulated here and amplified throughout the essay, pp. 146–91.

gesticulation" (p. 614), so that, as we might expect, his "mountebank bravado" has the assaultive force of "mountebank mockery" (p. 568).

When Fosco is killed off at the end of the novel, then, it is for reasons more like those that determine the fate of Mrs. Sparsit than like the relatively abstract, pious exigencies that prescribe Compeyson's death. Yet, before he can be killed, this outrageous parodist of panopticism of course has to be caught, and the way in which he is caught suggests the revenge of an outraged panopticism itself— for what is in more ways than one the scene of apprehension is set not just in a theater, but in a theater of paranoia that anticipates the similar one in *Great Expectations*. But whereas Compeyson, even as a spectacularized spectator, remains uncannily spectral, Fosco, ever the show-off, again insists upon playing the lead, this time from the audience:

> His oily murmur of approval, "Bravo! Bra-a-a-a!" hummed through the silence, like the purring of a great cat. His immediate neighbors on either side . . . seeing and hearing him, began to follow his lead. Many a burst of applause from the pit that night started from the soft, comfortable patting of the black-gloved hands. The man's voracious vanity devoured this implied tribute to his local and critical supremacy with an appearance of the highest relish.
>
> (p. 589)

More than his apparently more grievous offenses, it is Fosco's failure to limit this "vanity," I have been arguing, that requires that he now be caught, as it were, in the act. And if this scene aims to catch a falling star, what rises as a result is in some sense "the Novel" itself. Recognized by Walter Hartright—and, with the necessarily fatal consequences, by a fellow member of an Italian secret society— as a traitor to that society, Fosco implicitly relinquishes the privilege of panoptic spectatorship, which hence passes, unsurprisingly, to Hartright. But while Hartright, as critics have noticed, accordingly assumes the title of master detective—by which he is also entitled to become the book's ultimate wielder of patriarchal authority—his privileged seeing divests itself, or tries to divest itself, of its theatrical connotations. Not only must Hartright preside over the eradication of the theatricality produced by "the sins of the [previous] father": he must also eliminate the secondary, more "subjective" theatrical implication of the supervisory role itself, by revising that role in terms of his own hermeneutic command of the "long chain of circumstances" (p. 575) leading from the sinning father to the suffering child. The phallic errancy of Philip Fairlie, and the phallic threat posed by Fosco—that other, problematically transitional father figure, who reigns all the more despotically for the apparent incongruity of his "iron rod"—must be replaced by a more self-disciplined, as well as a more self-effacing, phallicism. Ending with a tableau of detheatricalized domesticity benevolently ruled by the patriarch-as-detective—concluding a project in which, as Miller shows, a number of things need to "get straight"—the novel thus interprets that new patriarch's phallic "resolution" (p. 33) as an essentially *narrative* (as opposed to a spectatorial) mastery.[35]

And yet, so intriguing a character is Fosco, and so blandly formulaic is the now-wholesome little family that survives him, that, even after the novel has done away with the villain, it cannot quite seem to let him go. (Even as censorious a contemporary critic as Margaret Oliphant admits, with perhaps unconsciously punning verve, that she "cannot understand how Hartright . . . finds it in his heart to execute justice upon so hearty, genial, and exhilarating a companion.")[36] As if bringing Fosco back by popular demand (though able to do so only by condescending to that demand as "the popular appetite for horror" [p. 642]), Collins finds it in *his* heart to provide us with one last image of that "hearty . . . companion." As Hartright is passing the morgue in Paris, he overhears a conversation about a corpse on display there, and realizes that the corpse is Fosco's. Succumbing (*à la* Fosco?) to the popular appetite that he pretends merely to name, Hartright "force[s] [him]self" (p. 643) to join the audience for his defeated adversary's final appearance: "Slowly, inch by inch, I pressed in with the crowd, moving nearer and nearer to the great glass screen that parts the dead from the living at the Morgue—nearer and nearer, till I was close behind the front row of spectators, and could look in" (p. 643).

Moreover, even though the star of the show is dead, with a knife or dagger wound "exactly over his heart" (p. 643), the subsequent

---

35. Miller, ibid., esp. pp. 164–66. For a valuable discussion of the way in which the novel images its own narrative procedures, and of the striking congruence between Fosco and Hartright as manipulators of narrative, see Walter Kendrick, "The Sensationalism of *The Woman in White*," *Nineteenth-Century Fiction* 32 (June 1977): 18–35.

36. Cited in Winifred Hughes, *The Maniac in the Cellar*, p. 143: ["Sensation Novels," *Blackwood's* 91 (May 1862): 567–68.].

spectacle proves as fascinating as any of Fosco's earlier performances: "The chattering Frenchwomen about me lifted their hands in
admiration, and cried in shrill chorus, 'Ah, what a handsome man!' "
(p. 643). Where the textualization of Mrs. Sparsit has the effect of
writing her off, the image here of Fosco as palimpsest, with the letter
T incised in his arm, "obliterat[ing] the mark of the Brotherhood"
(p. 643), intensifies, rather than diminishes, his allure. We have seen
how, in other cases besides Sparsit's, textuality would "obliterate"
theatricality; here, on the contrary, textuality ("in spite of itself")
promotes theatricality. And if that promotion gratifies nothing so
much as what Miller calls a "flushed moralism,"[37] whose inherent
instability paradoxically keeps it going (keeps it going paradoxically),
we might still take heart from the recognition that the novel's return
to the crime of the scene implicates Hartright in an almost Brontëan
voyeurism, which hardly becomes the master of the house. For when
Hartright, from his position just "behind the front row of spectators," ventriloquizes the "chattering Frenchwomen," he gets to join
them, in the best vicarious fashion, in their "shrill chorus" of "admiration." Though this nostalgic farewell to Fosco does nothing to
subvert the final domestic settlement that immediately follows it, it
points, provocatively enough, to what the chattering French might
term a *répétition* compulsion—an obsessive need to rehearse a supposedly transcended theatricality—in the very head of the family.
After all, the *Heimliche*, as Freud shows, has a tendency to turn into
the *Unheimliche*.[38] When Hartright comes back from France, he
comes back not as a star in his own right, but with some experience
as, let us say, a "chorus girl." At the end of the novel, that is, the
banished "twin-sister" "herself" may come back as the newly installed father.

My invocation here of certain Brontëan motifs—voyeurism, cross-
dressing, francophobia—might serve as a transition from *The Woman
in White* to Collins's next novel, *No Name* (1862). What is most recognizably "Brontëan" in the latter, however, is its heavily thematized opposition between the governess and the actress: while the
portentously named Magdalen Vanstone illustrates the evils of fe-

37. Miller, *The Novel and the Police*, p. 188.
38. See Sigmund Freud, "The 'Uncanny,' " in *The Standard Edition of the Complete
Psychological Works of Sigmund Freud*, 24 vols., trans. James Strachey (London: Ho-
garth, 1953–74), vol. 17.

male theatricality, her sister Norah, who submits to the degradations of the governess's lot, demonstrates the virtues and surprising rewards of female pedagogy. Unlike *The Woman in White*, then, *No Name* authorizes a correlation between the sisters it portrays and the "sisters" of Collins's more general, and more generic, family romance. Yet, at the same time that it would seem to punish the theatrical sister and to celebrate the "novelistic" one, it also distinguishes itself from its predecessor by assuming an *explicitly* theatrical form: as if to facilitate the stage adaptation for which it was in fact destined, *No Name* presents itself as a sequence of eight "Scenes," with epistolary exchanges and other documentary material positioned "Between the Scenes."

This overt contradiction between form and content exemplifies the "indeterminacy" that critics have discovered in sensation fiction as a whole. Not only does the novel's form appear to do the opposite of what its content appears to say, it is hard to know just what that apparent contradiction in itself does. On the one hand, this "self-deconstruction" might be seen, from the perspective of an increasingly familiar paranoia, as effecting not a relaxation but a refinement of discipline: the palpable "collapse" of theatricality into the very system of the narrative would serve both as evidence of, and as a graphic warning against, the potential pervasiveness of the theatrical threat. But by advertising that threat, the novel would also neutralize it: far from undermining the practices that the novel defends as those of "home-control,"[39] the calculated collapse of the stage into the novel would represent a positive *domestication* of theatricality.

On the other hand, such is the grammatical shiftiness of "home-control" that we may have reason to doubt its absolute finality. If only because Magdalen's identity as a "born actress" (p. 38) is signaled initially in a context of private theatricals, her ostensibly reassuring end, in which she acquiesces in her containment, would seem perversely to replicate her ominous beginning: it is not entirely clear whether the home will control her theatricality, or whether her theatricality will control the home. No more than in *The Woman in White*, to be sure, do these intimations of narrative circularity auto-

---

39. Wilkie Collins, *No Name*, ed. Virginia Blain (Oxford: Oxford University Press, 1986), p. 129. Subsequent references to the novel will be to this edition, and will be included parenthetically in the text.

matically ensure anything as spectacular as "subversion." For while
going in circles may be one way of balking the phallic imperative
of linearity, the figure thus inscribed also suggests a geometry of
closure: circularity squares all too easily with circumscription.

By the same token, the repetition that marks this narrative can
signify both a quasi-theatrical compulsion—sly or unwitting testimony to Magdalen's appeal—and a way of binding Magdalen's theatrical energy, of bringing her into line. In the course of the novel,
this performing heroine, seeking to regain her late father's fortune,
attempts not one but two elaborate projects of impersonation, both
of which fail—and one senses in Collins a certain sadism here—on
the verge of success. First, Magdalen (ab)uses her histrionic abilities
to trick the heir into marrying her; then, when her plan to inherit
his money is foiled, she assumes the role of a servant in order to
discover the Secret Trust, on which some chance of inheritance still
depends. Victory is snatched from her yet again, and by the time
Norah—who has finally married the new heir and thus "legitimately" recovered their father's fortune—presents her sister with
the Secret Trust, a reformed (i.e., exhausted) Magdalen can only tear
it up.

What compels Collins—Magdalen's ultimate adversary here—to
repeat the frustration of her scenarios may be his own need to display the lengths to which he will go in order to exercise his will to
power. Yet, as we have seen, display itself is a risky business. Indeed,
in his punitive relation to Magdalen, Collins oddly resembles Magdalen's most formidable rival *in* the text, the equally scheming (and
equally theatrical) housekeeper, Mrs. Lecount, who occasionally
"overact[s]" (p. 207) her part, and whose "cunning" thus ends up
"overreach[ing] itself" (p. 441). Flexing his authorial muscle a bit
more rashly than does, say, the Dickens of *Hard Times*, Collins not
only exposes himself to the danger of being compared with his
novel's equivalent of Mrs. Sparsit, but also inadvertently underscores his instructive affinity with the Brontë of *Villette*.

Critics have noticed a continuity between Brontë's novels and
sensation fiction, but that continuity has less to do with a shared
interest in madwomen and she-devils than with a tendency, discernible even in the "patriarchal" Collins, to "overreach" binarisms
of subversion and containment by inserting within them traces of
a less neatly symmetrical overdetermination or "overacting." At one

point in *No Name*, Magdalen's wily male co-conspirator observes of her, with as much dismay as admiration, that "She is capable of going a long way beyond the limit of dressing herself like a man, and imitating a man's voice and manner" (p. 186). Conversely, Collins's resemblance to Mrs. Lecount indicates his own capacity for female impersonation, or better—since Lecount is herself a francophone reinscription of the Count (who, also something of an "over-actor," is already impressively bilingual)—for figuring a variety of simultaneous cultural, sexual, and generic boundary-confusions that, without denoting "transcendence," point in their own right "beyond the limit" of simplifying polarities.[40] Instead of enforcing unambiguous "home-control," the novelist-as-(foreign)-house-keeper might keep the house strange, might keep domesticity from coinciding with itself.

This sort of authorial figuration by no means *erases* differences of, for instance, gender. But it should make it harder to follow Elaine Showalter in bracketing Collins as a "conventional" sensationalist while identifying his female colleagues as "subversive" sensation-alists.[41] Beginning with Austen, we have seen how, in the nine-teenth-century novel, theatricality, though highly politicized, is often at odds with or in excess of any given author's apparent po-litical intentions. One of the reasons for attending to theatrical effects in nineteenth-century texts is that they challenge the ideological assurances both of those texts themselves and of the critical pro-cedures that would situate them. And one advantage of such an approach is that, far from discovering a layer of signification that somehow lies "beyond" ideology, it can locate fault lines or pressure points *within* ideology. Thus, if our discussion of theatricality in Collins suggests the micropolitical complications of "conservative,"

---

40. In *Woman and the Demon: The Life of a Victorian Myth* (Cambridge: Harvard University Press, 1982), pp. 205–06, Nina Auerbach makes a related point when she claims that, in *No Name* and *The New Magdalen* (1873), Collins "celebrated the public woman with ambivalent intensity." It should be clear that I find Collins less cele-bratory than does Auerbach, and that I view his "ambivalence" as largely an effect of unwitting implication rather than conscious identification. Auerbach invests heavily in a "transcendent" theory of female theatricality: "Predicated on a belief in the transcendent truth of the public, performing woman, the novels can only fade away into unease once they reduce her to sincerity." Though I might endorse the latter part of this eloquent observation, I do not see how *No Name*, at any rate, is predicated on the belief that Auerbach claims for it.

41. See note 33 to this chapter.

male sensationalism, a brief look at a novel like Mrs. Henry Wood's *East Lynne* (1861) might offer an example of the interesting local vicissitudes that too sweeping a vision of "subversive" female sensationalism tends to elide.

For while the dominant, diachronic pattern of the novel's *narrative* in fact suggests its author's ultimate complicity in the Victorian project of "home-control"—where the home is, emphatically, the subject of control—some of the novel's synchronic elements hint at possible difficulties not only in assigning and securing "control" but also in knowing just where the boundaries of "the home" are to be drawn, and what its contents are supposed to be. Indeed, the agitating question that traverses *East Lynne* is that of the proper "discipline of [the] house."[42] When the bored Isabel Vane abandons her husband and children for an adulterous liaison, she melodramatizes the crisis of domesticity and the concomitant disturbance of gender relations that are at issue everywhere in the text. Yet what makes the question of domestic discipline most agitating here—and what must have accounted in large part for the phenomenal success of the stage version of this novel—is the subsequent movement of the plot, in which a disfigured and repentant Isabel, assumed to be dead, returns to her children and her (remarried) husband, but disguised as a governess, Madame Vine. That is to say, the wife and mother returns not only as a governess, but as an actress as well. "She had her *rôle* to play" (p. 340), the narrator reminds us in a characteristic moment of mingled vicariousness and *Schadenfreude*. But where the role of Jane Eyre—speaking of vicariousness and *Schadenfreude*—is to provide a psychologizing or detheatricalizing screen for the other members of the household, the performance of Wood's governess-actress would seem to have the opposite effect. As though her condition were contagious, the presence in her former home of the bicultural Madame Vine—"English by birth, but the widow of a Frenchman" (p. 334)—disfigures and estranges from itself that entire domestic space, turning it into one big stage set, on which the discipline Isabel Vane once neglected now gets played out as both tragedy *and* farce.

42. Mrs. Henry Wood, *East Lynne*, ed. Sally Mitchell (New Brunswick: Rutgers University Press, 1984), p. 341. Subsequent references to the novel will be to this edition, and will be included parenthetically in the text.

The best way of illustrating that point would be to examine the protracted scene at the deathbed of Isabel's young son; rather than offer an excruciating reenactment of that scene at the level of analysis, however, I would merely broach such an analysis by suggesting that one must have a heart of stone not to laugh at the death of little William. Although the narrator herself is more than willing to interpret this event, and everything else that happens to Isabel after her disguised homecoming, as just retribution for her sins against patriarchy, what this Christian moralism itself disguises is the considerable gratification afforded by the disgraced and "disgraceful" mother's return-with-a-difference. As one critic rather patronizingly puts it, "For a good third of the novel, Mrs. Wood indulges her heroine (and readers) in a prolonged, luxurious orgy of self-torture, as the miserable governess, in going about her humble duties, must watch the repeated caresses of her former husband showered upon his second wife, the hated Barbara Hare."[43] Contemporary readers who were themselves wives and mothers may have enjoyed in the final third of the novel the opportunity not only for masochistic identification, but also for seeing their appointed station, the pseudo-empowering "center" of the home, as and from its spectatorial margin, where marginality—as a locus of both criticism and fantasy—can mean more than just subservience.

In any case, while the narrative as a whole seems to push teleologically toward a domestication of theatricality, a passage such as the following, in which Isabel first sees her old home through the eyes of "Madame Vine," may allow us to glimpse the ambiguity of that disciplinary strategy:

> On she followed, her heart palpitating: past the rooms that used to be hers, along the corridor, towards the second staircase. The doors of her old bed and dressing-rooms stood open, and she glanced in with a yearning look. No, never more, never more could they be hers: she had put them from her by her own free act and deed. Not less comfortable did they look now, than in former days: but they had passed into another's occupancy. The fire threw its blaze on the furniture: there were the little ornaments on the large dressing table, as they used to be in *her* time, and the cut glass of the crystal essence bottles was glittering in the fire-light. On the sofa lay a shawl and a book, and on the bed a silk dress, as if thrown there after being taken

43. Hughes, *The Maniac in the Cellar*, p. 115.

off. No: these rooms were not for her now: and she followed Joyce
up the other staircase.

(p. 336)

The propagandistic function of such doting verbal photography is
obviously to captivate the potentially restive female reader; like the
proverbial page out of *House Beautiful*, this passage takes pains to
glamorize a domesticity that, as even the narrator admits, is all too
apt to appear tiresome. Yet the pain that it takes (as well as inflicts)
may produce a pleasure not entirely reducible to the *frissons* of commodity fetishism. For if the narrative can reinforce "home-control"
only by casting the home itself in an enthrallingly theatrical light,
the spectacle thus staged may be compromising in more ways than
one. To reframe the home as a desirable site, glittering with crystal
and silk, is to make it all the more intelligible (and all the more
vulnerable) as a site of desire. (If, coupling *mise en scène* with *mise
en abîme*, we imagine the book on the sofa to be a sensation novel,
the instability of the relationship between frame and picture becomes particularly evocative.) To the extent that it involves a theatricalization of domesticity, the domestication of theatricality has the
potential to get out of hand.

Although the inexorable logic of the larger narrative requires that
Isabel die in the end, the *sub*plot revolving around the far more
brashly and incorrigibly libidinous Afy Hallijohn intimates a comic
and even irreverently "feminist" *counter*plot. Admittedly, the greater
license granted to Afy has something to do with her lower-class (as
interpreted here, relatively inconsequential) status. But when she
says of her future husband, "I'm sure he'd let me turn the house
into a theatre, if I liked" (p. 447), she speaks a female desire that is
not necessarily class-bound, and that may resist being bound by
even the most accommodating or self-beautifying of domestic ideologies.

It is by now a common critical practice, especially in discussions
of narrative, to celebrate the ways in which the part impishly escapes
the manifest intention of the whole. Though my own emphasis here
has fallen on the tensions between global designs and local figurations or disfigurations, I want to insist again that I do not see these
tensions as inherently subversive. Nor, however, do I see them as
being automatically neutralized. My point, rather, is that, even as
they energize ideology by supplying it with its necessary "drama,"

they may cause unpredictable and often inconvenient changes in the script; precisely insofar as they provide suspense, they can also hold up the operation they are supposed merely to support. In keeping with my impulse to slow down the totalizing gestures of both the "paranoid" school and the avowedly *de*totalizing, "carnivalesque" criticism against which it defines itself, I wish to conclude this chapter by suggesting a particular genealogy of the concern I share with suspicious critics and their more fun-loving colleagues alike. I want to propose, that is, that sensationalism itself already offers the lineaments of a rather sophisticated discourse about the politics of literary parts and wholes, a discourse presented in terms of the relationship between narrative trajectories and the theatrical counterforces that threaten to interrupt them.

Some sense of this genealogy has been implicit, I hope, in my comments on the novels of Collins and Wood. I would like now to turn to what is perhaps the most theoretically articulate of sensation novels, Mary Elizabeth Braddon's *Lady Audley's Secret* (1862). Written by a former actress, *Lady Audley's Secret*, like *East Lynne*, was as extraordinarily successful in its stage adaptations as in its original novelistic form. Yet it should come as no surprise that this distinctly theatrical novel does not obviously embrace theatricality as a thematic value. The novel in fact demonizes a theatricality conceived as essentially female—embodying it in the villainous Lady Audley—and idealizes a narrative conceived as essentially male—associating it with the heroic efforts of the detective-like Robert Audley. Uncannily anticipating the political unconscious of mainstream cinema as explained by a feminist film theorist like Laura Mulvey, *Lady Audley's Secret* not only posits a "split between [female] spectacle and [male] narrative,"[44] but also represents the former as a quasi-castratory threat that has to be mastered by the latter. "Good heavens!" Robert declares, "what an actress this woman is. What an arch trickster—what an all-accomplished deceiver. But she shall play her pretty comedy no longer under my uncle's roof" (p. 219).

The novel tells a story, then, in which storytelling itself—the resolutely rational process of putting a "chain" together, "link by

44. Laura Mulvey, "Visual Pleasure and Narrative Cinema," in *Women and the Cinema: A Critical Anthology,* ed. Karyn Kay and Gerald Peary (New York: Dutton, 1977), p. 420.

link"[45]—scores a virile victory over a woman whose "hellish power of dissimulation" (p. 235) merely magnifies the tendency of *all* women to "go[. . .] through [life] as if it were a pageant or a procession" (p. 177). Tellingly, however, the image of the procession, with its linear implications, suggests both the precariousness of the governing oppositions here and the reasons why they have to be set up in the first place. Lady Audley is threatening, first of all, not so much because she stands outside of narrative altogether as because she would cross Robert Audley's narrative line with "plot[s]" and "scheme[s]" (p. 331) of her own. By the same token, the numerous references to her as a kind of pre-Raphaelite Medusa make clear that she represents not femaleness itself, but rather the confusion of stereotypically female traits (beauty, childishness, etc.) with a certain phallic aggressivity. Emblematizing the collapse of both sexual and generic polarities, Lady Audley thus takes her place alongside all those other hybrid figures whom sensationalism loves to hate. But if the novel contains her no less ambivalently than *The Woman in White, No Name,* and *East Lynne* house *their* respective monsters, it spells out with unusual acuity the stakes of such apparently defensive projects.

For it shows that what sensationalism appears to defend—by repeatedly producing—is the fiction (in both senses of the word) of the normative male subject. Lady Audley has usurped certain male privileges, as well as their signifiers, but far more troubling is the possibility she thereby raises—the possibility of an inverted male counterpart. The text takes this possibility seriously enough, albeit in a semi-comic way. At the beginning of the novel, Robert Audley, while not obviously feminized, exhibits an unmanly "indolen[ce]" (p. 52) and a mildly endearing but also mildly disquieting indifference to the importunities of heterosexuality. The protagonist's sexual "confusion," moreover, has as its characteristic literary manifestation an equally endearing and equally disquieting fondness for "reading French novels" (p. 27). Given the francophobia (or francophilia, which often comes to the same thing) that we have noticed in all of the other sensation novels, we can understand why the

45. Mary Elizabeth Braddon, *Lady Audley's Secret* (Harmondsworth: Penguin, 1987), p. 133. Subsequent references to the novel will be to this edition, and will be included parenthetically in the text.

crossing of this particular nationality with this particular genre might already suggest a small scandal in its own right. And to make that scandal complete, Robert fails to maintain any sort of hierarchy among his entertainments—to differentiate, for example, between a "new burlesque" (p. 339) he might attend and a novel he might read the same evening, even though it may only be a novel by Paul de Kock.

Thus, Robert Audley, like Walter Hartright before him, needs to be virilized, made more cocksure,[46] not just in the course of the narrative but, as it were, by virtue of narrative—and not just by assuming the plot-(re)constructing function of the detective but by virtually introjecting the mythic imagery of detective work itself: pursuing Lady Audley, Robert begins to demonstrate "a cold sternness that was so strange to him as to transform him into another creature—a pitiless embodiment of justice, a cruel instrument of retribution" (p. 232); he has come to "embody," that is—instead of merely using—the "links of steel in the wonderful chain forged by the science of the detective officer" (p. 104). And just as Audley, like Hartright, gets straightened out through this identification with his work, so the novel itself seems to sever both its French connection and its ties to theatricality, realigning itself with *narrativity*, a force that appears more conducive to the domestic order toward which *Lady Audley's Secret*, like *The Woman in White* (not to mention *No Name* and *East Lynne*), is teleologically—and, as Miller suggests, suicidally—aimed.[47]

And yet, having all but confirmed this normalization-through-narrative, Braddon engages in some curious last-minute equivocation. Although Lady Audley has been locked away in a Belgian *maison de santé*, a certain foreignness returns to the text in the form of Robert's fantasy of being haunted by the ghost of his friend George Talboys, whom he thinks (erroneously, we soon learn) Lady Audley has murdered:

"I haven't read Alexandre Dumas and Wilkie Collins for nothing," he muttered. "I'm up to their tricks, sneaking in at doors behind a

---

46. I borrow this pun from Terry Eagleton, *Literary Theory: An Introduction* (Minneapolis: University of Minnesota Press, 1983), p. 189. He offers "cocksure" as a translation of "phallogocentric."

47. Miller, *The Novel and the Police*, discusses the sensation novel's "wish to abolish itself" (pp. 165–66).

fellow's back, and flattening their white faces against window panes, and making themselves all eyes in the twilight. It's a strange thing that your generous-hearted fellow, who never did a shabby thing in his life, is capable of any meanness the moment he becomes a ghost."

(p. 340)

Coming just one page after Robert's profession of incredulous distance from his earlier, immature habits of novel-reading and/as theatergoing, this promiscuous coupling of Dumas and, of all English precursors, *Collins* would seem to risk bending the novel's laboriously straightened-out narrative line back into a circle.[48] That Dumas, like Collins, was a playwright as well as a novelist compounds our sense that the polarity (another straightening-out) of domestic sensationalism, on the one hand, and a "strange," more affirmatively theatrical fiction, on the other, has collapsed—or has *been* collapsed—on the verge of its triumphant consolidation. One might dismiss this passage, of course, as indicating one last anxiety that Robert must overcome on his way to normality; and indeed, he does overcome it, insofar as George, who turns out not to have been murdered at all, reappears at the end of the text in a reassuringly frontal way, "with his back to the window" (p. 373), rather than, as Robert's paranoid scenario would have it, "behind a fellow's back." Or, more ingeniously, one might exploit the grammatical ambiguity that makes Dumas and Collins look like ghosts themselves, and ascribe the paranoia of this passage to *the author*, reading the anxiety here as an anxiety of influence, whereby Braddon at once fantasmatically solicits an attack from Collins and, in linking him with the French (i.e., inferior) Dumas, gets him off her back.

Yet, while the anxiety of influence is not an exclusively male phenomenon, and while compelling cases have recently been made for the existence of a specifically female paranoia,[49] the more ingenious explanation, like the more "realistic" one, might rather ex-

48. Braddon thus seems incidentally to validate the otherwise unconvincing assertion, made by an anonymous contemporary reviewer of *No Name*, that "the sensation school, of whom Mr. Collins is by far the ablest representative . . . is a plant of foreign growth. It comes to us from France, and it can only be imported in a mutilated condition." See *Wilkie Collins: The Critical Heritage*, ed. Norman Page (London: Routledge & Kegan Paul, 1974), p. 134. Brantlinger, "What Is 'Sensational'?": 6–7, cites this review in relation to Braddon's characterization of Robert Audley's preferences as a reader.

49. See, for example, Naomi Schor, "Female Paranoia: The Case for Psychoanalytic Feminist Criticism," *Yale French Studies* 62 (1981): 204–19, and Mary Ann Doane, *The Desire to Desire: The Woman's Film in the 1940s* (Bloomington: Indiana University Press, 1987), esp. pp. 123–54.

plain *away* what is most interesting in the passage. For what both explanations elide is the overdetermination of the miniature narrative(s) that it inscribes. The "story" that Robert conjures up is in fact the "double" (p. 339) of an earlier one—"a morbid, hideous, yet entrancing story, which had once pleasantly congealed his blood" (p. 339). As a late, condensed rehearsal of the thrills that sensationalism cultivates only to "resolve," this passage may nonetheless signal the *pleasures* of the temporal doubling that is repetition itself—pleasures, moreover, that may attend paranoia without routinely being subsumed by it.[50]

At this point in the narrative, for example, Robert, one might think, should have "outgrown" the desires that such "morbid" recollections would seem to activate. Similarly, whatever anxiety Braddon may be managing here, with respect either to Collins or to her "responsibilities" as a novelist, may not entirely absorb her own pleasure in implicating both herself and sensationalism as a whole in the cultural and generic contexts that they appear to have put behind themselves. In Braddon's hands, the repetition and collapse, and the repetition *of* collapse, in which sensationalism specializes may become more than just the objects of a theory of the novel—a theory, that is, directed against them. Instead, these sensationalistic motifs may become the *means* of a discourse that, no longer necessarily wishing, as Miller says, "to abolish itself,"[51] dramatizes intimate relations not only between the novel and theatricality, but also between theatricality and theory. Braddon's novel exemplifies the way in which sensation fiction, relegated even now to the outskirts of the canon, adumbrates a commentary on the politics of more "serious" nineteenth-century novels. Articulating with considerable subtlety the terms of its resistance to, and covert restitution of, theatricality, the sensation novel indeed pulls nineteenth-century English fiction toward a kind of border or limit—a limit that George Eliot, for example, will confront, by turning against sensationalism and a sensationalized culture.

50. I agree with Langbauer, "Women in White," that "paranoia can be consoling as well as salutary, providing a structure that identifies those defined as male subjects with ultimate authority": 221. But I differ from her in that I find the paranoia of sensationalism (and of such a critic of sensationalism as Miller) less hegemonic and less easily legible in its performative effects than she does.

51. Miller, *The Novel and the Police*, p. 165.

5

Poetry and Theatricality in
Daniel Deronda

My Dear Lewes

I had to go out of Town this morning and have only time to write a line before post hour to say that I read Book Six [of *Daniel Deronda*] last night and have unbounded congratulations to send to Mrs. Lewes. She is *A Magician*. It is a Poem, a Drama, and a Grand Novel.

John Blackwood

Theodora. . . . As for the Jewish element in *Daniel Deronda*, I think it a very fine idea; it's a noble subject. Wilkie Collins and Miss Braddon would not have thought of it, but that does not condemn it. It shows a large conception of what one may do in a novel.

Henry James, "*Daniel Deronda*: A Conversation"

Until *Daniel Deronda* (1876), explicit theatrical themes and images appear rarely and fleetingly in George Eliot's novels.[1] For this reason, however, one senses a powerful pressure of authorial and textual self-reflection whenever one of the earlier novels does engage the issue of theatricality. One such moment occurs in *Middlemarch* (1872), and, although it was Eliot's "rule not to read contemporary fiction," the theatricality that it represents bears a strange resemblance to the extremism and the excess of the sensation novel.[2] At the end of

---

1. John Blackwood's letter is quoted in Gordon S. Haight, ed., *The George Eliot Letters*, 9 vols., (New Haven: Yale University Press, 1954–78), 6:227. Henry James's comment is reprinted in Haight, ed., *A Century of George Eliot Criticism* (Boston: Houghton Mifflin, 1965), p. 102; also reprinted as an appendix to F. R. Leavis, *The Great Tradition* (Harmondsworth: Penguin, 1972), p. 291.

2. Haight, ed., *Letters* 6:418. In *A Literature of Their Own: British Women Novelists from Brontë to Lessing* (Princeton: Princeton University Press, 1977), Elaine Showalter, pointing out Braddon's influence on Eliot, refers to Madame Laure as "a character right out of sensation fiction" (p. 171).

Chapter 15, which offers an account of Lydgate's psychology, the narrator explains Lydgate's "strictly scientific view of woman"[3] as a reaction against his infatuation, while a student in Paris, with an actress named Madame Laure, who was playing the part of woman who stabs her lover. After she has in fact stabbed and killed her husband (who played the lover) on stage, Laure explains the circumstances to Lydgate: "My foot really slipped." But when he hastens to agree that "it was a fatal accident," he is shocked to hear her say, "I did not plan: it came to me in the play—*I meant to do it.*"[4]

The force of this brief flashback comes from its suggestion that Laure's foot is not the only thing capable of slipping.[5] Her grammar, for example, wavers oddly between activity and passivity ("I did not plan," "it came to me," "I meant to"), while one wonders what logic—other than that of temporal distance—grounds the distinction between planning to do something and meaning to do it. The self-incriminating nature of her remarks notwithstanding, these very instabilities in fact contribute to Laure's acquittal: precisely because her husband's death occurs *on stage*—that is, in the essentially irresponsible, paradox-ridden world of "fiction," where unwilled volitions and unplanned meanings are virtually the order of the day—it can be deemed "accidental."[6] Ultimately, Laure owes her alibi to the general slippage whereby the fictional frame of her performance becomes indistinguishable from the reality of her (more precisely, her husband's) execution. We could characterize this slippage as that between art and reality, between the "act" and the fact of murder. And that dedifferentiation finally affects Lydgate, who, in this uncharacteristic but character-forming episode, slides from his "scientific" position as male spectator, to be taken in, as it were, by what Jacqueline Rose calls "the spectacle of the woman."[7]

3. George Eliot, *Middlemarch*, ed. W. J. Harvey (Harmondsworth: Penguin, 1981), p. 183.

4. Ibid., p. 182.

5. For a discussion that relates the instabilities staged in this scene to the nineteenth-century discourse on "monomania," see Simon During, "The Strange Case of Monomania: Patriarchy in Literature, Murder in *Middlemarch*, Drowning in *Daniel Deronda*," *Representations* 23 (Summer 1988): 92–93.

6. *Middlemarch*, p. 181.

7. Jacqueline Rose, "George Eliot and the Spectacle of the Woman," in Rose, *Sexuality in the Field of Vision* (London: Verso, 1986), pp. 105–22. Rose offers a deft analysis of this episode, as well as of related issues in *Daniel Deronda*. Like During and others, she develops the connection between Laure and Gwendolen.

Moreover, although *Middlemarch*, like *Jane Eyre*, attempts to get beyond its (equally French) theatrical prehistory, the potent confusions broached in this episode themselves slide, as it were, to a point near the end of the novel, in a passage whose theatricality, more typically of Eliot's pre-*Deronda* fiction, is implicit rather than explicit.[8] As an odd anticipation of *Deronda*, and as a clue to what is at stake in Eliot's shift toward a more open and sustained engagement of theatrical issues, the passage is worth quoting. Lydgate again has a starring role, and once again he breaks character: this time, with his male mastery compromised both by financial trouble and by Rosamond's recalcitrance, he goes to the infamous billiard-room, and, despite his aversion to gambling, loses himself, as Fred Vincy watches, in what the narrative evocatively calls "play":

> The last thing likely to have entered Fred's expectation was that he should see his brother-in-law Lydgate—of whom he had never quite dropped the old opinion that he was a prig, and tremendously conscious of his superiority—looking excited and betting, just as he himself might have done. Fred felt a shock greater than he could quite account for by the vague knowledge that Lydgate was in debt, and that his father had refused to help him; and his own inclination to enter into the play was suddenly checked. It was a strange reversal of attitudes: Fred's blond face and blue eyes, usually bright and careless, ready to give attention to anything that held out a promise of amusement, looking involuntarily grave and almost embarrassed as if by the sight of something unfitting: while Lydgate, who had habitually an air of self-possessed strength, and a certain meditativeness that seemed to lie behind his most observant attention, was acting, watching, speaking with that excited narrow consciousness which reminds one of an animal with fierce eyes and retractile claws.[9]

Just as Laure's slip of the foot intimated other, farther-reaching "accidents," so the "strange reversal of attitudes" here points to even more unsettling irregularities. If Laure's transgressiveness threatened Lydgate's status as objective spectator, implicating him in her equivocality, here, much later in the novel, Lydgate is "really" making a spectacle of himself, as Henleigh Grandcourt might say. Where the earlier scene hinted at a chiastic exchange of the "atti-

8. In *The Madwoman in the Attic: The Woman Writer and the Nineteenth-Century Literary Imagination* (New Haven: Yale University Press, 1979), p. 500, Sandra M. Gilbert and Susan Gubar make the comparison between the story of Laure in *Middlemarch* and the story of Céline in *Jane Eyre*.

9. *Middlemarch*, p. 724.

tudes" of male power and female vulnerability, the later scene compounds the ambiguity by figuring the biologically minded and proudly "superior" Lydgate not only as an animal and hence as *inferior*—Lydgate himself thinks of women as animals, and this association has a venerable pedigree in Eliot's novels[10]—but as an animal whose "fierce eyes and retractile claws" recall the violence performed by the homicidal actress. Like Laure and her less lucky English counterpart, Lady Audley, or—on a less obviously sensationalized plane—like Vashti and her prototype, Rachel Félix, whom George Henry Lewes called "the panther of the stage,"[11] Lydgate is simultaneously scary and pitiable. The passage thus illustrates a tendency of Victorian novels to make spectacularization and feminization virtually synonymous, and to invest both with the apparently contradictory attributes of danger and weakness.

And again like the earlier scene, this one, bizarrely featuring the man of science as a belated revamping of the murderous actress, combines sexual ambiguity with rhetorical or formal ambiguity: just as Lydgate occupies both male and female positions here, so the rather "excited" language that describes his inhabitual way of "acting, watching, [and] speaking" calls attention to it *as* acting, and to its narrative context as both represented reality and staged scene. The novel's realism almost threatens here to turn into the more obviously stylized and alienating mode of melodrama. At the same time, however, the passage gives us reason to believe that this sensationalizing may not be so easily contained. In keeping with a familiar pattern, the spectacle spreads out to include its spectators: although Fred Vincy's "inclination to enter into the play [is] suddenly checked," the rest of the passage suggests that he may already have been entered into *a* play—inserted within a frame—that supersedes individual inclinations and disinclinations. However welcome the check on Fred's bad habit, his sudden positioning as surrogate reader ironically reveals in him—or reveals him in—another, subtler kind of involuntarity: if Fred "look[s] involuntarily grave and almost em-

10. See, for example, Eliot's comparison of Laure to an "untamed ruminating animal" (p. 182), or Lydgate's view of Rosamond as an "animal of another and feebler species" (p. 719). Another Eliot novel replete with women-as-animals metaphors is *The Mill on the Floss*.

11. George Henry Lewes, *On Actors and the Art of Acting* (Westport, Ct.: Greenwood, 1968), p. 31.

barrassed as if by the sight of something unfitting," his uneasiness may stem from a sense that, like his brother-in-law Lydgate, he can all too easily be made to fit inside whatever it is that does not itself fit a realistic narrative. It is as though even the least astute characters in the novel somehow suspected that, just outside the represented world they inhabit, "Destiny"—whom Nina Auerbach celebrates as an "awesome stage-managing divinity"[12]—"stands by sarcastic with [their] *dramatis personae* folded in her hand," ready to impose the archness of a proscenium that would underscore their status as fictional creations rather than real people.[13]

Eliot's representation of Destiny as both female and sarcastic— that is, as embodying at once a specific kind of person and a specific use of language—serves to reinforce the point that, for all the rapid and startling combinations in these passages, they seem to require that their reader approach them with two distinct sets of analytic terms: while part of what is going on here is about sex and gender— about the sorts of concerns that might be denominated as "feminist" or more broadly as "historicist"—another, equally conspicuous part has to do with questions of rhetoric and epistemology—about the definitive preoccupations of a criticism often dubbed poststructuralist. Of course, at this stage of our inquiry, it should hardly seem surprising that one might have to use these two frames of reference concurrently. Indeed, one of the premises of this book is that, in both nineteenth-century novels and late-twentieth-century literary criticism, problems of textuality and écriture have an intimate and crucial relation to problems of social self-fashioning. What is new in *Daniel Deronda*—though already adumbrated in the passages from *Middlemarch* that we have been considering—and what makes Eliot's final novel especially pertinent in view of the polarizing tendencies of much contemporary criticism, is that it thematizes this relation not only insistently and sophisticatedly, but also in adversarial or even invidious terms.

As we saw in the previous chapter, a sensation novel like *Lady Audley's Secret*, in repeatedly staging the breakdown of the opposition between the realistic norm and the spectacular deviation, in-

12. Nina Auerbach, "Secret Performances: George Eliot and the Art of Acting," in Auerbach, *Romantic Imprisonment: Women and Other Glorified Outcasts* (New York: Columbia University Press, 1985), p. 264.
13. *Middlemarch*, p. 122.

scribes a rather sophisticated *theory* of the novel. Eliot may not have read much contemporary fiction, but the presence of sensational motifs in her novels, combined with her own high-powered theorizing, suggests an intertextual relationship of some importance. In *George Eliot and Blackmail,* Alexander Welsh has demonstrated some remarkable thematic affinities between Eliot's novels after *The Mill on the Floss* and the sensation fiction to which she might seem serenely indifferent.[14] I want to argue that, in addition to sharing the sensationalists' preoccupation with the control of information in an increasingly urbanized and increasingly anxious culture, Eliot is anxiously engaged in her own systematic misreading of sensationalism. If only as represented to her through Lewes's literary criticism, sensationalism may have posed something of a threat, a threat that condescending dismissals could not quite deflect.[15] Eliot's more coherent response, I would suggest, is to superimpose upon sensationalism the very "metalanguage" she has in fact elicited from it. If she cannot escape from sensationalism, at least she can try to regulate it. Containing within their lurid, ostensibly precritical narratives the lineaments of a theoretical discourse about the novel and its theatrical other, novels like *The Woman in White* and *Lady Audley's Secret* remind us that "theatricality," as its etymology reveals, signifies precisely the mutual implication of the theoretical and the spectacular. The effect of Eliot's intervention, however, is that, rudimentarily in *Middlemarch* and elaborately in *Daniel Deronda,* the theoretical discourse and the still-sensational narratives upon which it now appears to have been mapped, as if from outside, seem not mutually implied but antithetical or antagonistic. James's Theodora is thus in a certain sense responding on cue when she says of the "Jewish element in *Deronda*" that it is a "noble subject," and that "Wilkie Collins and Miss Braddon would not have thought of it."

Because this effect has been insufficiently acknowledged, the apparent competition between theory and sensationalism repeats itself across the more-than-a-century's distance since *Daniel Deronda* was published, in some of the most perceptive and influential readings

---

14. Alexander Welsh, *George Eliot and Blackmail* (Cambridge: Harvard University Press, 1985).

15. See, for example, Lewes's "Farewell Causerie," *Fortnightly* (December 1, 1866): "Sensation novels of course depend on 'exciting' situations, and breathless rapidity of movement; whether the movement be absurd or not matters little, the essential thing is to keep moving" (894).

of the novel. Cynthia Chase's "The Decomposition of the Elephants: Double-Reading *Daniel Deronda*," and Catherine Gallagher's "George Eliot and *Daniel Deronda*: The Prostitute and the Jewish Question"—to name two such readings—could be taken to epitomize, respectively, poststructuralist and feminist-historicist practices.[16] What would allow them to be taken thus is that, though each replicates the disjunctively theoretical sensationalism of Eliot's text, the former absorbs the sexual into an allegory of rhetoric while the latter subordinates the textual to an allegory of the sexual-economic. Chase's disciplinary technique may therefore be closer to Eliot's, but I want here to emphasize the curiously hybrid or self-divided quality that *both* essays share with the novel, a quality that to some extent exceeds, even as it motivates, their subsumptive endeavors. Gallagher's reading, for example, derives much of its interest from its displacement of classic deconstructive motifs like textuality and dissemination into a more worldly register of economic and sexual exchange, presided over by those seductive emblematic figures, the "almost always Jewish" moneylender and the prostitute: "The inflationary usurer and the infectious or combustible 'expensive' woman—these are the assured but dangerous inhabitants of the authorial sphere, the degradingly feminine sphere of exchange."[17] And while Chase is as intent upon referring referentiality itself to a citational *mise en abîme* as Gallagher is committed to regrounding the mystifications of writing in the realities of authorship,[18] her reading plays heavily upon the "scandal" of Deronda's unmentionable circumcision: "As a mark that tells too much of the conditions of history or too much of the limits cutting off signification or storytelling, circumcision is a sign that the story must evade or exclude or cut out: narrative must cut out or cut around the cutting short of the cutting off of narrative."[19]

My own reading of *Daniel Deronda* necessarily engages Chase's

---

16. Cynthia Chase, "The Decomposition of the Elephants: Double-Reading *Daniel Deronda*," *PMLA* (March 1978): 215–27. Catherine Gallagher, "George Eliot and *Daniel Deronda*: The Prostitute and the Jewish Question," in *Sex, Politics, and Science in the Nineteenth-Century Novel: Selected Papers from the English Institute*, 1983–84, ed. Ruth Bernard Yeazell (Baltimore: Johns Hopkins University Press, 1986), pp. 39–62.

17. Gallagher, ibid., pp. 43, 46.

18. I am echoing here Gallagher's statement that Eliot "replac[es] the mystifications of genealogy with the realities of economics" (ibid., p. 46).

19. Chase, "The Decomposition of the Elephants": 224. The phrase, "the scandal of the referent," appears on p. 223.

and Gallagher's powerful essays. Yet my aim here is not to "correct" them by resolving the contradiction that they tend rather to manage vertically. Nor am I sure that I would *want* to resolve it, even if the scope of the present study permitted such an effort: the tension in recent critical writing between theory and an almost irresistibly vulgar theatricality has been too productive to be defused unambivalently. Rather, I hope to show how, in her final novel, Eliot both sets up and attempts to settle a conflict between a certain formulation of the "rhetorical" and a certain formulation of the "social." I will argue that her model for their relationship, like her model for the relationship of the Jews to the Gentiles, is one of "separateness with communication,"[20] in which "communication," however, designates a unilateral and hierarchical exercise of power rather than a reciprocity of dialogical equals. That is, it should become clear in the pages that follow that the domination of the social by the rhetorical constitutes not a refusal of politics, but rather a new political technology. It should also become clear that, whether or not one approves of this project, it stands in an exemplary relation to some recent criticism in its most rigorous and energetic modes.

In May of 1875, while she was working on *Daniel Deronda*, Eliot wrote to one of her correspondents:

> We have been much interested lately in seeing Salvini, a genuinely great actor, play Othello. And on Monday we are hoping to see him in Hamlet. I wish you could have the same enjoyment. Great art, in any kind, inspirits me and makes me feel the worth of devoted effort, but from bad pictures, bad books, vulgar music, I come away with a paralyzing depression.[21]

What is striking here, first of all, is Eliot's testimony to the almost physical vulnerability of the spectator in the face of "bad" art, a vulnerability registered both in Lydgate's experience with Laure and in the "shock" Fred Vincy feels when he sees Lydgate gambling. "Great art," in contrast, surpasses the physical or the sensational: instead of "paralyzing," it "inspirits." The distinction between

---

20. George Eliot, *Daniel Deronda*, ed. Barbara Hardy (Harmondsworth: Penguin, 1982), p. 792. Subsequent references to the novel will be to this edition, and will be included parenthetically in the text.

21. Haight, ed., *Letters* 6:147.

"great art" and "bad" is of course one of the more prominent themes in the novel Eliot was then writing. Yet even the example of the great Salvini may suggest how easily that distinction can break down. For Eliot and Lewes saw Salvini not only in *Hamlet* and *Othello*, but also in a melodrama called *The Gladiator*, and in the latter performance, at least according to Lewes, they "were greatly disappointed in him."[22] Despite this disappointment, though, Lewes was "inspirited" to write an essay on Salvini, with which he ended his book *On Actors and the Art of Acting*, published in the same year. Since Lewes (in addition to serving as the definitive English interpreter of Rachel[23] and as a mediating link between Jane Austen and Charlotte Brontë) was both the foremost English drama critic of his time and George Eliot's "husband," this essay may merit a brief look; it may also tell us something about how, in the novel in which she was simultaneously engaged, Eliot was in fact developing a whole technology for regulating the relationship between great art and bad art.

After evaluating Salvini's interpretation of Othello (for which Lewes's enthusiasm, apparently more qualified than Eliot's, began to wane in the fourth act), the critic turns to the sorry spectacle of *The Gladiator*.

> One may say of the play, and of Salvini's acting, what Johnson said of a poem when Boswell asked him if it had not imagination: "No, sir; there is in it what *was* imagination once." Salvini showed us what had been dramatic expression: and so powerful is his mastery that many spectators accepted the conventional signs; just as many readers accept for poetry the splendid images and poetic thoughts which inferior writers gather from other writers far and wide, instead of expressing poetical feelings of their own.[24]

Like the passages from *Middlemarch* that I discussed above, these lines record the undesirable sliding of a formal or rhetorical boundary: where those passages imaged an increasingly comprehensive spectacularization, whose ultimate effect would be to turn the entire novelistic world into a stage, so Lewes here remarks Salvini's use of "conventional signs" to blur the line separating "dramatic expres-

---

22. From Lewes's Diary, May 17, 1875; cited in Haight, ed., *Letters* 6:142.
23. See John Stokes, "Rachel's 'Terrible Beauty': An Actress Among the Novelists," *ELH* 51 (Winter 1984): 771–93.
24. Lewes, *On Actors and the Art of Acting*, p. 229.

sion" from its "inferior" simulacrum. The reference to Johnson gives a nice authoritative punch to Lewes's indictment of this transgression, but Lewes seems to feel that his judgment needs additional support: in reaching out to *poetry* for a compelling analogy, Lewes exemplifies in miniature the strategy that Eliot elaborates in *Daniel Deronda*. For though the analogy appears to present poetry, which after all has its own counterfeiters, as simply the equivalent of acting, Lewes's next paragraph makes clear that poetry here is a synecdoche for a broadly metalinguistic level of analysis that by definition detaches itself from and exercises interpretive authority over the less theoretically articulate products of dramatic art.

> I do not blame Salvini for not having interested me in the Gladiator, for I do not think that any actor could have succeeded with such a patchwork. But I must blame his overacting—the apparent determination to get a multiplicity of effects out of materials which might have been more simply and massively presented. An illustration may be cited from his first scene. In telling the hideous history of his child, ripped from its mother's womb, he turned the narrative into a dramatized presentation, going so far as to repeat the words of the sorceress in high womanly tones. In his gestures there is always an excess in this direction: an excess which would not be felt indeed by Italians, since they are much given to what may be called pictorial gesture; but I cannot think it consistent with fine art, being, as it is, a remnant of the early stages of evolution, wherein gesture is descriptive, and not, as in the higher stages, symbolical: it bears the same relation to the expressive gestures of cultivated minds that picture-writing bears to the alphabet.[25]

Although the visible purport of this passage is that there are (as it were) "higher stages" of acting, which correspond to the putatively more evolved forms of writing as well as to authentic poetry, it is not hard to imagine how Lewes's aesthetic Darwinism might authorize the ranking of dramatic art as a whole below its ostensible analogues. For one thing, Lewes's expressive bias would seem to favor poetry, with its privileged relation to interiority, over the drama, which from this perspective always runs the risk of appearing superficial or rather crudely literalistic. It is telling, for instance, that Lewes faults Salvini for at one point "turn[ing] the narrative into a dramatic presentation." Isn't "dramatic presentation" precisely what Salvini's art is all about? Capable of evoking at once the embar-

25. Ibid., pp. 229–30.

rassing earliness of mere "picture-writing" and the decadent lateness of mere "conventional signs," acting in general would seem to be fundamentally hedged about by the danger of "overacting." For another thing, by marshaling a certain philosophical abstraction with which to "blame" the "excess" of Salvini's primitively "pictorial gesture[s]," Lewes symbolizes his own mastery of the very "symbolical" gestures he associates with "fine art" and "cultivated minds." To be sure, Lewes implies the possibility of some suitably refined mode of dramatic gesture; yet his language has the performative effect of appearing to transcend performance, of gesturing beyond gesture—if not to "poetry" in the strict sense, then to a superior, totalizing discourse of *poetics*.

That this poetic aspiration entails an equally hierarchical politics is clear from Lewes's patronizing remark about Italians, to say nothing of his attitude toward cultures that have not yet achieved the distinction of possessing an alphabet. Deploying both poetry and poetics in similar ways in *Daniel Deronda*, Eliot conspicuously opposes such ethnocentrism, although the immediate beneficiaries of her generosity are the Jews rather than the Italians. As we will see, however, in an important respect her metalinguistic project rejoins Lewes's in its racial ideology. For in Lewes's representation of Italian culture, as in Eliot's representation of Jewish culture, racial or national identity intersects with gender or sexual identity. It turns out, for example, that even in Salvini's "otherwise rare" portrayal of Hamlet, "there was a dissonance between the high plaintive tones and the massive animal force, both of person and voice—it was an operatic tenor, or *un beau ténébreux*, grafted on the tragic hero: an incongruous union of the pretty with the grand."

Shakespeare's play, Lewes observes, has been "cut down to suit Italian tastes."[26] And if those tastes betray a certain cultural immaturity, it comes as no great surprise that the cut that suits them suggests to Lewes's more sophisticated English sensibility "something [as] unfitting" as what a certain Freudian gaze might interpret as castration. Indeed, the implicit characterization of Salvini's acting as *childish*—significantly, the "hideous story" he tells in *The Glad-*

26. Ibid., pp. 232, 230. On the sexual implications of Italian politico-cultural "immaturity," see D. A. Miller, "*Cage aux folles*: Sensation and Gender in Wilkie Collins's *The Woman in White*," in *The Novel and the Police* (Berkeley: University of California Press, 1988), pp. 186–90.

iator is of a "child, ripped from its mother's womb"—leads with an almost proverbial inevitability to its implicit characterization as *effeminate*. He tells the story in, significantly, "high womanly tones." Like those tones, Salvini's "high plaintive tones" as Hamlet, yoked incongruously with his "massive animal force," reinforce the sense of a gender-confusion as objectionable as his effacement of the distinction between "great" and "bad" art.

Just as the spectacle of Lydgate in the billiard-room intimated at once a formal conflation (of realism with melodrama) and a sexual conflation (of masculinity with femininity), so, even in *Hamlet*, Salvini violates the laws of both genre and gender, "graft[ing]" the "operatic" onto the "tragic" and the "pretty" onto the "grand." In some sense, then, his characteristic moment remains that in which, illicitly mixing both literary forms and gender attributes, he "turn[s] the narrative into a dramatized presentation, going so far as to repeat the words of the sorceress in high womanly tones." Salvini always risks "disappointing" because, even at his best, he always threatens to embody the sensationalism whose promiscuous effects—whose scandalous mixture of the "great" and the "bad"—we examined in the previous chapter. As we saw, the notorious and definitive gesture of sensationalism—in which, as in Salvini's gestures, "there is always an excess"[27]—is that whereby it collapses the barrier erected between the masculine and the feminine and between "narrative" and "dramatic presentation." As in the identification of the "tragic" with the "grand" and of the "operatic" with the "pretty," sensationalism reveals the sex-gender system and the text-genre system as being closely and profoundly intertwined. Yet Lewes's strategy, like Eliot's, though on a much smaller scale, is to divide the latter against the former, abstracting from a hideously theatricalized narrative an apparently autonomous poetics with which to rule and, ultimately, to reform it. Although Lewes's theoretical comments about Salvini's acting, and about acting in general, may seem to constitute so much pedantic embroidery upon the more important particularities of theatrical criticism, they function as condensed versions of what happens so grandly in *Daniel Deronda*, where the criticism of theatricality gives way to the masterful discourse of "poetry."

---

27. "Excess" and "melodrama" are closely related, as suggested by the subtitle of Peter Brooks's *The Melodramatic Imagination: Balzac, Henry James, Melodrama, and the Mode of Excess* (New Haven: Yale University Press, 1976).

If Eliot's final novel represents a monumental expansion of Lewes's project in his essay on Salvini, it might also be read as a working through of the theatrical problems that surface briefly but disturbingly in her own earlier work. With hindsight, the account of Lydgate's experience with Laure and the description of his gambling, at any rate, begin to look like notes toward the supreme fiction that is *Daniel Deronda*. Not only is that novel famously preoccupied with actresses and acting, but it opens, just as famously, with a scene of gambling, in which the theatricality of that pastime is imaged more conspicuously than in *Middlemarch*, as if the anxieties such "play" arouses could thereby be addressed more directly and efficaciously.

The first chapter of *Deronda* seems to pick up where the scene in the Middlemarch billiard-room left off. Conducted into the casino at Leubronn, we observe an uncanny, sophisticatedly Continental replay of the scene around the Middlemarch billiard table. Having demonstrated the superficial heterogeneity of the international cast of characters, the narrator adds: "But while every single player differed markedly from every other, there was a certain uniform negativeness of expression which had the effect of a mask—as if they had all eaten of some root that for the time compelled the brains of each to the same narrow monotony of action" (p. 37). The casino seems to have the same "paralyzing" impact upon its clientele that bad art has upon Eliot. Again, we witness the contaminating effects of a negative, joyless theatricality, now at an advanced or even epidemic stage. The emptiness of exchange; the indiscriminate overriding of differences; the oppressive atmosphere of quasi-narcotic involuntarity; the narrowness of that artificial excitation—all of the elements of the earlier scene are here, magnified and transposed to a more ostentatiously worldly setting. It is as though the "Study of Provincial Life" itself set the stage for—that is, necessitated—its successor's study, and critique, of cosmopolitanism.

If, as Jacqueline Rose suggests, theatricality moves from the "outskirts" of *Middlemarch* to the "heart"[28] of *Daniel Deronda*, this movement indicates a shift not from insignificance to paramount importance, but from the status of repressed irritant to that of deliberately elicited and methodically targeted pathology. And if the latter novel's virtually obsessive deployment of theatrical tropes and topoi

---

28. Rose, "George Eliot and the Spectacle of the Woman," in *Sexuality in the Field of Vision*, p. 108.

intimates the difficulty of distinguishing between sickness and cure—
apparently, Eliot even considered writing *Deronda* as a play[29]—we
recognize once more the outlines of a tricky homeopathic strategy
of fighting theater with theater. Interestingly, however, there are no
literal "men of science" among *this* novel's *dramatis personae*. Instead, Science is figuralized here, and if that process entails a certain
displacement, Science may thereby find itself at once secondary and
seconded, at once deidealized and reinforced. Eliot's new and improved "scientific" method is announced from the outset, in the
often-quoted epigraph to the first chapter:

> Men can do nothing without the make-believe of a beginning. Even
> Science, the strict measurer, is obliged to start with a make-believe
> unit, and must fix on a point in the stars' unceasing journey when
> his sidereal clock shall pretend that time is at Nought. His less accurate
> grandmother Poetry has always been understood to start in the mid-
> dle; but on reflection it appears that her proceeding is not very dif-
> ferent from his; since Science, too, reckons backwards as well as for-
> wards, divides his unit into billions, and with his clock-finger at
> Nought really sets off *in medias res*. No retrospect will take us to the
> true beginning; and whether our prologue be in heaven or on earth,
> it is but a fraction of that all-presupposing fact with which our story
> sets out.
>
> (p. 35)

Just as Lewes's rather banal generalizations about poetry belie
their stringent disciplinary function, so the disarming modesty of
this Shelleyan deconstruction hides its extensive agenda: the epigraph establishes a metacritical frame for the ensuing narrative, and
prescribes the terms for its therapeutic technique. As critics have
noticed, the subtext of the reference to the prologue "in heaven or
on earth" is Goethe's *Faust*, with its two prologues. In a fine reading
of *Daniel Deronda*, David Marshall has argued that this allusion introduces the question of the historically and epistemologically complicated relations between the theater and the novel.[30] Yet the relations here involve not two terms, but four: it is a question not just
of the novel and/or the theater, but of the novel and/or the theater
and/or Poetry and/or Science.

---

29. See Gordon S. Haight, *George Eliot: A Biography* (New York: Oxford University
Press, 1978), p. 471.
30. David Marshall, *The Figure of Theater: Shaftesbury, Defoe, Adam Smith, and
George Eliot* (New York: Columbia University Press, 1986), pp. 193–94.

Appropriately, the novel begins by evoking a play (about a "scientist") that is also a poem, and whose first prologue, which takes place in a theater and consists of a discussion among a theater manager, a dramatic poet (*Theaterdichter*), and a comic character, explicitly stages a debate between the claims of poetry (*Dichtung*) and of the theater. But the force of Eliot's epigraph—which thereby becomes either less than or all too exemplarily "deconstructive"—is to decide in favor of the former. This is not merely a matter of billing: it is not just that the theatrical reference is relatively cryptic, while Poetry looms large. Personified, in this antigenealogical genealogical fable, as the grandmother of Science, Poetry enjoys a privilege that transvalues, even as it springs from, the apparent disadvantage of being "less accurate." Poetry is accorded a temporal and ontological priority that not only makes Science look a little derivative or belated, but also postulates a strong aesthetic alternative to the particularly unpleasant and un-Goethean version of the theater we are about to encounter.

Much of that strength, moreover, derives from the flexibility of "poetry": since, as every novel we have studied in this book makes clear, and as the passages we have considered from *Middlemarch* and *Deronda* would seem to confirm, the relative specificity of "the theater" gives way to the more insidious diffusion of "theatricality," "poetry" must emerge as even more expansive. It is crucial, in other words, that "Poetry," rather like Goethe's *Dichtung*, identify not just a specific literary genre, which can thus be isolated from lesser genres, but (as in many of Eliot's earlier uses of the term)[31] a general possibility of literariness, charmingly characterized as "make-believe"; once established in this latter, comprehensive sense, Poetry is free to inform those other genres—as it informs science—and, ideally, to rehabilitate them—as it might rehabilitate the novel and the theater, or the most disconcertingly contaminated form of all, the theatricalized novel.

As the author of so theatrical a novel as *Daniel Deronda*, Eliot herself could be called a *Theaterdichter*; but she will deploy a nov-

---

31. See, for example, "Notes on Form in Art," in *Essays of George Eliot*, ed. Thomas Pinney (New York: Columbia University Press, 1963), pp. 431–36. On Eliot's longstanding interest in "the poetry of experience," see Suzanne Graver, *George Eliot and Community: A Study in Social Theory and Fictional Form* (Berkeley: University of California Press, 1984), pp. 80–149.

elistic *Dichtung* that, far from being ruled by *Theater*, will rule it. At the risk of overschematizing, let me propose that, in accordance with the hierarchy of genres that the epigraph implicitly recommends, the narrative will elaborate and put into practice a "science" of poetry, or of poetic drama, whose aim is to appropriate and neutralize the theatricality that threatens to infect the novel. The defense of poetry comes to mean "poetry *as* the defense." Working together, grandmother and grandson allegorize a salutary, perhaps even life-saving, intervention. By opposing a poeticized theatricality to a more virulent theatricality, Eliot would turn the novel as well into a local variant of archi-Poetry, minimizing, if not eliminating, the potential for internal disorder.

The first epigraph is itself an example of the strategy it prescribes: its privileged status as a framing device allows it to *contain* not only the highly theatrical chapter it introduces, but the novel as a whole. Indeed, the relationship between the epigraphs in general and the rest of the novel epitomizes the discursive hierarchy we have been considering. For one thing, many of those epigraphs are themselves productions in verse, either by other authors or of Eliot's own invention. By the time *Deronda* appeared, Eliot had of course already published poetry, much of it, significantly, in the form of verse drama; for that matter, she had already instituted the practice of beginning chapters with mottoes (both poetic and nonpoetic, both original and borrowed) in her earlier novels. But with her poetic epigraphs to *Deronda*, she creates an aggressively systematic effect of discursive layering which, far from illustrating some sort of heteroglossic carnival, makes graphic the superiority of poetry to prose. Not only her own "fragments" of verse, and not only the quotations from other poets, but all of the epigraphs, even those written in prose, become sites of a master-discourse, in which a generalized and generalizing *poetics*—what we would nowadays call "literary theory"—exercises hegemonic control over less principled literary forms. And it is precisely when, like the first epigraph, these chapter heads advertise a certain ironic self-mockery that they enforce their policing power most effectively.

That Eliot incorporates into her novel a discursive apparatus that nonetheless persists in looking like an external authority perhaps suggests a certain "crisis" in the Victorian novel, a larger uncertainty about the future of that hitherto dominant form as the end of the nineteenth century approaches. Eliot's need to enlist the support of "poetry" would indeed seem consistent with the widely held view that the English novel loses something of its vitality and sense of purpose in the latter part of the nineteenth century.[32] It is as though, no longer sure of its own identity, the novel could know itself only obliquely, through a pitched battle between two more visible or more coherent forms, such as poetry and theatricality. Where novels like *Mansfield Park, Jane Eyre,* and *Villette* take shape through their own binary struggle with theatricality, many of the more canonical novels later in the century invoke the definitional help of some idealized third party, often for the sake of a compromise with an adversary they cannot hope to control more authoritatively. If Eliot summons "poetry," Hardy models his novels on Greek (poetic) tragedy, while James, as we will see, programmatically and insistently segregates "the theater" from "the drama," aligning himself of course with the latter. And it would be eminently plausible, not to say utterly conventional, to see this process as culminating in a generically eclectic work like *Ulysses* or in the "lyrical" novels of Virginia Woolf.

Yet this familiar story is usually told without reference to the remarkable body of texts that come between Austen and Brontë on the one hand and Eliot and her protomodernist and modernist successors on the other. Before the "crisis" of the novel makes itself felt in more recognizable forms, it is already staged in the sensational texts of Collins, Braddon, Wood, and the late Dickens. Inheriting the collapsed binarisms of the sensation novel, Eliot can claim novelty only by introducing a *third* term, only by using "poetry" to triangulate the relationship between the novel and theatricality. And if poetry here is a synecdoche for the poetics or the theoretical narrative that is itself latent in the sensation novel, the very abstractiveness of that figuration points to the process in the novel whereby enabling differences are imposed and space-making distances asserted.

Thus, although the first epigraph, with its personification of "Poetry" as a woman, may suggest a confluence of literary theory and a certain feminism, the narrative that follows attests to a separation

---

32. On the difference between earlier and later nineteenth-century novels, see Catherine Gallagher, *The Industrial Reformation of English Fiction: Social Discourse and Narrative Form, 1832–1867* (Chicago: University of Chicago Press, 1985), pp. 265–67.

of the "theoretical" from the "experiential." We soon discover, for example, that the affection accorded to that rather flatly allegorical grandmother does not seem to carry over to many of the more fully fleshed-out female characters in the novel proper. Indeed, no sooner do we learn to respect that paradoxically but benignly bodiless avatar than the narrative zeros in on a rather sinister Gwendolen Harleth, whose theatrical equivocality, reinforced by the fact that she is "occupied in gambling" (p. 35), is framed in the first paragraph with an almost clinical fastidiousness:

> Was she beautiful or not beautiful? and what was the secret of form or expression which gave the dynamic quality to her glance? Was the good or the evil genius dominant in those beams? Probably the evil; else why was the effect that of unrest rather than of undisturbed charm? Why was the wish to look again felt as coercion and not as a longing in which the whole being consents?
>
> (p. 35)

And what, we might add, has happened to the "deconstructive" nonchalance about arbitrariness and indeterminacy expressed in the epigraph? As seen by Daniel Deronda—much more adamantly a spectator and much less willingly a performer than female counterparts like Jane Eyre and Lucy Snowe—Gwendolen looks like a composite of Lydgate and Laure. (Lydgate, of course, also looks like a composite of Lydgate and Laure.) Viewing Gwendolen as "dramatic," Daniel necessarily treats her as an object of "scrutiny" (p. 37); once she is thus positioned, it follows that *her* relation to arbitrariness takes on the guilt associated with gambling, and that *her* indeterminacy gets moralized, in somewhat panicky but venerable misogynistic fashion, as duplicity. Like her sensationalized precursors in *Middlemarch*, Gwendolen conflates two kinds of conflation, embodying a rhetorical and epistemological scandal—she theatricalizes reality—and therefore, at the same time, a sexual scandal—arrogating to herself the powers of *ambiguity*, she almost automatically suggests a Medusa-like bisexuality, as evidenced by the references to her serpentine appearance (pp. 40, 41). Whereas certain deconstructive properties (if that is not a contradiction in terms) may be said to become a poetic grandmother, rather similar effects inspire "unrest," as at the sight of something unfitting, when associated with a "problematic sylph" (p. 38) performing on the stage of a casino.

Daniel's "unrest," of course, follows from his sense of spectatorial "coercion," a sense that—like Lydgate watching Laure, like Fred Vincy watching Lydgate, or like Robert Audley watching his "aunt"—he risks being drawn, involuntarily, into the sordid masquerade: not by assuming the "uniform," compulsory "mask" of the compulsive players, but merely by standing and looking. Where the expansive tendency of Poetry must not seem expansion*ist*, the spectacle of Gwendolen is at the center of a microcosm where "uniform negativeness" suggests a world grotesquely corrupted by a pervasive artifice. What's a nice boy like Daniel doing in a place like this? Catherine Gallagher has called attention to the similarity between the grown-up Daniel, whose mother traded him for a career as, precisely, a performer, and the little boy in the casino, who also seems to have been abandoned for "play."[33] The description of the child is particularly instructive in light of the context to which he constitutes an "exception":

> There was a deep stillness, broken only by a light rattle, a light chink, a small sweeping sound, and an occasional monotone in French, such as might be expected to issue from an ingeniously constructed automaton. Round two long tables were gathered two serried crowds of human beings, all save one having their faces and attention bent on the tables. The one exception was a melancholy little boy, with his knees and calves in their natural clothing of epidermis, but for the rest of his person in a fancy dress. He alone had his face turned toward the doorway, and fixing on it the blank gaze of a bedizened child stationed as a masquerading advertisement on the platform of an itinerant show, stood close behind a lady deeply engaged at the roulette-table.
>
> (p. 36)

Citing this first scene in the novel as a salient staging of "woman as spectacle," Jacqueline Rose and other feminist critics have hinted at an analogy between this spectacle's "dynamic quality" and certain definitive features of mainstream film, as theorized most notably by Laura Mulvey in her pioneering essay, "Visual Pleasure and Narrative Cinema"—an essay whose insights, as we noted at the end of the previous chapter, seem to be prefigured by a novel like *Lady Audley's Secret* as well.[34] Especially when informed by Mulvey's

---

33. Gallagher, "George Eliot and *Daniel Deronda*," in *Sex, Politics, and Science*, p. 53.

34. Laura Mulvey, "Visual Pleasure and Narrative Cinema," in *Women and the*

Lacanian interpretation, the cinematic analogy is highly suggestive.[35] If, as Mulvey argues, cinematic "structures of fascination" build upon structures of the patriarchal unconscious, then the passage about the little boy seems strikingly protocinematic, a fine example of what both film theorists and psychoanalysts would call "projection."[36]

For the image of the "melancholy little boy" is in some sense a defensive projection of a certain "exhibitionist" potential that, as we will learn, Daniel has good reason to fear in himself. Indeed, far from being "exceptional," the child is not nearly exceptional enough. Though he looks away from the tables, his is not the controlling male gaze of the normative cinematic spectator, but the "blank [i.e., screen-like and therefore feminized] gaze of a bedizened child stationed as a masquerading advertisement on the platform of an itinerant show." Again, we are reminded that one need not wear the mask of the player to pulled into the "narrow monotony" of the play. The language here, indeed, seems to be going out of its way to invest the boy (an uncanny offspring of Wordsworth's Blind Beggar?[37]) with theatrical attributes of the most culpably commercial and degradingly reified kind, as if to turn him into a miniature version of the "ingeniously constructed automaton" from which a French "monotone . . . might be expected to issue"; even his skin, which ought to be exempt from the general unreality, is dressed in the ornate periphrasis of a "natural clothing of epidermis." Where the epigraph's reversal and displacement of the Science/Poetry hi-

---

Cinema: A Critical Anthology, ed., Karen Kay and Gerald Peary (New York: E. P. Dutton, 1977), pp. 412–28. In addition to Rose, see Catherine Belsey, "Re-reading the Great Tradition," in *Re-reading English*, ed. Peter Widdowson (London: Methuen, 1982), pp. 121–35; Mary Wilson Carpenter " 'A Bit of Her Flesh': Circumcision and 'The Signification of the Phallus' in *Daniel Deronda*," *Genders* 1 (Spring 1988): 1–23. The phrase, "woman as spectacle," occurs in Belsey, p. 131.

35. Under the combined influence of *Nachträglichkeit* and Mulvey's striking formulations, one even begins to wonder if much in the modern cinema does not derive from certain *theatrical* moments in certain late nineteenth-century novels. On the relationship between films and nineteenth-century theatrical conventions, see William Rothman, "Virtue and Villainy in the Face of the Camera," in *The "I" of the Camera: Essays in Film Criticism, History, and Aesthetics* (Cambridge: Cambridge University Press, 1988), pp. 69–84.

36. The phrase, "structures of fascination," comes from Mulvey, "Visual Pleasure," in *Women and the Cinema*, p. 417. On projection, introjection, and exhibitionism, see ibid., pp. 416–22.

37. For a perceptive discussion of theatricality in Wordsworth, see Geraldine Friedman, "History in the Background of Wordsworth's 'Blind Beggar,' " *ELH* 56 (Spring 1989): 125–48.

erarchy occur within an ostensibly *gemütlich* vignette of grand-mother and grandson, the "deconstructive" paradox of natural cloth-ing emblematizes, only pseudocomically, a perversion of nature by culture, and might even—if we were to pause and imagine a suitably lurid shot of this scene—insinuate a whole melodrama of maternal negligence and child abuse.

As Gallagher suggests, Daniel will in fact discover that he has been inscribed in just such a melodrama. Yet the aim of the narrative as a whole, sustained by a projective energy like that of the passage we have been examining, is to write him out of it. If the novel raises the specter of *man* as spectacle, it does so in order to exorcise the danger posed by such fearful symmetry. Indeed, among all of the metaphors and similes conjured up to evoke the repellent quality of Grandcourt, perhaps none is more damning (or more surprising) than the one that likens him to, of all things, an "actress" (p. 145).[38] If only because of this association, one might argue half-fancifully, Grandcourt must die. What makes Daniel not only Grandcourt's would-be opposite number, but also the novel's titular hero, is the fact that he struggles manfully against the theatrical impingements of his own obscure history. Long before his revelatory meeting with the Princess Halm-Eberstein, Daniel takes great pains to deny the theatricality into which others, even with the best of intentions, might seem to coerce him.

One such denial is adduced in chapter 16, where Eliot takes us back into Daniel's boyhood, to trace his "invisible history." A certain invisibility, it turns out, is just what Daniel wants to achieve, and what the narrative works to secure for him. The traumatic scene that motivates this reactive project occurs "One morning after [Dan-iel] had been singing 'Sweet Echo' "—the Lady's Song from *Comus*, as Barbara Hardy points out (p. 890)—"before a small party of gentle-men" (p. 207) assembled at Sir Hugo Mallinger's house. Thinking to praise Daniel's "beauty" as well as his "thrilling boy voice" (p. 207), Sir Hugo asks him, in front of the audience:

> "What do you say to being a great singer? Should you like to be adored by the world and take the house by storm, like Mario and Tamberlik?"

38. In this regard, see Eliot's letter of April 18, 1876, to John Blackwood, in which she discusses charges from the critic of the *Spectator* that "the scenes between Lush and Grandcourt were not 'vraisemblable'—were of the imperious feminine, not the masculine character" (Haight, ed., *Letters* 6:240).

Daniel reddened instantaneously, but there was a just perceptible interval before he answered with angry decision—
"No; I should hate it!"

(p. 208)

Daniel's anger has its stimulus not just in the widespread Western phobia about the presumably feminizing objectification—to say nothing of the inevitably eroticizing "adoration"—of the adult male; it expresses also his recently crystalized suspicion that he is Sir Hugo's illegitimate child:

He had often stayed in London with Sir Hugo, who to indulge the boy's ear had carried him to the opera to hear the great tenors, so that the image of a singer taking the house by storm was very vivid to him; but now, spite of his musical gift, he set himself bitterly against the notion of being dressed up to sing before all those fine people who would not care about him except as a wonderful toy. That Sir Hugo should have thought of him in that position for a moment, seemed to Daniel an unmistakable proof that there was something about his birth which threw him out from the class of gentlemen to which the baronet belonged.

(p. 209)

As the figural relays of the narrative make clear, however, Daniel's fear of illegitimacy comments upon, rather than supersedes, his fear of theatricality: if to be theatricalized is to be feminized, to be feminized is almost automatically to be rendered illegitimate—if not in the strict legal sense, then in the more disturbingly inclusive sense of the almost sexually unfitting "play" in which Lydgate, Laure, Gwendolen, and, most spectacularly, Daniel's mother, the diva, are engaged.[39] His fear of illegitimacy in fact turns out be quite legitimate: in this novel, the "legitimate theater" would seem to be an oxymoron. "Vivid" indeed, the "image of taking the house by storm" cannot but give way to the less gratifying but even more indelible prospect of "being dressed up to sing before all those fine people who would not care about him except as a wonderful toy." It is as if Daniel's consciousness reached both backward and forward in the text at once, proleptically taking in the revelation of the not-

---

39. Compare Daniel not only with female performers in Eliot's earlier works (Caterina in "Mr. Gilfil's Love Story," Armgart in *Armgart*, etc.), but also with the musically inclined, feminized, and deformed Philip Wakem in *The Mill on the Floss*, with whom Eliot herself seems implicitly to be comparing him in this chapter (pp. 209, 215).

quite-extenuating circumstances of his birth and abandonment, circumstances that would cast him in the role that, from the very beginning of the novel, we see him trying to cast out: that of the illegitimately, even scandalously "bedizened" toy-like boy "stationed" as an "advertisement"—better, as an *avertissement*, both "warning" and "foreword"—on the second page of the text.[40] Project or be projected, throw out or be thrown out: such is the primitive logic of Daniel's sophisticated defense.

The projection of the melancholy figure of the boy indeed condenses a number of the anxieties that the therapeutic narrative thereby works to dispel. For if Daniel's fear of being thrown out "from the class of gentlemen" is obviously social as well as sexual, what he fears about such social dislocation is the loss not only of class identity but also of national identity. Recalling the "operatic tenor . . . grafted" onto Salvini's Hamlet, the references to Mario and Tamberlik echo the danger that Salvini himself embodied: that of incomplete or stunted development on both the individual and the cultural level, a condition suggested not only by the boy's distasteful aura of cosmopolitanism, but also by his appearance of having been "stationed"—indeed, rendered stationary—on a platform.

Before the end of chapter 16, however, Eliot indicates that, in order to prevent Daniel from turning into a plaything, it is also insufficient merely to reassure him, as Sir Hugo in fact does, of his predetermined role as an "English gentleman" (p. 212). The case of Grandcourt, after all, serves to remind us that that being "grand" in that sense does not necessarily preclude one's being thought "pretty": status as an English gentleman does not in itself confer immunity from the perils of theatricalization. To the extent that Daniel is the hero of a bildungsroman, his education entails a rather complicated dialectical itinerary; it is in the mapping out of that education that Eliot's project most clearly surpasses Lewes's in its scope and its subtlety. As a boy, Daniel seems to hover precariously at the outer edge of respectable English maleness; as a youth, he escapes the dangers of marginality, gravitating toward the centers of power and privilege in his culture (Eton and Cambridge, to be

---

40. See Gallagher, "George Eliot and *Daniel Deronda*," in *Sex, Politics, and Science*, pp. 52–58, on the interchangeability of apparently shameful "sexual exchange" and apparently admirable "artistic exchange."

exact); but then, to counteract the dangers attendant upon *that* phase
of identification, he reverses his direction and travels beyond the
England that has solidified him. Daniel explains to his "uncle" why
he wants to leave Cambridge and study abroad: "I want to be an
Englishman, but I want to understand other points of view. And I
want to get rid of a merely English attitude in studies" (p. 224).

And yet this laudably anti-ethnocentric program is not without
its own risks. At this point, we can see how Daniel's *Bildung*, or
formation, coincides with the (risky) formal experiment of the novel
as a whole. For the desire to extend "sympathy" to the sphere of
international relations accounts for the novel's own refusal, at the
level not only of subject matter but also of composition, of a "merely
English attitude": critics have observed that the novel's so-called
"Jewish half" would achieve for its reader what Deronda would
achieve for himself.[41] Yet Eliot is aware that the attempt "to understand other points of view" can land one, say, in the middle of the
casino at Leubronn, which, as it happens, is exactly where we find
Daniel at the beginning of the novel. And if Daniel's well-meaning
foreign study does not necessarily implicate him in the pervasive
artifice that he encounters in the casino, it still comes uncomfortably
close to the sort of cosmopolitanism that, before he was confirmed
in his career as a gentleman, had provoked in him such "unrest."

So insistent and multifarious, it seems, is the threat of theatricality
that the novel must exercise extraordinary vigilance and agility in
defending against it: the defense itself can become the disease.[42]
Gently pointing out the "demerits" of character foreshadowed by
Daniel's "boyish love of universal history, which made him want
to be at home in foreign countries, and follow in imagination the
travelling students of the middle ages," the narrator summarizes
them as a tendency to "linger . . . longer than others in a state of

41. See, for example, Avrom Fleishman, " 'Daniel Charisi': An Assessment of
Daniel Deronda in the History of Ideas," in Fleishman, *Fiction and the Ways of Knowing*
(Austin: University of Texas Press, 1978), pp. 86–109. See also Eliot's letter to Harriet
Beecher Stowe, in which, discussing responses to *Deronda*, she denounces the "in-
tellectual narrowness—in plain English, the stupidity, which is still the average mark
of our culture" (Haight, ed., *Letters* 6:302).

42. For a provocative discussion (albeit with reference to a rather different historical, political, and textual configuration) of the way in which defense can be implicated in disease, see Lee Edelman, "The Plague of Discourse: Politics, Literary
Theory, and AIDS," *South Atlantic Quarterly* 88 (Winter 1989): 301–17.

social neutrality" (p. 220). Though forgiving, the narrative cannot be neutral toward this neutrality. To be sure, as a definitive feature of Daniel's "travelling student" phase, it cannot simply be equated with the "neuter" fate that seemed to await the boy singer; *Daniel Deronda* is obviously not "Sarrasine." But Daniel's foreign study must not conclude his education, since its characteristic openness is still a far cry from the improved virility—the more-than-gentle-man-liness—at which, as we will see, his whole elaborate education is aimed. Far from promoting a mere worldly receptivity, which could just as easily be represented by, say, the sensational figure of Fosco, the narrative that would transform Daniel into more than just an English gent(i)leman requires, both for his postcollegiate career and for the valedictory legitimation of Eliot's career as a novelist, a very specific and rigorous foreign study indeed. Far from celebrating all things Jewish, that is, this narrative effects, as Gallagher has suggested, the systematic "alienation of all the negative things Jewishness stands for in the book," the most characteristic of which is precisely worldly receptivity—otherwise known as cosmopolitanism, internationalism, or, in Eliot's own terms, "social neutrality" itself.[43]

These negative things finally find their most eloquently self-damning avatars, as Gallagher shows, in Daniel's mother, Alcharisi, and in Mirah and Mordecai's father, Lapidoth. Actor, gambler, pander, Lapidoth floats from country to country, acting "like a woman" (p. 806) when the role suits him, and like a child in relation to his own children; near the end of this chapter, we will consider the mode of Alcharisi's demonized worldliness. For now, however, we are faced with a different question, one raised but not satisfyingly answered by Gallagher. Gallagher herself is so worldly a critic—"worldly" not in the sense of being socially neutral but in the sense of being socially engaged and socially acute—that she assigns relatively little specificity to the ostensibly "good" Jewishness that is left after the signs of "bad" Jewishness have been "alienated" or subtracted. This may be because "good" Jewishness (the term is mine, not Gallagher's) resembles what we might want to call the *un*worldly or the *other*worldly—what a more linguistically oriented critic than Gallagher might focus on, and what the narrative in fact

43. Gallagher, "George Eliot and *Daniel Deronda*," in *Sex, Politics, and Science*, pp. 56–58.

privileges, as "Poetry." Admittedly, recent developments in literary study have taught us to suspect distinctions between linguistic and social-historical criticism; and one does not have to be a student or a critic of literature to become more than a little nervous about a distinction between "good" (or "poetic") and "bad" (or "theatrical") Jewishness. But the reason I make these distinctions is that Eliot's novel, so concerned with the separation of "great art" from "bad," itself quite aggressively makes and enforces them: it is this rather violent "science" that the epigraph to the first chapter prefigures. However, I want also to show how the disjunctions or "alienations" in question make possible a whole system of hierarchical or disciplinary linkages, which entail a complex rhetorical procedure in their own right.

Two other epigraphs exemplify this procedure, each figuring Jewishness (or "Israel") not just in terms of separateness, but in terms of what the novel will identify as a proto-Zionist ideal of "separateness with communication" (p. 792). Here is Eliot's translation of the epigraph to chapter 42, from Leopold Zunz's *Die Synagogale Poesie des Mittelalters*:

> If there are ranks in suffering, Israel takes precedence of all the nations—if the duration of sorrows and the patience with which they are borne ennoble, the Jews are among the aristocracy of every land—if a literature is called rich in the possession of a few classic tragedies, what shall we say to a National Tragedy lasting for fifteen hundred years, in which the poets and the actors were also the heroes?
>
> (p. 575)

"Israel" here signifies both a separation and a communication: a separation, to be precise, of good Jewish communication from the bad Jewish communication that the novel personifies in characters like Alcharisi and Lapidoth. For Jewish history is defined here as a peculiarly *literary* history, a fusion of the literary and the historical that manifests itself in the theatrical genre of a "National Tragedy." Where theatricality in Eliot ordinarily stands for an undesirable admixture, a *con*fusion, of literature and experience, the particular tragedy of "Israel" represents theatricality redeemed, theatricality poeticized: insofar as the heroes are not only actors but *poets* as well, this tragedy constitutes an ideal "communication"—both between literature and history and, in Zunz's terms, between *Trauerspiel* and *Poesie*.

The second epigraph, which actually occurs earlier in the text, introduces chapter 34, and comes from Heine's *Prinzessin Sabbath*:

> Er ist geheissen
> Israel. Ihn hat verwandelt
> Hexenspruch in einen Hund.
> . . . .
>
> Aber jeden Freitag Abend,
> In der Dämmerungstunde, plötzlich
> Weicht der Zauber, und her Hund
> Wird aufs Neu' ein menschlich Wesen.[44]

Against Daniel's mother, the bad or witch-like Jewish princess we will meet later in the novel, this fragment of Heine's poem invokes a good Jewish princess, who (at least in the context of the novel) symbolizes a kind of counter-magic that restores Jewishness itself to its original, higher state. And if it is a question once again of separating good Jewishness from bad, it is also a question of establishing a therapeutic communication—this time between the Jewish ideal and the English culture it would cure. For the image here of a transformation of the dog (*Hund*) back into a human being (*menschlich Wesen*) seems, through an uncanny logic of textual displacement, to reverse the scene of reversal in *Middlemarch*, in which Lydgate resembled an "animal with fierce eyes and retractile claws." It is as though the Princess Sabbath, or the Jewish tradition that she emblematizes, had the power to turn Lydgate back into the superior being he once was—as though superior Jewishness provided the antidote to the poisonous magic of theatricality that already afflicts English culture.

Yet the specular relationship between these two images of metamorphosis implies a less reassuring reading of English-Jewish com-

---

44. His name is Israel,
    And a witch's spell has changed him
    To the likeness of a dog.
    . . . .
    But on every Friday evening,
    On a sudden, in the twilight,
    The enchantment weakens, ceases,
    And the dog once more is human.

The Works of Heinrich Heine, trans. Margaret Armour (New York: E. P. Dutton, 1906) 12:4.

munication: just as the humanizing process must be repeated every Friday evening (*jeden Freitag Abend*), so Jewishness in general may be seen not as a final solution to the English question but merely as its inverted repetition. For the communication between good Jewishness and English culture to be effective, the separation of good, *menschliche* Jewishness from bad, doggy Jewishness must be definitive: the cyclicality of Jewish ritual must be subsumed by a linear pattern, a narratable teleology.[45] Imposing that teleology, the bildungsroman centered on the Jewish-English hero thus traces not only his own visible and "invisible history" but also an invisible, (re)visionary history of Jewish-English relations. If Eliot devotes her usual care to the analysis of the protagonist's moral and intellectual growth, she does so not just for the usual purpose of "unravelling certain human lots, and seeing how they were woven and interwoven";[46] the painstaking precision with which she delineates Daniel's progress contributes to the foundation of a new *English* literary history, whose heroes and actors would also be its poets. In telling Daniel's story, Eliot asks not what the country can do for the Jews; she asks what the Jews can do for the country.

For example, the reason the ever-careful narrator demonstrates a certain tolerance toward Daniel's "social neutrality" is that, while it can degenerate into something dangerously like a narcotized theatricality, it can also be converted, through the appropriate disciplinary intervention, into the very poetic, or rather, poeticized, posture that the novel would affirm. In the important retrospective chapter that charts Daniel's progress from boy singer to English-gentleman-in-training to something ambiguously more or less than that, Eliot provides a clue as to how this risky ambiguity might be counteracted. For Daniel's social neutrality, which underlies his wanderlust, also manifests itself in the form of a "meditative interest in learning how human miseries are wrought—as precocious in him as another sort of genius in the poet who writes a Queen Mab at nineteen" (p. 219). While Daniel's cosmopolitan proclivities could, theoretically, turn him into a younger version of the unsavory Lapidoth—one of the novel's two examples of "bad" (or *merely* theatrical) Jewishness at its worst—the defensive poetics insinuated here,

---

45. On narrative and causality in the novel, see Chase, "The Decomposition of the Elephants": esp. 216–20.
46. *Middlemarch*, p. 170.

just as theoretically, hints that Daniel will instead turn into an example of "good" (or poetic) Jewishness at its best—in other words, into a Jewish version of that poetic defender whom the text invokes in the powerfully prescriptive epigraph to chapter one. Tellingly, Daniel is being compared to the very young Shelley, a Shelley who signifies *precocity* rather than fully developed genius; just as the author of *Queen Mab* had to ripen into the author of the "Defence of Poetry," so the hero of Eliot's peculiarly Shelleyan novel must progress beyond his boyish identification with the traveling students of the Middle Ages, to the point where he seems capable of having written that novel's epigraph. And just as Shelley also wrote plays, so the epigraph looks forward to the containment, through Daniel, of the theatrical by the poetic.

One might ask, of course, why England needs a Jewish version of Shelley when it can already claim the original as one of its own. Does this analogy imply a flatly specular relationship between the Jews and the English after all? I would argue that, instead of merely setting the Jews up as allegorical figures for more properly English concerns, Eliot is strategically focusing on and isolating a certain "Jewishness" inherent in English culture, so as to fortify it and ultimately to reintroduce it into that culture; again, separateness with communication offers the model for Eliot's procedure. Eliot's comments in a letter to Harriet Beecher Stowe suggest something of this dialectic of inside and outside:

> There is nothing I should care more to do, if it were possible, than to rouse the imagination of men and women to a vision of human claims in those races of their fellow-men and women who most differ from them in customs and beliefs. But towards the Hebrews we western people who have been reared in Christianity, have a peculiar debt and, whether we acknowledge it or not, a peculiar thoroughness of fellowship in religious and moral sentiment. Can anything be more disgusting than to hear people called "educated" making small jokes about eating ham, and showing themselves empty of any real knowledge as to the relation of their own social and religious life to the history of the people they think themselves witty in insulting? They hardly know that Christ was a Jew.[47]

As one who is both Jewish and English, the saintly (if not Christlike) Daniel would embody the essence of a saving difference or

47. Haight, ed., *Letters* 6:301–02.

alterity latent within England and waiting to be mobilized against other, more dangerous (and presumably less integral) alien influences.

One indication of the form this mobilization will take appears at the end of the long paragraph comparing Daniel to Shelley. Of Daniel's precocious sympathy, the narrator says: "In many of our neighbours' lives, there is much not only of error and lapse, but of a certain exquisite goodness which can never be written or even spoken—only divined by each of us, according to the inward instruction of our own privacy" (p. 219). That this exquisite goodness somehow resists the vulgarizing translations of both writing and speech betokens a movement away from the awkward exteriority of public experience toward the welcome interiority of private divination.[48] Mustering the familiar oppositions between inside and outside, and between private and public, this passage founds its hope for Daniel's future not only on the durable prestige but also on the well-known and "exquisite" incorporative capacity of the former term in each dyad.

Given the way the chapter in which this passage occurs insinuates a preemption of theatrical badness by poetic goodness, it seems appropriate that, in the next chapter, Daniel should discover and rescue a suicidal Mirah, who is of course Lapidoth's estranged daughter. In a sense (although a limited one, as we will see), it is as if Mirah and Daniel were rescuing each other—as if he were rescuing her from the cosmopolitan theatricality for which she has been professionally groomed by her father ("I hated our way of life" [p. 252]), and as if she were rescuing him from the same fate, for which he has been, as it were, genetically programmed by his mother. Early in their first conversation, Mirah asks Daniel, who has been singing the gondolier's song from Rossini's *Otello*, "Do you belong to the theatre?" (p. 232). Not surprisingly, he responds, "in a decided tone," "No; I have nothing to do with the theatre" (p. 232). As David Marshall notes, "This denial is rich in irony," since, "in many senses," both Daniel and Mirah, as well as the novel that contains them, "belong . . . to the theater and ha[ve] everything

---

48. Gallagher ("George Eliot and *Daniel Deronda*," in *Sex, Politics, and Science*) points out that, since Mordecai transmits his poetry cabbalistically, it can be seen in some sense to bypass the problematics of both authorship and textuality (p. 58).

to do with the theater."[49] But, unlike the previous chapter, in which Daniel's equally "decided" denial of theatrical implication ("No; I should hate it!") is reinforced by a merely insinuated poetic defense, this chapter comes ironclad, outfitted with an elaborate counter-theatrical, and therefore counterironic, armature. For though Daniel's singing, and Mirah's echoing of his words, would seem to insert them both inside a theatrical frame, what begins in this chapter is a long process whereby these two decidedly antitheatrical characters in fact escape from that frame, with the help of an increasingly decided effort of alienation and reconnection on the part of the narrative itself.

Though primarily apotropaic, the fantasmatic projection, in the previous chapter, of Daniel's career as a singer at the same time thrusts him both backward and forward to an unfitting, if merely hypothetical, theatrical fate; the representation, in this chapter, of Daniel's grown-up singing at once predicts and produces the saving effects of his intervening, if as yet incomplete, poetic education. The most obvious proof that Daniel himself is becoming proof against the theater is the chapter's insistence on associating music and song with (an always implicitly and essentially *lyric*) poetry, rather than with performance. Mirah may wonder if Daniel belongs to the theater, but his emphatic denial is seconded by the narrative's own emphatic attempt to disengage singing from the theatrical context it might have been thought to inhabit, and to relocate it in its proper poetic context, where it thus finally seems fitting. If Daniel's song comes from an opera by Rossini, and if that opera's Shakespearean source seems to underscore the threat of theatricality, what deflects that threat is Eliot's reminder that the song in question is actually one in which Rossini has "set to music the immortal words of Dante" (p. 227), and—in a footnote, no less—that "Dante's words are best rendered by our own poet in the lines at the head of the chapter" (p. 227). And indeed, at the head of the chapter are Tennyson's lines from "Locksley Hall."

This ostentatious flurry of more-than-allusive erudition suggests T. S. Eliot rather than the more stately intellectuality of George Eliot. But while this citational display seems a little showy, whatever in-

49. Marshall, *The Figure of Theater*, p. 196.

advertent theatricality it might imply is overborne by Eliot's authoritative way of doing the poetic police in different voices.[50] Perhaps it would be more "accurate" (if less poetic) to say that, in
reclaiming song for poetry, Eliot effectively poeticizes any theatricality that remains either in song itself or in her own discourse about
it. The different poetic voices here are thus all really the same mon-
ological voice: whatever seems to "belong to the theater" ultimately
belongs to poetry, precisely because the theater itself now belongs
to poetry. As a result of this redefined, nonreciprocal linkage, even
Shakespeare ends up looking more like a poet than like a playwright.

Yet it is on Daniel, of course, that the novel's poetic discipline
has its most important and most striking rehabilitative effect. Admittedly, he is still "angry" to find that even his assumption of the
male "gaze" can seem less "dreadful" (p. 226) than feminizing: "His
own face in the glass had during many years been associated for
him with thoughts of some one whom he must be like—one about
whose character and lot he continually wondered, and never dared
to ask" (p. 226). But if this speculation anxiously anticipates a specular relationship between Daniel and his mother, the virilizing
changes in his voice and body testify to the promise of phallogocentric "firmness" with which, like the novel itself, he will eventually dispose of her:

> The voice, sometimes audible in subdued snatches of song, had turned
> out merely a high baritone; indeed, only to look at his lithe powerful
> frame and the firm gravity of his face would have been enough for
> an experienced guess that he had no rare and ravishing tenor such
> as nature reluctantly makes at some sacrifice. Look at his hands: they
> are not small and dimpled, with tapering fingers that seem to have
> only a deprecating touch: they are long, flexible, firmly-grasping
> hands, such as Titian has painted in a picture where he wanted to
> show the combination of refinement with force. And there is some-
> thing of a likeness, too, between the faces belonging to the hands—
> in both the uniform pale-brown skin, the perpendicular brow, the
> calmly penetrating eyes. Not seraphic any longer: thoroughly terres-
> trial and manly; but still of a kind to raise belief in a human dignity
> which can afford to acknowledge poor relations.
>
> (p. 226)

50. In "Discipline in Different Voices: Bureaucracy, Police, Family, and *Bleak
House*," in *The Novel and the Police*, pp. 58–106, D. A. Miller alludes to this phrase to
evoke the recontainment of "subversive" difference.

Though the pictorial analogy indicates that Daniel remains susceptible to the operations of framing, this passage records, less ambiguously, his development *away from* the role of boy prodigy—a role in which there is apparently no real development but only degeneration into a rather phobically anatomized, equivocally sexed prodigiousness. The frame that necessarily objectifies Daniel also houses the portrait of one who, in accordance with the novel's normative scenario of male *Bildung*, promises to end up as a family man. While still something of a *beau ténébreux*, Daniel is no longer in any danger of becoming an operatic tenor: though high, his baritone sounds a reassuringly "subdued" note. Needless to say, the "dignity" thus secured for him hardly compromises his "manliness": for in "acknowledging poor relations," Daniel would merely offer further evidence of his capacity for patriarchal beneficence.

In a sense, that is just what he is doing in this chapter. Although Mirah will not in fact become his "relation" until the end of the book, when he marries her, they are already "related" not only by their shared Jewishness but also, less happily, by their echoing theatrical histories. However, by "acknowledging" Mirah as an "impersonation" of his own "misery" (p. 227), and by being "acknowledged" by her even before she repeats the words from his song, Daniel participates in a large-scale narrative movement that shifts the ground of their sympathetic performance from one of illicit publicity—thanks to her father, Mirah has almost literalized the metaphor of the actress as prostitute—to one of respectable intersubjectivity, ending in the institutionalization of interiority that is marriage. Indeed, in a sort of preview of that domestic bliss, the sympathy enacted in their scene of mutual recognition seems almost magically to transcend its own overdetermined theatricality, affirming, as in a Brontë novel, the preemptive claims of "the inward instruction of our own privacy":

> Her hands were hanging down clasped before her, and her eyes were fixed on the river with a look of immovable, statue-like despair. This strong arrest of his attention made him cease singing: apparently his voice had entered her inner world without her having taken any note of whence it came, for when it suddenly ceased she changed her attitude slightly, and, looking round with a frightened glance, met Deronda's face. It was but a couple of moments, but that seems a long while for two people to look straight at each other.
>
> (pp. 227–28)

Where David Marshall would elicit the inescapable ambivalence of such moments, underscoring their inherent theatricality, I want to stress the overarching developmental trajectory that would master that ambivalence by preparing Daniel to become the master of the house. Tending to minimize the gender politics of the narrative, Marshall thereby downplays its vigorously domesticating poetics as well.[51] Though, as I have argued, Daniel and Mirah indeed reinforce each other in their antitheatricality, this mutual poeticizing ultimately subserves what Eliot is quite willing to exhibit as the asymmetrical structure of patriarchal marriage, a structure that obtains not just in obviously unhappy families like the Grandcourts but in the novel's normative Jewish household as well.[52] The novel makes clear that, one way or another, in a male-regulated economy of gender roles, it is women who are bound to be the "poor relations," for it is they who are traditionally meant to be "framed": "framed," as Mirah's brother Mordecai says approvingly, "for the love which feels possession in renouncing" (p. 803); "framed," in Alcharisi's words, as "instruments" (p. 726) of solidarity between grandfathers and grandsons; or framed, as Rose has shown, by a "scientific" tradition that demands their spectacularization. Just as the narrative inserts the theater inside poetry, so Daniel sets up a domestic frame to contain Mirah's theatrical frame. Arranging for her to give *private* singing lessons (a kind of "inward instruction" in its own right) and *private* performances—conveniently, the appropriate authorities have pronounced her a mediocre actress, and have concluded that her voice "will never do for the public" (p. 256)—Daniel advances the process that will culminate in his accession to the traditional male role of the framer.[53]

51. For example, of Alcharisi's statement, "You can never imagine what it is to have a man's force of genius in you, and yet to suffer the slavery of being a girl" (p. 694), Marshall writes: "I want to suggest that the issue of sexual difference here is a specific manifestation of the more general question of difference that Eliot is insisting on in this chapter" (*The Figure of Theater*, p. 217).

52. For a reading of *Deronda* as a subversive critique of the traditional marriage plot, see Joseph Allen Boone, *Tradition Counter Tradition: Love and the Form of Fiction* (Chicago: University of Chicago Press, 1987), pp. 172–87.

53. See Carpenter, " 'A Bit of Her Flesh' ": 4–5, for a sophisticated account of Mirah's (and her mother's) singing as evocations of "women's freer access to the Imaginary."

For that final triumph to take place, however, Daniel's poetic character must undergo considerable disciplinary reconstruction. Although he demonstrates admirable sensitivity to "the presence of poetry in everyday events," and although that sensitivity already permits him to "raise" certain "faint" and "obscure" facts of Jewish history into the "region of poetry" (p. 414), in the middle of the novel Eliot still finds him wanting in "the chief poetic energy:—in the force of imagination that pierces or exalts the solid fact, instead of floating among cloud-pictures" (p. 431). Where the latter state suggests a vaguely effete lingering among stage sets, real or imagined, the more energetic alternatives of piercing or exalting the solid fact would characterize the figure Daniel has yet to become—the youth as virile poet. That is, to prove himself the worthy heir to his grandfather's proto-Zionist "vocation," Daniel must learn how to enforce his grandfather's "notion of separateness with communication" (p. 792), in which to "communicate" is precisely to apply the "force of imagination" to solid facts, thereby achieving a kind of *Aufhebung* of the realism, as well as of the reality, to which Eliot's earlier novels are monuments.

If it is Daniel's grandfather who symbolizes most forcefully and articulates most succinctly the novel's poetic imperative, there are two other characters who also help to define it. One of these is the brilliant Jewish composer and musician Herr Klesmer, whose trenchant critical powers—Mary Wilson Carpenter points out that the Yiddish word *klesmer*, which means "musical instrument," can also evoke instruments such as knives[54]—establish his credentials as a virtuoso of piercing. The other is the poet Mordecai, in whose "soul" "new psalms of exile live again" (p. 555), and whose resolutely prophetic discourse identifies him as a veritable professor of exaltation. Yet, as we will see, Daniel's accession to the chief poetic energy represents less an alternation between two discrete and specialized techniques—as though the "or" of "pierces or exalts" designated mutual exclusiveness—than their more impressive synthesis, whereby "or" betokens the apposition of near-synonymy. Furthermore, while this synthesis might be viewed as a form of "androgyny," in which the "masculinity" of piercing merges with the "femininity" of exalting, both techniques serve the purposes of a poetics

54. Ibid., 8.

directed by men against women and womanish men: Daniel's Titianesque "combination of refinement with force" (p. 226) eventually becomes a refinement *of* force, a new and improved tactic of domination. To exalt, here, is as phallocentric an act as to pierce. Through Klesmer and Mordecai alike, the novel shows how to enforce a piercing exaltation of a distressingly feminized culture.

For the world of solid fact that Daniel is trained to confront turns out not to be so solid after all—otherwise, it would not need confronting. Daniel practices his skills on the relatively tractable Mirah, yet it is Gwendolen in whom the effects of his energy must be most visible, since it is she, more saliently than even Grandcourt, who embodies the alarmingly unstable condition of English culture, a culture already infected by bad Jewishness. In the first scene of the novel, we see Gwendolen engrossed in the very activity of gambling that marks Lapidoth as such an embarrassingly inadequate Jewish father. Moreover, as the novel's central instance of woman-as-spectacle, and as a woman who at one point even thinks of taking to the stage, Gwendolen resembles the novel's other bad Jewish parent, Daniel's mother. Gwendolen's "problem," as it were, is that she wants to be what Daniel's mother is—namely, a Princess. And though not exactly a Jewish princess, Gwendolen is tellingly (if somewhat bemusedly) described, on two occasions, as a "princess in exile" (pp. 53, 71). In Gwendolen, one might say, a certain parodic, because too-worldly, version of Jewish exile is itself in exile. From the very beginning of the novel, and well into the penultimate Book 7, we are repeatedly reminded of how Gwendolen tries to transform the "narrow theatre" (p. 94) of her female experience into what Alcharisi calls "the wide world, and all that I could represent in it" (p. 693). In widening the theater of her performance, Gwendolen would paradoxically effect the dedifferentiation or narrowing of the distance between the world and representation that marks the sensationalism against which Eliot writes.

Thus, where critics like Henry James and F. R. Leavis admire the "good [Gentile] part" of the novel for its "deep rich English tone," viewing the "bad [Jewish] part" as a lapse from the "solid" into the "liquid,"[55] I am arguing that, especially as personified by Gwendolen

---

55. The terms "good part" and "bad part" come from Leavis, *The Great Tradition,* pp. 97–146 passim; the other quotations are from James's *"Daniel Deronda*: A Conversation," (reprinted in Leavis, p. 290).

(Leavis was of course prepared to delete the "bad part" and to name what was left of the novel after *her*), the "good part" is already tainted by bad Jewishness, and can be saved only by the good Jewishness of the "bad part." When Daniel first sees the "Austenian," or, indeed, "Jamesian" heroine in the casino, where the "atmosphere [is] well-brewed to a visible haze" (p. 35), he finds himself faced with an unwelcome reflection of his own floating existence in a world of "cloud-pictures." The vast remainder of the novel, much of which takes place back in England, might well be read as Daniel's attempt to save himself and the Jews by saving Gwendolen and the contaminated—that is, already bad-Jewish—English culture that that heroine represents. Or rather, since Eliot devotes so much space and time to the relationship between Daniel and Gwendolen, saving the Jews is merely a pretext for (and an unwritten sequel to) the more urgent business of saving the English novel and the culture that *it* represents. The goal of Daniel's vocational training is the founding of a separate Jewish state; but, as I have suggested, that apprenticeship involves, more immediately and maybe more crucially, extensive practical experience in the theoretical technique of separating good (virilizing) Jewish communication with the English from bad (feminizing) Jewish communication with the English. Before he can leave England to set up poetic house and homeland with Mirah, Daniel must acquire and exercise the chief poetic energy that will allow him to put in order an already dangerously theatricalized English house of fiction.

Daniel's major assignment in the novel, then, is to make sure that this actress manquée stays manquée: that Gwendolen's performance, like the much more cooperatively antitheatrical Mirah's, shrinks to fit the contours of an interiority (if not of a marital domesticity) whose only "width"—in a reversal of the first paradox—comes from the spiritualizing impact of humiliation. That Daniel finally succeeds in this project of shrinking Gwendolen explains why critics have characterized his role in relation to her as that of a psychotherapist in relation to a patient.[56] (Indeed, Eliot's poetic "science" might be adduced as one example of how, as Freud acknowledged, the poets had anticipated him.) But it is the great "professor" (p. 79) and musician Klesmer, who, in subjecting Gwendolen to the

---

56. See, for example, Welsh, *George Eliot and Blackmail*, pp. 264–369, and Gillian Beer, *George Eliot* (Bloomington: Indiana University Press, 1986), p. 217.

discipline of a certain "Jewish" science, first exemplifies the therapeutic technique Daniel will employ. Eventually, Gwendolen will in fact recognize that Daniel's "possible judgment of her actions was telling on her as importunately as Klesmer's judgment of her powers" (p. 381). But first, let us consider Klesmer's lesson in the techniques of piercing and exalting.

Significantly, Klesmer's penetrative effect—it is said that his genius "pierces the whole future of a life" (p. 282)—extends beyond, or through, Gwendolen to the larger English culture for whom "he has a deuced foreign look" (p. 290). Early in the novel, Klesmer's pupil and wife-to-be, Catherine Arrowpoint (whose name, Carpenter suggests, is itself fairly pointed)[57] says to Gwendolen: "Imagine what I have to go through with this professor! He can hardly tolerate anything we English do in music. We can only put up with his severity, and make use of it to find out the worst that can be said of us" (p. 79). The "severity" with which Klesmer pierces and deflates Gwendolen's fantasy of a career as a singer and actress therefore emblematizes an almost surgical intervention in both the English novel and the culture for which it stands, an operation in which a life-saving foreignness is implanted as a cure for the malignant one—the theater is presented here as an almost exclusively Jewish profession[58]—that has already spread too far. As Klesmer punctures Gwendolen's plan "to become the most approved Juliet of the time" (p. 307), her unhealthy desire for representation in the wide world indeed contracts to a more humble theatrical scale. Putting her theatrical project in its place, he tells her, "I must clear your mind of these notions, which have no more resemblance to reality than a pantomime" (p. 301). Having restored a certain realism, however, Klesmer must supplement poetic piercing with poetic exalting, lest Gwendolen's hopes *remain* "no better than the packed-up shows of a departing fair" (p. 306). That he possesses the energy or force of imagination necessary for such complex work is signaled, of course, by his musical genius, which in effect excuses his flamboyance. And

57. Carpenter, " 'A Bit of Her Flesh' ": 6.
58. On Jews and actors, see the paragraphs entitled, "On the Problem of the Actor," in Friedrich Nietzsche, *The Gay Science,* trans. Walter Kaufman (New York: Random House, 1974), pp. 316–17. For a comparison of antisemitism and antitheatricalism, see Jonas Barish, *The Antitheatrical Prejudice* (Berkeley and Los Angeles: University of California Press, 1981), pp. 464–69.

if, in calling himself "the Wandering Jew," and in being called "cosmopolitan" (p. 284) by Miss Arrowpoint, Klesmer seems implicated in the floating tendencies of those with lesser poetic energy, the Shelleyan defense that he offers immediately afterward marks the decisive difference between his powerful poetics of exile and Daniel's less efficacious mode of errancy: "We [artists] are not ingenious puppets, sir, who live in a box and look out on the world only when it is gaping for amusement. We help to rule the nations and make the age as much as any other public men. We count ourselves on level benches with legislators" (p. 284). Marshaling the force of the mature Shelley's definition of *poets* as the "unacknowledged legislators of the world," Klesmer draws a vigorously discrediting frame around the philistine notion of artists as so many stage properties.

But Klesmer's most commanding assertion of his poetic, and poeticizing, power occurs in his painful interview with Gwendolen, when he says, rather indignantly:

> I am not decrying the life of the true artist. I am exalting it. I say, it is out of the reach of any but choice organisations—natures framed to love perfection and to labour for it; ready, like all true lovers, to endure, to wait, to say, I am not yet worthy, but She—Art, my mistress—is worthy, and I will live to merit her. An honourable life? Yes. But the honour comes from the inward vocation and the hard-won achievement: there is no honour in donning the life as a livery.
>
> (p. 298)

By "exalting" the "frame" of "the true artist," Klesmer not only establishes his own good-Jewish credentials: as he communicates to Gwendolen the terms of his "inward vocation," he also provides her with a model for achieving an exaltation of sorts within the far more constricted frame to which his piercing words have just consigned her. Spelling out this prescription for a homeopathic cure of her *false* artistry, Daniel himself will advise Gwendolen that "a little private imitation of what is good is a sort of private devotion to it, and most of us ought to practise art only in the light of private study—preparation to understand and enjoy what the few can do for us" (p. 491).

What Klesmer does for Gwendolen, early in the novel, is precisely to give her forceful, if indirect, inward instruction, instruction in the inwardness to be secured through "a little private imitation" of good-Jewish "art." For in the famous scene of the *tableau vivant* from *The*

Winter's Tale, this princess in exile, posing as a "Rachelesque heroine" (p. 90), begins by imitating the statue-like queen Hermione, but ends up resembling the "statue-like" (p. 227) Mirah, inadvertently transcending her own rather bad or embarrassing "imitation of acting" (p. 90), thanks to Klesmer's improvised yet timely *musical* intervention:

> "Music, awake her, strike!" said Paulina (Mrs. Davilow, who by special entreaty had consented to take the part in a white burnous and hood).
> Herr Klesmer, who had been good-natured enough to seat himself at the piano, struck a thunderous chord—but in the same instant, and before Hermione had put forth her foot, the movable panel, which was on a line with the piano, flew open on the right opposite the stage and disclosed the picture of the dead face and the fleeing figure, brought out in pale definiteness by the position of the wax-lights. Everyone was startled, but all eyes in the act of turning towards the opened panel were recalled by a piercing cry from Gwendolen, who stood without change of attitude, but with a change of expression that was terrifying in its terror. She looked like a statue into which a soul of fear had entered: her pallid lips were parted; her eyes, usually narrowed under their long lashes, were dilated and fixed.
>
> (p. 91)

Like the private theatricals in *Mansfield Park* and *Jane Eyre,* this *tableau vivant* constitutes a densely significant scene of instruction. Though it precedes the interview with Gwendolen, in which Klesmer performs his brutally deflationary poetic piercing, the final image that his "good nature" produces here is one in which Gwendolen's pretensions have already been pierced—"struck" is the operative term—but have thereby been readied for the compensatory, "devotional" sublimation that Daniel, following Klesmer's lead, will be called upon to teach her both during and after the "long Satanic masquerade" (p. 831) of her marriage to Grandcourt. "Oh, the door was not locked; it was probably the sudden vibration from the piano that sent it open" (p. 92), reasons Gwendolen's uncle, Mr. Gascoigne. In terms of symbolic action, that vibration has far-reaching effects, since Klesmer's "thunderous chord" communicates to Gwendolen "a little privat[izing]" poetic energy, which she echoes in her "piercing cry." But that cry also betrays "a little" poetic receptivity to something like exaltation, however "terrifying": not, as Gwendolen will fantasize, through worldwide renown as an actress—no Vashti or Alcharisi is this would-be "Rachelesque heroine"—but rather, as the "fixed" yet "soulful" "dilation" of her "usually narrowed" eyes suggests, through an almost Jane Eyre–like expansion into inwardness, notwithstanding her revulsion from the prospect of life as a governess.

But while, in *Jane Eyre*, this inward expansion seems virtually definitive of "the novel" as against theatricality, Eliot's staging of this process depends upon the intermediation of a strikingly alien artist who is much more like a poet—and a highly theoretical one at that[59]—than he is like a novelist. Gwendolen's theatrical *tableau* becomes *vivant* only when Klesmer "fixes" her by forcing her to give life to the poetry of Shakespeare's script. And where the private theatricals threatened at first to be merely embarrassing—or, worse, to inflict the kind of "paralyzing depression" that is Eliot's response to bad art—this fixing of Gwendolen's bad theatricality implies, far more resonantly, her "mortification" (p. 93). Klesmer strikes the chord that both places and repairs the spectacle she embodies: he forces that spectacle to resonate with the humiliating but therefore redemptive note of a presumably *authentic* privacy, before which what starts out as the spectator's "unrest" gives way to gratifying intimations of *Gwendolen's* capacity for "spiritual dread" (p. 94). For although Gwendolen has "always disliked whatever was presented to her under the name of religion" (p. 94), when she is struck by music, or pierced by poetry, she indeed has an almost "Jewish" experience of "the vastness in which she seemed an exile" (p. 95). In the necessarily "little" world of her "narrow theater," that is, this English princess exchanges bad Jewish exile for good Jewish exile.

In the process, moreover, the narrative that contains this scene is saved from the embarrassment of seeming to have lapsed into the sensationalism of a novel like *Lady Audley's Secret*. Where Gwendolen's literally melodramatic seizure might recall the histrionic humiliation of that novel's equally histrionic heroine, Eliot takes great care to frame *her* heroine's self-betrayal as an instance of lyricizing *melos* rather than of hystericizing drama. Granted, Klesmer is tactful enough to recuperate what he "divines" is Gwendolen's "betrayal into a passion of fear" (p. 93) by praising it as "a magnificent bit of

---

59. See the description of Klesmer's composition, *Freudvoll, Leidvoll, Gedankenvoll*, as "an extensive commentary on some melodic ideas not too grossly evident" (pp. 79–80).

plastik" (p. 92) and as "good acting" (p. 93). Yet this divination hints that the true source of goodness lies in his own divine poetic antidote to the theatrical infection of reality by artifice: poetic force invades, spiritualizes, and thereby redeems both theatrical artifice *and* the reality it has infected. It is just such an antidote that Daniel will administer to Gwendolen when, after the "absorbing show" (p. 405) of her marriage has become a "Satanic masquerade" (p. 831)—whose end is prefigured quasi-sensationally in the frightening picture disclosed in the *tableau vivant*—*he* attempts to recuperate that bad spectacle by prescribing "private devotion" to "art" through "a little private imitation of what is good" in it.

But if Gwendolen finally accepts this painful treatment, there is one female character in the novel who persists in rejecting what's good for her. Daniel's mother, Alcharisi, the Princess Halm-Eberstein, the princess in exile par excellence, articulates the novel's strongest feminist refusal of the poetic therapy of patriarchal Jewishness. In the famous description of her "double consciousness," we see the last, extravagant revival of the spectacle (already unwittingly revived by Lydgate) in which the duplicitous Madame Laure once starred,[60] and which has haunted Eliot's writing ever since:

> The varied transitions of tone with which this speech was delivered were as perfect as the most accomplished actress could have made them. The speech was in fact a piece of what may be called sincere acting: this woman's nature was one in which all feeling—and all the more when it was tragic as well as real—immediately became matter of conscious representation: experience immediately passed into drama, and she acted her own emotions. In a minor degree this is nothing uncommon, but in the Princess the acting had a rare perfection of physiognomy, voice, and gesture. It would not be true to say that she felt less because of this double consciousness: she felt—that is, her mind went through—all the more, but with a difference: each nucleus of pain or pleasure had a deep atmosphere of the excitement of spiritual intoxication which at once exalts and deadens.
>
> (pp. 691–92)

The repressed that returns as Alcharisi is the disturbing catachrestic conflation of "sincerity" (or the real) and "acting" (or the fictive)

---

60. It was in a talk by Neil Hertz at Yale University that I first encountered the idea that Lydgate's scenes with Laure might be read alongside Daniel's scenes with Alcharisi.

that Eliot has been trying to rewrite *poetically* all through *Daniel Deronda*. Though Alcharisi's "double consciousness" suggests a kind of transcendence, her "excitement" is too reminiscent of the gambler's state of mind; though her "intoxication" may be "spiritual," it can hardly be "inspiriting," as Eliot calls great art. If the chief poetic energy pierces and exalts, the Princess's theatrical "nature" merely "exalts and deadens"; and while to deaden is not exactly to kill, we still sense that we are in the treacherous vicinity of a "panther of the stage" (as Lewes called Rachel), of an "animal with fierce eyes and retractile claws," whose piercing would be even more violent—and much less salutary—than, say, Klesmer's. Like Lydgate's "excited narrow consciousness" at the billiard table, or like the "narrow monotony of action" in the casino at Leubronn, Alcharisi's feverish private performance signifies the most spurious and insidious kind of "width," whereby the differences between "nature" and "representation," between "experience" and "drama," and between "consciousness" and delirium are all collapsed in an unhealthy "atmosphere" of coercion. Whereas Lucy Snowe, and Charlotte Brontë as well, take the uncanny doubleness of the imperiously suffering Vashti as an example or model for their own activities as writers, Daniel Deronda, and George Eliot, *make* an example of this later "Rachelesque heroine," punishing her for her deconstructive artistry.[61]

Neil Hertz has shown how this exemplary punishment of the "bad" surrogate author works to defend both the author herself and the " 'good' surrogate" who is Daniel: "the casting out of the princess, her abjection, is intended not to collapse the distance between author and surrogate, but to stabilize it as a chosen separation and thus to ground the multiple gestures of mimesis that make up the novel."[62] My own discussion suggests that the good surrogate and the bad surrogate embody a larger narrative power struggle between the good Jewishness of poetry and the bad Jewishness of theatri-

61. For a discussion of how Brontë and Eliot differ in their representations of Rachel, see Stokes, "Rachel's 'Terrible Beauty.' "

62. Neil Hertz, *The End of the Line: Essays on Psychoanalysis and the Sublime* (New York: Columbia University Press, 1985), p. 232. The terms "good" surrogate and " 'bad' surrogate" appear on p. 224. For a less theoretically sophisticated but still useful discussion of the difficulty of distinguishing between good and bad actors in Eliot's novels, see Karen B. Mann, *The Language That Makes George Eliot's Fiction* (Baltimore: Johns Hopkins University Press, 1983), pp. 156–65.

cality. Rejecting her father's prescriptive definition of her as "the Jewish woman" (p. 692)—that is, as a good or nice Jewish girl— Alcharisi nonetheless assumes a certain poetic identification: she becomes, after all, "the greatest lyric actress of Europe" (p. 703). Yet, unless properly regulated, opera can be dangerous, as we know from both Eliot and Lewes. The Princess's particular operatic conjunction of poetry and theatricality inverts what the novel deems the proper hierarchical relationship between the two forms, and threatens to undo the realignment of singing with the former: here, instead of giving itself up to the inspiriting sovereignty of the lyric, a deadening theatrical exaltation—more spiritu*ous* than authentically spiritu*al*— parodies and exceeds it, as when, adding insult to injury, Daniel's mother mocks Mirah's "attach[ment] to the Judaism she knows nothing of," sneering, "That is poetry—fit to last through an opera night" (p. 729).

If Grandcourt's odd resemblance to an actress seals his doom, that wisecrack is enough to get the Princess, for her part, expelled from the novel. As Marshall notes, Deronda's interviews with his mother teach him "the limits . . . of sympathy,"[63] and his sympathy certainly seems limited when he points out to her: "You renounced me—you still banish me—as a son. . . . But that stronger Something has determined that I shall be all the more the grandson whom also you willed to annihilate" (p. 727). The Princess herself recognizes all too well that her glamorous cameo appearance serves merely to "frame" her retroactively as an "instrument" (p. 726) for relations between men.[64] Functioning, to be sure, as the matrilineal proof of Jewishness, but therefore, in a more overtly thematized way, as a conduit in spite of herself for the transmission of "that stronger Something" that is the Name-of-the-(Grand)Father, the actress who "banishes" her son enters the narrative only to *be* banished from it.

But where Daniel's mother resents to the end the instrumentality imposed upon her, his wife accepts with the requisite docility her own supporting role in the homosocial transaction between Daniel and Mordecai. The marriage of Daniel and Mirah merely consolidates the "marriage of . . . souls" (p. 820) between Daniel and Mir-

---

63. Marshall, *The Figure of Theater*, p. 215.
64. See Eve Kosofsky Sedgwick, *Between Men: English Literature and Male Homosocial Desire* (New York: Columbia University Press, 1985).

ah's brother. And the absorption of Mirah into this male bond signals the triumph of poetry over a by-now domesticated theatricality. Mirah's childish tendency to interpret her life in theatrical terms ("What I have read about and sung about and seen acted, is happening to me," [pp. 800–801]) is not only checked by Mordecai's fraternal disapprobation ("My sister, thou hast read too many plays," [p. 803]): it is overruled and supplanted by Mordecai's "poet's yearning" (p. 537) for the realization of his visions. His most remarkable visionary success occurs when, "straining to embody" his "ideal self," he virtually wills the arrival, against a "golden background" (p. 550), of the "figure representative of [his] longing" (p. 531). "Visions," Mordecai tells Daniel, "are the creators and feeders of the world" (p. 555). "Darkened by the excess of light" (p. 531), the Miltonic Daniel rows along the Thames from fantasy into reality, thus conjoining those realms under Mordecai's powerful creative and nutritive—in a word, poetic—influence.[65] "Embodying" in Daniel the "ideal"—that is, figurative *and* literal—functions of both the father and the mother, Mordecai invests the hero with a *good* catachrestic power whose ultimate effect—notwithstanding that this process is called a "maternal transference of self" (p. 553)—would be to render real or living mothers and wives somewhat superfluous.

Having put its actresses in their place, having replaced contaminating (female) theatricality with visionary (male) poetry, the novel can finally separate its good Jewish characters from the English world with which they have been communicating. If the novel begins with poetry—the epigraph to the novel as a whole is a verse motto by Eliot herself—it, like Eliot's career as a novelist, also end with poetry, as Mordecai dies in Daniel's and Mirah's arms. Appropriately, the lines are from Milton's closet drama, *Samson Agonistes*. Reaching back before Shelley, to one of his own great precursors, Eliot invokes an earlier British poetic impersonation of Jewish identity, a canonical text signifying precisely that residue of "Jewishness" in English culture that she has been attempting to revitalize and to reactivate—not only against her culture's ambient philistinism, but also against another "Jewishness" that floats or

65. See pp. 571–73 for a meditation on the scientific versus the visionary (Mordecai), which elaborates upon the discussion of Poetry and Science in the epigraph to chapter 1.

wanders too indiscriminately throughout that culture. Now that theatricality has been safely contained—has, as it were, been given a home—Eliot can reward the Jewish hero who has helped her administer that domestication, envisioning an end to his exile as well: Daniel may travel to the East (with Mirah at his side), to create and feed a new and separate poetico-political reality.

Although this chapter is in large part about how a certain kind of literary theory defines itself against the sensationalism to which it nonetheless remains crucially attached, it was not until I had written most of it that I became aware of some of its own more significant performative implications and affiliations. To be specific, many of the themes identified here as central to Eliot's text—literary autonomy, the fate of the novel, cultural "decadence," and, most sensationally, "the Jewish question"—turned out (to *my* surprise, at any rate) to resemble the themes of the most sensational or sensation-causing text on the contemporary literary-theoretical scene, Paul de Man's recently discovered 1941 newspaper article, "Les juifs dans la littérature actuelle," accounts of which I read before beginning to write this chapter. For a number of reasons, this is not the place in which to analyze that article, much less to consider its role either within the extensive body of de Man's wartime journalism as a whole or, even more broadly, in relation to his later, more recognizably "theoretical" work. Not only am I inhibited by the sheer fact of not yet having read the wartime writings in their entirety: I am also sufficiently mindful of this chapter's warnings against the possible dangers of metacriticism to resist the temptation to begin constructing yet another interpretative frame, especially this late in the chapter.[66]

But I append these brief remarks in the hope that they may be usefully self-historicizing rather than "totalizing and (potentially totalitarian)," as de Man himself characterized the version of literary

---

66. See Paul de Man, *Wartime Journalism, 1939–1943,* ed. Werner Hamacher, Neil Hertz, and Thomas Keenan (Lincoln: University of Nebraska Press, 1988); and Hamacher, Hertz, and Keenan, eds., *Responses: On Paul de Man's Wartime Journalism* (Lincoln: University of Nebraska Press, 1989).

theory of which he was the acknowledged master.[67] The relevant information about my own history is that I first wrote about *Daniel Deronda* in the late 1970s in a dissertation under de Man's direction, and that, as one might have expected of a dissertation produced at that time and under that influence, I there subjected the novel's Jewish content to the same process of sublimation and exclusion—of sublimation *as* exclusion—that I have here been tracing in the novel itself. Generally speaking, the force of my reading consisted in its relentlessly formalizing subsumption of both "good" and "bad" Jews under the privileged rubric of "poetry," a move that effectively forestalled any consideration of the resistance offered to this process not only by the "bad" Jews but by the "bad" Jewishness that virtually pervades the novel's dramatis personae.

Now I suspect that most readers of this book are familiar, at least from all of the attendant and often gleefully vindictive publicity, with the outlines of de Man's disturbing *Le Soir* article. I would merely point out that, in its own obviously more spectacular way, that article performs similar gestures of sublimation and exclusion, and upon similar objects. After affirming that, "en gardant, malgré l'ingérance sémite dans tous les aspects de la vie européenne, une originalité et un caractère intacts, [notre civilisation] a montré que sa nature profonde était saine," de Man concludes that "la création d'une colonie juive isolée d'Europe" would in fact have negligible consequences for *la vie littéraire de l'Occident:* "Celle-ci perdrait, en tout et pour tout, quelques personnalités de médiocre valeur et continuerait, comme par le passé, à se développer selon ses grandes lois évolutives."[68] Unlike Eliot—whose final novel would also isolate the Jews from Europe, though for more attractive reasons—de Man implies no distinction between good and bad Jewishness; for him,

67. Paul de Man, *The Resistance to Theory* (Minneapolis: University of Minnesota Press, 1986), p. 19.

68. Paul de Man, "Les juifs dans la littérature actuelle," in Hamacher, Hertz, and Keenan, eds., *Wartime Journalism*, p. 45. I borrow Geoffrey Hartman's translation of this passage: "By preserving, despite the semitic intrusion into all aspects of European life, an originality and a character that have remained intact, our civilization has shown that it is healthy in its deep nature. . . . The latter [the literary life of the West] would lose, all in all, some people of mediocre value and would continue as in the past to develop according to its own great laws of evolution." Hartman, "Blindness and Insight," *The New Republic* (March 7, 1988), p. 26.

there is only "mediocre" Jewishness, which can be safely excluded precisely because its putatively polluting *influence* has always already been sublimated to the point of mere *ingérance*, or meddling.[69] And what guarantees the health of *notre civilisation* is nothing other than the aesthetic autonomy that de Man locates in the *grandes lois évolutives* of Western literary life.

To do no more than adduce this article as yet another candidate for some hypothetical anthology of theoretical sensationalism would be to repeat the formalizing move that this chapter has attempted at least to slow down, if not to reverse. Nor, after having problematized the distinction between "good" Jews and "bad" Jews, am I about to propose a distinction between the "good" Paul de Man and the "bad" Paul de Man. My aim is rather to situate this chapter more explicitly than I was able to do as I was writing the bulk of it. Imagining a separation of the Jews from *la littérature actuelle*, de Man ends up celebrating its "great evolutive laws." Critics will be arguing for some time to come about whether or not those "laws" were reenacted decades later as the canonical principles of deconstruction. For my part, rereading *Daniel Deronda* has meant not only uncovering a certain system of "great art" as a set of laws in its own right—laws that I myself enforced in an earlier reading—but also according a certain space and a certain play to some of the figures in the novel on whose performing bodies those laws get enforced. As Foucault and others have shown, if laws require enforcers, they also require violators. And if, as previous chapters of this book have indicated, it is thus not a simple question of "authority" versus "subversion," the present chapter has nonetheless been written in the name of the "bad" Jewishness that Eliot's novel, among other more or less well-intentioned agents of Western ideology, punishes so grandly.

69. De Man begins the article by ascribing to "vulgar anti-Semitism" the view that, as a result of Jewish influence, all of contemporary literature must be considered *polluée et néfaste*. A few paragraphs later, he writes: "À examen quelque peu proche, cette influence apparait même comme extraordinairment peu importante" (ibid., p. 45).

6

Making a Scene
Henry James's Theater of Embarrassment

The pleasure that comes of exercising a power that questions, monitors, watches, spies, searches out, palpates, brings to light; and on the other hand, the pleasure that kindles at having to evade this power, flee from it, fool it, or travesty it. The power that lets itself be invaded by the pleasure it is pursuing; and opposite it, power asserting itself in the pleasure of showing off, scandalizing, or resisting. Capture and seduction, confrontation and mutual reinforcement: parents and children, adults and adolescents, educator and students, doctors and patients, the psychiatrist with his hysteric and his perverts, all have played this game continually since the nineteenth century. These attractions, these evasions, these circular incitements have traced around bodies and sexes, not boundaries not to be crossed, but *perpetual spirals of power and pleasure.*

Michel Foucault

If in *Daniel Deronda* George Eliot enforces the laws of a certain "poetry" over and against the infractions of a certain "theatricality," Henry James seems at once to continue "the great tradition" by maintaining law and order and to imperil it, almost sensationalistically, by blurring the distinction between discipline and transgression. In one of the most lucid and articulate literary-critical applications of Foucault's ideas[1], Mark Seltzer has argued that the novels of Henry James exemplify "a criminal continuity between the techniques of the novel and the social technologies of power that inhere in these techniques."[2] Yet, though richly suggestive in its account

---

1. The passage by Michel Foucault quoted at the beginning of this chapter appears in Foucault, *The History of Sexuality I: An Introduction,* trans. Robert Hurley (New York: Vintage, 1980), p. 45.

2. Mark Seltzer, *Henry James and the Art of Power* (Ithaca: Cornell University Press, 1984), p. 57. For a more explicit criticism of Seltzer's assumptions and strategies than

of the surprising affinities between the novelist—especially *this* novelist—and "the police," Seltzer's reading remains oddly abstract in
its sense of the repeatedly asserted *criminality* of their connection:
what is "criminal," it would seem, is merely that the connection,
systematically disavowed by James and his critics alike, exists in the
first place. Seltzer's otherwise acute representation of the detective-
as-novelist will not allow us to get much beyond the truism according to which—"since Oedipus," we are almost required to say—
the detective and the criminal resemble each other to the point of
being identical.

At least one of James's contemporary critics, however, was willing
to go further in speculating about the novelist's "crimes." In 1902,
in an article provocatively entitled, "The Queerness of Henry
James," F. M. Colby wrote: "In a literature as well policed as ours,
the position of Henry James is anomalous. He is the only writer of
the day whose moral notions do not seem to matter. His dissolute
and complicated Muse may say just what she chooses. This may be
because it would be so difficult to expose him. Never did so much
vice go with such sheltering vagueness."[3]

Taking it upon himself to "police" Seltzer's unlikely "policeman"—when the subject is the "politics" of literature, quotation
marks seem inevitable—Colby conducts an investigation that results
in both the acquittal and the conviction of its subject. For while
Colby concludes that, in James's late fiction, "nobody sins because
nobody has anything to sin with,"[4] this very disembodiment—what
the critic seems to have in mind when he refers to James's "queerness"—constitutes a kind of offense in itself. For Colby, James's
"sheltering vagueness" may appear to mitigate his "vice," but in
some sense that vagueness *is* his vice: "indeed, it has been a long
time since the public knew what Henry James was up to behind
that verbal hedge of his, though half-suspecting that he meant no
good, because a style like that seemed just the place for guilty se-

---

I can offer here, and for a discussion of the literary-theoretical context of Seltzer's
reading, see my "Back to the Future: A Review-Article on the New Historicism,
Deconstruction, and Nineteenth-Century Fiction," *Texas Studies in Literature and Language* 30 (Spring 1988): 120–49.

3. F. M. Colby, "The Queerness of Henry James," *Bookman* 15 (June 1902); cited
in Roger Gard, ed., *Henry James: The Critical Heritage* (London: Routledge and Kegan
Paul, 1968), p. 337.

4. Ibid.

crets."[5] Purporting to find James innocent, Colby manages at the same time to make the novelist's "verbal hedge" ("a style like that") look culpably shady in its own right. To attest that James is "difficult to expose" is thus, conveniently enough, already to expose him.

And yet, if Colby puts James in the position of the "suspect," he offers yet another illustration of the remarkable fluidity, almost the reversibility, that Foucault, in the epigraph to this chapter, discerns in the broader historical transactions between scandal and surveillance. For Colby begins his investigation on a curiously confessional note: "A year ago, when Henry James wrote an essay on women that brought to our cheek the hot, rebellious blush, we said nothing about it, thinking that perhaps, after all, the man's style was his sufficient fig-leaf, and that few would see how shocking he really was."[6] As though what compels him to write the present exposé were remorse over his own silent complicity in the cover-up, Colby performs the almost ritually expiatory gesture of dramatizing his guilt: "the hot, rebellious blush" that (re)appears on his cheek— although a certain "sheltering vagueness" prevents him from making clear against *what* that blush is rebelling—betokens his own implication in the "circular incitements" that, "since the nineteenth century," according to Foucault, "have traced around bodies and sexes . . . *perpetual spirals of power and pleasure.*"

That the putative cause of Colby's blush was James's "essay on women," and that the prosecuting critic has to name, as codefendant, James's "dissolute and complicated Muse," suggests, however, the need for heterosexual triangulation of what might otherwise appear to be an affair exclusively "between men," in Eve Kosofsky Sedgwick's phrase; without the homophobic interposition of "women," the critic's preoccupation with the author's "fig-leaf," and with what "shocking" evidence it may conceal, might itself, given the focus on "queerness," begin to look "suspicious" in more ways than one.[7] In other words, though Foucault explicitly opposes the spirals of power and pleasure to "boundaries not to be crossed," we see here

---

5. Ibid., p. 335.
6. Ibid.
7. For a full-scale elaboration of this homophobic-homosocial paradigm, see Eve Kosofsky Sedgwick, *Between Men: English Literature and Male Homosocial Desire* (New York: Columbia University Press, 1985). On the "telling ambiguity" of the phrase "suspicious characters," see D. A. Miller, *The Novel and the Police* (Berkeley: University of California Press, 1988), p. 161.

that the "game" being "played" may not be able to dispense entirely with certain imaginary boundaries or buffer zones. The offending essay was probably James's piece on Matilde Serao, the Italian author whom he characterized as "a lady-novelist . . . confessedly flushed with the influence of Emile Zola."[8] And while the rhyme of Serao's flush with Colby's blush may stand synecdochally for the essay's "shocking" recognition of female sexual and textual desire as a force to be reckoned with, the rather supercilious case that James in fact bases on the "lady-novelist['s]" "confession" reminds us that, for his own part, he can still carry out the police work of keeping the woman writer in her place, not only *between* men but also conspicuously *under* men—under their "influence," that is. Colby, we might conclude, has less to worry about than he would have us believe.

My aim in teasing out these intertextual strands is twofold. On the one hand, I want to supplement Seltzer's Foucauldian emphasis on James's policial techniques with what I take to be an equally Foucauldian emphasis on the incessant *mobility* of the power relations between "the police" and the objects of their surveillance. James's "criminality" extends beyond the mere fact of his involvement in power, insofar as power itself "lets itself be invaded by the pleasure it is pursuing." On the other hand, I want to complicate or to fill in Foucault's scenario by underscoring within the field of circular incitements, "not boundaries not to be crossed," but boundaries that are all the more consequential for *being crossed*, in ways apparently accidental and self-compromising, but in fact strategic and potentially self-enhancing. Power in James may depend, as Seltzer argues, upon the panoptic privilege of "seeing without being seen,"[9] but James's novels also show how power gets a charge out of appearing, at selected moments, to make a spectacle of itself. From the point of view of power, the game that Foucault delineates brings rewards because it entails calculated risks, and it is the calculation of those risks that I hope to uncover in James's writing.

Though I will be using Foucault's metaphor of the game, I will be taking advantage of the cognate notion of "play" to incorporate

8. "Matilde Serao," in Henry James, *Literary Criticism: French Writers, Other European Writers, The Prefaces to the New York Edition*, ed. Leon Edel and Mark Wilson (New York: Library of America, 1984), p. 961.
9. Seltzer, *Henry James*, p. 41.

the ludic within a larger, *theatrical* frame of reference. As I have suggested in previous chapters, the theatrical analogy tends to be more inclusive, more dynamic, and more useful than the ludic one; even when, as in *Middlemarch* and *Daniel Deronda*, play turns into the sinister activity of gaming, that activity owes its special aura of danger to its conspicuous theatrical overlay, rather than to any intimation of a degenerative principle inherent in play itself. My interest, in short, is in what, taking my cue from the title of James's 1896 collection of stories, *Embarrassments*, and from the embarrassing results of his attempted career as a playwright, I would call James's veritable *theater* of embarrassment, which comprises not just the late works that Colby and so many others love to make fun of, but indeed virtually all of James's writing.[10] The term *embarrassment* appears frequently enough in James's work, though it sometimes has the older meaning of "obstacle" or "impediment" rather than the newer one, current when James was writing, of "abashment" or "discomposure." My focus, however, is less on "embarrassment" as a signifier than on embarrassment (for which, as we will see, James has his own favorite terms) as a complex signifying *mechanism* within the Jamesian text—a mechanism, moreover, that is almost indistinguishable from the large and complex thematic-metaphorical apparatus of the theatrical itself.

It has long been recognized that, beyond the local fact of his concrete engagement with the theater, theatrical terms and techniques have a privileged position throughout James's writing. Among the novelists discussed in this book, only Dickens and Collins rival James in the prominence and durability of their interest in the theatrical. That all of these authors are male is no doubt significant: one could argue that writing about the theater (and writing theatrically) is as precarious a business for nineteenth-century women as is acting itself, and that nineteenth-century men enjoy greater freedom in this as in virtually every other walk of life. But this argument would have to be qualified by an acknowledgment of James's difference from Dickens and Collins. In the next section of this chapter, I will try to define that difference as a function both

10. With predictable cruelty (and perhaps a certain obtuseness), an anonymous contemporary reviewer of the 1896 collection wrote: "Really these stories are often *Embarrassments* in a sense other than that intended by their author." Cited in Gard, ed., *Henry James*, p. 259.

of historical change and of James's sexual (as distinguished from gender) specificity, which, if it is not reducible to the masculine/ feminine binarism, has an intimate relation, as has often been remarked, to a certain cultural construction of "the feminine."

James writes in a period when theatricality has acquired meanings that it did not have—could not have had—for earlier writers, male or female. Moreover, as I will show, James's experience as a desiring subject is such that these meanings cannot but impinge upon him with particular force. The result of this convergence of historical and biographical specificity is that, for James, embarrassment and theatricality all but constitute each other, so that to speak of a "theater of embarrassment" verges on redundancy; we are far from Gwendolen Harleth's "mortification," whose effect was essentially *counter*theatrical. Although the embarrassments of James's excursion into the actual theater in the 1890s may appear as so many misfortunes befalling him as it were from outside, we will see that that painful episode in his life merely literalizes the *inherence* of embarrassment in the Jamesian "theater." But to guard against the perception of that "theater" as James's *alone*—as the sublimely solipsistic creation of a unique and transcendent aesthetic sensibility—I hope to relate the power plays that take place in James's writing to performances on other salient stages of late nineteenth- and early twentieth-century culture.

We have already seen in the case of one of James's critics how, instead of disabling the project of surveillance, the staging of one's own embarrassment may motivate it. It is significant, moreover, that in employing this strategy the critic, hot on the trail of James's "guilty secrets," at the same time displays the guilty secret of his own almost specular collusion with James. At least in the relatively circumscribed milieu of James's readership, a certain combination of sadism and exhibitionism does begin to assume the kind of formal regularity that indeed suggests the repeatable playing of a game. Though terms like *sadism* and *exhibitionism* might seem to signal the insistence (in both this text and the texts that it discusses) of Charlotte Brontë, it would be more appropriate here to point out their relevance to a discourse that is precisely contemporary with James, and that in fact shapes the more immediate context not only of his own production but of his reception as well.

I refer of course to the discourse with which Foucault concerns himself in *The History of Sexuality*, that of nineteenth-century psychiatry and sexology. The mode of James criticism that this discourse informs is not the obviously "powerful" (i.e., "conservative") ideological enterprise that accomplished, in Fredric Jameson's witty formulation, "the remarkable transformation of Henry James from a minor nineteenth-century man of letters into the greatest American novelist of the 1950s."[11] Rather, it is a question here of a less celebratory exercise of critical power, one in which my own reading of James no doubt takes part and which is in evidence both before and after the great period of James's canonization. Not only James's more recent, avowedly suspicious critics but many of his contemporary readers as well—even ostensibly friendly ones—at once act out a certain "pathology" and adopt the vocabulary that would control it.[12]

Though Edith Wharton, for one, was both a friend and a reader of the novelist, her participation in the game we might call "embarrassing Henry James" indeed raises questions as to whether or not she should be viewed as a friendly reader. The name of the game is deliberately ambiguous: as Wharton demonstrates, to get into the act of embarrassing James is to risk being embarrassed *by* him, finding out just how embarrassing *he* can be. But where the "flushed" Matilde Serao functions as an instrument of male power relations rather than as a player in her own right, Wharton is a "lady-novelist" who takes up a position of her own in the interpretative relay. That is to say, she picks up the game where F. M. Colby left off. In her autobiography, *A Backward Glance* (1934), Wharton, having described the aging master's painful sensitivity to the discomforts of heat and travel, captures him in an even more poignant scene of embarrassment:

11. Fredric Jameson, *The Political Unconscious: Narrative as a Socially Symbolic Act* (Ithaca: Cornell University Press, 1981), p. 222.

12. For examples of early responses to James that apply the languages of psychopathology, see the unsigned review of *The Author of "Beltraffio," Etc.*, the selections from Robert Buchanan's "The Modern Young Man as Critic" and from William Watson's "Fiction—Plethoric and Anoemic," and the essay by H. G. Dwight, all in Gard, ed., *Henry James*.

A similar perturbation could be produced (I later learned, to my cost) by asking him to explain any phrase in his books that did not seem quite clear, or any situation of which the motive was not adequately developed; and still more disastrous was the effect of letting him know that any of his writings had been parodied. I had always regarded the fact of being parodied as one of the surest evidences of fame, and once, when he was staying with us in New York, I brought him with glee a deliciously droll article on his novels by poor Frank Colby, the author of "Imaginary Obligations." The effect was disastrous. I shall never forget the misery, the mortification even, which tried to conceal itself behind an air of offended dignity."[13]

Subjecting James, "with glee," to Colby's "deliciously droll article," Wharton does more than just reenact Colby's quasi-juridical proceeding as a quasi-medical scene of exposure, in which what comes to light is not so much James's hidden "vice" as his "morbidly delicate sensibility."[14] Or rather, to the degree that she does continue Colby's work of putting James on the spot, she also follows "poor Frank Colby" in exposing herself along with James. If this anecdote, like the two that come after it, refuses to let James's "mortification" "conceal itself," it also exhibits Wharton's own embarrassment. For in rehearsing these incidents, she makes a point of noting their "cost" to herself. Yet, just as the specific valence of Colby's "hot, rebellious blush" remains somewhat elusive, so Wharton—apparently unaware, for instance, of the aggression betrayed by the "glee" with which she shows Colby's in-itself–aggressive article to James— partially and perhaps unwittingly conceals the exact nature and extent of that "cost," which thus, like James's own phrases, does "not seem quite clear."[15] As we read on, however, we begin to see that a significant, determinate relationship obtains between embarrassment and indeterminacy (or "vagueness") itself. Introducing the last of her three anecdotes of the master in distress, Wharton begins: "Once again—and again unintentionally—I was guilty of a similar blunder."[16] She then recalls how she complained to James about the manner of his late novels, observing that

13. Edith Wharton, *A Backward Glance* (1934; rpt. New York: Charles Scribner's Sons, 1964), p. 189.
14. Ibid., p. 190.
15. Roger Gard observes: "in view of what Colby actually wrote, I wonder if her account should be quite so much admired as it commonly is." Gard, ed., *Henry James*, p. 342.
16. Wharton, *A Backward Glance*, p. 190.

his stage was cleared like that of the Théâtre Français in the good old days when no chair or table was introduced that was not *relevant to the action* (a good rule for the stage, but an unnecessary embarrassment to fiction). Preoccupied by this, I one day said to him: "What was your idea in suspending the four principal characters in 'The Golden Bowl' in the void? What sort of life did they lead when they were not watching each other, and fencing with each other? Why have you stripped them of all the *human fringes* we necessarily trail after us through life?"

He looked at me in surprise, and I saw at once that the surprise was painful, and wished I had not spoken. I had assumed that his system was a deliberate one, carefully thought out, and had been genuinely anxious to hear his reasons. But after a pause of reflection he answered in a disturbed voice: "My dear—I didn't know I had!" and I saw that my question, instead of starting one of our absorbing literary discussions, had only turned his startled attention on a peculiarity of which he had been completely unconscious.[17]

Echoing Colby's paradoxical point about the "embarrassment" of a certain Jamesian abstraction, and likening that effect to an inappropriate theatrical style, Wharton discovers that, if James's embarrassing theatricality constitutes a "system," it is not "a deliberate one" but one "of which he had been completely unconscious." In addition, Wharton *displays*—but as though "unintentionally"—a striking resemblance between, on the one hand, the very unintentionality of her own recurrent "blunder[s]" and, on the other hand, James's unconsciousness with respect to the systematic embarrassment he has produced. Yet, as we should recall from Colby's exposure of Jamesian "vagueness" as something of a scandal in itself, unintentionality and unconsciousness—the grounds for the "surprised" author's plea, "I didn't know I had!"—are not secondary or contingent features of the theater of embarrassment, but primary or essential ones: they are as necessary to that theater as to the famous "other scene" of Freudian psychoanalysis. Indeed, rather like "the fact of being parodied," which, though "one of the surest evidences of literary fame," also testifies to the elements of automatism and expropriability in one's discourse, embarrassment—the experience of making a spectacle of oneself—presupposes one's lack of complete cognitive control over one's own signifying power, whose consequent "excesses" become available for identification, interpretation, and supervision by others.

17. Ibid., pp. 190–91.

We should also remember, however, that Colby suspects James's "vagueness" of having a "sheltering" function. What if, instead of denoting, say, the irreducible blindness that enables one's insights, unconsciousness serves, less ontologically but just as felicitously, as a kind of alibi, deflecting or limiting the responsibility that an author might otherwise have to acknowledge? This might explain, for example, why, even though Wharton's embarrassing questions to James repeatedly represent her as knowing more about his work than he knows—or claims to know—she must characterize this "criticism" as "quite involuntary."[18] On one level, this assertion of involuntarity suggests Wharton's retaliatory use of "the velvet glove," to cite the title of James's short story that may have her as its subject.[19] Along the same fairly obvious psychological lines, the plea of involuntary criticism may bespeak a strategy of defense—in some sense a stereotypically "female" one—as well as of attack: Wharton may be shielding herself from an awareness of the aggression we have noticed in her supposedly innocent conduct toward "perhaps the most intimate friend I ever had."[20] This point might become less banal if we remark that Wharton's tendency to remystify the subjective conditions of her demystifying criticism seems to recapitulate the larger, transferential politics of interpretation that we discussed in the chapters on Charlotte Brontë. That is, by maintaining a semblance of vagueness concerning the "cost" to herself of the "perturbation[s]" that she inflicted upon James, and that she now restages in her narrative—Does she really not know, one wonders on second thought, how much the anecdote about Colby's "deliciously droll article" reveals about her own motives?—Wharton may also manage to obscure the *profit* that accompanies such a "cost."

For if the satirical governess-author and the demystifying academic critic both assume an ambiguous cultural instrumentality by virtue of the "sheltering shadow" in which they work, Wharton's "involuntarily" embarrassing critical practice, while appearing to make her more visible and hence more vulnerable than those masked unmaskers, may afford her greater discursive power, and

18. Ibid., p. 190.
19. For a discussion of "The Velvet Glove" (1909) in the context of James's relationship with Wharton, see Leon Edel, *Henry James: A Life* (New York: Harper and Row, 1985), pp. 655–57.
20. Ibid., p. 173.

hence greater discursive pleasure. Or better, Wharton suggests a way in which later styles of demystification may themselves diverge from the Brontëan model. Like James and Colby, Wharton of course occupies the historical space between Brontëan criticism and its modern analogue, a space that makes a difference. That difference is the vast nineteenth-century disciplinary formation that Foucault and others have anatomized. This formation, I have indicated, is governed not only by perpetual spirals of power and pleasure, but also by a perpetual sense of danger. If even those who deploy the discursive machinery cannot help crossing the boundary line separating their own conscious authority from the embarrassments of which they have taken charge, then the "pleasures" (not to mention the "pains") under analysis must be so pervasive and so insistent as to approach universality. Given this potentially anarchic state of affairs, the various technicians of surveillance—including, along with doctors and psychiatrists and educators, novelists and literary critics of a particularly suspicious cast—can never be *too* suspicious: they must become ever more alert to the constant possibility of aberrations not only in others but in themselves as well. Yet their intensified vigilance does more than promise a more reliable policing of the social body: it also quietly bespeaks the importance of their specialized analytic expertise, which, far from having been discredited, has been rendered all the more fascinating—even sexier, as it were—by the demonstration of its own susceptibilities.[21]

In the ongoing search for emblems of demystifying literary criticism, I would not, however, simply replace the self-effacing governess, or Charlotte Brontë herself, with the racier and more glamorous figure of Edith Wharton. Rather, I would propose that we consider both figures in tandem, and that we note their surprising similarities. For just as, for instance, the phenomenon of "out-gov-

---

21. It is in this light, for example, that one might understand a gesture that has become almost compulsory in many varieties of poststructuralist criticism—namely, the critic's acknowledgment of his or her own implication in whatever rhetorical contradiction, ideological procedure, or psychic structure he or she happens to be examining. (My compulsion to acknowledge my own performance of that gesture earlier in this chapter merely represents another turn of this familiar discursive screw.) The point is not to invalidate such methodological self-reflexivity, but to signal its less obvious situational effects. I discuss below the strategic advantages of a more or less canonical instance of analytic self-embarrassment, Freud's apparently inadvertent demonstrations of his own "hysteria."

ernessing the governess" showed that Brontëan self-effacement entails its own kind of exhibitionism, so we should bear in mind that
the theater of embarrassment is also a shelter. But I hope to have
indicated why this sheltering function should not be equated with
the mere illusion of immunity or impunity. Though the plea of
unconsciousness may serve to exculpate the individual author, what
the unconscious protects most successfully is discourse itself: its
systematically and continually substantiated force and immensity
guarantee that there will always be more to investigate and more
to diagnose, more to show and more to say. In the theater of embarrassment, what every act of exposure shadows forth is the inex-
haustible reserve of the unconscious. Like a canny impresario (or
like an impresario of the *un*canny), the specialist in embarrassment
knows how to captivate an audience with the promise of endless
surprises in store.[22]

22. This account, I realize somewhat tardily, has certain congruences with the
reading of Rousseau's *Confessions* in the final chapter of Paul de Man's *Allegories of
Reading: Figural Language in Rousseau, Nietzsche, Rilke, and Proust* (New Haven: Yale
University Press, 1979), pp. 278–301. I would call attention to a passage such as the
following:

> The more crime there is, the more theft, lie, slander, and stubborn persistence
> in each of them, the better. The more there is to expose, the more there is to
> be ashamed of; the more resistance to exposure, the more satisfying the scene,
> and, especially, the more satisfying and eloquent the belated revelation, in the
> later narrative, of the inability to reveal. This desire is truly shameful, for it
> suggests that Marion was destroyed, not for the sake of Rousseau's saving
> face, nor for the sake of his desire for her, but merely in order to provide him
> with a stage on which to parade his disgrace or, what amounts to the same
> thing, to furnish him with a good ending for Book II of his *Confessions*. The
> structure is self-perpetuating, *en abîme*, as is implied in its description as ex-
> posure of the desire to expose, for each new stage in the unveiling suggests
> a deeper shame, a greater impossibility to reveal, and a greater satisfaction in
> outwitting this impossibility.
>
> (pp. 285–86)

The similarity between de Man's reading of Rousseau and my remarks about the
self-implicating rhetoric of late nineteenth-century surveillance might raise questions
about the historical specificity of the latter. Without going into the whole issue of
the way in which "the lesson of Paul de Man" has influenced the present book—an
issue that I could only broach at the end of the previous chapter—I would merely
say that my aim here is not to "overcome" the allegorical nature of reading by
appealing to history, but rather to conceive of different, and perhaps differently
useable, narrative (which is to say, historical) frames in which the allegorical nature
of reading can be activated. In any case, if anyone thought that "allegory" and
"history" are antonyms, the recent rereading of de Man's work on guilt and excuses
in Rousseau in light of the discovery of de Man's wartime journalism would suggest
otherwise. What I mean is that to reread, as many people are now doing, the essay

This impresario, of course, is also necessarily a performer as well—in Wharton's case, obviously a *female* performer. Nor is it insignificant that our avatar of the embarrassing critic, like our "model" for the unmasking critic (and I echo deliberately the language of fashion), is a woman writer. Not only does this assignment of roles evoke the cultural stereotype of literary studies as a feminized institution: it also has to do with the close historical relationship between a discipline like psychiatry and a figure like the mythically and often actually female hysteric. As critics and historians have shown, the nineteenth-century hysteric appears in a distinctly theatrical light: instructively exhibited, for example, on the stage of what Charles Bernheimer calls Charcot's "hypnotic theater," the hysteric herself is seen to stage a split between "socially commendable and socially censurable roles," enacting the latter in the relatively safe form of symptoms issuing from the "other scene" of the unconscious.[23] Indeed, her very illness has been interpreted as an "involuntary . . . criticism" of her culture.[24] Again, however, we must avoid reducing unconsciousness and involuntarity to the status of mere excuses: as a performer of the unconscious, the hysteric not only adopts a legitimizing cover for her "criticism," but becomes, as Nina Auerbach has suggested, an almost glamorous figure—a kind of cover girl in her own right.[25] As demonstrated, moreover, by a series of shrewd

on the *Confessions*—an essay that is palpably haunted by the specter of Freud—as itself the allegory of de Man's historical experience as a particular kind of postwar intellectual would have the effect, among many others, of bringing both that essay and "Rousseau" much closer to the cultural context in which I am trying to locate James.

23. Charles Bernheimer, Introduction: Part One, in Charles Bernheimer and Claire Kahane, eds., *In Dora's Case: Freud-Hysteria-Feminism* (New York: Columbia University Press, 1985), p. 7. For a historian's account of hysteria as a socially acceptable form of deviation from traditional female roles, and for a discussion of the complicities of male doctors with female patients and of the concomitant countertransferential hostilities, see Carroll Smith-Rosenberg, "The Hysterical Woman: Sex Roles and Role Conflict in Nineteenth-Century America," in her *Disorderly Conduct: Visions of Gender in Victorian America* (New York: Oxford University Press, 1985), pp. 197–216.

24. Taking off from the dialogue between Hélène Cixous and Catherine Clément in *La jeune née*, and from the question of whether the hysteric contests or conserves the patriarchal family, Jane Gallop's "Keys to Dora" (in Bernheimer and Kahane, eds., *In Dora's Case*, pp. 200–220) offers a witty and expansive discussion of the politics of hysteria.

25. In *Woman and the Demon: The Life of a Victorian Myth* (Cambridge: Harvard University Press, 1982), Auerbach writes: "Like Trilby's voice, . . . Dora's dreams function in this case history as a token of a transforming power that enervates her increasingly paralyzed master" (p. 30). Interestingly, in light of the present context,

readings of Freud's case history of "Dora" (in which, we recall from the chapter on *Jane Eyre*, the figure of the governess also looms large), the interdependence of doctor and hysteric at times intimates a confusion of identities, so that the spectacle of *Freud's* hysteria almost ends up eclipsing that of his patient's.[26] As a critic of the Jamesian unconscious who simultaneously insists on the unconsciousness of her own criticism, Edith Wharton (who had in fact suffered from a hysteria-like condition) aptly embodies the analytic self-hystericization that constitutes a definitive act in the theater of embarrassment.[27]

To be sure, one hardly comes away from the essays on Freud's hysteria with the impression that he *planned* to embarrass himself: on the contrary, these readings indeed imply the *cost* to Freud—as well as to the patriarchal economy that psychoanalysis serves—of such ostensibly accidental self-exposure. Without denying that this phenomenon often has a "painful" effect not unlike the "surprise" that Wharton observes (and induces) in James—an effect as gratifying to the reader as it seems inimical to the master and his discourse—I would argue that being "surprised" has surprising advantages as well. For while Freud's apparently unconscious identification with "Dora" may seem to compromise his authority, that identification may also work positively, to mediate his relations with other men. This is not the place to rehearse the intricate interplay of transferences and countertransferences in the case history, especially since that interplay has already been explored so extensively and so deftly by so many others. It should suffice to mention that, as one gathers from those previous readings, "Dora"'s sense of herself as an "object of barter" applies not only to the way she facilitates exchanges

---

she goes on to characterize "the central emotion of the case history" as "the teller's [i.e., Freud's] affliction, like that of an emotionally eroded Jamesian narrator, with what might be called 'dream envy' " (p. 31).

26. Many of these readings have been collected in Bernheimer and Kahane, eds., *In Dora's Case*.

27. In her thirties, Wharton was afflicted by what she described as a "form of neurasthenia." According to R. W. B. Lewis, *Edith Wharton: A Biography* (New York: Harper and Row, 1975), "This condition was customarily diagnosed at the time as hysteria"(p. 83); she eventually came under the medical supervision of the famous (or infamous) Dr. S. Weir Mitchell. For an account of this period in her life, see Lewis, pp. 65–79.

between her father and her would-be lover, but also to her function as both conduit and screen for Freud's own desirous symbolic transactions with those other men, as well as with certain male colleagues.[28] Allowing himself to become identified *with* the hysteric, Freud at once invites and forestalls identification *as* the "pervert." The most hysterical thing about Freud, one might say, is his own enactment of the relationship, not between "socially commendable and socially censurable roles," but between one censurable role and an even more censurable one.

Freud's performance, moreover, might shed some light on the strategy whereby Colby invokes James's "Muse" and his "essay on women" so as to heterosexualize his own interest in James's "queerness." For Colby's blush in response to that essay begins to resemble a hysterical symptom: in the process of heterosexualizing himself, he also feminizes himself. And if that "feminine" identity nonetheless constitutes a sort of mask, this shelter, as Colby himself might call it, is in turn open to suspicion. In the theater of embarrassment, the more one seems to conceal, the more one seems to display; the more self-conscious one seems, the more accident-prone one seems. Yet, as I have suggested, submitting oneself to these ironies does not necessarily undermine one's power: indeed, as evidenced by the enormous and ever increasing cultural prestige of both Freud and James (if not of "poor Frank Colby"), it can even enhance that power by advertising a certain heroics of interpretation.

To prevent my own embarrassment (though it may be too late for such defensive measures), I should acknowledge here that my relation to Edith Wharton, the other author-critic in this scene of reading, repeats the familiar pattern in which a suspicious male interpreter articulates his interest in other men's "secrets" through the figure of a woman. Like Freud's identification with "Dora," and like Colby's impersonation of James's "dissolute and complicated Muse," my casting and promotion of Wharton in the role of the embarrassing critic does more than just serve—not least as a respectably "feminist" gesture—to grant a certain legitimacy to my own act of surveillance: as an implicit instance of what Elaine Sho-

28. For suggestions of this insight, see, for example, the essays in *In Dora's Case* by Toril Moi, Jane Gallop, and Neil Hertz.

walter calls critical cross-dressing, it no doubt looks like a teasing, attention-getting ploy.[29] Of course, if I hereby seem to subvert rather than to defend myself, this self-exposure may be expected to have its own ironically recuperative function. Yet I will risk perhaps more serious embarrassment by attempting to justify my use of Wharton as more than just a move in a game or a ruse in a series of power plays. I hope, that is, not merely to reenact but also to explore a significant aspect of the dynamics of power and pleasure in and around James's texts. Specifically, I would argue that, as dramatized in the passages I have quoted from her autobiography, Wharton's relation to James itself plays out—but in reverse, which may be to say, with a difference—what one might call the primal scene of Jamesian embarrassment, a scene virtually constituted by James's own framing and appropriation of a certain female role.

James describes this scene in *A Small Boy and Others* (1913), the first volume of *his* autobiography. It took place almost sixty years before, in the summer of 1854, at a cousin's house in Rhinebeck, New York, and unfolds, in James's narrative, against the backdrop of a family crisis brought about by the grave illness of an aunt and uncle. The main players are another aunt and uncle, their daughter, and James himself, though he installs himself here, as throughout this volume, in the position of the quintessential spectator-*flâneur*, embracing "the so far from showy practice of wondering and dawdling and gaping." As we will see, it is characteristic of James to deny the "showiness" of this "practice" with one hand and to embarrass *himself* by showing it off with the other: "But I positively dawdle and gape here—" he adds a few sentences later, "I catch myself in the act."[30] This dual stance is already discernible in his account of the scene in question, in which the eleven-year-old James both plays the detached observer who merely watches as his "spoiled" cousin Marie, "exactly of my own age," *makes a scene*— his own phrase—and projects himself into her performance. What precipitates this scene-within-a-scene is Marie's father's expression

29. Elaine Showalter, "Critical Cross-Dressing: Male Feminists and the Woman of the Year," *Raritan* 3 (Fall 1983): 130–49.

30. Henry James, *Autobiography: A Small Boy and Others, Notes of a Son and Brother, The Middle Years*, ed. F. W. Dupee (Princeton: Princeton University Press, 1983), p. 17.

of "the strong opinion that Marie should go to bed," an opinion
whose strength James proceeds to qualify:

> It had been remarked but in the air, I feel sure, that Marie should
> seek her couch—a truth by the dark wing of which I ruefully felt
> myself brushed; and the words seemed therefore to fall with a certain
> ironic weight. What I have retained of their effect, at any rate, is the
> vague fact of some objection raised by my cousin and some sharper
> point to his sentence supplied by her father; promptly merged in a
> visible commotion, a flutter of my young companion across the gallery
> as for refuge in the maternal arms, a protest and an appeal in short
> which drew from my aunt the simple phrase that was from that mo-
> ment so preposterously to "count" for me. "Come now, my dear;
> don't make a scene—I *insist* on your not making a scene!" That was
> all the witchcraft the occasion used, but the note was none the less
> epoch-making. The expression, so vivid, so portentous, was one I had
> never heard—it had never been addressed to us at home; and who
> should say now what a world one mightn't at once read into it? It
> seemed freighted to sail so far; it told me so much about life. Life at
> these intensities clearly became "scenes"; but the great thing, the
> immense illumination, was that we could make them or not as we
> chose. It was a long time of course before I began to distinguish
> between those within our compass more particularly as spoiled and
> those producible on a different basis and which should involve de-
> tachment, involve presence of mind; just the qualities in which Marie's
> possible output was apparently deficient. It didn't in the least matter
> accordingly whether or no a scene *was* then proceeded to—and I have
> lost all count of what immediately happened. The mark had been
> made for me and the door flung open; the passage, gathering up *all*
> the elements of the troubled time, had been itself a scene, quite enough
> of one, and I had become aware with it of a rich accession of pos-
> sibilities.[31]

"The passage . . . had been itself a scene": similarly, the scenic
"intensities" of this *narrative* passage epitomize the interpenetration
of stage and page in virtually all of James's work. Yet if in his writing
James may thus be said regularly to "make a scene," with all the
connotations of conscious craftsmanship that "the simple phrase"
can bear, the particular scene described here stands out as "epoch-
making" or primal not only because of its obvious oedipal lineaments, but also because it enables, forecasts, and "illuminat[es]," a
productive peculiarity of Jamesian scene-making in general—
namely, that it partakes of both consciousness and *un*consciousness,

31. Ibid., pp. 106–07.

of both craft and "witchcraft": "Life at these intensities clearly became 'scenes'; but the great thing, the immense illumination, was
that we could make them or not as we chose."

Admittedly, in its apparent celebration of autonomous, even omnipotent aesthetic volition, this statement might seem merely and
unambiguously to override or ignore the ordinary implications of
"making a scene." Even in everyday life, one can of course "choose"
to "make a scene," but this "choice," more often menacingly announced than actually put into practice, suggests the desperation of
the last resort. As Marie, for one, might have confirmed, the very
"simplicity" or conventionality of the phrase invests it with a remarkable capacity to reveal how easily one's behavior, so far from
answering to one's unique semantic intentions, or from attesting to
one's "detachment" and "presence of mind," can be named, framed,
and stigmatized by others, especially if one is a child and those
others are adults. Significantly, it is not Marie but her mother who
has the power to wield "the simple phrase," and it is her mother's
"insistence" on Marie's "not making a scene" that in effect produces
what it proscribes, transforming Marie's "protest" and "appeal" *into*
a scene. And yet, the power relations depicted in this scene of scene-
making may not be entirely one-sided. In view of the fact that Marie
is "spoiled"—it is telling, for instance, that her father's "strong opinion" rapidly finds itself up "in the air"—this little tableau of domestic
"commotion" might indeed be said to typify the game of circular
incitements that Foucault sees as having been played in so many
arenas of our culture since the nineteenth century. In what would
thus be the home version of that game—after all, as Foucault points
out, "parents and children" get to play, too—Marie may well be
"showing off, scandalizing, or resisting" the power that, in its interpretative absolutism, would seem to have rendered resistance
impossible.

If it turns out that Marie has greater control over her performance
than we might think, then, conversely, James's apparently unambiguous affirmation of the magisterial ego may, like his uncle's unsettling words to Marie, "fall with a certain ironic weight." James
in fact seems to signal this irony by playing on the contrast between
the ordinary or "simple" understanding of "making a scene" and
the heroic or "portentous" meaning that the eleven-year-old spectator, who "had never heard" the expression, manages "preposter-

ously" to "read into it."[32] To be sure, if the small boy identifies decisively with the performance he appears merely to observe, the seventy-year-old autobiographer makes a point of differentiating between youth and maturity: "It was a long time of course before I began to distinguish between those [scenes] within our compass more particularly as spoiled and those producible on a different basis and which should involve detachment, involve presence of mind; just the qualities in which Marie's possible output was apparently deficient." But if the equivocation of "*possible* output" strengthens the distinction by weakening Marie, that of "*apparently* deficient" strengthens Marie by weakening the distinction. What are we to do with such "indeterminacy"? How much should we "read into" these "ironies"? On the one hand, we could use them to catch James in the act (as he might say), where the act is one of unwitting, hubristic self-deconstruction: in this reading, James would be seen ironically to regress in the very attempt to mark his progress, to trip himself up in the very process of positing a firm "basis" for the opposition between his "presence of mind" and Marie's "deficiency"; asserting his "detachment," he would seem instead to get entangled in his own unstable binarisms, finally and fatally weakening *himself* through what Harold Bloom would call his weak misreading, whereby "spoiled" ends up meaning merely "inferior." On the other hand, these rhetorical knots might be explained in terms of an older, more honorific sense of Jamesian "irony," according to which the author, precisely making scenes or not, as he chooses, would turn out to have embarrassed *us*, his would-be debunkers, by masterminding all of the "embarrassments" in which we imagine we have caught *him*. Whereas the first explanation would not so much abolish the magisterial ego as surreptitiously reassign it to the critic, the second, evoking the aura of a certain American Romanticism, would return that transcendental consciousness, exalted by the very audacity of its self-contradictions, to its proper or more traditional place.

32. James's phrasing here brings to mind that of Freud in an anecdote from his *History of the Psychoanalytic Movement* which Neil Hertz discusses in his essay on Freud's hysteria, "Dora's Secrets, Freud's Techniques," in Bernheimer and Kahane, eds., *In Dora's Case*, pp. 221–42, esp. pp. 236–42. In that anecdote, Freud, striking "the note of the ingénue," as Hertz observes (p. 240), remarks that he "had never heard of such a prescription" as that which constitutes the punch-line of a colleague's knowingly risqué joke.

I want to argue, however, that the rhetorical performance of James-ian embarrassment exceeds, even as it seems to solicit, both of these ways of reading. To be sure, if the passage we have been considering is indeed "itself a scene," it does more than just describe or discuss the phenomenon of making a scene as one chooses: it *exemplifies* that phenomenon, but in so doing it places the trope of voluntary scene-making beyond the familiar torsions of self-deconstruction and self-recuperation alike. James—the grown-up narrator—"makes a scene" here by contradicting himself; yet, having placed such em-barrassment explicitly under the aegis of choice, he also makes it difficult for us to think that, even more "grown-up" or sophisticated than he, we have uncovered the telltale signs of a genuine authorial inadvertence. Reading James, we thus have the sense that he is playing games with us, a sense all the more discomfiting for our not quite knowing what those games *are*. Or, to put it more accurately: our playing along with him means that we, too, have to engage in such "embarrassed" professions of "vagueness." What is at stake in this play?

I would like to propose that, instead of reducing these relations between author and reader to a question of who's duping whom, we see them as local effects of the general structure of power and pleasure defined by Foucault: as an especially articulate instantiation of that structure, what I have been calling James's theater of em-barrassment shows both author and readers moving back and forth across the footlights. In subjecting James to one's analytic gaze, one tends, that is, to expose oneself as well, repeating the author's double role as spectator *and* performer. In neither case, I have suggested, does this self-doubling have to signify self-defeat; yet in neither case, I would add, should it be assimilated too quickly to what Mark Seltzer calls the "double discourse" of power, whereby power is at once disavowed and ironically reinscribed.[33]

For in the Jamesian theater of embarrassment, if not in the larger Foucauldian structure, power's identification with "the pleasure it is pursuing" has specific performative implications beyond those of an always-already-*aufgehoben* self-disavowal. Seeing himself, how-ever ambivalently, in Marie's role, James assumes a certain female position. The position is female not only because of the gender of

33. Seltzer, *Henry James and the Art of Power*, p. 174.

his cousin, but also because her ultimately and perhaps strategically indeterminate scene-making resembles that of the prototypically female hysteric. Significantly, James associates "the vague fact" of Marie's scene with "witchcraft," the category often invoked in the middle ages, as Charles Bernheimer points out, to "explain" hysterical symptoms.[34] But if Freud's identification with "Dora" serves as a surprising medium for his analytic power and pleasure, the advantages of James's similar relation to the "spoiled" Marie may be even more surprising.

Of course, where Freud can count on the protection of a preexisting, certifiable identification as a heterosexual male, James's standing in the symbolic order of patriarchy is itself constitutively "vague." And as we learned from the example of F. M. Colby, in the contemporary context "vagueness," far from representing a mere failure of meaning, is already viewed as suspect in its own right, not despite but because of the fact that it is also seen as an alibi: by seeming not to mean anything much, it is taken to mean something in particular, and that something, however obliquely named— whether as "queerness," to cite Colby, or as "perversity" or "effeminacy," to cite other readers of James—is homosexuality, well established, by James's time, as the proverbial name of the unnameable.[35] "Effeminacy" in particular reminds us that, given the enduring popular conception of same-sex desire in terms of "inversion," (female) hysteria might easily appear to stand less in front of than simply *for* (male) homosexuality.

Yet if James's conspicuously "vague" identification with "witchcraft" (performed not by Marie alone but, tellingly, by Marie and her parents together) thus seems almost dangerously *trans*parent, he nonetheless marks in that experience a "rich," albeit necessarily unspecified, "accession of possibilities." Figured as a "door flung open," this accession constitutes not so much an emergence from the closet as a "passage" into any number of possible *future* "passages"—into countless possibilities that "preposterously . . . 'count' " toward the writing/staging of a whole career's worth of passages/

---

34. Bernheimer, Introduction: Part One, in Bernheimer and Kahane, eds., *In Dora's Case*, pp. 3–4.

35. For contemporary examples of this coding, see the essays in Gard, ed., *Henry James: The Critical Heritage*, by William James, Vernon Lee, J. P. Mowbray, and George Moore.

scenes in which one simultaneously conceals and displays one's own "scandalous" sexual investments. Not so much a coming-out, then, as what we might call an open-and-shut case, the recounting of this "epoch-making" scene *re*covers the process whereby James *dis*covers, in a domestic drama centered on a kind of female masquerade, the lineaments of his own highly theatrical, inside-outside, now-you-see-it-now-you-don't, *écriture gaie*.[36] Perhaps it is not inconsequential that Marie was "named in honour of her having been born in Paris"; along with her reputation for being "spoiled," this foreignness, "marking sharply her difference from her sisters, so oddly, so almost extravagantly testified, . . . [makes] her in the highest degree interesting."[37] "The mark had been made," indeed: "Marie's possible output"—itself equivocally in and out—makes possible, for both the small boy and the big man who fondly re-collects him, a rich array of extravagantly equivocal markings of difference.

If I accentuate the positive here, I do so not to deny, by idealizing, the homophobic oppression that makes such rhetorical caginess necessary. But I prefer to see Jamesian equivocation as more than just a tacit concession to a surveillance that it thus fails to escape. Although, for example, Colby's accusatory attitude toward James's "vagueness" unpleasantly recalls the overzealous prosecutor's longing to drag the suspect out from his shelter and to publish his "crimes," the rather prurient, coyly periphrastic language of Colby's own investigation attests, as we have seen, to his fascinated involvement in the game of embarrassing Henry James. Like many of James's would-be exposers, both early and late, Colby seems not-so-secretly to *take* pleasure—what, after all, makes his writing "deliciously droll"—from the *pursuit* of pleasures that, while they never

---

36. On James and homosexuality, see Robert K. Martin, "The 'High Felicity' of Comradeship: A New Reading of *Roderick Hudson*," *American Literary Realism* 11 (Spring 1978): 100–108; Michael Moon, "Sexuality and Visual Terrorism in *The Wings of the Dove*," *Criticism* 28 (Fall 1986): 427–43; Georges-Michel Sarotte, *Like a Brother, Like a Lover: Male Homosexuality in the American Novel and Theater from Herman Melville to James Baldwin*, trans. Richard Miller (New York: Doubleday/Anchor, 1978); Eve Kosofsky Sedgwick, "The Beast in the Closet: James and the Writing of Homosexual Panic," in Ruth Bernard Yeazell, ed., *Sex, Politics, and Science in the Nineteenth-Century Novel: Selected Papers from the English Institute, 1983–84* (Baltimore: Johns Hopkins University Press, 1986), pp. 148–86. For an extended theoretical discussion of the relationship between homosexuality and writing, see Lee Edelman, "Homographesis," *Yale Journal of Criticism* 3 (Fall 1989): 189–207.

37. Henry James, *Autobiography*, p. 106.

really evade him, he can never quite catch, so teasingly do they hover on the borderline between meaning and not-meaning. And as long as they continue to hover there, the game itself can continue.

To call this process a game is not, however, to imply that it has been rigged. On the contrary, much is at stake in many games, including this one. At stake here, for instance, is both the possibility and the significance of being *surprised*, whether painfully or pleasurably. "Surprise," to use Wharton's term, is a tricky but important concept. If I have tried to argue against the image of James as a furtive and anxious cultural policeman inevitably betrayed by the truth of his own "criminal" desire, I want equally to resist the move that turns him into a generalized and thereby heterosexualized agent of an all-seeing but unseen power—a power that somehow seems to function a little too smoothly and predictably. What gets elided in Seltzer's account, at any rate, is a sense of James's specificity as an agent of power who, by virtue of his homosexuality, is also one of the most visible and laboriously constructed *objects* of that power. As I have suggested, this specificity by no means restricts James's capacity for enforcement: indeed, it may even increase that capacity. Yet the homosexual difference has nonetheless to be marked, and figured into the calculus of power and pleasure. Between the disavowal and the reinscription of power comes the difference that James brings to this double operation, a difference that "mark[s]" itself as "sharply" and "oddly" and "extravagantly" as does Marie's "difference from her sisters." This difference is registered in the Jamesian text as an effect of what James himself calls catching himself in the act. Precisely *as* an effect, of course, this self-catching is bound to seem somewhat staged. Yet to say that something is staged no more automatically implies spuriousness than to say that something is a game. It should be clear by now that "the stage," with its derivatives, designates an inextricable relationship, at least in certain nineteenth-century texts, not between authenticity and inauthenticity, but between control and surrender, between artifice and chance. Like "making a scene as one chooses," "catching oneself in the act" evokes the indeterminate juncture of consciousness and unconsciousness—the very site, as it were, of surprise—that makes the Jamesian theater of embarrassment not only "odd" but "in the highest degree interesting" as well.

My aim in the rest of this chapter will be to look at some of the acts in which James catches himself—acts, to recall his own example, like "dawdling and gaping," where surveillance begins to resemble what might nowadays be referred to as "cruising." Intelligible in the form of textual marks, these acts, I hope to show, mark a "vaguely" eroticized extravagance (literally, a wandering beyond bounds) on the part of one canonical author to whom power has been delegated. To catch himself in the act—and James does so again and again in all the various genres in which he works, from the beginning to the end of his career—James must first have *lost* himself (as he also likes to say) in the act; this pattern of flirtatious self-dissolution (as opposed to hapless self-deconstruction) and sharp self-arrest (as opposed to masterful self-recuperation) inscribes, I propose, a "double discourse" within the larger, more abstract double discourse of disavowal and reinscription that Seltzer allegorizes through James.[38] I hope to have made it clear why the "vagueness" of the former double discourse is not the same thing as the abstractness of the latter. If, moreover, the more specifically Jamesian double discourse constitutes a difference within (rather than a difference from) the more general one, that difference might also allow us to signal a certain "gay writing" between the lines of the Foucauldian social text towards which this chapter began by orienting itself. It should go without saying that, in so doing, we would not be moving away from Foucault, but closer to him.[39]

Telling of James's childhood, but from the perspective of his old age, *A Small Boy and Others* figures the capacity of the Jamesian theater of embarrassment to comprehend virtually everything the

---

38. It would be useful to set this Jamesian pattern against the backdrop of another recent critical paradigm besides Seltzer's—namely, John Kucich's elaboration of a Victorian form of repression whereby the self-negations of desire, instead of leading outward toward visions of community, are seen to produce a radically asocial subjectivity. James is not one of the authors whom Kucich considers; it is therefore interesting to speculate as to what the inclusion of James would do to Kucich's paradigm. My guess is that, in addition to complicating the rather oppressively predictable politics described by Seltzer, a recognition of James's specific sexual-discursive situation might open up, in the rather oppressively psychological construct whose sheer density and persistence Kucich demonstrates so well, certain possibilities for reengaging and refiguring the social. See John Kucich, *Repression in Victorian Fiction: Charlotte Brontë, George Eliot, and Charles Dickens* (Berkeley: University of California Press, 1987).

39. For a helpful discussion of ways in which a gay rereading of Foucault might proceed, see Ed Cohen, "Foucauldian Necrologies: 'Gay' 'Politics'? Politically Gay?" *Textual Practice* 2 (Spring 1988): 87–101.

author wrote. But since the scope of this chapter hardly permits a full-scale exploration of this vast and prodigiously elaborated theater, I will limit the discussion to one especially pertinent novel from James's middle period, *The Bostonians* (1886). That the novel is in some sense about lesbianism has certainly been recognized, though until recently the recognition has most often taken the form, as Judith Fetterley has demonstrated, of homophobic and misogynistic misprision.[40] That the novel is also about the inescapable theatricality of late-nineteenth-century American culture has been recognized as well. What has *not* been recognized, much less compellingly analyzed, is the novel's articulation of its lesbian theme with its theatrical theme, to say nothing of its articulation, on a more "formal" level, of a certain homosexual semiosis with a certain internalized narrative stagecraft. In the following pages, I will attempt to show how such questions—both "thematic" and "formal" ones—might be recognized and analyzed; as we will see, an important consequence of this project would be to begin seeing Olive Chancellor in a new light—no longer merely as the rather unlovable victim or even as the tragic heroine that she can easily seem to be, and that the text indeed permits readers to think her to be, but rather as the focus of a surprisingly affirmative textual-sexual-theatrical practice.

This is not to say that the novel takes a completely rosy—or even a completely sympathetic—view of Olive and what she signifies. At the levels of both *discours* and *récit*, there are innumerable traces in *The Bostonians* of the revisionary, countertheatrical impulse toward "detachment" and "presence of mind" that we noted in James's autobiographical account of the primal scene. In the following chapter, in fact, I will consider the increasing predominance of this impulse in James's next two novels after *The Bostonians*—*The Princess Casamassima* (1886) and *The Tragic Muse* (1890), which, together with *The Bostonians*, constitute what may be regarded as James's theatrical trilogy, and as a rehearsal for his embarrassing engagement with the actual theater in the 1890s. For now, however, let us turn to the richly embarrassing *Bostonians*, to see the inventiveness—rather than

---

40. See the chapter on *The Bostonians* in Judith Fetterley, *The Resisting Reader: A Feminist Approach to American Fiction* (Bloomington: Indiana University Press, 1978), pp. 101–53.

just the passivity or the complicity—of its response to some of the
new inflections of theatricality toward the end of the nineteenth
century.

In the thoroughly theatrical world of *The Bostonians,* making a scene
becomes a regular spectator sport. If, as we have seen, the Jamesian
theater of embarrassment runs the affective gamut from "surprise"
to "mortification," with an array of blushes and blunders and pre-
posterousness in between, *The Bostonians* would appear to constitute
a virtual compendium of the various degrees and kinds of productive
"perturbation." As we might expect, many of the novel's *female*
characters, at any rate, seem particularly given to illustrating this
repertoire. At one end of the spectrum of embarrassments—its point
of least intensity—we might locate the "naturally theatrical" Verena
Tarrant's impressive yet relatively uncomplicated and uncompro-
mising scene-making, as viewed with rather patronizing admiration
by Basil Ransom: "If at Miss Birdseye's, and afterwards in Charles
Street, she might have been a rope-dancer, today she made a 'scene'
of [her parents'] mean little room in Monadnoc Place, such a scene
as a prima donna makes of daubed canvas and dusty boards."[41]
Somewhat further along that same spectrum, we could place the
more agitated (if less agitating) scene-making of the unfortunate Mrs.
Luna, who characteristically threatens an intrusive reporter by saying (again the "simple" but no less "portentous" phrase), "If you
have the impertinence to publish a word about me, or to mention
my name in print, I will come to your office and make such a scene!"
(p. 410).

Yet the most interesting performer in this novel's theater of embarrassment is the one who stands at the opposite extreme from the
admirable-laughable Verena, the one who, in the tradition of such
other avowedly nontheatrical heroines as Fanny Price, Jane Eyre,
and Lucy Snowe, ends up stealing the show. I am referring, of course,
to Olive Chancellor. Like her Austenian and Brontëan predecessors,
Olive derives her peculiar star quality precisely from the panicky

41. Henry James, *The Bostonians,* ed. Charles Anderson (Harmondsworth: Penguin, 1985), pp. 77, 230. Subsequent references to the novel will be to this edition,
and will be included parenthetically in the text.

urgency with which she can insist, "Oh dear, no, I can't speak; I have none of that sort of talent. I have no self-possession, no eloquence; I can't put three words together" (p. 63). For it is just Olive's apparent inability to "possess" herself that permits her to become the magnetic icon of the highest degree of embarrassment that the Jamesian canon affords—humiliation. If other characters make possible—and are made possible by—James's imaginative projection of milder forms of embarrassment (e.g., silliness, gaucherie, discomfiture), Olive Chancellor, emblazoned from the outset of the novel as "visibly morbid" (p. 41), provides a wonderfully hospitable textual site for the excruciating, exquisite *mise en scène* of James's own "morbidly delicate sensitivity" at its most acute, in both senses of the word.

Now, it may be difficult to accept this characterization of author-character relations with the same enthusiasm with which it seems to have been proffered. I am myself "sensitive" to the possibility that some readers will infer from it not only a particularly unsavory exploitativeness on the part of the author, but, even worse, a willingness on my own part to aestheticize that exploitativeness. As I have indicated, the versions of female impersonation practiced (however vicariously) by both James and many of his male critics can evoke all too readily the sleaziness (to say the least) of the patriarchal "traffic in women." Yet I want to suggest that, while James invests heavily indeed in Olive's victimization, that investment makes her a far more resilient, more resourceful, and more compelling figure than even sympathetic critics have recognized. I would even go so far as to claim that, for all their ostensible sex appeal, the two other major characters in the novel look rather flat and vacuous in comparison with Olive.

For although Verena's brief but brilliant theatrical career, and her powerful erotic effect on others, testify to her "charisma," much of her success, as Jennifer Wicke has shown, consists in her "nullity."[42] And while the initial, quasi-pornographic description of Basil ("His discourse was pervaded by something sultry and vast, something almost African in its rich, basking tone, something that suggested the teeming expanse of the cotton-field" [p. 36]) seems promising

---

42. Jennifer Wicke, *Advertising Fictions: Literature, Advertisement, and Social Reading* (New York: Columbia University Press, 1988), p. 98.

enough, the ethical and ideological "ugliness" (p. 328) that becomes increasingly apparent in him as the novel progresses has the rather counterintuitive effect of simplifying, diminishing, and de-eroticizing him. In relation to her two fellow players in the novel's triangular drama, Olive is odd woman out in more ways than one: not only is she necessarily excluded (unlike *The Woman in White*'s genially assimilable Marian Halcombe) from the heterosexual configuration with which the narrative cuts itself off; more important, the very fact that she is thus left out and left over serves as an index of her role, at numerous points in the novel, as a particular kind of *genius loci*, where the place in question is an improbable, inert-looking semiotic residue in the narrative machinery, a residue that even the more astute critics have not begun to notice, much less activate.

Though Judith Fetterley, for example, was one of Olive's first and most eloquent defenders against an army of malevolent or merely obtuse "phallic critics," and though she affirms that *"The Bostonians* is finally Olive Chancellor's book," what she finds in that book's final scene, where Olive presents herself to the angry audience at the Boston Music Hall, is a depressing apotheosis of "masochism" and "self-destructiveness."[43] Almost everyone agrees that Olive's fate at the end of the novel is an unhappy one, and that it culminates the lengthy series of insults, indignities, and threats that she has had to endure throughout the narrative. I hardly wish to deny that Olive suffers; still less do I want to elide the reasons *why* she suffers. Nor is it my purpose to recast her self-sacrifice at the end as an unequivocally triumphant theatrical debut, a sort of Victorian anticipation (in the manner of Lucy Snowe's last-minute conscription into the *vaudeville*) of the Hollywood fairy-tale motif whereby the understudy goes on in place of the fallen leading lady and comes back a star; as we will see, the final paragraphs of the text discourage any excessive optimism about Olive's reception, to say nothing of the prospects for her career in the theater of American feminism. Yet it is important, I think, not only to acknowledge the extent of Olive's pain, and to take into account its causes in the culturally legitimized sexism and homophobia of which Basil Ransom is the novel's foremost representative—to ask, as Basil does not, "Why was she morbid, and why was her morbidness typical?" (p. 41). It is

---

43. Fetterley, *The Resisting Reader*, pp. 134, 151.

important also to ask what that pain does, what imaginative relations it makes possible—beyond the alternatives of exploitation and commiseration—between the gay author and the lesbian character, and between those two figures and a resisting reader, to use Fetterley's term, who would resist both the temptation to validate their oppression and—what comes to the same thing—the temptation to glamorize it.[44]

In a fascinating essay on the pervasive theatricalization of late-nineteenth-century American culture, Philip Fisher unpacks the self-contradiction of Olive's "almost hysterical privacy."

> One of James's greatest accomplishments in his novel is the notation of the painfully physical shyness that is Olive's one performance. Her white-lipped anger, her sudden tears, her tense expectation, as well as her passion are all transparent in her face and tense bearing. For such a person, although she dreads being in public, there is never any genuine privacy, because her aspect broadcasts her mood in spite of her will. Blushes, frowns, clipped-off words, breathlessness, blazing eyes—she has no hidden feelings at all. She is a martyr of involuntary publicity.[45]

Fisher's evocation of Olive's "martyrdom"—her resonantly symbolic status—reminds us that hysteria is an inherently theatrical con-

---

44. For a more general discussion of these and other, related questions, see Eve Kosofsky Sedgwick, "Across Gender, Across Sexuality: Willa Cather and Others," *South Atlantic Quarterly* 88 (Winter 1989): 53–72. Looking briefly at *The Bostonians*, Sedgwick discerns there "a woman-hating and feminist-baiting violence of panic" (67). Though I would not deny that James's text exhibits such violence, this chapter attempts to show that there may be other, less phobic forces at work in the relationship between James and Olive Chancellor. Needless to say, James's cross-gender identification with Olive cannot constitute a lesbian-feminist politics and poetics; nonetheless, something in addition to (and more affirmative than) gynephobic defensiveness seems to be playing itself out in the space between the gay male author and the lesbian character.

After completing this chapter, I read Claire Kahane's "Hysteria, Feminism, and the Case of *The Bostonians*," in *Feminism and Psychoanalysis*, ed. Richard Feldstein and Judith Roof (Ithaca: Cornell University Press, 1989), pp. 280–97. As its title suggests, Kahane's essay has certain affinities with my own reading of James's novel: in addition to its interest in hysteria, and specifically in the representation of hysteria in Freud's case history of "Dora," Kahane's interpretation resembles mine in its attention to the complex relations between author and characters and in its recognition of the ambiguity of the novel's ending. But while Kahane is concerned mostly with questions of gender, I focus more insistently on questions of sexuality, or on the intersection of gender and sexuality in the Jamesian text.

45. Philip Fisher, "Appearing and Disappearing in Public: Social Space in Late-Nineteenth-Century Literature and Culture," in *Reconstructing American Literary History*, ed. Sacvan Bercovitch (Cambridge: Harvard University Press, 1986), p. 185.

dition, an "involuntary" staging or externalization of what would seem most private or internal. Interestingly, it is through Basil, from whom the diagnosis of Olive as "morbid" immediately issues, that James confirms this interpretation, even allowing the reactionary protagonist to name hysteria, in his memorable diatribe, as one of the major symptoms of a diseased public life: "It's a feminine, a nervous, hysterical, chattering, canting age" (p. 327). The reason why it is "interesting" that Basil gets to speak this line is that the rhetorical and ideological position from which he speaks it constrasts markedly with the rhetorical and ideological position from which the diagnostic discourse in James usually proceeds. As I have suggested, James, like so many modern practitioners of surveillance, employs a strategy of self-implication, a strategy that, instead of reacting against the ways in which hysteria deconstructs the opposition between public and private, makes the most of those deconstructive breakdowns. When Basil denounces the hystericization of the "age," however, the force of that denunciation comes from his implicit assumption that there can and should be such a thing as what Fisher calls "genuine privacy." It is to this recovered private space, of course, that Basil would consign Verena, and that he is busy mapping out as he watches her feminist performance for Mrs. Burrages's New York friends.

> The idea that she was brilliant, that she counted as a factor only because the public mind was in a muddle, was not an humiliation but a delight to him; it was a proof that her apostleship was all nonsense, the most passing of all fashions, the veriest of delusions, and that she was meant for something divinely different—for privacy, for him, for love. He took no measure of the duration of her talk; he only knew, when it was over and succeeded by a clapping of hands, an immense buzz of voices and shuffling of chairs, that it had been capitally bad, and that her personal success, wrapping it about with a glamour like the silver mist that surrounds a fountain, was such as to prevent its badness from being a cause of mortification to her lover.
>
> (pp. 269–70)

While Basil does not appear to find Verena herself "hysterical," he clearly views her "success" as another sign of the general hysteria that he identifies in his tirade. For just as this general hysteria represents a widespread boundary-confusion, so Verena's "success" indicates that "the public mind [is] all in a muddle." What is "muddled" there, for example, is the distinction between the public *tout court* and "something divinely different"—the sacred space of "privacy," for which Verena appears to be "meant." Yet, far from feeling threatened by this otherwise pandemic confusion, Basil, blissfully inattentive to what Verena is saying, positively basks in the assurance of his own immunity. He expresses his sense of self-exemption most tellingly when he congratulates himself, not once but twice, for being impervious to "humiliation" and "mortification." After all, these are the characteristic experiences of that "typical" or "representative woman" (p. 284) of her hystericized age, Olive Chancellor. Tacitly demonstrating his own divine difference from the "martyr of involuntary publicity," Basil thereby demonstrates as well considerable confidence in his ability to redraw the line between public and private.

That project will of course begin at home, where Verena is destined to wind up after Basil abducts her from the Music Hall, in which she is to present her lecture on "A Woman's Reason." Especially given James's final, ominous prediction about Verena's future as a married woman, it is difficult to imagine that, once domesticated, her peculiar theatrical "badness" will resemble Jane Eyre's in inscribing a disruptive potential within the privatizing enclosure. On the contrary, the novel leaves little doubt that that "badness" will merely be dissolved into the mystifying regime of doublespeak that Basil models for Verena when he says of her "gift":

> I want to give it another direction, certainly; but I don't want to stop your activity. Your gift is the gift of expression, and there is nothing I can do for you that will make you less expressive. It won't gush out at a fixed hour and on a fixed day, but it will irrigate, it will fertilize, it will brilliantly adorn your conversation. Think how delightful it will be when your influence becomes really social. Your facility, as you call it, will simply make you, in conversation, the most charming woman in America.
>
> (pp. 379–80)

When Daniel Deronda, echoing Klesmer's "divining" intervention in Gwendolen Harleth's bad acting, prescribes for her "a little private imitation" of "art," the outlook for that theatrical heroine, as we have seen, seems dreary enough. Yet one must view with still greater skepticism the benevolence ostensibly underlying Basil's similar reinstatement of the divine difference between public and private. Even without James's final, gloomy forecast, and without the implied characterizations of Basil as a kidnapper, a rapist, and an assassin, there is ample reason to regard Basil's seductive speech, in which he promises to turn Verena's "gift" into so much fertilizer, as itself a kind of pernicious (if high-grade) bullshit. In its literalizing violence, his last, sinister gesture, whereby he "thrust[s] Verena's long cloak over her head, to conceal her face and her identity" (pp. 432–33), makes clear that his "charming" vision of her domesticated theatricality already performs a murderous cover-up in its own right.

Thus, though we must refrain from placing Olive's story under the mythical heading of "A Star Is Born," it would not be entirely inaccurate to title Verena's, "A Star Is Killed." If we restrict our analysis of theatricality in *The Bostonians* to the heterosexual "love" story between Basil and Verena, what emerges, with a depressing inevitability, is the outline of a lurid scenario that has become all too familiar in our own time—the scenario in which an increasingly insistent and dangerous "fan," intent on turning into a shroud the "glamour" with which a particular female performer is "wrapp[ed] about," pursues her with a vengeance. Like most lurid scenarios, this one obviously has its own "morbid" attraction; late-twentieth-century culture, at any rate, seems irresistibly drawn to it. Yet it does not in fact provide James with much of a focus for his own "morbidity." It is not that James's imagination recoils from such "melodramatic" subject matter; as Peter Brooks has shown, "melodrama" occupies a privileged place in the Jamesian oeuvre.[46] Rather, what empties the Basil-Verena plot of any effective interest for the author is that, like the militantly retrograde Basil himself, it moves inexorably backward, away from the possibilities of scene-making that make James's writing "count" as it does, and toward the restitution of binarisms that the most powerful (and the most pleasurable) nineteenth-century discourse works to unsettle.

This is not to say that the heterosexual plot can be reduced to its teleological end: the final tableau of Verena under wraps and of Basil thus ready to unmuddle "the public mind" from his foothold in the *Rational Review* is not, as it were, the whole story. We could no doubt show that, like most regressive-repressive trajectories, this narrative movement is necessarily problematized by its own violent

---

46. See Peter Brooks, *The Melodramatic Imagination: Balzac, Henry James, Melodrama, and the Mode of Excess* (New Haven: Yale University Press, 1976), pp. 153–97.

wishfulness. We could return, for example, to the climactic scene in the Music Hall, and juxtapose Basil's usual smug self-exemption— "He was not one of the audience; he was apart, unique, and had come on a business altogether special" (p. 414)—with the sentence, a few lines below, that interprets his "uniqueness" rather more ambiguously: "There were two or three moments during which he felt as he could imagine a young man to feel who, waiting in a public place, has made up his mind, for reasons of his own, to discharge a pistol at the king or the president" (p. 414). In view of the novel's cultural-historical frame of reference, the allusion to John Wilkes Booth seems all but undeniable; that Basil is being compared to an assassin who not only committed his (highly theatrical) crime in an actual theater but who was himself an actor calls into question, at the very least, the neatness of his earlier self-heroicizing formulation.

Yet, however revealing, Basil's impercipient self-contradiction here does not offer the "rich accession of possibilities" that James discovers in the emblematically self-contradictory figure of "involuntary publicity" and "almost hysterical privacy" whom the heterosexual teleology leaves out. As Basil and Verena recede into the post-narrative death that is marriage, Olive, "unmarried by every implication of her being" (p. 47), "mark[s] . . . her difference" from them ever more "sharply" and "oddly" and "extravagantly." And it is the sharpness of this marking that gives point to the growing acuteness of her discomfort. Olive is unmarried, that is, but as a rich and richly elaborated reincarnation of James's "spoiled" cousin, she is hardly un-Maried. Indeed, the signifying potential of Olive— who is, after all, rather "spoiled" herself—suggests an even greater embarrassment of riches than does Marie's, and not just because the former is a major character in a long novel while the latter is limited to a cameo role in someone else's autobiography. "Almost hysterical," Olive, like Marie, opens up a world of difference for James; yet, as if anticipating "Dora," she represents what might be called a double difference, since she possesses the further theatrical virtue of "perversion." Olive's thoroughgoing and definitive unmarriedness, that is, has "implications" for James himself that remain camouflaged by Marie's (relatively) unmarked sexuality.

The advantage for James (along with the "risk") lies not so much in Olive's greater specificity per se as in the more specific articulation

of her socially meaningful "vagueness." To Marie's evocatively indeterminate quasi-hysterical "output," Olive adds a provocatively
opaque homosexual mode of signification, much like James's own
inside-outside rhetorical obliquity, whereby he can simultaneously
disclose himself and withhold himself in the process of "study[ing]
. . . one of those friendships between women which are so common
in New England."[47] "In the course of our history," writes James in
the role of the "ironic" narrator, "I shall be under the necessity of
imparting much occult information" (p. 41): we expect by now that
a great deal of that "information" will be as much about himself as
about his characters.

What both James's and Olive's provocative "styles" provoke is a
desire in others to join in the evasive game that gets played, for
instance, by "the psychiatrist with his hysteric and his perverts."
Not even Basil Ransom can help getting into the act. The same
impulse that motivates Colby's innuendos about James's "queerness" ("nobody sins because nobody has anything to sin with," and
so on) lies behind Basil's not-so-deliciously droll reflections on "Olive Chancellor's sex": "(what sex was it, great heaven? he used
profanely to ask himself)" (p. 324). As we have seen in relation to
Colby, this is an impulse at once to "impart" and to keep "occult"—
to impart *by* keeping occult—the "guilty secrets" of unorthodox sexual practice. Both Colby and Ransom play knowingly on the easy
rhetorical interchange between, on the one hand, the indeterminacy
or underdetermination of a putative *a*sexuality and, on the other
hand, the determinate sexual meaning for which it almost always
seems to front.

But where James, I have argued, gives us the impression of *playing
along*—not only of being in on the game but even of having written
its rules—Olive does not at first appear to share in the fun. Indeed,
in his representation of her numerous torments throughout the
novel, James seems abundantly to bear out Basil's initial classifi-
cation of her as one of "the people who take things hard" (p. 41).
If, however, while directing his analytic gaze at the morbid Olive,
James manages at the same time to inhabit her vulnerable subjectivity, she herself can claim far more agility than one might think:

47. *The Complete Notebooks of Henry James,* ed. Leon Edel and Lyall H. Powers
(New York: Oxford University Press, 1987), p. 19.

in the diagnostic theater that the novel maps out, Olive is not merely confined to the role of abject specimen. Nor, for that matter, is her mobility simply an effect of her trying to escape surveillance by rushing to embrace the almost equally rigid identity of the detached spectator. Admittedly, just as a remarkable connection obtains between James and Marie, so there are instructive affinities between Olive and *her* cousin. As critics have pointed out, Olive and Basil, like so many antagonists, are in some sense "mirror images of each other."[48] Especially in their dealings with Verena, they exhibit strikingly similar totalitarian tendencies; Fetterley reminds us, for example, that they perform "the same symbolic gesture" of covering Verena with a cloak.[49] For our purposes, the most significant resemblance between the cousins consists in the way in which they both assume a position outside and above what they perceive as the *vulgarity* inherent in the pervasive theatricalization—the "Barnumization," to use Jennifer Wicke's felicitous term—of late-nineteenth-century American culture.[50]

But while Basil adheres to that position tenaciously—if, as we have indicated, imperfectly—Olive's relation to it, like James's, is surprisingly provisional and open-ended. On the one hand, in taking charge of Verena's career Olive wants to "rescue the girl from the danger of vulgar exploitation" (p. 104). On the other hand, although Olive persuades herself that while "Miss Tarrant might wear gilt buttons from head to foot, her soul could not be vulgar" (p. 101), the narrator's *style indirect libre* rather gives away the game (on the same page, in fact), letting it be known that Verena's vulgarity accounts in large part for Olive's fascination with her:

> It was just as she was that she liked her; she was so strange, so different from the girls one usually met, seemed to belong to some queer gipsy-land or transcendental Bohemia. With her bright, vulgar clothes, her salient appearance, she might have been a rope-dancer or a fortune-teller; and this had the immense merit, for Olive, that it appeared to make her belong to the "people," threw her into the social dusk of that mysterious democracy which Miss Chancellor held that the fortunate classes knew so little about, and with which (in a future possibly very near) they will have to count.
>
> (p. 101)

48. Fetterley, *The Resisting Reader*, p. 136.
49. Ibid., p. 147.
50. Wicke, *Advertising Fictions*, p. 90.

That the image of Verena as "rope-dancer" occurs to and has a distinctly stimulating effect on both Olive and Basil reveals that neither of them is exactly unambivalent toward her vulgarity. Yet while Basil would ultimately destroy the vulgarity or "badness" that excites him, Olive ends up not so much "rescuing" Verena from it as identifying with it—or with the difference ("she was . . . so different from the girls one usually met") that it signifies in its own "queer" way.

As he surveys the scene in the Music Hall, Basil notes contemptuously that Olive, in her capacity as Verena's manager-producer-collaborator, has "conform[ed] herself to a great popular system" of "enterprise and puffery" (p. 415). It is not certain, however, that Olive's conformance is readable only as the "sacrifice" (p. 415) that Basil takes it to be. For on at least two occasions, Olive lets on—though we can never know how "involuntarily"—that she might actually derive considerable vicarious pleasure from the kind of popular success that she engineers for Verena. Just before her "Oh dear, no, I can't speak" speech, Olive tells Mrs. Farrinder: "I want to do something—oh, I should like so to speak!" (p. 63). And later, in a passage from which I have already quoted, Olive acknowledges via the narrator one of her motives for agreeing to bring Verena to New York: "Lastly, Olive was conscious of a personal temptation in the matter; she was not insensible to the pleasure of appearing in a distinguished New York circle as a representative woman, an important Bostonian, the prompter, colleague, associate of one of the most original girls of the time" (pp. 283–84).

We have already seen how Olive in fact becomes the "representative woman" of her culture, albeit in a sense other than that which she appears to have in mind here. Again, however, I would maintain a certain caution in judging the degree to which this development is "involuntary." For, *pace* Fisher, there is no more reason to assume that Olive is simply betrayed into publicity than there is to assume that James, in the passage from *A Small Boy and Others*, is the dupe of his own self-deconstructing rhetoric. The proximity of author and character in the theater of embarrassment is nicely suggested by one of James's notes for *The Bostonians*: "There must, indispensably, be a type of newspaper man—the man whose ideal is the energetic reporter. I should like to *bafouer* the vulgarity and hideousness of this—the impudent invasion of privacy—the extinction of all conception of privacy, etc."[51] If James sounds like Basil here, he also sounds like the Olive who "despise[s] vulgarity" (p. 129) and whose "highest indulgence" is a vision of domestic *Ge-mütlichkeit*, "with falling snow outside, and tea on a little table, and successful renderings, with a chosen companion, of Goethe" (p. 107).[52] Yet his desire "to *bafouer* the vulgarity" of a Barnumized culture produces another example of Jamesian scene-making, since, for all its "distinguished" Frenchness, *bafouer*, according to at least one French-English dictionary, means "to heckle." While Basil gets framed as John Wilkes Booth, James, that is, stages his own self-contradiction by projecting his satire into the less criminal but no less embarrassing performative mode of the spectator who insists on making a spectacle of himself. The heckler is indeed the extreme, vulgar—even "carnivalesque"—version of a familiar figure in the game of embarrassing Henry James: the critic who, in the act of embarrassing someone else, succeeds at the same time in embarrassing him- or herself.

To be sure, Olive is no heckler; her "tragic shyness" (p. 41) ensures that, when she makes scenes, at least she does not do so obnoxiously. But it also ensures that her scene-making will nonetheless have an extravagance of its own, an extravagance that, though wrapped about with the high-cultural "glamour" of tragedy as a literary form, does not therefore cut itself off from a sustaining vulgarity, whose force consists to a great extent in its susceptibility of both class determinations (as when "vulgarity" means "commonness") and sexual ones (as when, in more recent usage, "vulgarity" means "indecency"). For when, in the novel's melodramatic final scene, Olive finds her tragic fulfillment in taking Verena's place on the Music Hall stage, it is as though she were finally installing herself at the site of the energizingly coarse theatricality that has attracted her to Verena all along. Having settled up until this point for the vicarious, behind-the-scenes gratification of her "occult" representational desires, Olive at last moves out from the protective cover of her role as "prompter" and steps into the spotlight that Verena—herself cov-

51. Edel and Powers, eds., *Notebooks*, p. 19.

52. For a discussion of Olive's valorization of privacy as an instance of the "romantic" mystification that James indicts in this novel, see Robert K. Martin, "Picturesque Misperception in *The Bostonians*," *Henry James Review* 9 (Spring 1988): 77–86.

ered now irrevocably, it would seem—once occupied. Even before she decides to replace Verena, Olive seems virtually ablaze with a certain garish star-like intensity. Here is Ransom's final view of Olive, just as he is about to take Verena away from her:

> The expression of her face was a thing to remain with him for ever; it was impossible to imagine a more vivid presentment of blighted hope and wounded pride. Dry, desperate, rigid, she yet wavered and seemed uncertain; her pale, glittering eyes straining forward, as if they were looking for death. Ransom had a vision, even at that crowded moment, that if she could have met it there and then, bristling with steel or lurid with fire, she would have rushed on it without a tremor, like the heroine that she was.
>
> (p. 431)

"Bristling with steel or lurid with fire" seems to modify "death," but its metonymic link with Olive's "rigid" bearing and "glittering eyes" suggests that the phrase could describe her as well. We do not need, in any case, to dwell on the image here of a violent, boundary-collapsing sexual consummation to see that Olive, as "heroine," is inscribed not only in the discourse of tragedy but also in the more frankly vulgar one of sensationalism: the word "lurid" alone suffices to indicate where James's melodramatic imagination is ultimately most in force. Unlike Gwendolen Harleth, whose rewriting as a tragic heroine is designed precisely to rescue her from the vulgarity of sensationalism, Olive Chancellor enjoys, one might say, the best of both worlds: she gets the chance to figure, luminously, as "in the highest degree interesting" and, in so doing, to charge herself with the peculiar energies of power-pleasure that only vulgarity affords.

And when Olive comes out from behind the stage to assume Verena's vacated position as "the cynosure of every eye" (p. 270), as "a New England Corinna" (p. 265), James, I would argue, gets to reenact his primal scene of embarrassment, putting himself once again in the place of the "representative woman." As Olive "rush[es] to the approach to the platform" (p. 431), one almost hears the sound of a door being "flung open" a second time, so that, while the author does not "come out" any more overtly than does his heroine, he thereby accedes to a renewed possibility of putting *himself* on the line between gay meaning and equally gay not-meaning.

> She rushed to the approach to the platform. If [Basil] had observed her, it might have seemed to him that she hoped to find the fierce

expiation she sought for in exposure to the thousands she had disappointed and deceived, in offering herself to be trampled to death
and torn to pieces. She might have suggested to him some feminine
firebrand of Paris revolutions, erect on a barricade, or even the sac-
rificial figure of Hypatia, whirled through the furious mob of Alex-
andria.

(pp. 431–32)

If Olive takes pleasure from her "exposure" here—at least as "it
might have seemed to" Basil—that pleasure would doubtless come
under the heading of "masochism." But the novel isn't quite over
yet, and Olive's performance hasn't really begun; the passage—both
Olive's "approach to the platform" and the narrative space in which
it is described—has yet to become, as James might say, itself a scene.
Although, just before going on stage, Olive announces, "I'm going
to be hissed and hooted and insulted!" (p. 432), what Basil hears a
few moments later as he makes off with Verena suggests that, just
as James, precisely by playing Olive here, is half in and half out, so
Olive is in fact poised at a threshhold of her own, between certain
disaster and surprising success—at a site of significant liminality that
gets reread not in terms of "fierce expiation" but, oddly enough, in
terms of "embarrassment."

> As they mingled in the issuing crowd he perceived the quick, com-
> plete, tremendous silence which, in the hall, had greeted Olive Chan-
> cellor's rush to the front. Every sound instantly dropped, the hush
> was respectful, the great public waited, and whatever she should say
> to them (and he thought she might indeed be rather embarrassed) it
> was not apparent that they were likely to hurl the benches at her.
> Ransom, palpitating with his victory, felt now a little sorry for her,
> and was relieved to know that, even when exasperated, a Boston
> audience is not ungenerous.
>
> (p. 433)

Our sense of Olive's chances is of course mediated by Basil's
spectatorship—more accurately, by his auditorship. But what I want
to stress is the marginality of the ironizing narrative frame that Basil
gets to draw around Olive's incipient performance. Given what
James might call the "intensities" that this performance seems to
promise, Basil's condescending pity—his feeling "a little sorry for"
Olive—looks remarkably banal and inadequate as a critical response.
While Basil is peremptorily wrapping up the novel itself as well as
Verena, Olive, by virtue of the very indeterminacy of her "possible
output," manages to exceed the opposition between framer and

framed, between cover and covered. "She might indeed be rather embarrassed"; but she thus marks what remains, on stage and in the text, after the brutal binarisms of heterosexuality have been imposed. And if James, by drawing the frame that encompasses the novel as a whole, can claim "detachment" and "presence of mind," a large part of him, I like to imagine, stays behind (with) Olive, to imagine for his own part the pains and pleasures and powers that embarrassment can bring.

Actress, Monster, Novelist
Figuration and Counterplot in The Tragic Muse

He was so accustomed to living upon irony and the interpretation
of things that it was new to him to be himself interpreted and—
as a gentleman who sits for his portrait is always liable to be—
interpreted all ironically. From being outside of the universe he
was suddenly brought into it, and from the position of a free com-
mentator and critic, an easy amateurish editor of the whole affair,
reduced to that of humble ingredient and contributor.

Henry James, *The Tragic Muse*

Although published in the same year as *The Bostonians*, 1886, *The
Princess Casamassima* follows it in order of composition. As a later
text, it registers a development that we could chart over the long
course of James's career—namely, his growing uneasiness about the
implications of embarrassment. In some sense, it seems that that
career in itself recapitulates the pattern of theatrical "deviation" and
theoretical "correction" that we traced from the sensation novel to
Daniel Deronda. Admittedly, since we have located the paradigm of
Jamesian embarrassment in an even later text, *A Small Boy and Others*
(1913), our history may seem somewhat at odds with itself. Yet it is
not necessary to resolve this apparent contradiction by claiming, for
instance, that after *The Bostonians*, James begins to experience a
revulsion from his characteristic theatrical strategies—a revulsion
that one might expect to have reached its climax as a result of his
disappointing excursion into playwriting—but that, in the last few
years of his life, he somehow undergoes a conversion *back* to those
strategies. As has been suggested by numerous studies of James's
relation to popular forms, the sensationalistic and the "Eliotic" are
inextricably entangled *throughout* his work. I would agree that one
can in fact discern a persistent and coherent structure of ambivalence
in James's writing. Both as early as in *The Bostonians* and as late as

in *A Small Boy*, the author can be seen to seek "detachment" from the theater of embarrassment as much as involvement in it. Conversely, texts like *The Princess Casamassima* and *The Tragic Muse* (1890) evince a continuing engagement—indeed, a fascination—with the very practices of scene-making that they want at the same time to keep at a distance. Such changes that take place in the course of James's career are changes of emphasis and degree, rather than of fundamental attitude.

Yet it is important, I think, both to acknowledge those changes and to ask what they might have to tell us about certain contiguous changes in the culture itself. Thus, in the Conclusion to this book, I will be suggesting that the anxiety one can notice in the revised text of *The Tragic Muse* has something to do with the more-than-embarrassing "case" of Oscar Wilde, whose *Picture of Dorian Gray*, moreover, itself published in the same year as the *original* version of *The Tragic Muse*, comes a bit too close to the latter for James's comfort. Most of the present chapter will indeed be given over to a discussion of the revised version of *The Tragic Muse*, which appears in the New York edition of 1909.[1] But before turning to that text, I want to look very briefly at *The Princess Casamassima*, since this middle novel in the theatrical "trilogy" reveals a significant renegotiation within the larger theater of the Jamesian oeuvre as a whole.

Of Hyacinth Robinson, the "little hero" of *The Princess Casamassima*, James writes: "he was to go through life in a mask, in a borrowed mantle; he was to be, every day and every hour, an actor."[2] In this respect, Hyacinth is as "typical" of his environment as Olive Chancellor is of hers. For although theatricality in *The Bostonians* manifests itself most obviously as an ineluctable, vulgarizing publicity, while theatricality in *The Princess Casamassima* is bound up, rather

---

1. The passage quoted at the beginning of this chapter appears in Henry James, *The Tragic Muse*, 2 vols. (New York: Charles Scribner's Sons, 1908), 2:410. James is referring to Gabriel Nash, who is about to disappear from the novel, and to fade away from the canvas on which his portrait is being painted. Subsequent references, to both the novel and its preface, will be included parenthetically in the text. In a few instances, I have used the first edition of the novel (1890) where I preferred its phrasing to that of the New York edition. These exceptions will be noted accordingly.

2. Henry James, *The Princess Casamassima*, ed. Derek Brewer (Harmondsworth: Penguin, 1987), p. 109. Subsequent parenthetical references to the novel will be to this edition, which reproduces the text of the 1886 version.

differently, with a thematics of political paranoia and revolutionary conspiracy, both novels depict thoroughly theatricalized worlds. And if we were to articulate the question of theatricality-as-theme with that of theatricality-as-mode, we might begin to see how these two apparently dissimilar theatrical novels in fact overlap with each other. What I have in mind, specifically, is the insistence of a certain "vulgarity" as an overdetermined and increasingly problematic figure for the embarrassments of James's own discourse.

As was noted in the previous chapter, "vulgarity" in James gets coded not only as that which is "low" in terms of class hierarchy, but also—in anticipation of more recent usage—as that which is "low" (i.e., disreputable) in terms of sexual behavior or sexual representation; in James, "vulgar" means "common," yet it begins to approach "obscene" as well. Desiring Verena, finally almost *becoming* Verena, Olive Chancellor, we saw, is drawn to the very social-sexual vulgarity that she professes to "despise." Olive's not-so-secret desire for and identification with this vulgarity, moreover, opens a space for *James's* enactment of his own similar relationship to what he would *bafouer*. Now, if Olive Chancellor offers such opportunities, one would think that a character like Hyacinth Robinson might provide even richer possibilities for authorial investment. For James's own liminal stance, as both in and out of the closet, as both for and against the embarrassment of vulgarity, finds a promising analogue in the double "vagueness" of Hyacinth's *social* identity—is he the son of his aristocratic father or of his proletarian mother?—and of his *sexual* identity—is he in love with, say, the Princess Casamassima and Millicent Henning or with, say, Captain Sholto and Paul Muniment?

On the whole, the critics who have written about this novel have a great deal to say about the former, social kind of indeterminacy and almost nothing to say about the latter, sexual kind.[3] Although Hyacinth's name alone seems resonant enough, it would appear that, despite or perhaps because of their preoccupation with the

3. On those rare occasions when they do take up the question of Hyacinth's sexuality, critics tend to display a drearily predictable heterosexist bias. Writing as recently as 1987, for example, Derek Brewer, in his Introduction to the Penguin edition, opines: "Hyacinth fails to realize the full sexual [i.e., heterosexual] desire that would be natural to a lively and reasonably well-fed young man, except when he has cause to be jealous of Paul Muniment with the Princess. He has a kind of impotence" (p. 20).

novel's "political" theme, critics are content to overlook its concern with the politics of sexuality. To be sure, James himself is characteristically evasive about this issue, but to the extent that this evasiveness leaves traces in both the novel and its preface, it demands all the more to be *read*. Though such a reading cannot be my project here, I would nonetheless point to certain places where that project might begin.

For one thing, one might want to determine what it means that James employs a technique of dispersion in this novel, establishing not one but at least two main figures of embarrassment. For in addition to Hyacinth, whose increasing chagrin ends only with his literal (self-)mortification (that is, with his suicide), there is the chronically embarrassed, strikingly Olive-like Lady Aurora Langrish, whose frustrated attraction to Paul Muniment in many ways replicates Hyacinth's. And while this dispersion might bespeak a productive refinement of the technology of embarrassment—along the lines of Olive's enrichment of the possibilities inherent in the figure of James's cousin, Marie—it is hard to see just what that refinement produces. Where Olive's very *exclusion*, I hope to have shown, allows for the activation of significant imaginative energies in James himself, both Lady Aurora and Hyacinth, each eventually encountering an intolerable erotic impasse, suggest instead a recalcitrant *occlusion* of performative possibilities. Similarly unlucky in love, Olive nevertheless ends up intimating, for James, something evermore about to be. But at the end of Book Fifth, in the final, vaguely rueful interview between Hyacinth and Lady Aurora, when they sit "looking at each other, in a kind of occult community of suffering" (p. 539), the author seems to be marking less his difference *with* them than his difference *from* them. In short, his relationship to these two characters and to the dispersion that they underwrite indicates not greater *investment* in their embarrassed "community" but rather *divestment*, dissociation from it.

In his preface to the novel, James explicitly differentiates himself from "little Hyacinth Robinson," even as he emphasizes their connection.

> To find his possible adventure interesting I had only to conceive his watching the same public show, the same innumerable appearances, I had watched myself, and of his watching very much as I had watched; save indeed for one little difference. This difference would

be that so far as all the swarming facts should speak of freedom and ease, knowledge and power, money, opportunity, and satiety, he should be able to revolve round them but at the most respectful of distances and with every door of approach shut in his face. For one's self, all conveniently, there had been doors that opened—opened into light and warmth and cheer, into good and charming relations; and if the place as a whole lay heavy on one's consciousness there was yet always for relief this implication of one's own lucky share of the freedom and ease, lucky acquaintance with the number of lurking springs at light pressure of which particular vistas would begin to recede, great lighted, furnished, peopled galleries, sending forth gusts of agreeable sound.

(p. 34)

Asserting a simultaneous identification with and detachment from the "possible adventure" of another, this passage seems strikingly like the one from *A Small Boy and Others*, where James posits the origin of his peculiar vocation in the scene made by Marie. What is telling here, however, is the way in which James sets himself apart from Hyacinth. While the difference between James as narrator and Marie as character was primarily a difference of age—it would take "a long time of course" before James himself would learn to "distinguish between" inferior and superior scenes—the "one little difference" between James and Hyacinth is clearly one of class: it is obvious why if, "for one's self, all conveniently, there had been doors that opened," for Hyacinth "every door of approach shut in his face."

Much as one admires the candor and perspicacity with which James recognizes his own social and economic privilege, one also has to wonder what deeper "implication" his thematizing of class difference works to conceal. From what embarrassment do the sentences announced by the phrase, "save one little difference," save James himself? I would argue that if, as James admits, he and Hyacinth are fellow spectators of "the same public show," comrades in their enjoyment of "the ripe round fruit of perambulation" (p. 33), James is nonetheless prepared to leave Hyacinth at the door, at the point where the pleasure of urban voyeurism threatens to turn into the pain of rejection—or worse. Doors must get shut in Hyacinth's face not just because of his lower-class affiliation but because the "fantasy of surveillance" that, as Mark Seltzer has shown, he shares with James risks emerging a little too ripely as a *sexual* fantasy, raising the possibility of more, and more specific, embarrassment than James may want to entertain.[4]

If James, staging his own disappearance into a space of "good and charming relations," ostentatiously saves himself from "little Hyacinth['s]" fate—and that miniaturizing, distancing nomenclature echoes the novel itself—he thereby exempts himself, at least this time, from the experience of liminality; *this* passage—out of the street and into the protective recesses of a specialized, rarefied, and sanitized locus of the "social"—is designed precisely to *avoid* becoming "itself a scene." The doors that are flung open for James here are to be seen as permitting neither exit from nor entrance into anything as determinate as a closet; rather, what he supposedly accedes to is the saving difference of, in his terms, "knowledge and power"— knowledge and power as construed in the most blandly abstract light.

The novel itself does not withhold clues as to why the author might want to part company with his protagonist. One might look, for instance, at the curious scene in chapter 28, where Hyacinth, having arranged to have an eminent West End doctor pay a housecall to the dying Pinnie, is disconcerted to find himself the object of the medical gaze: "The great man . . . gazed at Hyacinth over his spectacles (he seemed rather more occupied with him than with the patient)" (p. 369). Perhaps the differentiation on which James insists, both in the novel and in its preface, reflects his own unwillingness to undergo the kind of surveillance imposed with increasing fixity by the new "spectacles" of medicalized discipline. In any event, despite James's avowed affinities with Hyacinth, his relationship to this character often resembles a disappearing act.

Having indicated the outlines of that relationship, I turn now to James's next novel, *The Tragic Muse*, where vulgarity, no longer mitigated, as in Hyacinth, by virtue of being mixed with "refinement," takes center stage, and where, as a result, James's defensive disappearing act—and I am aware of the paradoxical implications of

4. Mark Seltzer, *Henry James and the Art of Power* (Ithaca: Cornell University Press, 1984). Seltzer's first chapter (pp. 25–58) is "*The Princess Casamassima*: Realism and the Fantasy of Surveillance."

the term—becomes more systematic and elaborate. It is not a question here merely of exposing James's anxiety, of transforming him from an adroit practitioner of self-embarrassment to an unwitting case of male hysteria. Though the contradictions we observe in the author's discourse may look at first like so many symptomatic gaffes, they may turn out to be sophisticated new techniques in the repertory of embarrassment. For if James seems to want to avoid embarrassment here, that very "desire" might in fact *promote* embarrassment. The major difference between the present chapter and the previous one is that, whereas I was concerned there with the strategic value of embarrassment, I will be paying greater attention here to its affective content. I will try, that is, to convey some of the *experience* of embarrassment for Henry James as he revises his always-already revisionary novel of 1890.

In his history of antitheatricalism through the ages, Jonas Barish identifies *The Tragic Muse* (1890) as a major instance of nineteenth-century *pro*theatricalism. Where earlier novels like *Mansfield Park*, *Vanity Fair*, *Villette*, and *Daniel Deronda* use the theatrical temperament to represent duplicity and ontological indeterminacy, *The Tragic Muse* celebrates actors and acting, and demonstrates affectionate respect for the art form at which James would soon fail so dismally. Many other nineteenth-century novels with theatrical themes tend to view the theater as their demonic other, so that it comes to stand not only for various kinds of moral inadequacy, but also as a foil, a negative backdrop, for the novel itself as an artistic form. Barish argues that James, however, "links the fate of the theater firmly with that of all the arts, makes the theater into a paradigmatic case *for* the arts, and sees society's downgrading of it as a symptom of its hostility to art in any form that presumes to be serious."[5]

In his preface to *The Tragic Muse*, James underlines the paradigmatic status of the theater in his text, but he does not do so in quite the same spirit that Barish's account would suggest.

> The late R. L. Stevenson was to write to me, I recall—and precisely on the occasion of *The Tragic Muse*—that he was at a loss to conceive how one could find interest in anything so vulgar or pretend to gather fruit in so scrubby an orchard; but the view of a creature of the stage,

5. Jonas Barish, *The Antitheatrical Prejudice* (Berkeley: University of California Press, 1981), p. 385.

the view of the "histrionic temperament," as suggestive much less, verily, in respect to the poor stage *per se* than in respect to "art" at large, affected me in spite of that as justly tenable.

(1:xvi)

What is at stake in this metaphorization is the possibility of refining the "vulgar" literality of "the poor stage *per se*" out of the theatrical theme, so that what remains can be appropriated as a "suggestive" paradigm of "'art' at large." Once purified *as* metaphor, the theatrical theme is no longer susceptible to Stevenson's reproach. For on the thematic level the metaphor itself now becomes, as it were, a stage for its own technical or formal assimilation, an assimilation whose product is what critics will call James's scenic method or dramatic mode.

Indeed, many critics have followed James in identifying *The Tragic Muse* as a pivotal text in his career, since it combines his older, painterly approach with a newer, more dramatic one.[6] Earlier in the preface, James explains how this formal innovation centers on the novel's most prominent "creature of the stage," the actress Miriam Rooth:

> The emphasis is all on an absolutely objective Miriam, and, this affirmed, how—with such an amount of exposed subjectivity all round her—can so dense a medium be a centre? . . . Miriam *is* central then to analysis, in spite of being objective; central in virtue of the fact that the whole thing has visibly, from the first, to get itself done in dramatic, or at least in scenic conditions—though scenic conditions which are as near an approach to the dramatic as the novel may permit itself and which have this in common with the latter, that they move in the light of *alternation*. This imposes a consistency other than that of the novel at its loosest, and for one's subject, a different view and a different placing of the centre. The charm of the scenic consistency, the consistency of the multiplication of *aspects*, that of making them amusingly various, had haunted the author of *The Tragic Muse* from far back.

(1:xv)

6. See, for example, Robert Falk, "*The Tragic Muse*: Henry James's Loosest, Baggiest Novel," in *Themes and Directions in American Literature*, ed. R. B. Browne and Donald Pizer (Lafayette, Ind.: Purdue University Studies, 1969), pp. 148–62; Judith E. Funston, "'All Art Is One': Narrative Techniques in Henry James's *Tragic Muse*," *Studies in the Novel* 15 (Winter 1983): 344–55; William R. Goetz, "The Allegory of Representation in *The Tragic Muse*," *Journal of Narrative Technique* 8 (Fall 1978): 151–64.

In posing the initial question as to how a character as dense or opaque as Miriam can function as a center, James calls attention to the contrast between his more famous "centers of consciousness" and the "absolutely objective" center exemplified by this dramatic protagonist, whom we never "go behind" (1:xvi) but whom we see "in the light of [scenic] alternation" that permits both a "multiplication of *aspects*" and the tightness of "consistency." "The sense of a system," writes James, "saves the painter"—not to mention the dramatically oriented novelist—"from the baseness of the *arbitrary stroke*" (1:xiv). Any baseness or arbitrariness resulting from the attempt to "do the actress" (1:xvi) disappears once this central figure is seen as motivating a new technical system, as serving a higher purpose than that of mere entertainment. By using the theater as a metaphor for " 'art' at large" and then establishing a second stage to the theatrical metaphor—that is, by constructing the novel itself according to dramatic principles—James completes the process of refining the "vulgarity" out of his theatrical subject and of distinguishing himself from those whose interest is captured by "the poor stage *per se*."

Though they interpret James's use of the dramatic analogy variously, most critics seem to accept his claim for the "consistency" of this method.[7] Fredric Jameson, for example, regards the method as an instrument of conservative mystification—especially compared with Conrad's narrative strategies—but he assumes its unity and efficacy:

> The secondary model which organizes Jamesian point of view is the metaphor and ideal of theatrical representation. As in the development of perspective (itself the end product of a theatrical metaphor), the structural corollary of the point of view of the spectator is the unity of organization of the theatrical space and the theatrical scene; hence the obsessive repetition throughout the nineteenth-century novel of theatrical terms like "scene," "spectacle," and "tableau," which urge on the reader a theater-goer's position with respect to the content of the narrative. Such terms are also abundant in Conrad, yet

7. Some, like Funston, praise James's use of the dramatic analogy for its conduciveness to the creation of "living, breathing characters": 352. Others view it as enabling the subterfuge of an "amusingly various" pseudomultiplicity in the service of an authoritarian ideology. In addition to Jameson's Marxist perspective, see the Foucauldian formulation offered by Seltzer in *Henry James*, pp. 155–56.

they are reappropriated by the perceptual vocation of his style, which
undermines the unity of the theatrical metaphor.[8]

Yet the stability of the theatrical metaphor in James is by no means
self-evident. One could argue, in fact, that it is unnecessary for
Conrad to undermine its "unity," since James—or a certain powerful
insistence in James's text—has already done so. While the scenic
method works to convert the theater into a sufficiently abstract representation of representation, any notion of the formal purity and
coherence of " 'art' at large" is destabilized, earlier in the preface,
by certain representations of the "largeness" of art, images that call
into question the extent to which James has succeeded in transforming the theater from a vulgarly literal milieu into the guarantor
of a "consistency other than that of the novel at its loosest." "It
seemed clear," James admits, "that I needed big cases—small ones
would practically give my central idea away; and I make out now
my still labouring under the illusion that the case of the sacrifice for
art *can* ever be, with truth, with taste, with discretion involved,
apparently and showily 'big' " (1:viii).

Indeed, no sooner has James complained of the risks to "health
and safety" posed by certain nineteenth-century novels he calls
"large loose baggy monsters, with their queer elements of the accidental and the arbitrary" (1:x), than he implies that *The Tragic Muse*
may come close to joining this unhealthy company: for the looseness
of his own literary structure is embodied, ironically, in its central
character. Central though Miriam may be, "again and again, perversely, incurably, the centre of my structure would insist on placing
itself *not*, so to speak, in the middle" (1:xi). James attempts to differentiate Miriam from the "vivid monsters" (1:xviii) of Anatole
France, who in his *Histoire comique* has also " 'done the actress' "
(1:xvii). Yet, as the novel's ostensible center, Miriam lurks somewhere
behind or within James's striking emblematization of his asymmetrical novel as a "loose" monster in its own right:

> In very few of my productions, to my eye, *has* the organic centre
> succeeded in getting into proper position.
>   Time after time, then, has the precious waistband or girdle, studded
> and buckled and placed for brave outward show, practically worked

8. Fredric Jameson, *The Political Unconscious: Narrative as a Socially Symbolic Act*
(Ithaca: Cornell University Press, 1981), p. 231.

itself, and in spite of desperate remonstrance, or in other words essential counterplotting, to a point perilously near the knees—perilously I mean for the freedom of these parts.

(1:xi)[9]

The oddness of James's evocation of the monstrous text, which
"insists," "perversely," on finding its own place, and whose waistband or girdle "works itself" out of proper position, suggests that
this beast enjoys a certain autonomy, acting against its creator's
better judgment. It is as if the "creature of the stage" somehow
resisted James's attempt to dignify her as the presiding genius of
the novel's compositional procedure and "insisted" instead on a
more unsettling kind of centrality, a centrality characterized by the
very largeness, looseness, bagginess, and monstrosity that James
attempts to preclude by turning the theater into a metaphor for " 'art'
at large."[10] Here is a center that wanders from its assigned post,
pervading and disfiguring the text that tries to master it. Far from
being insufficiently central, this creature is *too* central—central to the
point of incorporating the text and remaking it in its own image.
Where James had hoped to achieve the "charm of . . . scenic consistency" and the beauty of formal control, he confronts instead the
meretricious spectacle of an "outward show" much too "showily
'big.' "

But it would be a mistake to conclude that this return-of-the-
repressed, this reinstatement of theatrical vulgarity on the level of
the novel's very form, represents a failure of metaphor, whereby
the delicately figurative or spiritual ideal (" 'art' at large") gives way
to the brute force of the literal ("the poor stage *per se*"). Rather,
James presents a more complex version here of the relationship

9. An indication of the uneasiness that *The Tragic Muse* still inspires in its author
is the somewhat cagey obliquity with which he discusses its status in relation to his
(other?) decentered "productions": "As to which in my list they are, however, that
is another business, not on any terms to be made known" (1:xi). Despite the aura of
mystery James creates here, he spends much of his time in the preface trying to
determine the degree to which this novel is or is not adequately centered. Not surprisingly, the results are contradictory: at some points he praises the book's "unity
of tone" (1:vii, 1:xxii), while at others he judges it "false," "dissembling" (1:xiii), or
"imperfect" (1:xiv).

10. John Carlos Rowe notes in *The Theoretical Dimensions of Henry James* (Madison:
University of Wisconsin Press, 1984), that "Miriam is central to analysis only because
she permits a certain alternation of relations and an unsettling of the center." Though
I agree with this formulation, I think it important to stress that, for James, "alternation" should not lead inevitably to "unsettling" (p. 247).

between the figurative and the literal, in which figurative language is no longer opposed to, but implicated in, the baseness of the literal; metaphor is no longer charmingly aloof from the "queer elements of the accidental and the arbitrary" but inhabited by them from the outset. For example, James's image for the novel's extravagance— the figure *en déshabillé*—is not only an extravagant figure in its own right, with its showy syntax and its irrepressible imagery: it also displays the convergence of figure-as-rhetorical-trope with figure-as-bodily-form, where both body and trope are at once theatrically vivid and theatrically mediated, bound up flamboyantly in a "waistband or girdle, studded and buckled and placed for brave outward show."

Given the theatricality of metaphor, it becomes increasingly difficult to distinguish the figural force of James's theatrical metaphor from the literality of the theater. Thus, his statement, "the centre of my structure would insist on placing itself *not*, so to speak, in the middle"—an apparent affirmation of a split between the literal (the middle) and the figurative (the center)—has to invoke the figurative indirection of "so to speak" to name that literal term. No wonder, then, that in looking back at *The Tragic Muse* James refers to it as "the maimed or slighted, the disfigured or defeated, the unlucky or unlikely child" (1:vi). For the novel, like its preface, is precisely about the dis-figuration that results when a certain ideology of metaphor or figurative language—an ideology that supports in turn a highly metaphysical abstraction of " 'art' at large"—breaks down.[11] Both *The Tragic Muse* and its preface exhibit the dis-figuring effects of novel-writing itself, an activity that not only engenders monsters but also threatens to uncover a certain "monstrosity" in the unlucky parent.

What James, in the passage cited above, calls "desperate remonstrance" or "essential counterplotting" is nothing other than a system designed to ensure his own "health and safety" by deflecting this threat. But when James points out that "the sense of a system" triumphs over the base and the arbitrary, he also admits that "it was but half a system" to rely on Miriam to accomplish such a task:

11. The term "disfiguration" plays in important role in some of the later essays of Paul de Man. See, for example, "Autobiography as De-facement" and "Shelley Disfigured," in de Man, *The Rhetoric of Romanticism* (New York: Columbia University Press, 1984), pp. 67–81, and 93–123.

"That device was to ask for as much help as it gave" (1:xiv). For if James "delight[s] . . . in an organic form" (1:x), the "form" of Miriam Rooth turns out to be "organic" in ways that James cannot regulate or normalize into a coherent counterplot or strategy of resistance to the novel's decentering or disfiguring force. The problem is that, although Miriam may assist in this counterplot, she also serves as the "medium" that conducts the monstrous theatricality, against which that defensive system is directed, from the literal into the figural realm. The monstrosity transmitted from her "form" to the "form" of the novel as a whole keeps drifting toward the "form" of Henry James, who would play the role of external author-subject to Miriam's "absolutely objective" character, but who repeatedly finds himself imperiled by the baseness and arbitrariness embodied in his own inescapably theatrical metaphors.[12]

Four years after he wrote *The Tragic Muse*, James complained to his brother William about the "humiliations and vulgarities and disgusts" he was then enduring as a remarkably unsuccessful playwright: "The whole odiousness of the thing lies in the connection between the drama and the theatre. The one is admirable in its interest and difficulty, the other loathsome in its conditions."[13] In *The Tragic Muse* James attempts to evade the "odiousness" of that "connection" by ridding the theater of its unpleasantly literal "conditions" so that it can be incorporated, thematically and technically, into the higher form of the novel.

Many critics have noted that *The Tragic Muse* situates the theater among other, competing modes of representation, and that much of its interest derives from James's ordering of these modes—novelistic,

12. The subject of the theater tends to crystalize the particular ambiguity of James's notion of "form." For an interesting example of this oscillation between aesthetic and somatic registers, see the letter to his brother William in which he describes the "fever of dramatic production" and the exhilaration it brings: "Now that I have tasted blood, *c'est une rage* [of determination to *do*, and triumph, on my part], for I feel at last as if I had found my *real* form, which I am capable of carrying far, and for which the pale little art of fiction, as I have practised it, has been, for me, but a limited and restricted substitute." *Letters*, 4 vols., ed. Leon Edel (Cambridge: Harvard University Press 1974–84) 3:329.

13. Edel, ed., *Letters* 3:452.

pictorial, even political—in relation to one another.[14] As would-be emblem of the novel's "dramatic" method, Miriam occupies a central position in the text, but this very centrality indicates her intermediate status on James's ethico-aesthetic scale, where her artistry stands below that of the novelist or painter but above that of the politician. Gabriel Nash, the text's resident novelist-critic-aesthete, best artic- ulates this aesthetic hierarchy. When Nash calls acting "the lowest of the arts," and Peter Sherringham asks, "Lower than politics?," Nash replies: "Dear no, I won't say that. I think the Théâtre Français a greater institution than the House of Commons" (1:55).[15] But then, to complete the scale, Nash delivers his opinion on the institution of the theater in general, condemning its dependence upon

the *omnium gatherum* of the population of a big commercial city at the hour of the day when their taste is at its lowest, flocking out of hideous hotels and restaurants, gorged with food, stultified with buy- ing and selling and with all the other sordid preoccupations of the age, squeezed together in a sweltering mass, disappointed in their seats, timing the author, timing the actor, wishing to get their money back on the spot—all before eleven o'clock. Fancy putting the exquisite before such a tribunal as that! There's not even a question of it. The dramatist wouldn't if he could, and in nine cases out of ten he couldn't if he would. He has to make the basest concessions. One of his prin- cipal canons is that he must enable his spectators to catch the suburban trains, which stop at 11:30. What would you think of any other artist— the painter or the novelist—whose governing forces should be the dinner and the suburban trains? . . . What can you do with a character, with an idea, with a feeling, between dinner and the suburban trains? You can give a gross rough sketch of them, but how little you touch them, how bald you leave them! What crudity compared with what the novelist does!

(1:66–67)

14. Goetz's essay is particularly rewarding as a discussion of these different rep- resentational modes. For Seltzer, *Henry James*, p. 155, the novel is "virtually an in- ventory of aesthetic and political modes of representation, and their entanglement."

15. Significantly, however, Nash chooses a French rather than an English theatrical "institution." The most aggressive characterization of the difference between the two comes from Miriam's tutor, the great old actress Madame Carré: "Je ne connais qu'une scène—la nôtre. . . . I'm assured by every one who knows that there's no other" (1:122). For James's comparisons of the Parisian and London stages, see the essays collected in *The Scenic Art*, ed. Allan Wade (New Brunswick: Rutgers University Press, 1948). For an extremely interesting and informative study of James's views in the context of late-nineteenth-century discussion of the French theater versus the English theater, see D. J. Gordon and John Stokes, "The Reference of *The Tragic Muse*," in *The Air of Reality: New Essays on Henry James*, ed. John Goode (London: Methuen, 1972), especially pp. 127–40.

Amplifying James's notion of the vulgarity of the "poor stage *per se*," Nash identifies the contemporary theater as a site of degrading intercourse, of an oppressively close and insistent physicality: the philistine modern audience is notable primarily for its sensual over-indulgence—imaged as overeating—and for its "sordidly" commercial associations. The dramatist, for his part, must pander to its appetites, squeezing himself into the structures of capitalist reality, neatly condensed here as the inevitabilities of "dinner and the suburban trains." And if the dramatist is a pander, the implications for the social and economic status of the actress are clear. Where he can at least hide behind the scenes, her contact with the "sweltering" masses is more compromisingly direct.

The novelist and the painter suffer no such exposure. But if, by the end of Nash's speech, the painter has implicitly dropped into second place, leaving only the novelist completely immune from the "crudity" of the age, this differentiation may have something to do with the fact that the kind of painting represented in this novel is portraiture, of which Nash says, albeit approvingly, that it "offer[s] a double vision" (2:52), one that reveals the painter as well as the subject painted. At its most essential, however, art is supposed to be characterized by singleness, solitude, and autonomy. Hence James's remark in the preface about the difficulty of depicting the true artist:

> The most charming thing about the preference for art is that to parade abroad so thoroughly inward and so naturally embarrassed a matter is to falsify and vulgarise it; . . . under the rule of its sincerity, its only honours are those of contraction, concentration and a seemingly deplorable indifference to everything but itself. Nothing can well figure as less "big," in an honest thesis, than a marked instance of someone's willingness to pass mainly for an ass.
>
> (1:viii)

Especially in light of our discussion in the previous chapter, this distinction between embarrassment and vulgarity may strike us as being somewhat tenuous: it is as though James had concluded that, since embarrassment is inevitable, the best he can hope for is to be "*naturally* embarrassed." But the point here seems to be that, if the novelist cannot help "pass[ing] mainly for an ass," he thus gets to turn his back on the vulgar parade that others must join. Eschewing all figurative "bigness," the novelist is the least theatrical of artists.

Instead of being ruled by the constraints of "dinner and the suburban trains," he obeys only the "rule" of "sincerity" and the dictates of "honesty." The "indifferent" novelist stands alone, answerable only to himself. Even the portrait-painter, in the apparent seclusion of his studio, finds himself forced *outward* into a kind of intercourse with otherness and difference, insofar as he must submit to the doubling of his vision. The hierarchy that James has Nash suggest, then, points to the aesthetic supremacy of the novelist who defines this hierarchy in the first place.[16]

James himself seeks to emplot—or, as he would have it, to counterplot—this distancing of his artistry as a novelist from that of the artists within his novel, by having them try to distance themselves from the vulgarity of their own lesser arts. Thus, Miriam must develop from an "artlessly rough" (1:130) and "rude" (1:131) theatrical novice into an "exquisite" dramatic "revelation" (2:430) as Juliet, and Nick Dormer must give up his political career for the nobler calling of the portrait-painter. Together, the "theatrical case" (1:ix) and the "political case" (1:ix) should illustrate "the conflict between art and 'the world' " (1:v). As they advance arduously from " 'the world' " to "art," Nick and Miriam—especially Miriam, since her chosen art form straddles the line dividing the "loathsome" theater from the "admirable" drama—should dilate the distance between their creator and the vulgar entanglements from which he labors to extricate them. Snatching Nick from " 'the world' " and pointing him toward "art," saving Miriam from the theater and training her for the drama, James stages a "conflict" whose terms reinforce his own singular authenticity.

But just as the outrageously "affected" (1:173) Nash may seem too much like James at times, so Nick and Miriam—especially Miriam—

16. A number of critics have taken special pains to deny any identification of Nash, the artist-critic, with James himself. In doing so, they enforce the differential system whereby a divinely self-contained author, though his attributes are invested judiciously in his various characters, avoids the contamination that affects those characters. See, for example, R. P. Blackmur, Introduction to the Laurel edition of *The Tragic Muse*, rpt. in Blackmur, *Studies in Henry James*, ed. Veronica A. Makowsky (New York: New Directions, 1983), pp. 202–12; Oscar Cargill, *The Novels of Henry James* (New York: Macmillan, 1961), pp. 182–202; Leon Edel, *Henry James: The Middle Years, 1882–1895* (Philadelphia: Lippincott, 1962), pp. 259–60; Dorothea Krook, *The Ordeal of Consciousness in Henry James* (Cambridge: Cambridge University Press, 1962), pp. 62–105.

threaten to abbreviate, rather than expand, the distance between James and a "world" from which he would "contract." And just as many critics strive to reassert the ironically stabilized differences between James and Nash, so James himself deploys the counterplot of aesthetic development and refinement against the risk of his own infection by vulgarity. In describing the task shared by Nick and Miriam as one of "postponing the 'world' to their conception of other and finer decencies" (1:xvii), the author describes the role of the counterplot as well: difference and deference are underwritten by narrative deferment, by a more or less "desperate" putting-off of the "world" designed to look like a transcendence of the world's base and arbitrary conditions.[17] For James to present the counterplot as one of deferment is for him to recognize the danger of his own implication in the theatrical "plot" against which that counterplot struggles, a plot whose dangerous theatricality is embodied in Miriam Rooth.

James took the title of the novel from Reynolds's portrait of Sarah Siddons, and at several points in the text Miriam is compared to that other Jewish actress, the legendary Rachel Félix.[18] At the beginning of the novel, however, any comparison between Miriam and such luminaries seems inconceivable. "*Notez bien*," says Madame Carré, the great actress whom Miriam engages as a tutor, "Rachel wasn't a *grosse bête*" (1:133). Yet, as Peter Sherringham recalls, Miriam "had looked slightly *bête* even when [he] . . . said to Nick Dormer that she was the image of the Tragic Muse" (1:190). The early Miriam combines overtones of stupidity, even perhaps of beastliness, and of a subtle but undeniable sexual immodesty, to

17. An interesting and complex issue, but one beyond the scope of the present essay, is that of James's compulsive use of quotation marks. This ironizing gesture tends to undermine or put into question the literal status of virtually any term, to turn all discourse into endless catachresis. If James can speak both of " 'art' at large" and of "the 'world,' " neither of these supposedly antithetical terms seems clearly literal—or, for that matter, clearly figurative. For provocative discussions of related rhetorical problems in James, see Deborah Esch, "A Jamesian About-Face: Notes on 'The Jolly Corner,' " *ELH* 50 (Fall 1983): 587–605; William R. Goetz, *Henry James: The Darkest Abyss of Romance* (Baton Rouge: Louisiana State University Press, 1986); Ruth Bernard Yeazell, *Language and Knowledge in the Late Novels of Henry James* (Chicago: University of Chicago Press, 1976).

18. For a discussion of James's use of the Reynolds painting as a compositional model, see Falk, "*The Tragic Muse*," in Browne and Pizer, ed., *Themes and Directions*, pp. 152–53.

yield an image of the monstrosity her aesthetic education will have to dispel. This implication of sexual impropriety is most evident in Sherringham's obsessive and ambivalent reflections on the actress:

> It struck him abruptly that a woman whose only being was to "make believe," to make believe she had any and every being you might like and that would serve a purpose and produce a certain effect, and whose identity resided in the continuity of her personations, so that she had no moral privacy, as he phrased it to himself, but lived in a high wind of exhibition, of figuration—such a woman was a kind of monster in whom of necessity there would be nothing to "be fond" of, because there would be nothing to take hold of. He felt for a moment how simple he had been not to have achieved before this analysis of the actress. The girl's very face made it vivid to him now—the discovery that she positively had no countenance of her own, but only the countenance of the occasion, a sequence, a variety—capable possibly of becoming immense—of representative movements. . . . The expression that came nearest belonging to her, as it were, was the one that came nearest being a blank—an air of inanity when she forgot herself in some act of sincere attention.
>
> (1:189–90)

This monstrous woman whom one cannot "take hold of" looks in many ways like a more "vivid" or more particularized incarnation of the large loose baggy novel that its author can barely hold together. Juxtaposed with this passage from the novel, the description of the figure in the fallen waistband or girdle begins to assume a sexual specificity that James's indeterminate language occludes, and the fallen girdle suggests the garment appropriate to a fallen woman or a woman of "loose" virtue: a woman like Miriam who can "make believe she had any and every being you might like." Though essentially "blank," Miriam confronts Sherringham with a disquieting potential for "immensity" that recalls the uncontrollable text and thus inscribes the novel's technical or structural problem in a more "strikingly" anxious context. Indeed, in this light, James's remark that the garment has "worked itself . . . to a point perilously near the knees," with its curious qualification, "—perilously I mean for the freedom of these parts," takes on a more plausibly nervous tone, as if to hint that James is more concerned about the parts that might be exposed than about the parts that might be constrained. To all the other attributes that make Miriam "a kind of monster," then, we may add one more—a theatrical tendency to conflate the form-giving ideal of "figuration" with the fraudulence of "personation," so that the loftier ambitions of representation are reduced to the cheapness of "exhibition."

With her initial air of aesthetic and sexual impropriety, Miriam is just a notch above the politician, who offers the most egregious affront to the novel's notion of representation. James indicates the stigma attached to political representation when he allows Nick to define the profession he will eventually abandon:

> It's an appeal to everything that for one's self one despises . . . to stupidity, to ignorance, to prejudice, to the love of hollow idiotic words, of shutting the eyes tight and making a noise. Do men who respect each other or themselves talk to each other that way? They know they'd deserve kicking! A man would blush to say to himself in the darkness of the night the things he stands up on a platform in the garish light of day to stuff into the ears of a multitude whose intelligence he pretends he rates high.
>
> (1:103)

If, as Sherringham says, one "half" of Miriam's profession is "brilliant" while "the other's frankly odious" (2:199)—the brilliant half corresponding to the "admirable" drama and the odious half to the "loathsome" theater—the "detestable side" (1:xxi) is contiguous with the irredeemable world of politics, wherein, as Nick's remarks imply, theatricality becomes virtually synonymous with prostitution. For the politician "stands on a platform in the garish light of day" and "pretends" sympathy for a "multitude"; "shutting the eyes tight and making a noise," he enacts a travesty of love. And what he "loves," or pretends to love, is itself a travesty, a perversion of language into "names and phrases" and "hollow idiotic words." In his "appeal to . . . stupidity," this *bête* epitomizes monstrosity as an aberration at once intellectual, sexual, and rhetorical.

As the narrative of *The Tragic Muse* unfolds, the "brilliant" side of the actress should gradually eclipse her "odious" side: she should move further away from the politician and closer to the novelist, just as the (reluctant) politician in the novel rises to the rank of painter. Yet her association with political grandstanding—with theatricality at its worst—never quite disappears, so that her "brilliance" always seems a bit too close to mere "garishness." Even on the verge of her triumph as Juliet, when she ends up apotheosized as an "incarnation" uttering the "truest divinest music that had ever poured from tragic lips" (2:430), she reminds us of her earlier, more palpably carnal self, of the "strange girl" who thinks that to act is "to go and exhibit one's self to a loathsome crowd, on a platform, with trumpets and a big drum, for money—to parade one's body and one's soul" (1:162). It is as if, even as Miriam begins to deserve the comparison with Rachel Félix, she could degenerate into that other, presumably "great" Jewish precursor, Sarah Bernhardt, of whom James writes, in another context: "She has in a supreme degree what the French call the *génie de la réclame*—the advertising genius; she may, indeed, be called the muse of the newspaper."[19] Here is the Tragic Muse in her penultimate dramatic triumph, as observed by a starstruck Peter Sherringham:

> Miriam had never been more present to him than at this hour; but she was inextricably transmuted—present essentially as the romantic heroine she represented. His state of mind was of the strangest and he was conscious of its strangeness, just as he was conscious in his very person of a lapse of resistance which likened itself absurdly to liberation. He felt weak at the same time that he felt inspired, and he felt inspired at the same time that he knew, or believed he knew, that his face was a blank. He saw things as a shining confusion, and yet somehow something monstrously definite kept surging out of them. Miriam was a beautiful actual fictive impossible young woman of a past age, an undiscoverable country, who spoke in blank verse and overflowed with metaphor, who was exalted and heroic beyond all human convenience and who yet was irresistibly related to one's own affairs.
>
> (2:326–27)

If, even at this late stage, Miriam still suggests "something monstrously definite," we can see why James calls the remonstrance of his counterplotting "desperate." This "monstrously definite" substance neither coincides with nor cancels out the sense of "shining confusion," because Miriam, like Lucy Snowe at her most histrionic, possesses an uncanny plasticity that flouts the either/or logic of realistic mimesis. That this defiance has an erotically illicit under-

---

19. James, *Scenic Art*, Wade ed., p. 129. The figure of the Jewish actress looms large in such other novels of theatricality as *Villette* and *Daniel Deronda*. Barish, *The Antitheatrical Prejudice*, pp. 464–69, has an interesting discussion of the conventional association of actors with both Jews and prostitutes. The present chapter is also significantly indebted to Catherine Gallagher, "George Eliot and *Daniel Deronda*: The Prostitute and the Jewish Question," in *Sex, Politics, and Science in the Nineteenth-Century Novel: Selected Papers from the English Institute, 1983–84*, ed. Ruth Bernard Yeazell (Baltimore: Johns Hopkins University Press, 1986), pp. 39–62. I discuss Gallagher's reading in the final section of this chapter.

current appears in Miriam's overpowering influence on her ecstatic beholder. Admittedly, she no longer strikes us—or Sherringham— as either stupid or vulgar. Yet her monstrosity persists, as a rhetorical transgression manifested in her "overflow[ing] with metaphor." From the point of view of the counterplot, metaphor is not supposed to overflow, but to stay within bounds—indeed, to reinforce the bounds between theatricality and " 'art' at large." What thwarts the counterplot here is not just the skewing of the narrative line that would trace a progression from vulgarity to sublimity: in addition to diminishing the proper distance between the novel's beginning and its end, Miriam's overflow crosses the line separating male spectator from female performer, subject from object.

As William R. Goetz notes, Miriam "upsets the duality upon which representation is normally based."[20] For Sherringham now exhibits many of the same peculiarities that he noticed in Miriam when he performed his "analysis of the actress." Miriam appeared there in the dazzling light of contradiction: on the one hand, she had "any and every being you might like," and suggested a "variety—capable possibly of becoming immense"; on the other hand, because she lacked "moral privacy" she offered "nothing to 'be fond' of" and "nothing to take hold of," and "had no countenance of her own," except for an expression resembling "a blank—an air of inanity."[21] Here, Sherringham's own face becomes "a blank," a receptive surface on which the contradictory effects of theatricality are inscribed: acknowledging a "lapse of resistance" which at the same time feels like "liberation," feeling at once "weak" and "inspired," seeing things as both "a shining confusion" and yet at the same time "somehow . . . monstrously definite," the spectator now becomes the site of the very oscillation between lack and excess that he found in his loved and dreaded object. His body, like hers, has become a text. And if, by dint of these oxymoronic constructions, the "beautiful actual fictive impossible" actress always seems both "irresistibly real" or "vivid" and strangely "make[-]believe" or

20. Goetz, "Allegory": 150.
21. The notion of the actor as a paradoxical being has a venerable history. Diderot may be the exemplary theorist in this regard, but Hazlitt would serve as a useful nineteenth-century English instance. Of actors, he wrote, "It is only when they are themselves that they are nothing," "On Actors and Acting," in *Essays*, ed. Rosalind Vallance and John Hampden (London: Folio Society, 1964), p. 23. I am concerned here with the anxieties that may inform this virtually proverbial construction.

"inextricably transmuted" into a "heroic" figure "beyond all human convenience," the spectator himself is now affected by this same inconveniently and distinctively theatrical doubleness, in which "his state of mind [is] of the strangest and he [is] conscious of its strangeness."[22]

Yet James by no means celebrates this "shining confusion." For all the brilliance and energy of this passage, it occurs alongside others that characterize Miriam's metaphorical overflow in more stringent terms. Where James calls Sarah Bernhardt "the muse of the newspaper," Gabriel Nash offers his own "joyous amused amusing"—and condescending—vision of Miriam as the "predestined mistress" of the "roaring deafening newspaperism of the period":

> Gabriel brushed in a large bright picture of her progress through the time and round the world, round it and round it again, from continent to continent and clime to clime; with populations and deputations, reporters and photographers, placards and interviews and banquets, steamers, railways, dollars, diamonds, speeches and artistic ruin all jumbled into her train. Regardless of expense the spectacle would be and thrilling, though somewhat monotonous, the drama—a drama more bustling than any she would put on the stage and a spectacle that would beat everything for scenery.
>
> (2:197)

The interest of this passage lies in its displacement and reversal of the image of Miriam as the novel's center. Instead of being the stabilizing object around which everything turns, Miriam herself does the turning here, in a dizzying "progress through the time and round the world, round it and round it again." Miriam's aesthetic progress now takes on the mock-apocalyptic guise of a bizarre, pointless, unending revolution. Moreover, this confused and confusing circulation—much like that of a newspaper—indicates a rhetorical disorder, where the paradigmatic discourse of metaphor has deteriorated into an indiscriminately heterogeneous contiguity: Miriam becomes a destructive force, arbitrarily dragging "the world" along in her touring company, mixing up linguistic with non-lin-

---

22. Just before this extraordinary passage Sherringham hears Nick Dormer remark that Miriam's face is "finely made up—perhaps a little too much" (2:326). Sherringham's subsequent meditation on Miriam reveals how a brilliant or "shining" performance overflows the protective boundary between spectacle and audience, implicating the viewer in an exhilarating fictionality that might feel like the garishness, even the vulgarity, of wearing "too much" make-up.

guistic forms of transport, verbal with nonverbal forms of exchange, whirling around with "reporters and photographers, placards and interviews and banquets, steamers, railways, dollars, diamonds, speeches and artistic ruin all jumbled into her train." This "jumble" makes her triumphant overflow look like a perversion of metaphor into metonymy, a displacement that undoes the hierarchical and idealizing perspective of metaphor itself. If metaphor establishes a stable relationship between the fictive and the real, this displacement allows for the fluidity of relations that her "overflow" effects.[23]

For the "drama" and "spectacle" of her career will be more "bustling" and "scenic" than any of her real productions—if it makes sense to speak of "real productions" when the difference between the real and the fictional, between ground and figure, has succumbed to the general "artistic ruin." Symptoms of the "artistic ruin" that Nash sees Miriam as effecting can be found in the "shining confusion" that theatricalizes Peter Sherringham as he watches her perform; for though this seems, on the one hand, like a tribute to Miriam's heroic talent, it serves on the other hand as a sign of her disruptive potential, a sign that she might pull other characters besides Sherringham into her monstrous entourage.

Those who would object that this reading is predicated upon Nash's antitheatrical prejudice, which James himself does not endorse, may wish to exempt the author less from Nash's antitheatricalism than from the theatrical way in which he chooses to express it. For Nash, too, resembles Miriam insofar as his pronouncements about the importance of "style," and about the need to protect it from the vulgar public, strike other characters—including Miriam— as exercises in "histrionics" (1:208).[24] Nash's mysterious disappear-

23. Nina Auerbach, *Woman and the Demon: The Life of a Victorian Myth* (Cambridge: Harvard University Press, 1982), p. 206, sees the Victorian actress as the embodiment of that era's fascination with the "rich fluidity of self." I would emphasize that, while James may celebrate this fluidity, he also finds it disturbingly close to dissolution. In a perceptive discussion of James's criticism of women novelists, Evan Carton writes that James "characterizes 'the feminine element' in a series of related ways: it is a 'turn for color' rather than for composition, a sensitivity to impression rather than a power of reflection, a 'fatal gift of fluency' (James repeatedly describes the feminine style in terms of liquids, fluids, currents)—fatal because it implies for him the effacement of the traceable self in a flood of irrationalism, an inescapable and ultimately incommunicable wave of private impulse." "Henry James the Critic," *Raritan* 5 (1986): 132.

24. For an excellent discussion of the way in which virtually any artistic representation—including Nash's antitheatrical posturings—is in some sense theatrical, see

ance near the end of the novel, when he vanishes "without a trace" (2:412), just as his image is beginning to fade from the canvas where Nick is painting his portrait, may in fact identify him as the novel's scapegoat, who must be punished and expelled for advertising a theatricality that other characters exhibit as well.[25] Indeed, Nash, whom many in the novel consider a "mere *farceur*" (1:170), is no less immune from this theatricality than is Sherringham—or even Nick Dormer, who at one point late in the story turns against portraiture because even the works of its greatest practitioners fall short of "the idea" and become mere "performances."[26]

The desire to restrict this theatricality betokens a similar nostalgia for "the idea"—the idea of the omnipotent author and of the unified work of art. When Miriam overflows with metaphor, it seems as if *she* authored those metaphors in the very process of uttering them. And if the actress appears to usurp the authorial prerogative, her author may begin to look like an uncontrollable performer. Indeed, certain critics would deny what James himself acknowledges—that the text's monstrous overflow results from his own "vice," a "particular vice of the artistic spirit" (1:xi). If James encourages their nostalgia, it is in the wake of Miriam's more spectacular metaphoric

---

Gordon and Stokes, "The Reference of *The Tragic Muse*," in Goode, ed., *The Air of Reality*, pp. 86–114.

25. This "disappearance" (2:412) constitutes one of the more extreme, if not exactly terroristic, instances of James's counterplotting. Nash is made to vanish immediately after he boasts, "I dare say I'm indestructible, immortal" (2:411). It is not clear, however, whether he is punished for claiming an invulnerability that James would reserve for himself alone, or whether his offense is that of making this claim with "such a literal air" ([Harmondsworth: Penguin, 1978], p. 511), and in a manner "so nearly witless" (2:412). Perhaps Nash has exposed too great a similarity between the true artist's "willingness to pass mainly for an ass" and a vulgar—not to say *bête*—parody of that same willingness. Whatever its logic, this disappearing act (performed not so much by Nash as on him) is explicitly likened to the kind of thing one might find in "some delicate Hawthorne tale" (2:412). It is as though James wanted to break out of the realistic mode of the novel and to align himself with the precursor whose feelings about the "d——d mob of scribbling women" he knew well. That James also associates this fantastical event with the conventions of "a fairy-tale or a melodrama" (2:412) suggests, however, the persistence of a certain theatricality, alongside or even within a certain delicacy or ethereality.

26. Here, I quote from the 1890 version (ibid., p. 418). For "performances," the New York edition substitutes the more attenuated and less interesting phrase, "palpable polished 'toned' objects" (2:266). Significantly, even when Nick rededicates himself to his painterly calling, he retains the theatrical metaphor: "Art was *doing*—it came back to that—which politics in most cases weren't. He thus, to pursue our image, planted his supports in the dimness beneath all cursing, and on the platform so improvised was able, in his relief, to dance" (2:267–68).

overflow, which washes away any solid ground on which authors and characters alike might take absolute or unambiguous stands.[27]

Nash merely elaborates, then, upon what Sherringham recognizes much earlier, when he says to Miriam (as Daniel Deronda might have said to his mother): "Your feigning may be honest in the sense that your only feeling *is* your feigned one. That's what I mean by the absence of a ground or of intervals. It's a kind of thing that's a labyrinth!" (1:211). In the absence of a ground, it becomes extremely difficult to posit, with Nash, the polarity of the "dull, dense, literal prose" (1:170) of everyday life on the one hand and "our treatment of the material, our rendering of the text, our style" (1:172–73) on the other.[28] The integrity of what Nash calls "one's form" (1:173) is compromised by a monstrous rhetoricity that overflows from Miriam to pervade the novel's dramatis personae—including even its non-artistic characters—and to encroach upon the high ground staked out by the novelist himself.[29]

Thus, when Sherringham exclaims, "It's a kind of thing that's a

27. Significantly, James's admission that responsibility for the novel's tendency to overflow its designated formal limits lies not with Miriam or with some mysterious external force but with his own "particular vice" conflicts with his earlier stricture that associates the "preference for art" with self-effacement and inwardness: "to parade abroad so thoroughly inward and so naturally embarrassed a matter is to falsify and vulgarise it" (1:viii). As dramatized in the novel, Miriam's "parade," her theatrical effect, exposes the willfulness of any such opposition between the "inward" and the "vulgarised," between the "natural" and the "falsified." The overflowing theatricality of Miriam's metaphors threatens the circumscription of James's own theatrical metaphor; for anyone who overflows with metaphors as "naturally" as James does risks being pulled along in the "jumble" of Miriam's train. Given this confused state of affairs, what is to prevent "charmingly" introverted makers of metaphor from jostling against their less "embarrassed" fellows in her entourage? How are we to distinguish artistic virtue from artistic "vice"?

28. When Nash defends his "manner" as "a part of my little system," but then equates this "manner" with "candour" (1:170), he provides a miniature allegory of how a defensive system, little or big, can end up replicating the very confusion of the literal with the figurative—of "feeling" with "feigning"—that it seeks to forestall.

29. At the end of the novel, for example, Julia Dallow invites Nick, his mother, and his sisters to spend the Christmas holiday at her country estate. In the spirit of this "supremely sociable time," even the novel's most dourly and decorously anti-theatrical characters are hard put to resist getting into the act: "[Julia] was a perfect mistress of the revels; she had arranged some ancient bravery for every day and every night. The Dormers were so much in it, as the phrase was, that after all their discomfiture their fortune seemed in an hour to have come back. There had been a moment when, in extemporised charades, Lady Agnes, an elderly figure being required, appeared on the point of undertaking the part of the housekeeper at a castle who, dropping her *h*'s, showed sheeplike tourists about; but she waived the opportunity in favour of her daughter Grace. Even Grace had a great success; Grace dropped her *h*'s as with the crash of empires" (2:416).

labyrinth," he might be describing not so much Miriam herself as her effect on the structure of the novel as a whole: the neuter "it" points to a less narrowly personal and more widely textual concern. By representing metaphor as something more like metonymy, Miriam enacts the breakdown of James's hierarchically oriented theatrical metaphor into a trope of promiscuity—a trope that casts all the novel's artists, as well as some of its critics, as "jumbled" composites of the arbitrarily figurative and the basely literal. The theatrical metaphor, despite its initial purpose, ends up inscribing upon those characters the "grosser signs" (as Nash would say; see 1:34) of theatrical self-display.[30] For the text in which Miriam performs as a perversely decentering center demonstrates not how the art of the novel absorbs and reorganizes other art forms, but how the notion of " 'art' at large" shifts toward a transgressive theatricality that affects and redefines all modes of representation. If the resulting "system" is syntagmatic rather than paradigmatic, labyrinthine rather than hierarchical, this revision forces us to expand our understanding of how the various representational practices in the novel interact in a context not merely "artistic" but social as well.

For just as Miriam's spectacularly inclusive orbit conjoins the aesthetic with the journalistic and the commercial, so her transgression of the line between the stage and the audience figures the power of theatricality to render problematic the very division between art and "the world" that the counterplot seeks to maintain. In an essay written ten years before *The Tragic Muse,* James acknowledges these implications of theatricality, without concealing his dismay. Lamenting the rampant theatricalization of everyday life, he writes:

> It sometimes seems to an observer of English customs that this interest in histrionic matters almost reaches the proportion of a mania. It pervades society—it breaks down barriers. If you go to an evening party, nothing is more probable than that all of a sudden a young lady or a young gentleman will jump up and strike an attitude and begin to recite a poem or speech. Every pretext for this sort of exhibition is ardently cultivated, and the London world is apparently filled with stage-struck young persons whose relatives are holding them back from a dramatic career by the skirts of their garments.

---

30. The consequence of this general disfiguration, moreover, is yet another "jumbling," this time of the vocationally and generically stratified relations among the characters, and so of the progressive counterplot that sustains, and is sustained by, this relational system.

Plays and actors are perpetually talked about, private theatricals are incessant, and members of the dramatic profession are "received" without restriction. They appear in society, and the people of society appear on the stage; it is as if the great gate which formerly divided the theatre from the world had been lifted off its hinges. There is, at any rate, such a passing to and fro as has never been known; the stage has become amateurish and society has become professional. . . . It is part of a great general change which has come over English manners—of the confusion of many things which forty years ago were kept very distinct. The world is being steadily democratized and vulgarized, and literature and art give their testimony to the fact. The fact is better for the world perhaps, but I question greatly whether it is better for art and literature.[31]

Theatricality, in this vision, democratizes and vulgarizes "society," stretching it to the vastness of "the world." Almost thirty years later, in the preface to *The Tragic Muse*, James returns to this theme, but in tones of bemusement reminiscent of Gabriel Nash:

There had hovered before me some possible picture (but all comic and ironic) of one the most salient of London "social" passions, the unappeasable curiosity for the things of the theatre; for every one of them, that is, except the drama itself, and for the "personality" of the performer (almost any performer quite sufficiently serving) in particular. This latter, verily, had struck me as an aspect appealing mainly to satiric treatment; the only adequate or effective treatment, I had again and again felt, for most of the distinctively social aspects of London: the general artlessly histrionised air of things caused so many examples to spring from behind any hedge.

(1:vii)

This "possible picture" of an abandoned approach to the theatrical subject appears, like much of the preface, to continue the effort to protect the novelist from the contamination of theatricality. The passage calls up the forgotten "germ" (1:v) of the work, reconstructing the dream of a privileged novelistic site, one unpolluted by the "general artlessly histrionised air of things" that would nonetheless constitute the novel's subject matter. Here, the almost maniacal "interest in histrionic matters" would remain safely quarantined behind the *cordon sanitaire* of "satiric treatment," sealed off in such a way that it can do no damage to the "health and safety" of the satirist himself.

31. James, "The London Theatres, 1879," in *Scenic Art*, Wade, ed., pp. 119–20. In the novel, 1:150–51, Nash holds forth to similar effect.

Whether or not the novel treats the theatrical passion satirically, it inscribes the monstrous confusion of the formal ("treatment") with the literal ("matters") as a recurrent feature of its plot; and while the characters who inhabit it keep getting "histrionised," this theatricalization keeps threatening to reveal their producer as another "thing of the theatre" himself. In fact, in its rehearsal of *The Tragic Muse*, the preface at once anticipates and reenacts the novel's search for refuge from this taint of theatricality: a refuge in which James could escape the most reprehensible of " 'social' passions"—the passion "for the 'personality' of the performer (almost any performer quite sufficiently serving)." Refusing to be "histrionised" (even artfully so), James would withdraw from the social in the broadest and most unnervingly comprehensive sense of the term. For he pictures society as an immense theater, in which passions play themselves out none-too-exclusively, and in which he himself could figure as merely one more "performer" at the service of a promiscuous public.[32]

After Nick has painted Miriam as the Tragic Muse, she suggests that he do another portrait of her, this time as the Comic Muse. Sherringham, however, objects: "The Comic Muse? Never, never. . . . You're not to go smirking through the age and down to posterity— I'd rather see you as Medusa crowned with serpents. That's what you look like when you look best" (2:215–16). Yet for Miriam to "look best" as Medusa is precisely for her to function as the comic muse, since this comparison partakes of a scenario as reassuringly "comic and ironic" as the satirical project James recollects in the preface. Sherringham is not alone in adverting facetiously to this "mild Medusa" (2:336): Nick Dormer, for his part, enjoys characterizing her as "the dishevelled actress" (2:423), or, more archly, as "the dishevelled one."[33] Indeed, as a result of the novel's counterplotting, one

32. It is important, of course, to keep in mind James's remarkable ambivalence toward this public. For all his attacks on it, he desired its recognition at the same time. See, for example, the poignant letter to William Dean Howells, in which he writes: "I *have* felt, for a long time past, that I have fallen upon evil days—every sign or symbol of one's being in the least bit *wanted*, have [sic] so utterly failed." *Letters*, Edel, ed. 3:511.

33. *Muse* (1890; Penguin, 1978), p. 519.

has trouble knowing just how seriously to take these evocations of Miriam's monstrosity.

It is precisely this indeterminacy, however, that the counterplot works to achieve. For the urbane irony with which James invokes the stereotype of woman as "the demon, the devil, the devourer and destroyer" (2:254) does not make his remonstrance any the less desperate: the suavely comic tone of the references plays a crucial role in an elaborate defensive process, one that James executes adroitly but that he by no means invents. The image of Medusa, as Neil Hertz has shown, links a surprising number of texts by nineteenth-century male writers, and articulates a veritable canon of apotropaic counterplots.[34] Though not mentioned by Hertz, James's anatomy of the actress displays the very features that make the Medusa oddly attractive—rather than merely terrifying—to male writers of the age. Just as Miriam is "a kind of monster" because she combines excess (of "personations") with lack (of "moral privacy"), so the decapitated Medusa—as Hertz develops Freud's and Jean Laplanche's remarks on the subject—images at once an overabundance of snaky or phallic hair and the "castration" of the female genitalia. "The symbol of the Medusa's head is reassuring" to male writers, Hertz observes, "not only because its elements can be read in those ways, but because it is a symbol."[35]

Explaining in the preface why Miriam looms so large in the novel, James writes:

> The idea of the book being, as I have said, a picture of some of the personal consequences of the art-appetite raised to intensity, swollen to voracity, the heavy emphasis falls where the symbol of some of the complications so begotten might be made (as I judged, heaven forgive me!) most "amusing": amusing I mean in the blest very modern sense. I never "go behind" Miriam; only poor Sherringham goes, a great deal, and Nick Dormer goes a little, and the author, while they so waste wonderment, goes behind *them*: but none the less she is as thoroughly symbolic, as functional, for illustration of the idea, as either of them, while her image had seemed susceptible of a livelier and "prettier" concretion. I had desired for her, I remember, all man-

34. Neil Hertz, "Medusa's Head: Male Hysteria under Political Pressure," in *The End of the Line: Essays on Psychoanalysis and the Sublime* (New York: Columbia University Press, 1985), pp. 161–93. Hertz's essay is followed by responses by Catherine Gallagher, pp. 194–96, and Joel Fineman, pp. 197–205, to which Hertz adds a reply, pp. 206–15.

35. Ibid., p. 166.

ageable vividness—so ineluctable had it long appeared to "do the
actress," to touch the theatre, to meet that connexion somehow or
other, in any free plunge of the speculative fork into the contemporary
social salad.

(1:xvi)

Here, James recontains Miriam's showy bigness under the rubric of
"symbolic . . . illustration." Though inflated until she mirrors the
"gorged audience" of Gabriel Nash's diatribe, Miriam, in her immensity, now emblematizes a robust plenitude of meaning. Instead
of embodying a perilous and distressing vulgarity, Miriam permits
an "amusing" specificity, a " 'prettier' concretion," and a "manageable vividness." "Pretty" though she may be, Miriam offers the
added—or programmatically necessary—attraction of an almost Ra-
belaisian ribaldry: as symbol, she perforce bears the "heavy emphasis" of "complications . . . begotten" in the name of "the art-
appetite raised to intensity, swollen to voracity," and remotivated
to assume a centrality not exactly metaphorical but no longer loosely
metonymic either. James designs a Medusa who is both beauty and
beast—at whom the male characters gaze in "wonderment," but
whom we never "go behind."

It is no accident, moreover, that what Miriam "symbolizes"—the
"art-appetite"—reappears at the end of the passage, though in a
much lighter, and ostentatiously light-hearted, form: James confides
that he had wanted to "do the actress" by means of a "free plunge
of the speculative fork into the contemporary social salad." He acknowledges his own "art-appetite," but he does so as if to demonstrate its dissimilarity to Miriam's, its status as a mere figure of
speech. By now, however, the neutrality or innocence of figurative
expression is highly suspect. Hertz suggests that the Medusa scenario converts figurative language, whose meanings often exceed authorial control, into the "manageable vividness" and "functional"
predictability of symbolism: symbolism would serve as a kind of
exorcism, restoring the health of male writing by "casting out something that resembles it a bit too closely for comfort."[36] Thus Miriam's
"art-appetite" swells to voracity so that James's may seem to shrink
from such vulgar and corporeal connotations.

The constitution of Miriam as a symbol, then, permits James to

36. Ibid., p. 179.

project onto her—and to expel from himself—the twin evils of a certain theatrical expansiveness and a certain rhetorical "bigness." We recall James's comment about the "preference for art," according to which, in its most "natural" form—a form "falsified and vulgarized" by Miriam—the artistic spirit is never "large," but always "contracted" into itself, utterly free of the expansionistic "vices" that produced novels like *The Newcomes, The Three Musketeers,* and *War and Peace,* to name James's examples of large loose baggy monsters.[37] As long as James can shift the burden of this vice from himself to Miriam, he may recede into the safety and self-containment of his private pursuit, leaving the actress and the novel she represents to circulate among the likes of Thackeray and Dumas and Tolstoy and their bloated, *un*naturally embarrassed and embarrassing fictions.

For it is these precursors, among others, whom James would cast out as well. When he insists, as he does so often in his career, that he has that within which passeth show, he disavows not only the theatricality of his own rhetoric, but also the theatricality—the self-exposure, the commercial realities, the aesthetic compromises—imposed upon any novelist publishing at the end of the nineteenth century. Time and again, James speaks of literature and the theater as alternatives, but his writing is haunted by the sense that the two careers have much in common.[38] A number of critics have written interestingly about James's complex, ambivalent relationship to the dominant traditions of the English, American, and French novel, especially insofar as the overwhelmingly public and popular character of nineteenth-century fiction impinged upon his own ideal of literary vocation.[39] What has not been recognized sufficiently is the

37. James in fact refers to Tolstoy's novel as *Peace and War* (1:x). Blackmur, in *Studies in Henry James*, Makowsky, ed., p. 129, speculates interestingly on the significance of this reversal.

38. What is probably James's most famous, and moving, assertion of the incommensurability of the "sow's ear" of the theater and the "silk purse" of literature (*Letters,* Edel, ed., 3:509) appears in his *Notebooks.* Just after the failure of his play, *Guy Domville,* James wrote: "I take up my *own* old pen again—the pen of all my old unforgettable efforts and sacred struggles. To myself—today—I need say no more. Large and full and high the future still opens. It is now indeed that I may do the work of my life. And I will. x x x x x I have only to *face* my problems. x x x x x But all that is of the ineffable—too deep and pure for any utterance. Shrouded in sacred silence let it rest. x x x x x" (*The Notebooks of Henry James,* ed. F. O. Matthiessen and Kenneth B. Murdock [(New York: Oxford University Press, 1947)], p. 179).

39. See Carton, "Henry James the Critic," 124–36, and Rowe, *The Theoretical Dimensions,* pp. 68–118, as well as Alfred Habegger, *Gender, Fantasy, and Realism in*

extent to which *The Tragic Muse* and its preface allegorize this predicament. Turning away from the "parade" in which Miriam figures
a long line of recent and not-so-recent novelistic "personalities,"
James cultivates an inviolable and magisterially free-standing authorial identity, whose only outward sign is its serene "indifference
to everything but itself."

Just as the trade of the actress entails constant intercourse with
an overfed audience, and just as the business of the playwright
requires all sorts of vitiating concessions to popular taste, so the
enterprise of novel-writing involves a host of unwelcome contigu-
ities, not just with unappreciative readers but with other authors as
well, authors whom one may resemble "a bit too closely for comfort." "One must go one's way and know what one's about and
have a general plan and a private religion," James wrote to his
brother; "—in short have made up one's mind as to *ce qui en est*
with a public the draggling after simply leads one into the gutter.
One always has a 'public' enough if one has an audible vibration—
even if it should only come from one's self."[40] Although these remarks sound like a condemnation of the stage, they were written
in the year in which *The Tragic Muse* was published, and concern
the book's probable commercial failure. But they also hint that, even
if the public ignores the book, James will have been theatricalized
by his own internal "public" of fellow performers, the "audible"
audience installed within himself as an inevitable consequence of
his historicity.

The same letter goes on to allude to Milton's description of Satan's
fallen legions: "Thick as autumnal leaves that strow the Brooks /
In *Vallombrosa*." This intertextual opening points ironically to the
subversion of James's Satanic desire to appear "self-begot, self-
rais'd, by [his] own quick'ning power." In the more immediate context, of course, it is not Milton who occupies and divides James from
himself: it is to the "vibrations" of predecessors and competitors in
the art of the novel that James cannot help attending, since these
resonances have defined and continue to define his own voice. An

American Literature (New York: Columbia University Press, 1982), and William Veeder,
*Henry James—The Lessons of the Master: Popular Fiction and Personal Style in the Nine-
teenth Century* (Chicago: University of Chicago Press, 1975).
    40. *Letters*, Edel, ed., 3:300.

echo-chamber filled with other voices and other texts, James's consciousness emerges as a densely crowded stage: he performs both for and with a thick legion of conspicuously public artists, including Thackeray, Dumas, and Tolstoy, to be sure, but reaching back to Austen and Hawthorne and Balzac, and extending through Trollope and Eliot to Zola and Howells and Mrs. Humphrey Ward.[41] To end with this popular female novelist is to suggest the heterogeneity of influences that renders James himself heterogeneous by constructing his authorial self as a theater overflowing with prior and contemporaneous selves, each profoundly jumbled and histrionized in its turn.

Behind Miriam's overflow, which James can no more withstand than can Peter Sherringham, we glimpse, then, not some primal anarchic essence of metaphor, but the forces of literary history and social reality. Yet these forces cannot be dissociated from the rhetorical forms in which they present themselves and by means of which they shape the intertextual milieu of nineteenth-century fiction. In an important reading of *Daniel Deronda* that we discussed in Chapter 5, Catherine Gallagher has shown how women writers in the nineteenth century had to "avoid or transform" the metaphor of the author as prostitute, as agent of circulation rather than of production.[42] Gallagher argues that this metaphor was oddly attractive, despite its obvious disadvantages, because it represented an alternative to the metaphor of the author as father: it helped the woman writer to "evade . . . any specifically patriarchal authority that her literal and literary forefathers might try to impose, replacing the mystifications of genealogy with the realities of economics."[43]

Our reading of *The Tragic Muse* shows how the metaphor of the author as prostitute leads to the notion that the authoring of meta-

---

41. For James, Balzac is perhaps the epitome of monstrous literary productivity. See his remarks on the latter's "monstrous duality," in the 1902 essay, "Honoré de Balzac," in *The Portable Henry James*, ed. Morton Dauwen Zabel, rev. Lyall H. Powers (New York: Viking, 1968), p. 466. On the Balzac-James relationship, see Carton, "Henry James the Critic," 124–27, and Peter Brooks, *The Melodramatic Imagination: Balzac, Henry James, Melodrama, and the Mode of Excess* (New Haven: Yale University Press, 1976). With its theatrical plot, Mrs. Humphrey Ward's *Miss Bretherton* (1884) is an important source for *The Tragic Muse*. See James's entry in his *Notebooks*, Matthiessen and Murdock, eds., for June 19, 1884, pp. 63–64.

42. Gallagher, "George Eliot and *Daniel Deronda*," in Yeazell ed., *Sex, Politics, and Science*, p. 40.

43. Ibid., p. 46.

phors is a kind of prostitution in its own right. What does it mean, though, for James to inherit and to engage—if only to fend off—this metaphor? In its belatedness, *The Tragic Muse* can claim a revisionary novelty, for it interprets the patriarchal trope of genealogy and the (ambiguously) feminist trope of prostitution not as mutually exclusive, but as virtually identical. While James's textual practice opens not only onto Hertz's male tradition of naturalizing self-mystification but also onto Gallagher's female tradition of anti-natural self-commodification, it rewrites each tradition as the other's uncanny double. Indeed, for Miriam Rooth to become an actress is precisely for her to act out the destiny ordained by her paternal genes: "the Hebraic Mr. Rooth, with his love of old pots and Christian altar-cloths, had supplied in the girl's composition the aesthetic element, the sense of colour and form" (1:220). Jewish art and Jewish commerce converge in the Name-of-the-Father, which dictates, from the grave, Miriam's professional itinerary. Likewise, for Nick Dormer to pursue the career of the politician is for him to honor—not to abjure—the "consecrated name" (1:84) imprinted upon him by the "paternal dedication" (1:85) that compels him to follow his father's footsteps into Parliament.

To be sure, the parallel trajectories of Nick's and Miriam's stories seem to promise a way out of this double bind by having the protagonists transcend or repudiate the patriarchal imperative to sell oneself to the public. Yet neither evasion quite succeeds: Miriam ends up marrying her manager, consolidating her status as a commodity even in her apotheosis as the "divinest" Juliet, and Nick ends up giving in to the "bribery" of the politically ambitious Julia Dallow, who seems ready to lure him away from an aesthetic priesthood he has by now reconceptualized, in any case, as a displaced form of theatricality.[44] As Gabriel Nash predicts, Julia will "recapture" Nick as her husband and "swallow [his] profession," by remaking him as a fashionable amateur painter and setting him up as a "great social institution" (2:406)—exactly what he thought he was renouncing.

Thus, the supposed liberation of the prostitute—fruit of a seed she only seems to scatter—and the supposed autonomy of the male

---

44. In the *Notebooks*, Matthiessen and Murdock, eds., p. 90, James says of Julia's relationship to Nick: "She tries to seduce him—she is full of bribery."

artist—heir to a dubiously empowering legacy—parody and demystify each other. If the plot of *The Tragic Muse* collapses the distance between patriarchal genealogy and anti-patriarchal economics, this "deconstruction" narrows, instead of broadening, the ground available for a redemptive counterplot: in refiguring literary history, the novel by no means lifts James out of it. Of course, if male and female metaphors prove equally entrapping—and entrappingly equal—there is always androgyny. As David Carroll has noted, James's prefaces often portray the artist as both father and mother, both disseminating and inseminated by the "germ" that becomes the novel. Carroll also demonstrates, however, that this "artist/father/mother" repeatedly recognizes in its work "the 'monster' which has been produced in spite of itself."[45] Not surprisingly, James classifies the "disfigured" *Tragic Muse* as a "poor fatherless and motherless, a sort of unregistered and unacknowledged birth" (1:v). Yet this urge to disown the "unlucky" child may stem from a disquieting awareness of a similarity between authorial androgyny and textual monstrosity, a similarity readily suggested by the bisexual Medusa, who may well stand for what James, near the end of his life, would call "that queer monster, the artist."[46]

45. David Carroll, *The Subject in Question: The Languages of Theory and the Strategies of Fiction* (Chicago: University of Chicago Press, 1982), pp. 62, 65.
46. *Letters*, Edel, ed., 4:706.

Conclusion

The Picture of Dorian Gray first appeared in *Lippincott's Monthly Magazine* in 1890, the same year in which James published *The Tragic Muse*. In the following year, an expanded version of Wilde's novel appeared in a single volume. I have suggested that James's revisions of *The Tragic Muse*, itself already a revisionary or counterplotting text, may be seen in part as a defense against the ways in which Wilde's uncannily similar novel threatens to bring James further out of the closet—what one of Wilde's recent critics has dubbed "the closet of representation"—than he is willing to go.[1] This is not the place to begin exploring the fascinating intertextual relationship between James and Wilde, a relationship that goes back at least as far as 1882, when James characterized Wilde as "an unclean beast," and that constitutes in itself a highly instructive chapter in the intertwined histories of theatricality, the novel, aestheticism, modernism, and gay-male self-fashioning.[2] I want merely to signal here the unsettling pressure of *Nachträglichkeit* that Wilde's notorious novel

1. Ed Cohen, "Writing Gone Wilde: Homoerotic Desire in the Closet of Representation," *PMLA* 102 (October 1987): 801–13.
2. Leon Edel, *Henry James: A Life* (New York: Harper and Row, 1985), p. 273. Analysis of the James-Wilde connection (or disconnection) would have to take into account not only their very different relations to the genre of the novel (of theatricality) but also their sharply contrasting, though contemporaneous, careers as playwrights. Were one to cast this analysis in narrative (and dramatic) terms, one might begin with the poignantly telling scene of an extremely nervous James's attendance at Wilde's successful *An Ideal Husband* on the opening night of his own notoriously unsuccessful *Guy Domville*. For more information about this episode, see Edel, pp. 409–21.
   In his biography of Wilde, Richard Ellmann says of the "unclean beast" image and the like: "The images are so steamy as to suggest that James saw in Wilde a threat. For the tolerance of deviation, or ignorance of it, were alike in jeopardy because of Wilde's flouting and flaunting. James's homosexuality was latent, Wilde's was patent. It was as if James, foreseeing scandal, separated himself from this menace in motley." Richard Ellmann, *Oscar Wilde* (Markham, Ontario: Penguin, Canada, 1987), p. 171. This sounds right, but for another way of reading the steaminess of James's images, see below.

exerts over James's, whose purpose seems to be precisely the *avoid-ance* of notoriety.

Even if one knows *Dorian Gray* only superficially (which, as Wilde might have claimed, may be the best way to know it), one cannot read *The Tragic Muse* without finding Wilde's text already written between the lines.[3] The striking resemblance between the two works extends well beyond the fact that the fading portrait of Gabriel Nash, while explicitly framed as evoking "some delicate Hawthorne tale," seems to anticipate even more conspicuously, not to say more prox-imately, the famous supernatural conceit on which *The Picture of Dorian Gray* hangs. On a more general level, both novels present the configuration of three men and an actress, and though Miriam Rooth occupies a more "central" place in this configuration than does the unfortunate Sibyl Vane, *Dorian Gray*, no less than *The Tragic Muse*, could be read as an allegory of how a male-identified "art of the novel" (and of literary criticism) responds to the peculiar dis-turbance represented by a female-identified theatricality. Many read-ers have taken the novelist-critic Gabriel Nash to be a veiled portrait of Wilde himself, an inference rendered all the more irresistible by the parallelism between Nash and that novelist manqué, Lord Henry Wotton. James's figure of the painter, Nick Dormer, finds his Wildean counterpart in Basil Hallward. And for all their differences, Peter Sherringham and Dorian Gray are equivalent in the curious, quasi-homicidal abstractness of their relation to the actresses that they purport to "love."

Those differences, of course, are considerable, and they tell us a great deal about the kind of novel that James would probably rather not be seen as having written. For the eponymous hero of Wilde's novel embodies and thereby stimulates the relatively open homo-eroticism that circulates through it, lending an unmistakable charge to all of the transactions between and among the male characters. Now, it is hardly the case that men's dealings with one another in *The Tragic Muse* lack erotic content; indeed, the male bonds here—especially the bond that links the male characters in general with the author who, as he says, "goes behind *them*" (but never behind

3. In much of what follows, I am indebted to a letter from Eve Kosofsky Sedgwick, in which she offered some provocative suggestions about the *Tragic Muse–Dorian Gray* intertext.

Miriam)—derive their distinctive intimacy, their intensity, and their tension from the systematic interplay of certain elaborate laws of same-sex desire that traverse the entire Jamesian oeuvre.[4] But what is equally distinctive and equally systematic here is the author's way of investing those relations with the "vagueness" that is one of his stylistic hallmarks. And though, as we have seen, that vagueness perhaps epitomizes James's *écriture gaie*, it nonetheless underwrites a complicated process of evasion which figures much less rigorously in the discourse of and around Oscar Wilde, particularly after his very public trials in 1895.

In other words, if Jamesian "vagueness" provides a set of highly theatrical strategies for simultaneously revealing and concealing gay meaning itself, the connection between theatricality and homosexuality in Wilde's novel tends to be not only stylistic but also thematic—which is to say, all the more recognizable. I would suggest, although I cannot demonstrate here, that, while a certain theatricality determines all the transactions among James's male characters, and (more important) between those characters and James himself, Wilde, with the help of *his* male characters, turns certain theatrical modes of signification into specifically gay *signifieds*. The point is best illustrated with reference to the contrasting functions of the novels' actresses vis-à-vis their respective male "critics." As we have seen, the "monstrous" Miriam Rooth—unlike, say, the "hysterical" Olive Chancellor—achieves "symbolic" centrality in James's novel precisely so as to distract our attention from the "art-appetite" of James and his male characters. Sibyl Vane, however, seems to have almost the opposite function: instead of sustaining the "heavy emphasis" that falls on Miriam, Sibyl dies halfway through the book, and her disappearance, not surprisingly, has the effect of underscoring the sexualized theatricality that links the surviving male characters. With the actress out of the picture, as it were, theatricality does not, that is, fade away; rather, for the men who remain on the scene, it gets displaced and generalized, both in a comic or prototypically "gay" register (as the seductive epigrammatology of "in-

---

4. For a suggestive discussion of the way in which this representation of "going behind" illuminates the "Jamesian phantasmatic," see Kaja Silverman, "Too Early/Too Late: Subjectivity and the Primal Scene in Henry James," *Novel* 21 (Winter/Spring 1988): 147–73. Silverman remarks in passing the use of the term "going behind" (165) in the preface to *The Tragic Muse*.

sincerity" expounded by Lord Henry) and in a tragic or potentially homophobic one (as the guilt-ridden, lugubrious thematics of coverture and secrecy surrounding the portrait itself).

Despite its title, *The Tragic Muse* studiously eschews such "tragedy"; and despite, or because of, its avowedly comic counterplotting, it equally stops short of the kind of "comedy" that Wilde serves up so prodigally. Yet, if it is important to take note of these differences, it is equally important not to hypostatize them. As I have indicated, they take shape and make sense only against the backdrop of a similarity that threatens to reabsorb them. In revising *The Tragic Muse*, James seeks to reinforce the "vagueness" that has always informed his writing, well before the publication of *Dorian Gray*, but that now, retrospectively, seems always to have been prepared for the Wildean solicitation. And if this readiness suggests not only a sense of threat but also a sense of attraction, not only anxiety but also desire, there may be good reasons for not taking James's project of differentiation entirely at face value. Just as *Dorian Gray*'s striking departures from *The Tragic Muse* may in fact serve to tease out its erotic subtext—with all the provocative flirtatiousness that such teasing can connote—so James's apparent refusal of this intertextual foreplay may instead be seen to advance it.

Given what we know about the Jamesian theater of embarrassment, at any rate, it is not inconceivable that, in appearing to save face, James may deliberately be setting the stage for losing it again. One should beware of attributing too much sexual stage fright to the author who, in the same paragraph where he inflates Miriam Rooth into a "symbolic" alibi, reminds us of how he "goes behind" her male admirers. There is doubtless much more to be said about the later Henry James than I have been able to hint at in this book, and much more than even the most conscientiously antihomophobic and psychosexually astute of recent James critics have had time to explore. Since so much work remains to be done, it might seem appropriate to conclude the present study by widening the focus, allowing biographical questions to intimate "larger" historical ones. One might, for instance, point out the ways in which the tricky pas de deux that James performs with Wilde prefigures the fate of theatricality in the twentieth-century novel. Glancing at works by authors like Edith Wharton, Ford Madox Ford, James Joyce, and Virginia Woolf, one could sketch a historical narrative whose trajectory would describe either the development of the theatrical novel along ever more sophisticatedly contestatory lines, or the gradual consolidation of techniques that recuperate the scandalous potential of the form, or, most satisfyingly, some "dialectical" combination of the two. In view of my reservations about the subversion/containment dyad, though, I think it would be wiser to forgo such totalizing gestures (however modestly they would be made), and turn the spotlight one last time on my own critical performance.

I would begin by explaining that my brief discussion of Wilde here is intended not only to mark a particularly relevant context for James's theatricality, but also to acknowledge the hidden presence of *Dorian Gray* throughout the present book. That is, in a sense I have read not just *The Tragic Muse* but all of these novels, starting with *Mansfield Park*, as though they were on the verge of turning into *Dorian Gray*. For example, at the back of my reading of Fanny Price's withdrawal into the abandoned schoolroom, that architectural emblem of her pursuit of interiority, has been the image of the abandoned schoolroom into which Dorian—a rather different kind of protagonist, it would seem—retreats to be alone with his awful portrait. This does not imply, I hasten to add, some sort of teleological scheme whereby every other novel secretly aspires toward the pure, subversive theatricality that Wilde's text finally realizes. For one thing, the salience in that text of a heavy-handed theatricality of the closet—centered on the repressive "masking" of the portrait and the "sins" that it records—effectively disqualifies it as an instance of pure subversiveness, whatever that may be. For another, while I have been concerned to situate these texts in a kind of history, I have been reluctant all along to posit any simple linear progression, either from more "conservative" novels of theatricality to less "conservative" ones, or vice versa. One of this book's lessons, I think, is that theatricality in novels tends to have an antinarrative effect; my resistance to historical schematization may represent something of a mimetic tribute to my subject. Instead of revealing an underlying historical design, the silent, anticipatory inscription of *Dorian Gray* in these other novels signifies my own desire to read them, so to speak, against the grain—not to make them say things that they do not say, but to show how they indeed do say what they may not *want* to say.

This sort of anthropomorphic projection, of course, can easily beg the question that I am trying to answer—that of the position from which I have been discovering not just theatricality but a certain "bad" or "perverse" theatricality in such seemingly unlikely places. To define that position, I might revise myself somewhat, and propose that my interest here is not so much in what novels do not want to say as in what certain tendencies in literary criticism, as well as in the surrounding cultural discourse, make it harder to see in them. I have in mind primarily a version of deconstructive practice in which the social embeddedness of texts gets subordinated to a general problematic of textuality. Heavily as my readings here draw on the extensive analytic repertoire of deconstruction, I am engaged, like many others, in articulating an insufficiently recognized difference within deconstruction. In my case, this difference is explicitly named as "theatricality": if "textuality" can be formulated as a tension between the constative and the performative functions of language, I have deployed "theatricality" here in an attempt to put the performance back in the notion of the performative, not by reducing Rhetoricity to History, but by emphasizing the specific social implications of certain more or less local instances of rhetorical instability.

This insistence on the social typifies the way in which many critics in the past decade have responded to what one might call "high deconstruction," North American deconstruction in its most intensely language-centered projects of the 1970s. For although one of the most valuable and enduring lessons of that criticism was a tenacious suspicion of such psychological and would-be ethical categories as "the self" and "subjectivity," its inclination to universalize problems of signification in some sense coincided with the desocializing work performed through those very categories at other, more "popular" levels of the culture. When the large-scale thinning-out of our language of social experience becomes visible *as* performance, critical intervention in that process becomes possible. That intervention can take various forms, examples of which are available in some of the recent criticism that has inspired the present study. My own decision has been to focus on a group of canonical (and almost canonical) nineteenth-century novels, since, as others have argued, the nineteenth-century novel has proven to be a remarkably fertile site for the production of modern antisocial ideology. In my readings, I have attempted to catch that production in the act, to "go behind" the scenes where such supposedly universal, natural, transparent—in short, nontheatrical—"values" as sincerity, inwardness, privacy, and domesticity are being constructed and wheeled into place.

I hope, then, not only to have defamiliarized these novels but also to have defamilialized them. To return for a moment to the example of *Mansfield Park*: if my aim in interpreting that novel can be encapsulated as a desire to blur the distinction between the schoolroom where Fanny Price goes to be alone with her books and plants and the schoolroom where Dorian Gray goes to be alone with his picture, the impression created by such blurring should not be that of an arbitrary conflation, but rather that of an undeniable, though hitherto unnoticed, aperture built into a structure that otherwise appears oppressively closed. That structure, corresponding to a series of boxes within boxes, consists of Fanny's subjectivity, the room in which it seeks shelter, the house that contains the room, the novel named after the house, and the presumably air-tight ideology of the family that seems to enclose them all. One hardly needs to repeat that there is nothing intrinsically liberatory about the closeted moralizing that suffuses the Wildean counterscene. But to see that lurid counterscene as already implied by what one can no longer help recognizing as the staging of Fanny's interiority is to begin opening both novels out onto a stage whose fourth wall, though always hypothetically in place, is always necessarily broken down.[5]

Always broken down but always in place: we find ourselves back within the metaphorics of deconstruction, from which we may never have departed in the first place. But I cannot acknowledge this "predicament" without indicating one other way in which Wilde may have been exemplary here. For it has been customary to praise Wilde (without, however, having to pay much attention to him) by identifying him as a precursor of Derrida and of deconstruction itself; my earlier reference to Wilde's "epigrammatology" played on this truism. Like Lord Henry, *Dorian Gray*'s indefatigable theorist of an-

---

5. For an interesting discussion of the "fourth wall" in relation to Cold War stagings of male homosexuality, see Lee Edelman's essay, "Tearooms and Sympathy; or, The Epistemology of the Water Closet," in his book, *Homographesis* (New York: Routledge, forthcoming).

tireferentiality, Wilde indeed qualifies as what Paul de Man called an archie Debunker.[6] But like the Brontëan governess-actress and like Edith Wharton in her guise as a James critic—like, that is, the other paradigmatic figures in my (anti-)family romance—Wilde combines his demystifying practice with a theatricality that, if only for its almost proverbial association with a certain "gay sensibility," can prove something of an embarrassment, at least to those who like their Wilde respectably disrespectful. Not only in *Dorian Gray* and in his plays, but in texts like "The Critic as Artist" and "The Decay of Lying"—texts, interestingly enough, that recall James's experiments in the genre of criticism-as-theater—Wilde offers a model for articulating deconstruction with and through an erotically affirmative theatricality that it need not generalize as free play. He intimates scenes of reading and of writing to which, one hundred years later, literary criticism may just now be learning how to respond.

6. See the famous essay, "Semiology and Rhetoric," in Paul de Man, *Allegories of Reading: Figural Language in Rousseau, Nietzsche, Rilke, and Proust* (New Haven: Yale University Press, 1979), p. 9.

INDEX

Text: 10/13 Palatino
Display: Palatino
Compositor: Impressions
Printer: Edwards Brothers, Inc.
Binder: Edwards Brothers, Inc.